MOROCCO

الحمد لله وحده

بختم: الحمد لله محمد ربي وحسبي ومولاي

اذ نا يقول الله بجاه ملنا محمد لمنبيارك ومريدا لحر النصيحيد والجودكرة بالما مون مرسوم بلوداء ايل نشاء الشعيد الذو جئنانا وبلوداء الغبائل المغروبة بالعدراء وكذلك غنيان كبلاء زعير وزمور وايت يوسي وغيرمنا بيد سلهم بلد دات البرير لما يحتشر عليهما مرالخطر والامان الجودكرة نما بما قدل من المواقف علينه مرخلا منا وولاية اقرنا المعتز بالله اله يكوت على بال من منها وجولا نهما بابا ئد وبفرض جدرا ستنما حتو يجر جا مر شرا بنا ويبا خذ ستردبهما بهما عشوركات يعرض نهما جندك وببنتوصي خيرا بهما ويعرجهما بالحول المحوز بدا با نئت وبجيرهما مر النوجه لد وكا نيسا عدد ميتا عليند واداربها تجر واذلك بيشرع عليهما وبجوز خطها بذلك وابج نم بينات لد حوز يشمر عليهما بذلك نم بينا عد ثما ويستعمل الحست والمغرور و تحصيلهما على اراد الخيرة بونت جمع وكذا ثنة لا ظلام والطلام

وي 22 شعبا علم 1315 هـ

FACSIMILE OF THE SULTAN'S SAFE-CONDUCT.

TRANSLATION.

A Letter from the Sultan, with Instructions to the Amels.

The Imperial Seal.

WE hereby grant permission to the bearers of the present communication, MM. de la Martinière and Morel, both of them French citizens, to travel in our Empire over the regions of the plains where they may journey in safety, but not in the mountains nor through the territory of tribes known by their misdeeds, such as the Kebaïls of the Zaïrs, the Zemmours, the Aït Youssi, and other Kebaïls of the Berber country, so that no fear may be entertained for their safety and no danger be incurred by them in their excursions.

In consequence, we order any of our servants who shall take cognizance of our Imperial Rescript to provide for the safety of these gentlemen during their travels in our Empire, placing them under their protection, while in their respective provinces. We also order our servants to minister to all their wants, to receive them kindly and in a friendly spirit, to point out to them dangerous spots, to dissuade them from proceeding to such places and not to aid them in the undertaking; but should these gentlemen refuse to follow their advice and to listen to their warnings, our servants shall enter a protest and demand of them a declaration in writing of such refusal, and should they decline giving the declaration, the fact shall be recorded by the Adouls. After which, our servants shall proffer their aid and do all in their power to facilitate their travels and enable them to reach the goal. He who does his duty and all that is in his power cannot be blamed.

HAIL TO ALL

22 Chaaban 1301 (17 June, 1884).

[Before reading the above letter (which is termed Sherifian), the Moroccans would gaze with emotion on the seal, place it on their forehead, then kiss the document.]

MOROCCO

*JOURNEYS IN THE KINGDOM OF FEZ
AND TO THE COURT OF
MULAI HASSAN*

WITH ITINERARIES CONSTRUCTED BY THE AUTHOR AND A
BIBLIOGRAPHY OF MOROCCO FROM 1844 TO 1887

BY

H. M. P. DE LA MARTINIÈRE, F.R.G.S.

MEMBER OF THE GEOGRAPHICAL SOCIETY OF PARIS AND OF
THE TOPOGRAPHICAL SOCIETY OF FRANCE

WITH A PREFACE BY
LIEUT.-COLONEL TROTTER
93RD HIGHLANDERS

LONDON
WHITTAKER & CO., WHITE HART STREET
PATERNOSTER SQUARE
1889

NOTE.

THE following work was translated from the MS. of M. de la Martinière, and printed during his absence on a scientific expedition in Morocco. The publishers regret that various errors, especially of orthography, have in consequence remained uncorrected, except in the index, to which readers are referred for the correct transliteration of the proper names.

CONTENTS.

	Page
PREFACE	xiii

CHAPTER I.

Gibraltar, the starting point—The Passage—The Scenery on either Side of the Straits—View of Tangiers—The Monkeys' Mountain—The Arrival—Tangiers—Description of the Streets—The Great Mosque—The Legations—The Postal Establishments of the different European Powers—Scene in the Soko or Market Place—Story-telling—Danger to a Sceptical European—Pretended Oriental Dancing and Imposition on Foreigners—His Sherifian Majesty's Foreign Secretary—His skill in Entangling Diplomatic Affairs—The Governor's Palace—Its Marvels—The Prison and its Horrors—The Beggars—The Old Wazïr of the Arabian Nights, . . 1

CHAPTER II.

History of Tangiers—M. Tissot's Researches—The Town under the Romans—Invasion of the Vandals—The Mussulman Conquest—The Chief Ocba—The Portuguese Occupation—The British Occupation—Sherif Abd-es-Selam, and the Curious Amusements of His Friends who pay dearly for Them—Tangiers Bombarded—System of Defences of the Town—The Armstrong Guns and the Gunners—The Transaction of Diplomatic Business, a Farce—The Press at Tangiers—The European Population—The Climate—Dismal Appearance of the Town in Winter—The Environs—Shooting and Pig-Sticking—Trick played by the Beaters on successful Sportsmen—View from Cape Trafalgar—Archæological Researches—Cape Spartel, ... 20

CONTENTS.

CHAPTER III.

Preparation for an Expedition—Purchase of Horses and Mules—Treatment of Beasts of Burden by the Arabs—Visit to the Sherif—the Sherif and His Household—the Start—Our Trouble with the Muleteers—The Marshy State of the Country on the Road to Alqaçar—Difficulties on the Way—The Site of Ad Mercuri and the Ruins—The Site well-chosen by the Romans—The Country People—Discovery by M. Tissot—Our Mule Bagatelle, ... 40

CHAPTER IV.

On Our Way to Alqaçar—The Saint's Tomb—Our Soldier—All the Chatterboxes of the Country pay us a Visit—Our Cook and our Groom—A Group of Menhirs—Arthur Brooke's Opinion Concerning these—Origin of the Race of Inhabitants—The Roman Station of Ad Novas—The Battle of the Three Kings—Arrival at a dchar—Pleasant Reception—The Cheik—Chaouch the Horse Dealer—The Town of Alqaçar—Its History—Horrible State of the Town, a Hot-Bed of Fever—Description of the Town, ... 64

CHAPTER V.

Roads from Alqaçar to Dcharchiera—Traces of the Portuguese Occupation—The Wad el Kous—We Cross the River—Change in the Temperature—Red Partridges plentiful—Resemblance of this Region to Spain—The Orange Tree Garden of the Sherif of Wazzan—Dcharchiera—A Specimen in support of Darwin's Theory—Our First Night Encampment at Dcharchiera—Warlike Tendencies of the Berbers—Dolce Far Niente—Ben Chimol Family, ... 80

CHAPTER VI.

Departure—The Start—The Deserted Aspect of the Country—Unexpected Meeting with an English Lady—Our Soldiers Terrified—The Sherif's Country House—Our Alarm—The Djebel Sarsar—We are not allowed to ascend the Mountain

CONTENTS.

—Excursion to the Ruins of Basra—History of Basra—the town of Barca—The Qaïd—We Lose our Way—The Marauders—Excursion to the Hill north of the Dohar—Features of the Surrounding Country—The Thaleb—Departure for Wazzan, ... 92

CHAPTER VII.

Wazzan—Antiquity of the Town—It is supposed to have been the Roman Military Post called Vopiscianæ—M. Tissot's opinion concerning Ancient Ezaguen—Leo Africanus—Marmol—A few Words on its History—Influence and Organisation of the Religious Brotherhood of Mulai Taïeb, a National Order peculiar to Morocco—Its Chief the grand Sherif El Hadj Abd es Selam ben el Hadj el Arbi is in Favour of European Customs and Notions—Influence resulting from his Marriage with an English Lady, ... 106

CHAPTER VIII.

Description of the Town of Wazzan—Climate—Population—Mosques—Tolerant Spirit of the Disciples of Mulai Taïeb—Tomb of the Old Chiefs of the Brotherhood—Veneration of the Population—The Town and Part of the Rif Frontier Region—Incursion of the Berber Tribes—Dangers of an Excursion to the Orange Tree Gardens—The Sherif's Guard—Their Armament—Tragical Astronomical Surveys—Our House and its Discomforts—Wazzan, the Promised Land of Rheumatism—Dampness of the Tingitane again—A Cold Bath Interrupted—Feudal Life in Morocco—The Two Sons of the Sherif—Sidi el Arbi and Sidi Mohammed—Political Conversation—Tea à la Marocaine—The Tonkin at Wazzan—Our Host's Followers—The Sherif's Estates—Commonplace Appearance of the Architectural Style in the Town—Relations of the Order of the Taïeb with the Touat and the Oulad Sidi Cheik—Influence of the Senousîya—Hurried Departure of our Hosts—Once more the Fear of a *Coup de Main* on the Part of the Sultan—Our Preparations for Departure, 124

CHAPTER IX.

Route from Wazzan to W. Wargha—A Hydrographic Problem to Solve—The Sherif's Escort—A Runaway Mule—Camping at Sok el Arba d'Aouf—View of the Dj. Kourt—Numerous Remains of Antiquity—The W. Rdat—The Valley of the Wargha—Fertility—Comparative Geography—The Dj. Setta and the Roman Town of Assada—We Cross the River—Incidents—We Encamp among the Oulad Messenana—Disease in the Rural Districts, ... 145

CHAPTER X.

From the Wargha to the Sebou—Geographical Description of the Country—The Present Information Insufficient—Difficulty of Scientific Explorations—Hills which separate the Slopes—Travelling on Foot—Aspect of the Valley of the Sebou—The Basin of the Sebou—Commercial Roads in the Moghreb—The Moqaddem of the Zaouïa—A Moorish Fantasia—Gastronomic Achievements—The Passage of the River—Adieux to our Friend the Moqaddem—We Encamp—The Qariya of the Qaïd Embarek ben Chleuh—The Zarhoun—Roman Roads in Morocco—Roman Antiquities—Volubilis and M. Tissot's Works—Mula Idris and the Fanaticism of its Population—Tocolosida—Environs of Meknas—Arrival in the Gardens—We enter the Moroccan Versailles, . . . 163

CHAPTER XI.

A Glance at the Origin and Historical Development of the City of Meknas—The Reign of the Sultan Mula Ismaïl, and the works undertaken by him—Treaties with the English—Antiquity of Relations with France—Want of Prosperity in Meknas—Insecurity of the Neighbourhood in the South—The Direct and Indirect Line of Communication between Meknas and the Atlantic littoral, ... 197

CHAPTER XII.

Evening on the Terraces—Scenes therefrom—Woman: her Condition and Life among the Mussulmen—Slavery in Morocco—The Influence of France on the Trade of the Sahara, . 219

CONTENTS.

Page

CHAPTER XIII.

The ever-recurring Ambassadorial Ceremonies—The Manner of Living in Morocco—Our Quarters—First Visit to the Sultan—His Personality and Pursuits—A Morisco School—The Morisco Politicians of the Future—Education in the Moghreb: the Narrowing Influence of Mussulman Bigotry and Fanaticism—Manner of Bringing up Children—Pitiful Influence of Residence in Europe on Morisco—Science in the Moghreb—The Sultan as a Chemist and Photographer—A Morisco Disguised as a Spanish General—Beauty of Arab Ornamentation—Good Quality of Morisco Goods, ... 238

CHAPTER XIV.

The Makhzen—Military Resources of the Sherifian Government—The Tribes of the Makhzen—Their History and Organization—The Moroccan Cavalry—How Recruited and Mounted—The Degeneracy of the Moghrebian Races—The Armament and Equipment of the Service—Military Tactics—Want of Homogeneity, ... 258

CHAPTER XV.

The Sherifian artillery: Its Composition—Armament, Material, and Instruction—The Infantry—The Prevailing Disorder—The Wretched Accoutrements—Mode of Recruiting—The Harrabas Battalion and the Qaïd Maclean—The French Military Mission—Its Diplomatic Object—History of the Christians in the Moroccan service, . . . 283

CHAPTER XVI.

A Moroccan Court of Appeal and Justice—Taxation—Presents to the Sultan—The Government Budget and the Emperor's Fortune—The Expenditure—The Harem and how Recruited—The Europeans who figure in it—Administrative Disorder—The Influence of Renegades—History of two such Celebrities—Our Andalusian Servant, a hoary old Renegade Assassin, 306

CONTENTS.

Page

CHAPTER XVII.

The Sultan at the Mosque on Fridays—The Ceremonial—His drives—His Carriage—Mulai Hassan on horseback—Various customs of the Moroccan Army—The Sultan a man of war—His good intentions—The procrastination displayed by his orthodox entourage—The deplorable influence on the destiny of Barbary of the black Soudanese element—The probable effects of the Derkawa and the Senousiya—Incessant political and religious rivalry—The intellectual pabulum of a Moroccan Sultan in the 16th century—Ignorance of the Court—The real capital and camp of the Emperor—Want of prestige on the part of the Government—The abuses arising out of the insufficiency of the salaries—Military supplies—The story of a gun battery—Imperial favour obtained by means of a watch, ... 324

CHAPTER XVIII.

The excessive Fanaticism of Meknas—Our perfect security—Tranquillity assured by the system of Collective Responsibility—The Aïssawa—Their practices—History of the Confraternity—Our projected journey to Tafilalt rendered uncertain—Departure for Fez—The Route—Mehdouma—The Adventure of the Sultan's Musician—Insecurity of the Country—Arrival at Fez, ... 344

CHAPTER XIX.

Our Installation in the City of Mula Idris—A Gaoler and his Houris—Too flattering opinion of an Arab Chronicler—Necessity of following M. Zola's method in describing Fez—The Hydraulic System—Impurity of the Water a certain Factor in Fever and Dysentery—Deplorable State of the Streets—Primitive Method of Cleaning them—Suffocating Temperature—Population—Moral Disorder—The Universities—Destruction of Old Literary Treasures—The Students—Carping Spirit of the Populace—The Feast of Tholba—A Visit to a Pacha—Scandals and Abuses of the Protective System in Morocco—The Principle of Collective Responsibility, ... 366

CONTENTS.

CHAPTER XX.

Strategical View of Fez—Defences of the City—Siege of City by Mulai Hassan—Importance of its geographical position—Historical survey—Etymology of Fez—Invasion of the Merinides—Foundation of Fez Djedid—District of El Qaïraouiyn and of Andalusia—Commercial Importance—Algerian Influence—Insecurity of the commercial routes—Local Industries—Jewish Brandy—Neighbouring Salt Mines—Illness of my companion—Visit of a great Moroccan personage—The Moroccans at the house of a sick man—The Kiff and native medicine—Preparations for departure—The Consular Agent of France at Fez—Departure from the town—General Aspect—Overwhelming Heat—Route to Safrou—Revolt at South of Empire—The Qasbah of Qçabi es Shorfa—Aït Isdig and Aït Youssi—Impossibility of continuing journey—Route to Meknas—The Qariya of the Aït Ouelal and of the Béni Methirs—Return to Meknas—A Sultan as photographer—Farewell to Military Mission—Departure for Tangiers—Route of the Ambassadors—Valley of W. Rdem—Plain of Sebou—The Qariya of El Habbassi—The Marabout of Lella Mimouna—Succinct orography and hydrography of the region—Arrival at El Araïsh—History of the town—Spanish Occupation—French Expedition under Du Chaffaut—Estuary of the Kous, and Commerce of the Town—Azila—Portuguese Occupation—Episode in the siege—Passage of the Tahedart—Return to Tangiers, ... 385

BIBLIOGRAPHY OF MOROCCO, 1844—1885, . . 423
LIST OF MAPS AND CHARTS OF MOROCCO, . . 455

LIST OF ROUTE-MAPS AND PLANS.

Tangiers to Alkazar,	to face page	49
Alkazar to Wazzan,	,,	81
Wazzan,	,,	126
Wazzan to Zaouia of El Mazeria,	,,	145
R. Sebou to Meknās,	,,	177
Meknās,	,,	196
Meknās to Fās and Saforo,	,,	420

PREFACE.

The shallow scratches made in the still almost virgin soil of Morocco by historians and travellers have increased the thirst for any really useful and scientific information regarding that country; for since the time of Leo Africanus a long blank occurs, filled up, indeed, by such writers as Windhus and Leared in the last century, and, in our own time, by the more practical researches of Rohlfs, Tissot and Sir Joseph Hooker; but while these works have all their separate interests, the volume now to hand will occupy in its turn a special page in the History of the northern division of Morocco. It is with reluctance I have acceded to M. de la Martinière's request to write a few lines of Preface to his book, but my former connections with the country, and the fact of my being able, as far as my own knowledge goes, to testify to the accuracy of his statements, have induced me to make the attempt.

When, in 1881, I published the account of a "Mission to the Court of Morocco," I indulged in a too confident hope that some practical results might accrue from the Conference of Madrid, which followed immediately after the return of H.M. Envoy from the Sherifian Court. That such anticipations have not been altogether fulfilled is apparent to any who have followed the course of events in that part of North Africa during the last seven years; and the account of the condition of affairs, as portrayed in the present work, shows that the Ministers of Mulai Hassan are not alone in this 19th century in pursuing a system which, to use the now historical words of an eminent statesman, is "assuredly tending, through violence and rapine, to the dismemberment of the Empire."

The question of the future of Morocco is of such wide and ever-increasing importance, that it is matter of congratulation to find the subject treated by one who, from long personal association with the country, is competent to undertake the task; considering, also, the tension between France and England, which exists in another part of Africa, the nationality of the author will, while ensuring him the indulgence of English readers, not detract from the interest of his work.

It is, indeed, an ambitious and delicate task for a Frenchman to write, for the English public, of a country whose future may, possibly, be the cause of diplomatic difficulties between the two nations, and it is probable the views of the author may not be considered sufficiently advanced by some of his own compatriots; but past experience, and careful study of French, English and Spanish policies, as they bear upon the Morocco question, appear to have impressed M. de la Martinière with the conviction that an *entente cordiale* between his country and ours is as essential to the advancement of Morocco, as it would be conducive to preserving peace in the South of Europe; and representing, as the author does, the views of many of the more moderate of his countrymen, both in military and political circles, his opinions on the diplomatic situation will be received with attention.

Geographers and professional men who are interested in maps of hitherto unknown districts, will appreciate the admirable series which accompanies this volume, and they, as well as politicians, will derive advantage from the maturely considered deductions of this observant traveller. All will admit that individual opinions are valuable in proportion to the data on which they are formed, and there is no doubt that events may occur to concentrate, more than at present, the eyes of Europe on Morocco. The "Happy Realms" of the Sultan have always been an attractive bait, and if M. de la Martinière has helped to show that the Great Powers concerned may better combine to forward their several interests by the civilising effects of commerce and of exploration than by the sword, he will have rendered a service alike to diplomacy and to science.

The Moorish Army does not seem to have made much progress since, at the Sultan's request, I drew up a report on it in 1880; the system of recruiting indeed—according to M. de la Martinière—appears somewhat similar to that practised by the English in the early days of the Anglo-Egyptian Army, and, as the material is, at all events, of a no less warlike type, it is possible that the satisfactory results obtained in Egypt, may be rivalled by equally brilliant achievements on the part of Mulai Hassan's unwilling levies. More points of similarity than this might indeed be found between affairs in Morocco and those in Egypt, and pessimists in France and England who dread, mutually, a foreign occupation of either of these corners of North Africa might do worse than consider, with M. de la Martinière, that the most unlikely tactics of an invader are to place arms in the hands of the Aborigines, and to teach them their use.

P. D. TROTTER, *Lt.-Colonel.*

CURRAGH CAMP, *April,* 1889.

MOROCCO.

CHAPTER I.

Gibraltar, the starting point—The Passage—The Scenery on either Side of the Straits—View of Tangiers—The Monkeys' Mountain—The Arrival—Tangiers—Description of the Streets—The Great Mosque—The Legations—The Postal Establishments of the different European Powers—Scene in the Soko or Market Place—Story-telling—Danger to a Sceptical European—Pretended Oriental Dancing and Imposition on Foreigners—His Sherifian Majesty's Foreign Secretary—His skill in Entangling Diplomatic Affairs—The Governor's Palace—Its Marvels—The Prison and its Horrors—The Beggars—The Old Wazir of the Arabian Nights.

GIBRALTAR is generally the starting point for those who wish to cross to Tangiers, as there is no regular service of boats from Cadiz, and few travellers care to run the risks of a passage in the tiny bark which carries the mails from Tarifa to Morocco.

The journey of 35 miles across channel is effected in four hours by small steamers which are neither swift nor comfortable, and which are certainly redolent of the most frightful odours, their decks serving on the return journey to convey oxen and provisions for the victualling of Gibraltar. When the sea runs high in the Straits, the passage is indeed a truly painful ordeal; the frail vessel is tossed about by the waves like a mere shell, and, being almost at the mercy of the swift currents, ships so many seas that it is quickly half-filled with water. Passengers, who, under these circumstances, have neither the leisure nor the wish to admire the fine panorama on either side, find themselves in a truly pitiable state. In fine weather, the journey is, on the contrary, a most pleasant one, especially as the course followed between Spain and Africa allows no portion of the shore to escape notice.

The boat steams from the end of the bay—or rather gulf of Algeciras—where the commerce of Gibraltar, with its facilities for victualling, attracts a large array of merchant ships. The roads, with their commercial activity, offer a strange contrast to the lifeless and deserted appearance of the Spanish shore. They are enlivened by the incessant arrival and departure of steamers which stop here to take in their fuel from the huge hulks, the remains of some glorious frigates now doing duty as coal stores.

You leave the mole under the vigilant eye of the British sentry whose red coat stands out on the grey line of fortifications, each embrasure of which must appear as an eternal challenge to the Spanish officers of Algeciras. The town, with lines of houses rising like an amphitheatre, is commanded by an imposing mass of rocks, and, from the bridge of boats, one can admire all the grand details of the scenery. The barren rock might be taken for some crouching monster now transformed, by severe and incessant toil, into an impregnable fortress. Some illusion even of being in the country has been procured for the inhabitants, by the costly formation of a square planted out as a garden, whose mass of verdure contrasts favourably with the tints of the rocks scorched for centuries by the fierce sun. In the mountain itself every crevice has been cunningly taken advantage of and arranged so as to allow of a few shrubs sprouting there. The undertaking is certainly praiseworthy; and, bearing in mind what has been accomplished, we might ask ourselves what would Gibraltar be in the hands of the Spaniards? Those who are unacquainted with the Spanish administration would be enabled to speculate on the probable result by simply making an excursion to Algeciras. To mention only one instance: a small dyke may be seen, which was entirely destroyed some years ago, and has been left ever since in its ruinous state by the Andalusian administration, the consequence being that very complicated and cautious manœuvring is necessary to ensure a safe landing when the sea runs high.

The decks of the small steamers already mentioned, are generally crowded by that motley throng to be met with only in the neighbourhood of Eastern countries. Greasy Jews in hideous costumes, renegade Arabs, who are callous enough to trade without a pang of remorse on Christian land, and who add to their natural Eastern duplicity all the vices of civilization: such are the elements of the first picture which meets our gaze, and which does not leave on us a very favourable impression.

Among the devoted adherents of modern civilization, who have allowed themselves to be carried along by the wave of progress, adopting the hat and black frock-coat, are many with suspiciously hooked noses and olive complexions, and, as we gaze upon them, we are enlightened as to the facility with which the sons of Israel in Morocco assume the European garb. Their success in passing themselves off for Christians will enable them to surmount many difficulties as well as save their shoulders from too frequent an application of the stick. Should he be lucky enough to enjoy the protection of some foreign government, Abraham, Jacob, or Moses, is assured of being enabled to put to good use the store of gold bequeathed him by his forefathers.

The boat steams away from the European cape and leaves Algeciras on its right, which, in a short time, appears only as a white spot, whilst Gibraltar stands out in all its details. We can yet make out the signals of the semaphore and the blue ensign waving from the distant light-house. After passing the cape of Carnero our boat, now fairly on its course, hugs the Spanish coast as far as Tarifa so as to keep clear of the swift currents which run from the Atlantic into the Mediterranean and make the passage a difficult one even for a steamer. This northern coast is highly interesting, and as the boat hugs the shore no details of the scenery are lost.

The small beaches ensconced at the foot of towering cliffs, crowned by ruined towers, together with the cottages of the custom-house officers which rise unexpectedly as if to defy the smugglers—who are bold and numerous on this part of the coast—form many pretty features of a picturesque scene. Across the straits looms the lofty "Monkeys' Mountain," which protects Ceuta, whose houses appear in the distance like white sea-fowl resting on the shore. This chain of barren heights which, at all times, has attracted the attention of sea-farers, owing to its position on the edge of the great sea highways, was well known to the ancients. The "Monkeys' Mountain" of the Sierra Bullones is no other than the Djebel Bellyounech, a ridge called "Septem Fratres" by the Romans. By some effort of the imagination one of the peaks which command the channel may appear to have the form of an elephant. This "elephant" is the Djebel Mouça, which towers above the channel at its narrowest point.

The mountainous mass vies in boldness of outline with the rock of Gibraltar and surpasses it in altitude (2574 feet). Almost constantly shrouded in a thick mist, it soars above the neighbouring peaks, but on a close inspection it proves to be nothing more than a confused heap of scattered rocks with a few shrubs clinging here and there to the edges of deep precipices.

It is not easy to discern, on that jagged coast, the tiny island of Peregil about which some diplomatic difficulty between England and Spain arose in 1859. These shores consist mostly of deep ravines, fringed by a belt of white foam formed by the breakers on the reefs, which for centuries have been lashed and beset by the waves of the Straits of Gibraltar—(Gaditanum Fretum of the "Anonyme of Ravenne").

Just before we pass the heights of Tarifa we are able to discern, with the aid of the glass, a white tower, on the summit of a promontory of the African coast. At this point commences the bay of Tangiers, which bursts quite unexpectedly on our sight. The boat then alters its course, and, cleaving the wave, shapes its way direct towards ancient Tingis leaving Tarifa with its lighthouse and weak defences far behind. We then perceive the clusters of houses which glisten in the sun and rise in tiers along the hillside. The scene around us is full of interest. Far in the rear lies the Spanish coast, ending precipitously in the waters made famous by Hercules, and forming the extreme point of Europe, whose civilisation rises threateningly opposite these shores of Morocco, where a fanatical race preserve, in an undefiled sanctuary, the fierce precepts of Islam.

Tangiers offers a most attractive sight, with its white terraces, china minarets, and sparse palm-trees. It is situated on the northern slopes of a hill, along whose sides half the houses straggle up in tiers,—gilded and illuminated, like all African towns, by that glorious sun which, as if by magic, transforms everything under the blue sky. At the entrance of the bay we pass by a promontory, from which rises the Torre Blanca. This is the Malabatta, covered with laurel shrubs which grow in the midst of masses of rock. Before the boat was hove to, the whole of the Kasbah has been reviewed, together with its old ramparts and sandy beach, stretching as far as the old walls of the town. The whole vista is shaded by the green but gloomy foliage of a grove of cedars, situated just above the town. It must be mentioned that during the last few years some modern-looking buildings have been erected, but the glaring red of their roofs and the ugly style of architecture savour too much of the prosaic railway station. The impression they leave on you is soon dispelled, however, by the truly Eastern appearance of the minarets standing out against the blue African sky, tinged with crimson streaks by the setting sun. You experience, indeed, the sensation of being really in the East when the boat stops alongside the jetty, which, built by the English and destroyed by them when they evacuated the place in 1685, now offers some danger to navigation.

We at last cast anchor, and then a number of small boats full of Arabs and Jews row swiftly up, and cling to the sides of our bark. Scarcely have the steps been lowered than a swarm of these boatmen, the descendants of ancient pirates, climb up, agile as monkeys, and invade the deck, where they begin to quarrel for the possession of passengers and their luggage. A struggle ensues, fierce shouts rend the air, they rush about like madmen, and the inexperienced tourist, seeing them seize his portmanteaus and lay violent hands upon himself, perceives at once that *he* is the prize they are fighting for. Shameless interpreters offer their services, giving glowing accounts of the comfort offered by this or that hotel. At last, hurried away into a boat, with his baggage tossed in anyhow after him, the unlucky passenger finds himself completely bewildered and stunned by the horrible din of these worthies, who yell out a horrible mixture of all the languages in creation. The guide, on landing, will naturally take you to the hotel which allows him the highest premium for his prey; and the unfortunate traveller will have to sustain a fresh and terrible onset, when all the ragtag and bobtail of the harbour will claim from him as much money, all put together, as would perhaps buy up the whole of Morocco.

The tribulations and fearful ordeals which travellers have to go through are witnessed with interest and satisfaction by the loafers of the town. The dandies of the place are to be seen here on the arrival of the boat, amusing themselves, and viewing the misfortunes of the passengers with a silly and would-be ironical smile. But, when you get acquainted with the place, nothing of the kind will befall you as you know how to treat the obtrusive ones according to their deserts, and, once fairly on shore, you strike forthwith across country, and seek some cottage where you may enjoy the peaceful and enthralling life of the East.

To the tourist unacquainted with the Mohammedan

world all seems strange in Tangiers, where everything affords evidence of the backward state of civilisation of the disciples of the Arab Prophet; and yet Tangiers is, in certain respects, a European town—a town accursed, as good Mohammedans will say—and wholly given up to the unfaithful.

The entrance to the town is by the gate Babel Mesra, which fronts the sea at the landing point. Here may be seen a small pavilion, used as the Custom house. Some assistant officials examine the luggage outside, whilst inside the building are three officers of the Customs, fine looking men who squat on cushions with Eastern calm and stolidness, and keep a watchful eye on the doings of their subordinates. It seems as if these handsome Moors had been stationed there to give the foreigner an idea of the beauty of the race. These noble looking Orientals, with oval faces, silky beards, calm expression, and spotless white haïk flowing about their persons in majestic folds, are, indeed splendid specimens of humanity, The fineness of their hands, the elegance of their robes made of the richest and most delicately coloured stuffs, are the distinctive characteristics of a refined race, which has well nigh fallen back into a state of barbarism, but to which Spain owes much of her art and architecture. The streets of Tangiers are extremely narrow. They are designed, like everything else there, with the view of protecting the inhabitants against the fierce rays of the sun. The main street runs through the town from end to end, and leads from the harbour to the Soko or market-place. At certain hours of the day, the Soko is thronged by a large crowd of turbaned Moors, and swarthy Arabs in snowy flowing robes, who stop now and then to make purchases. How common-place a European looks in this bright picture under the cloudless blue African sky!

All the traffic of the town, which numbers about 15,000 inhabitants, takes place here. The other streets are nothing but dirty and tortuous lanes which a donkey with its pack will block up, and compel you either to retrace your steps or to stand on the threshold of a doorway. The luxury of paving-stones offered by the main street, horribly sharp and slippery though they be, is denied to the other parts of Tangiers. Herds of oxen and strings of camels block up the narrow ways, and nothing can be more unpleasant than to be jammed with one's steed between two of these huge animals. I recollect *à propos* of such disagreeable accidents the misadventure which befell a party of tourists who got entangled in a caravan of camels. The driver was a wild-looking Bedouin, who perhaps had never beheld so large a concourse of Europeans, or had his attention distracted from his duties by the sight of their strange attire. At any rate, he did not think of restraining the progress of his animals, some of which made a fierce onset on the pretty bonnets of the ladies, making a meal of the flowers and fruits which adorned the fashionable productions of some Parisian modiste or other. The result was comical in the extreme, the victims uttering loud cries for assistance, to which, naturally, I instantly responded.

It must be said that if one runs the risk of being trampled upon in the streets of Tangiers, there is no danger of being run over by vehicles for the simple reason that no such conveyances exist, owing to the absence of suitable roads and the narrowness of the streets.

The main street is lined by a number of quaint little stalls, where the stallkeepers find scarcely sitting room for themselves. Here they squat all day waiting for purchasers but seemingly unwilling to sell anything to anybody. The floors of these holes are carpeted with matting, and the furniture consists of one or two cushions occupied sometimes by a visitor who has come to have a conversation with his friend in the low and mysterious tone peculiar to Eastern people. A few of these shops or rather cupboards are tenanted by lawyers or some kinds of notaries, the knees of the occupant doing duty for a writing desk. The consultations are generally protracted, thanks to the figurative character of the Arabic tongue. The lawyer listens without moving a muscle, and when the client has left he closes his office, puts on his babouches, and retreats with his cushion under his arm to his dwelling at the bottom of some narrow lane.

In the main street are to be seen a few buildings the importance of which is great in the estimation of the inhabitants. Here rises the great mosque which no Christian, no infidel, is suffered to defile with his "accursed presence." Outside stand some ragged beggars whose fanaticism does not prevent them from soliciting alms from the Roumis. A kind of large curtain and a double wooden barrier screen the sanctuary from inquisitive eyes. On one solitary occasion, however, I was enabled to enter its precincts, but at a lonely hour and under favour of a *jellaba*. The details were of no particular interest. A fountain at which the faithful perform their ablutions occupies the centre of the first court, the galleries are carpeted with mats, and the greatest simplicity reigns here. In a corner are stowed away the stretchers used at burials and in front is erected the Imaum's pulpit.

The Spanish Legation looks on the small square halfway up the main street. The former building was destroyed during the war of 1860, and the large massive structure which replaced it is of no particular interest as far as architecture is concerned. The Spaniards have their post-office in the square, and at one of the corners, at the entrance of a pestiferous lane, the English post-office is situated. The French and Spaniards possess decent accommodation for their postal establishments—why then should Her Majesty's service be reduced to take shelter in a miserable shop in the midst of most awful odours?

This crossway which is alive with the commercial movement of the town is, till two o'clock, generally full of women They offer milk, butter, and eggs for sale. They arrive early in the morning, and do not look very prosperous—poor old women with parchment-like skin and emaciated countenance, proffering their wares with hands wrinkled and tanned, like those of a mummy. A few have on their heads those immense straw hats, which serve at the same time as parasols in this country where a parasol is the exclusive emblem and privilege of sovereignty.

On ascending the High Street may be seen the new Catholic Chapel and the Christian school, both under the direction of Spanish ecclesiastics. You then come up to the town gate known by the name of the gate Soko.

The Soko or market-place is full of scenes to which the brush alone could do justice. In what other way indeed, can you depict the mass of picturesque rags, quaint faces, and mad gesticulations of people who, for a few flouss, will curse and abuse one another in the vivid and rich language of the East? Here you have ample means of marking the difference between the apathetic Moor squatting in his shop and the country Arab and the Berber who both live in the open air and are robust and healthy.

In the midst of a cloud of reddish dust, under a scorching sun, a thousand excited bawling and shrieking fellows move amongst heaps of vegetables, fruit, and numbers of wretched chickens tightly fastened together, whose shrill notes swell the universal concert of sheep, goats, and lean cows, donkeys, horses, and mules. Now and then, one of the latter will escape, and galloping furiously through the crowd will smash the china wares of some poor old women who have toiled painfully to bring them up to market. The dogs, the horrible Eastern dogs, more like famished wolves than our own affectionate European animals, take advantage of the disorder to snatch a piece of meat or some offal from the stall of a butcher. In one corner an Arab veterinary surgeon conscientiously applies a red-hot iron to some unfortunate animals, making the air unpleasantly redolent of burnt grease and tar. No Europeans are to be seen here, with the exception perhaps of an old innkeeper, followed by a young Arab who takes charge of his purchases. I never visited the Soko without my curiosity being as keen as ever, or without feeling interested in this mobile picture, with its bright and beautiful light transparent atmosphere.

But towards the close of day, at the charming and poetical hour when the sun sinks behind the heights of Cape Spartel, and the ordinary crowd have retreated, there may be seen on that same market-place groups which show to better advantage the naive features and quaint characteristics of the population.

Around a story-teller, whose spirit and *verve* elicit shouts of laughter, and awaken keen curiosity, a large audience is seated on the ground in a three-deep circle. The clever orator, who alone is standing, chants a long prayer, listened to in religious silence. Now and then all the heads are bowed, and from all mouths comes forth a general Amen. Woe to the European sceptic who lingers to gaze with a sarcastic smile on this phase of Eastern life! More than one eye will flash with a fierce glance at the accursed Roumi, and presently he will be taken to task by the tale-teller and form the theme of an extempore anecdote. Should he linger, he will see the whole audience turn their eyes towards him, laugh and show their glistening teeth in a broad grin; and unable to realize to what extent his common-place attire and appearance have been ridiculed by the mocking listeners, the tourist, highly satisfied with his lounge and with himself, will that night relate at the table d'hôte all that he has heard concerning the impending holy war.

The Arab story-tellers have always appeared to me to be incomparable actors, whether they seek to fan into flame the smouldering passions of their audience by religious and warlike poems, charm by marvellous accounts the dreamy imagination of their hearers, or strive by means of an apologue to impress upon them some philosophical truths. They bring into play all the resources of ingenious pantomimic action—simple, though highly expressive and picturesque. The play of their features attracts the eyes, whilst their speeches charm the ears and stir the soul. Their gestures, now grave, now comical, now violent, but in constant and perfect harmony with the thoughts or images which they seek to convey, the noble gracefulness of their movements, the long snowy drapery flowing from their heads, with its many folds gathered under the arm or thrown back over the shoulder, form an *ensemble* which gives the orator an appearance of power and antique grandeur.

Occasionally, an orchestra consisting of tambourines and

fifes will aid in heightening the emotions and rapture of the audience. The melody begins with deep bass notes, which support the recital and make it more forcible; then follows a short, rapid, violent beating of tom-toms, and finally a rolling succession of raps as an accompaniment to the feelings of the orator when he sums up his improvisation in poetical and passionate accents. At this point the fifes, tambourines and tom-toms, burst out together into a frightful discord. The musicians throw their instruments up in the air, and with comical skill catch them again as they descend, without much interruption to their performance. Finally, they all rise to solicit some small reward from the audience.

Tandjah or Tindja-t-el-Baïda[1] the white, as the Moriscos call the town, hardly deserves an appellation which would place her on a level with Cairo. Many nooks and corners, however, have arrested the attention of the painter by their picturesque quaintness. Such artists as Henri Regnault and Benjamin Constant have visited Tangiers and found here subjects for their masterpieces.

It must be confessed that, in point of architecture, the town does not offer many features of interest. The lower part, inhabited by Christians, Jews, and a few Arabs, is common-place enough. Tangiers does not possess, as other towns of Morocco, a "mellah" or separate quarter for the disciples of Moses. Owing to this fact, as well as to the presence of the foreign diplomatic representatives, the Mussulman portion of the population is singularly tolerant in most matters, so that it is hardly possible for one who visits Tangiers to form therefrom a general opinion of the inhabitants of Morocco.

[1] It is thus spelt by El Bekri.

Nevertheless, a ramble through the maze of its crooked and narrow streets will fully repay the traveller. Unless you are well acquainted with the topography of the place you will return several times to the starting point, but at each turning are to be found spots worthy of inspection. The uniformity of white walls is not unbroken, and here and there you find vestiges of the picturesque and primitive East which civilisation has as yet left untouched. There are low arches under which a horse can scarcely stand, slippery flagstones, on which one has to slide rather than walk, and walls with such little space between that a narrow strip of azure is all one can see of the sky. Then, the olfactory organs are sometimes offended by strange smells, of which the natives do not seem to take the slightest notice. Rancid butter, sticky masses of dates, are spread out in the sun, and are soon covered by black swarms of flies. And it is only when the shopman serves a customer, wiping the while his hands across his brow, that you become aware of the nature of the merchandise. You soon grow accustomed to the odours, however, and they make you appreciate more keenly the delicious fragrance of the eau de rose with which every Mussulman knows so well how to sprinkle you on fitting occasions.

The Arab cafés are not worthy of notice, being frequented by the scum of the doubtful characters who levy blackmail on the stranger. Often when a distinguished European puts up at an hotel, the cunning guides, for a consideration to the landlord, get the café closed to the public, and bring there a few Jewesses, or girls of indifferent character, attired in Moorish costume. The distinguished foreigner is then escorted to the place, and is treated to some so-called Oriental dancing. After having been thus cheated and fleeced he departs, fully convinced that he has witnessed one of the most original and curious scenes of Eastern life. In winter similar performances are given almost every evening.

In the lower town stands the Kasbah, the seat of Government and the dwelling of the famous Sidi Mohammed Bargash, his Sherifian Majesty's Foreign Secretary, whose duty is to act as intermediary between the representatives of the ambassadors and his august Sovereign.[1] In this capacity S. M. Bargash used to show great skill in minimizing the importance of diplomatic incidents, and great ingenuity in temporizing and bringing into play all the artifices of Oriental cunning.

High up in this second town are the prisons, and in this quarter dwell a certain number of Mussulmen, who decline to live side by side with Christians and Jews. The road leading to it is steep, and brings you to a plateau which lies in front of the great gate, and whence a fine view is obtained of the straits, the lower town, and the country. It was on this spot that executions used to take place, but now the death penalty is rarely carried out. This leniency is not due to motives of philanthropy, for the culprit, in fact, generally falls a martyr to the horrible state of the prisons, or is allowed to perish of starvation. People repair to the plateau in the evening to enjoy the fine view; and Moorish women may be seen at sunset coming up to the Moghreb, for at this hour their husbands are at the mosque. This is the time for gossiping. They pay visits to one another, and climb from terrace to terrace, showing much agility and talent for gymnastics in the operation. How little do they then resemble, in their bright costumes, made more con-

---

[1] S. M. Bargash died 1886. His successor is S. M. Torrès, of Hispano-Moorish descent.

spicuous by the snow-white of the walls, the walking phantoms to be met in the streets, clad in the enormous and heavy haïk, from under which peep a couple of red babouches.

The Kasbah is commanded by a pretty octagonal minaret adorned with graceful arabesques and elegant ogives. As for the palace of the governor, it is certainly worthy of a special visit. I was much impressed when, on a glorious sunny morning, I had the honour to be ushered into the presence of the illustrious S. M. Bargash, an old grey-haired, red-bearded Arab, with a German-looking face, and gold spectacles. He showed us the utmost courtesy, and was obliging enough to do in person the honours of the old palace. My sensations were such, when I entered this magnificent specimen of Oriental architecture, that I was hardly conscious of the presence of my distinguished guide. The ceiling and walls in a succession of small halls are profusely decorated with lace-like delicate arabesques, and painted in a hundred vivid colours. Here and there some charming nooks, full of a dim, soft light, evoked in my imagination a vision of those mysterious harems of which we cannot possibly form any idea under our dull, leaden skies. We threaded many passages with abrupt turnings, small staircases topped by cupolas, recalling the splendours of the Alhambra, and leading to beautiful apartments with marble floors, on which rest slender and fragile-looking pillars of wood and plaster. Capitals made airy with intricate designs like lace-work, serve as cornices, and delicately carved windows—real masterpieces of decorative art—complete the ensemble, whilst pretty flower-beds load the air with delicious perfumes, and a thread of rippling water alone breaks this truly Oriental calm and silence. The palace has no occupants but His Excellency, who dwells at one end of the building, leading the life of a philosopher who has renounced the vanities of society, or of a government official fearful of exciting the jealousy of his master. When you leave the ruins of the beautiful place, you cannot help thinking how much these Moors must have degenerated to allow the architectural grandeur of their forefathers thus to fall into decay.

I will now say a few words of the prisons, and of the penitentiary system, so primitive and so cruel.

The prison of Tangiers lies at the very doors of the Pacha's dwelling. On entering within its precincts we gaze through a constantly open wicket, and our eyes rest on a frightful scene. The imprisoned culprits, who do not receive enough food to sustain life, would die of starvation if their friends did not come to their succour. Several hundreds of these poor wretches, some chained up to the wall, others wandering about like lugubrious ghosts, live on the bare stones, amidst horrible filth, and covered with vermin. Some of these half-naked prisoners have not seen the sun for years, and lead such a life of misery that for them death would indeed be a blessing. Others have been thrown into this abominable dungeon for the most trifling fault, and the thief and murderer live side by side with the innocent man, out of whom the Pacha wishes to squeeze some extra taxes.

The Pacha, taking up his station under an elegantly designed porch at the bottom of a kind of blind alley near the prison, deigns on certain mornings to administer justice. The scene, though simple, is not bereft of grandeur. Seated on a heap of cushions, with his secretary by his side, the representative of Sherifian authority listens attentively and passes judgment. An acquittal is of rare occurrence, as it brings less than would a conviction to his greedy purse. The soldiers lead in the prisoners, who, after sentence, are at once conveyed to the frightful place of which we have spoken, and which, in the Pachalik of Tangiers, is the sole expression of the Penitentiary system. In the square of the Kasbah may be seen a curious building, with a portal of Portuguese origin. It was used a few years ago as a storehouse for the chests containing the coin which the Sultan obtained from the French Mint, and on the other side is the lazar-house, a kind of shed, where the poor wretches suffering from skin diseases seek shelter. I will not dwell on these horrible sights, which soon cause you to avert your eyes.

Beggars, with a few picturesque rags which barely cover them, are numerous in Tangiers. Here a mulatto, with a huge black wig on his head and twanging the strings of a guitar, is squalling at the foot of a wall, and displays his legs swollen by elephantiasis. Further on, an ancient hadgi, in an old faded green cafetan, supports his mutilated body on crutches. His parchment-like face, and large eyes, deadened by the use of narcotics, but flashing now and then with a strange light, give him the appearance of some wazīr of the Arabian Nights. Covered with strings of quaint charms, and leaning on a kind of lance, this curious old fellow looks like an Indian fakir rapt in some fanatical trance.

CHAPTER II.

History of Tangiers—M. Tissot's Researches—The Town under the Romans—Invasion of the Vandals—The Mussulman Conquest—The Chief Ocba—The Portuguese Occupation—The British Occupation—Sherif Abd-es-Selam, and the Curious Amusements of His Friends who pay dearly for them—Tangiers Bombarded—System of Defences of the Town—The Armstrong Guns and the Gunners—The Transaction of Diplomatic Business, a Farce—The Press at Tangiers—The European Population—The Climate—Dismal Appearance of the Town in Winter—The Environs—Shooting and Pig-Sticking—Trick played by the Beaters on Successful Sportsmen—View from Cape Trafalgar—Archæological Researches—Cape Spartel.

I WILL now devote a few lines to the history of Tangiers, and to the vicissitudes of the unfortunate city, which was once the capital of the Tingitane Mauretania, and after reaching the height of its prosperity, was nearly destroyed during the invasion of Islam.

The lamented M. Tissot, to whom we owe many learned researches on the antiquities of Mauretania, has established beyond doubt that the ancient Tingis or Tingi of the Romans occupied the very site on which Tangiers now stands. Its origin, however, has not been traced, and the tradition according to which Antæus was its founder proves, at any rate, that previous to the first Oriental migrations, it must have been one of the principal centres of the native race. As to the origin of the Arab word Tandjah, it would be difficult to establish that it is derived from any but the Berber tongue, which again borrowed it from the Lybian, and, in supporting this theory, Tissot remarks that on the coast of Tunisia there exists a place called Tindja.

The Bay of Tangiers has always been of considerable geographical importance. Owing to its position at the base of the lesser slopes and its severance from the Atlantic and Mediterranean basins formed by the prolongation of the Djebel Andjera from Ceuta to Cape Spartel it partly commands the Straits. Very few traces of the Roman period are to be found at Tangiers, as the different foreign occupiers have scarcely left anything standing save some Corinthian or composite columns and capitals adorning the lobby of the Kasbah, and two granite columns which have lain for centuries by the side of the old mosque. In the time of Abou Obeïd el Bekri, there still existed some memorials of the past, such as arches, crypts, aqueducts, and a number of marble statues. When these ruins were excavated, says the Arab writer, jewels of various kinds were discovered, especially in the ancient tombs. The soil has indeed been explored so thoroughly that nowadays nothing is found but worthless debris.[1]

When founding colonies in the Mauritania, Augustus had granted to the inhabitants of Tangiers the title of Roman citizens. The history of the Roman power and civilization

---

[1] We may mention also as traces of the Roman occupation the remains of an aqueduct, or at least of subterranean ducts supplying water to the town which now has none during the great heat. These works are in such a good state of preservation that Mr. W., formerly an officer in the British navy, thought they might be repaired and used for the waterworks of a company to be established at Tangiers.

in this part of Africa is still obscure. The part played later on by the Tingitane[1] seems to have been almost insignificant. Albinus, the procurator appointed by Galba, seemed to entertain some design of making himself independent, but he was defeated and killed by Claudius Rufus whom Vitellius sent against him, A.D. 69. The weakness of the ties between the Empire and its provinces shows itself again in the insurrections which took place in the reign of Hadrian, who, in A.D. 122, was compelled to quell them in person, as the governors Lucius Quietus and Martius Turbo were unequal to the task. Under Antoninus, revolts broke out afresh, and under Marcus Aurelius, a Roman expedition seems to have penetrated even as far as the Atlas, A.D. 138. Finally, in the reign of Alexander Severus, the Roman troops were engaged in perpetual conflict with the rebel mountaineers.

When, in A.D. 292, Maximus Hercules shared with Constantius Chlorus the western provinces, he kept Africa for himself but joined the Tingitane to Hispania, and assigned them both to his associate.

Two centuries later, the northern part of the country was invaded by Vandals from Spain, at the bidding of Boniface, who wished thus to revenge himself on his perfidious rival Actius. These invaders, to the number of 80,000, including some Sueves, Alans, and Goths, crossed the Straits, and marched through Mauritania against Carthage. Most probably they hardly touched the Tingitane, as their goal lay elsewhere. In any case, their sway in the East was of

---

[1] The genuine Mauritania or country of the Moors, which from the ancient city of Tingi or Tangier, was distinguished by the appellation of Tingitana, is represented by the modern kingdom of Fez. *Gibbon*—"Decline and Fall of the Roman Empire."

short duration; the Moors made incessant attacks on them after the death of Genseric, A.D. 477, and drove them back as far as Numidia. Belisarius, at the time of the Greek conquest, wrested Africa from the Vandals, A.D. 533-534; but Justinian reinstated the Tingitane among the seven African provinces, under the rule of the pretory of Carthage. It was entrusted to a consular governor, and the greatest precautions seem to have been taken at that very epoch to prevent the recurrence of invasions from Spain. Septa (now Ceuta) was fortified, and Belisarius established himself there in a strong position.[1]

In spite of all these precautions, the Greeks did not rule undisturbed, and their power was shaken by the continual revolt of the natives. The Visigoths, therefore, taking advantage of the waning strength of the Byzantines, crossed the Straits, probably in the reign of Suintila, A.D. 621-631, and established themselves in Tingis at Septa, and perhaps at other spots which no historical records have made known to us.

The unfortunate Tingitane was then wholly given up to the exactions of a barbarous race, whilst the Berbers were striving to rid themselves of a yoke which was soon to be replaced by one far more terrible. The famous Obka-ben-Nafé or, according to the Arab spelling, 'Ok'ba-ben-Nafê, the then Emir of Yezid I., who made his appearance in A.D. 681, fell like a thunderbolt on Moghreb el Acsa.[2] After a march

---

[1] It must have been at this time that they erected the works whose ruins are to be seen nearly two miles from the town, towards the eastern side of the shore, and known as old Tangiers (Tandjah el Balia). The same may be said of the battered bridge over the neighbouring river, called the "Roman Bridge," but which, in reality, dates from the Byzantine period.

[2] Moghreb el Acsa, *i.e.*, "the extreme West" or Morocco.

which it would be no easy matter to trace, he arrived in front of Tangiers, overthrowing or driving back all the forces which were seeking to oppose his progress. He was making preparations for crossing the Straits, when a Roumi[1] nobleman of the name of Yulan came to meet the conqueror, and, bearing him presents, offered his submission. Obka, having learnt that the Spanish coast was well defended, inquired where the chiefs of the Roumis and Berbers might be found. "As for the Roumis, you left them behind you," replied Yulan, "but on your road, you will find the Berbers, and God knows the number of their cavalry. They dwell at Sous-el-Adna. They are men without any religion, who devour dead bodies and drink the blood of their cattle; in one word, they are people who live like beasts, for they neither believe in God, nor have they even heard of Him."[2]

The Emir, burning with the fierce fanaticism of Islam, assembled his companions, and proceeded southwards, as far as the territory of the Lemtouna Berbers. Having fought some bloody battles, he captured a number of women of such marvellous beauty that they fetched as much as a thousand golden mithcals on the Eastern markets.[3]

Having then reached the shores of the Atlantic, says the story, he spurred his horse into the sea, and raising his hand

---

[1] It is easy to trace the derivation from Roman.

[2] There exists but few documents concerning the religion of ancient African natives. They deified their former chiefs, such as Antæus, and offered up human sacrifices. In any case, the Lybian origin of the Berbers, and the influence of the Punic colonies of the coast may be traced far up into the mountainous regions of the interior.

[3] According to "Ibn-el-Khaldum" ("History of the Berbers," vol. i. p. 333,) it seems that it was at Taroudant, that the conqueror gained the first victory which enabled him to enter the Sous-el-Adna.

towards heaven, exclaimed : " Lord, if these waters did not arrest my progress, I would go to distant lands and to the Kingdom of Dou-l'-Carnein, to fight for Thy religion and slay the infidels who worship other gods than Thee."

I quote the above only to give an instance of Mussulman fanatical zeal, and to show what an easy prey Morocco, then given up to anarchy, must have been.

The incidents of the taking of Ceuta, a prelude to the irruption of the Arabs into Spain, are worthy of record. The Visigoths had just lost Tangiers, but they had retained possession of Ceuta, whose strong position could probably defy any attack. Nevertheless, the town was given up, and in the same way that Boniface had formerly opened Africa for the Vandals, Julian the governor opened Spain for the Arabs, by surrendering the passage of the Straits.

Tarek[1] was the first to land on the rock of Calpe which ever since has borne his name. He visited the point of Algeciras[2] and returned in order to prepare with his master, Mouça, for the landing of his troops in the following year, and for the victory of Xeres which was to be the signal for the downfall of the Iberian monarchy of the Visigoths.

It is easy to perceive that all the northern region of Morocco must have been of great importance for the conquerors, who were enabled thence to watch the Straits. The bay of Tangiers, the point of Alqaçar, the islet of Peregil, or El Coral on the west side of Ceuta, are familiar names in the history of the Conquest of Mauritania. These were the starting points for the Moorish fleets when they sailed for the conquest of Spain.

[1] Gibraltar, a corruption of Djebel Tarek or Tarik.
[2] Algeciras, a corruption of El-Djezirat-el-Radra or the Emerald Isle.

At the point of Alqaçar, you see nothing but a small number of hovels. Some ruins, almost disappearing under the brambles and sand, form the only traces of the town founded by Iacoub el Mansour in the 12th century. We are informed that these constructions were posterior to the Qaçar Masmouda, of very old Berber origin. This was the place of embarking for Tarifa, the straits there being only nine miles wide. For that reason, it attracted the notice of the Portuguese who seized upon the town in 1458. They left it in 1540 and since that epoch the little place seems to have been left alone. King John I. of Portugal, who had some designs upon Ceuta, was lucky enough in 1415 to obtain possession of that city which was to become so suitable a starting point for African expeditions. The revolution of 1640 delivered up the town into the hands of the Spaniards. It was in 1471, under Alphonso V., that the Portuguese took possession of Tangiers, which was forsaken by its inhabitants when they heard of the surrender of Arzilla at the sight of the Christian fleet.

The Portuguese occupation, which lasted for nearly two centuries, does not appear to have left any important traces in the town. It is almost impossible to discover in the entire site of the Kasbah any architectural remains [1] which might enlighten us on that period. Besides the portal which I have already mentioned, there exist, however, among the buildings attributed to the Portuguese, several

---

[1] It may be surmised that the cannon balls of the Prince de Joinville have had something to do with the absence of structures, for in the bombardment of 1844 the artillery of the French squadron made remarkable practice, in spite of the stormy weather, on the structure of the Kasbah which was taken as a butt in order to spare European interests.

important churches, some monasteries, and in the upper part of the town, in the south, a large hospital.

Tangiers was transferred to the British Crown on the marriage of Charles II. in 1662 with the infanta Catherine of Portugal. The Portuguese, when in possession of the town, had included it in a system of blockade, thus becoming the masters of the commerce of Morocco, whereas the English occupied it only partially; an incomprehensible error which must have deprived Great Britain of an important strategical position. The English again fortified Tangiers, and its much enlarged harbour was improved by the building of a fine jetty. Nevertheless, the occupation seems to have been no more than a long siege in which the English had to defend themselves against the Berbers of the Riff at first, and then against the troops of the powerful Muley Ismael. This prolonged desultory warfare entailed sacrifices out of all proportion to the importance of the town at that epoch. The British Parliament refused to vote the funds, and it was resolved to evacuate the place after blowing up the principal defences of the jetty.

The acquisition of Gibraltar induced England to establish satisfactory relations with Morocco. During the war with Spain, in which Gibraltar was besieged by land, the garrison of the town was compelled to have recourse to the resources offered by Tangiers. Hence the origin of the commerce between the two cities, which daily increases on account of the possibility of purchasing at Gibraltar, free of duty, all articles manufactured in Europe.

The long period of agitation caused by the Revolution and the wars under the first Empire, gave Tangiers peace for a while; and only the echoes of the cannon at Trafalgar were reverberated to Cape Spartel. Though unaffected by the European war, it suffered grievously from the plague brought in 1818 by an English frigate, "The Tagus," which had on board a number of pilgrims from Mecca. It is estimated that one-fifth of the inhabitants of the town fell a prey to this terrible scourge.

When the relations between Morocco and France became somewhat strained in consequence of some military events in the conquest of Algeria, there occurred a curious incident at Tangiers. The chief figure in the story is, according to a vague rumour, one of the relatives of a great religious personage now officially protected by France.—On a summer's day in 1842, Sherif Abd-es-Selam and other fanatics began to fire off their muskets on the boats of the French frigate "L'Américaine," then at anchor in the roads of Tangiers. The French Consul sent an account of this strange proceeding to Commander Turpin then stationed at Cadiz. This officer soon appeared upon the scene, and supported by the energetic representations of the consular agents, sent word to the Pacha that he must give satisfaction within twenty-four hours. The Sherif and ten of his friends who had thought fit to amuse themselves in such a strange manner were then brought to the harbour much to their disgust, with ropes round their necks and irons on their legs. They were stretched on the sand under a broiling sun, and received a castigation which the merciful Consul abridged at once, but which sufficed to act as a forcible warning.

Two years later, Tangiers was bombarded by the fleet commanded by the Prince de Joinville, whose political and military action deserves universal recognition. The ships did not open fire until Mr. Hay, the British Consul, had been put in safety on board one of the men of war. The Moriscos on the occasion had 220 killed and 400 wounded.

In the war with Spain in 1859, Tangiers was threatened with another bombardment and with assault, but luckily for the town, the intervention of England (by means of energetic diplomatic action) arrested the march of the victorious Spanish Army after the taking of Tetuan and the battle of W. Ras.

Since then the history of the town does not record any warlike events, though the place has been the object of the covetousness of many different European political parties.

The system of defences of the town is eminently primitive. In spite of the numerous guns with which the batteries commanding the bay are provided, one cannot help smiling on seeing every evening, how carefully the guards close the worm-eaten gates, which, however, will fly open at any time of the night, the mysterious "Sesame" being nothing else than a small fee to the porters. The walls would not stand ten minutes' shelling from a man-of-war anchored in the roads; while the small dilapidated fort, armed with two guns minus their carriages, on the other side of the W. el Halk, at the end of the beach, may be a valuable archæological structure, but it certainly is not a work capable of any serious defence.

The marine or landing harbour is commanded by two long batteries, which rise up in tiers and are divided by a long passage opening into the main street. Further on to the east, are yet to be seen under the windows of an hotel a few very old-fashioned cannon resting on quaint-looking cast-iron carriages. The guns are close together, and a single well aimed shell would cause dire havoc there. A few of these batteries possess no embrasures! The powder magazines are not more servicable. The duties of the artillery consist in duly saluting the men-of-war flags and in celebrating the victories which the Sultan now and then gains over the wretched tribes on whom his army has levied blackmail. The supervision of the batteries and carefully built works near the Kasbah, in the upper parts of the town, is entrusted by the Sherifian government to a Spanish engineer who is attired on the occasion of grand ceremonies in a splendid uniform glittering with gold. These defences were erected by engineers from Gibraltar. Three of the batteries are composed of twenty-ton Armstrong guns, which would offer serious resistance if there existed some corps of artillery well instructed in working and firing the guns or even in keeping them in proper order. The existence of such a corps seems doubtful when you behold the steel monsters sleeping with true Morisco nonchalance under a thick layer of dust. This defensive artillery is under the charge of a small body of about 200 gunners whose office is an heirloom bequeathed from father to son. The guns are fired with any kind of gunpowder, the charge being measured by the eye; as for using tangent scales, that is too complicated an operation. The rusty condition of the cannon is explained by the fact that the gunners drink the oil provided for the cleaning and preservation of the ordnance!

The weakest part, from a strategical point of view, is above the Soko, and from that spot entire command of Tangiers can be obtained. After landing under the protection of Malabatta point in the direction of the little beach of Calle Grande, it would be an easy task to penetrate into the town.

It is a well-known fact that in Morocco the representatives of the Powers are located at Tangiers where the Sultan never comes and probably never will come, as His Majesty visits each of his three capitals, Morocco, Meknas, and Fez, at indefinite periods, subject only to the unforeseen circumstances of some expeditions. A kind of foreign minister who resides at Tangiers, serves as a medium for diplomatic correspondence and attends to actual business, his duty being above all to attenuate the effect of remonstrances and complaints. The " modus vivendi " has the advantage of maintaining an easy communication between the Sultan and the agents of foreign governments, as the postal service to the capitals is pretty regular, in spite of the imperfect state of an exceedingly primitive system. But every picture has its dark side.

Let us then see how things are managed. On a trivial occasion, or even when the most insignificant question arises, the European agent applies to the official whom I spoke of in the account of my visit to the Kasbah. Then begins a farce which may be amusing, but which, when protracted, will ruffle even the blandest of diplomatists. His Excellency reads the despatches, or pretends to examine minutely the documents sent him, but, not being invested with any right of final decision, he contents himself with forwarding the papers to the Sultan. The suspicious document, carefully wrapped up in pieces of oil-skin, is consigned to the wallet of a rekkas—that is, a foot messenger. It will reach Morocco after a journey which lasts in winter from fifteen to twenty days. The most elegant diplomatic prose over which the Drogmans of the Legation have spent so many hours, transforming the plain, unvarnished speech of the foreign agent into an elaborate epistle full of flattering and conciliatory assurances, will fail to produce much effect on Muley Hassan, for his agent in Tangiers has taken care to revise the work in such a manner as to alter the sense of the despatch, and thus to protract the negotiations.

In the time of the former minister, these little manœuvres were still more complicated, as Sidi Mohammed Bargash much preferred to sojourn at Rabatt, where he had some important commercial transactions. The height of Oriental procrastination was then reached, for a secretary replaced him at Tangiers, and forwarded to him the documents for transmission to the government. If you add to this that the reply of the Sultan is seldom final, but is rather a request for further information, no astonishment need be felt at the slow progress in the settlement of business matters in the Moghreb.

Procrastination is, indeed, the essence of Morisco policy which continually aims at procuring the support now of one European power, now of another, so as to profit by their rivalries. By such means it evades any too pressing demands which might give rise to difficulties.

It often occurs that the solution found after all these delays cannot be of any utility, there having arisen meanwhile other questions whose more immediate importance causes the others to sink into oblivion. The Sultan is aware of this, and his ministers naturally reckon on the weariness which seizes the claimant in consequence of their unconscionable procrastination.

The foreign representatives sometimes cut matters short, when presenting their credentials, by settling then and there all affairs which have been accumulating under their predecessors, or by leaving on a special mission when the unfinished mass of negotiations has become, at last, too cumbersome. But of course the complicated organization and costly journeys of diplomatic missions cannot be of frequent recurrence.[1]

It has often been remarked that the want of accredited diplomatic agents to attend the Sultan in his different sojourns, was the greatest hindrance to the development of Morocco under European influence. But the question is really intricate, for, besides the difficulty of obtaining from the Sultan permission for the diplomatic corps to reside near the Makhzen (*government, administration*), it would be hardly possible to adjust to the requirements of etiquette the wandering mode of life of the Emperors of Morocco who rarely dwell in the capitals, and who spend several months on the road. Should the European diplomatic body, during the torrid heat, or during the season of diluvian rain, have to follow His Majesty, the Powers ought to be represented by military men, for it cannot be demanded of old diplomatists that they should accompany so warlike a Sultan on his toilsome journeys.

This question which I wish only to touch lightly upon, shows the difficulty of transforming the country and giving it the advantages of Western civilisation. All that has been written on the transfer of these embassies to the interior affords evidence of the little knowledge people possess about those regions, their administration, and fanaticism. A Paris newspaper went so far as to declare some time ago that the Sultan was willing to accept the changes proposed, provided the feminine portion of the legations never went out unless veiled!

[1] In the spring of 1882, the English diplomatic mission under Sir John Hay, was compelled, when travelling from Casablanca to Morocco, to follow a road other than that which M. Ordega had formerly taken, in order to spare the tribes the heavy burden of providing a second time a *mouna*, or provisions, for the caravan.

Who would ever imagine that Tangiers, which scarcely reckons 1800 Europeans, boasts of five newspapers? Fierce controversies are sometimes carried on between these journals.[1] Being often short of news, they are compelled to extemporise sensational articles in which the most ordinary incidents are wilfully misrepresented. Should a minister contemplate a short journey, or some official land in Morocco, the journalists are soon hard at work in exaggerating the significance of the simple event, and their excitement rises to a feverish pitch on the report of some insurrection in the interior. Making comments on the articles of the European press, conveniently arranging them for their own use, these prints, accustomed to see everything through a magnifying glass, sincerely believe at last that Morocco alone occupies the minds of the great Powers whose most secret designs are supposed to have for their sole object the acquisition of that portion of Africa. The worst of it is that the situation is always represented as being most critical. No importance would be attached to these local effusions, if some of the papers were not secretly supported by a grant in money from the legations. It is to be wished that some correspondents, writing from Tangiers, would enlighten the great European press by furnishing them with information less trivial and more trustworthy than that supplied by the above journals. The European public would then know something at least of what really takes place in the Moghreb. As the communication would have to pass through the editorial office, more than one *canard* hatched in the vicinity of the Soko would have its wings cut off, or at

---

[1] These are in chronological order: Al Moghreb el Acsa (in Spanish); Times of Morocco; le Réveil du Maroc, and the defunct le Commerce au Maroc.

least properly clipped, and the idea that the country is constantly on the eve of a terrible conflagration would no longer be entertained. These sensational articles are specially injurious when they are published at the time of the Arab religious festivals. The writers then complain of the intolerable position in which the obstruction or the fanaticism of a barbarous country places them. Why, it may be asked, do they not leave it and cross the Straits to enjoy the sweets of Spanish administration?

The European colony at Tangiers is a mixed one. Some years ago, a work conceived in a rather malicious spirit was published, pretending to raise the curtain of private life in the legations by disclosing a number of insignificant scandals, but no one put any faith in these statements. The nationality of the author having been disclosed, it was noticed that the legation of his own country was the only one on which he did not pour the vials of his wrath. Far from this, he extolled the purity of the lives of its members, the rectitude of their policy, the liberal views of the minister and the unimpeachable integrity of his actions.

It is necessary to live in a small town in the East, in the midst of a limited European society, to know with what readiness malevolent tongues will set themselves going. Tangiers forms no exception to the rule, but I, too, must avoid being guilty of the same offence, and I will therefore refrain from reviving the scandals occasioned by the conduct of a clever but not over scrupulous drogman, which are still fresh in the memory of all who have lived in Morocco.

Changes take place pretty often in the diplomatic world. Sir John Hay himself, the senior member of the diplomatic corps in Morocco, the man who possessed the best knowledge of a country where he had been brought up, is no longer the representative of Great Britain, the strict rule of the limit of age having been applied in his case. France and Germany, following the wise example of England, now send as their agents only those who are acquainted with the manners and language of Morocco.

France possesses, in the person of M. Féraud, an Arabic scholar, a learned and able representative who gave proof of the greatest tact and firmness in most difficult circumstances at Tripoli.

The European inhabitants, with the exception of a few respectable merchants and hotel keepers, suffer much from their proximity to Spain, which does not always send among them the choicest specimens of Andalusia, or even of Ceuta. The place abounds in low adventurers; and there are a number of interpreters, guides, and servants not worth their salt, who model, after their own image, a whole generation of Moors.

It is a matter of some difficulty to make an estimate of the numbers of the European colony, but every winter many tourists come here in quest of a quiet and careless life. Living is cheap, and the surrounding country is interesting to all those who are fond of archæological remains, or are devoted to hunting and riding. A mount can easily be got in this country of cheap nags, as the Sultan has forbidden the exportation of horses. Several hotels—the "Continental" especially—offer to travellers a degree of comfort which is truly surprising in this corner of Africa.

The shipping trade at Tangiers seems to be in a prosperous state, though the harbour, half filled up with the débris of the jetty destroyed by the English, has very little depth, and vessels are compelled to anchor at a distance in the roads, which are anything but safe in winter. Jews are the agents in almost all kinds of commercial transactions, and export hemp and untanned skins; whilst the French and English traders bring cargoes of ironmongery, cotton stuffs, tea, sugar, and candles. Several European banks have established branch offices here. With the exception of wheat, all kinds of corn are shipped to foreign countries. Wax and oil are also among the articles of export, and traders even carry to Algeria and Tunis those fine yellow slippers which adorn the feet of Orientals. Cork bark, which was at one time an important article of foreign commerce, cannot now be taken out of the country, probably on account of the diminution of the number of cork trees. Severe penal laws enforce the prohibition of the exportation of horses, but you can easily get round the Pacha, and, for a consideration, obtain permission to break the rule in that respect. The horses given away as presents from the Sultan are exempted from these stringent restrictions, and a kind of certificate must be delivered along with the animal. But, should the latter be sold by its owner, the free pass sometimes becomes, in the hands of some Jew agent, the subject of financial speculation. Although it is a difficult matter to take horses out of the country by shipping them surreptitiously, one utterly fails to perceive how, with such vague frontiers as Morocco possesses, the deportation of horses can be entirely prevented.

The consumption of tea in Morocco involves the use of an enormous quantity of sugar, since the beverage is taken in the form of a syrup. Honey is produced in abundance and is reserved for the making of sweet-meats and for the concoction of those extraordinary Arab dishes in comparison with which the Russian rabbit and chocolate sauce is a primitive gastronomic attempt. Naturally, bees' wax is found in large quantities; but great profit must be derived from exporting it or selling it to native distilleries, for the wax candles from Marseilles are, and deserve to be in favour here. Wealthy natives prefer them to the prettily coloured old-fashioned candle.

Tanneries are numerous in the country, and at Tangiers itself some of them—not to mention the heaps of goat-skins laid out in the Soko to dry—give most disagreeable evidence of their presence by exhalations which pervade the whole of the Eastern quarter near the shore. They turn out the well known Morocco leather, of good quality and remarkable for its fine red or yellow tint. The first colour is obtained by the use of cochineal brought from the Canary Islands, and the second from the rind of pomegranates. This kind of leather is artistic, but only answers certain purposes. Morocco saddlery leaves much to be desired as regards durability, and the native harness needs constant repairs. The Arabs not possessing the art of tanning leather properly, suppose all our European trappings to be pig skin. "Hallouf," they say, with a contemptuous look, and the fanatical attendants of the Sultan at Meknas, would not even touch the good stout French leather of our mule pack-saddles.

The climate of Tangiers deserves special mention, because its excellence has been exaggerated, or rather because it has been credited with qualities it does not possess. It is frightfully damp towards the end of autumn, in winter, and at the beginning of spring, and therefore scarcely satisfies the requirements of a hibernal resort. During the long wet winter days, when the rain pours down incessantly, the outlying districts are soon turned into a marsh, and the streets become regular sewers in which all kinds of garbage and filth float about. Tangiers and its inhabitants then assume a singularly wretched and uninviting appearance. All is colourless, the charm is dispelled, and of the whole town thoroughly illuminated by a glorious sun there remains only an agglomeration of houses whose walls now have turned to a dirty grey.

The Arabs have an awkward look when wading clumsily in the flooded streets with their yellow babouches and white haïks. They always reminded me then of the white *pierrots* and magnificent lords of the olden time seeking for a coach under a down-pour of rain after a Parisian bal masqué. The country people do not seem much hampered by the state of the weather; tucking up their jellaba, and taking off their babouches, they flounder boldly about like tall water-fowl, and swiftly make their way through the narrow lanes. After admiring Tangiers bathed in sunlight, and then seeing it deluged with rain, you have on the whole the impression of gazing upon stage scenes in full day light; the magical features have disappeared and the disenchantment is complete. The winter storms are severe, and at Cape Spartel, when the gale is raging, the ocean is furiously lashed into enormous yellowish waves with whitish crests, which scud along and dash against the rocks with a terrible din scarcely surpassed by the dismal roar of the wind.

Snow sometimes falls in great quantities on the Riff. I remember seeing it cap the summits of the mountains for four days in February 1883, and I was told that it even lay on the quays of Tangiers in 1871.

The great humidity of the climate of Tangiers may be explained by the fact that the whole of Morocco is included in the zone of the trade winds and by the position of the town exposed to the moist winds, which career in the Straits of Gibraltar. During the winter, the aërial currents proceed from the north-west, their course being parallel to the chains of the Atlas. The region is constantly soaked in a damp atmosphere and this accounts for the prodigious number of rheumatic complaints, for the facility with which metals are oxidized, and the plentiful dew with which the fields are covered. Even the easterly winds, generally so dry in the vicinity of the Mediterranean, bring an abundant supply of moisture to the mountains on the coast, and the chains of the Riff are then covered with clouds. These winds are very unpleasant; they blow for periods of three, six, nine, or twelve days; clouds of dust invade the dwellings; going out of doors becomes a painful ordeal when the eyes are not protected by strong spectacles. The means of communication with Europe, already so meagre, are suspended; the boat from Tarifa no longer carries the mails, and the one from Gibraltar, being unable to land its cargo, anchors in the harbour. The traveller must then either wait for the return of calm weather or take passage in a vessel from London, Marseilles or Oran capable of defying the atrocious weather; and for all these reasons, wintering in Morocco is to be avoided by those who wish to enjoy a climate similar to that of Egypt. In summer, on the contrary, residence there is exquisite; the country is a real paradise, and the temperature which is constantly cooled by the sea breeze, makes it a most delightful dwelling place.

The out-lying districts of Tangiers are perfectly safe for travellers. I have made many excursions, at all seasons, travelling nearly twenty miles at a time, by day and by night, in European or native costume, and I never met with any disagreeable adventure. You may go from Tangiers to Tetuan, a long day's march, without needing the protection of a military escort. I draw attention to the latter fact, for it is a rare occurrence to see a tourist unaccompanied by a magnificent Mokhazni, whose useless services may be secured at a cost of about seven francs. The natives work upon the fears of travellers to induce them to hire the escort, but if there were any risk of being attacked, it would most likely be owing to the sight of the chechia of the Pacha's horsemen. As for the aid to be expected from these horsemen, in an emergency, it is of no more value than their armament. In the neighbourhood of Sefrou, south of Fez, when we were among the Aït Youssi (a tribe of Berber race and not over friendly to the Sultan), the horsemen of our escort used to conceal their insignia which would have revealed their character to the population. Should you be travelling in Morocco, provide yourself with an excellent servant, or if you are fortunate enough to have a soldier already in your service, then train him for the work before setting out on an excursion. But above all, avoid encumbering yourself with a Mokhazni who will rob you and only take you to places where his own interests call him.

The soldiers attached to legations form an exception to the rule. Instructed in their special duties by long intercourse with Europeans, they prove to be valuable servants; but those furnished by the Pacha of Tangiers are the worst of all, and have not the least scruple in cheating travellers. On the other hand, the Mokhazni, assigned as attendants to travellers favoured with the Sultan's attentions, are old, trusty servants able to bear privations and fatigue.

There is no lack of game in the country round Tangiers, though the quantity decreases every year in consequence of the depredations of traders, who export it in all seasons to Gibraltar. But, in order to rival the exploits of certain sportsmen who kill in one day hundreds of partridges, it would be necessary to go far into the interior. Rabbits are abundant, but they diminish in number as you go south, and increase again beyond the Bou-Regrag, a river which empties itself into the ocean at Rabatt. The only monkeys indigenous to these regions belong to the species found on the rock of Gibraltar. They are to been seen in the northern extremities of the chain of Beni-Hassan, near Ceuta, but no trace of them appears in the south. Hares, like partridges, for a like reason, are becoming scarce, but thousands of quails sometimes descend upon the fields to seek rest before taking flight across the Straits.

Pig-sticking is a favourite sport at Tangiers. It is pursued by the officials of the legations, a few gentlemen of the town, and tourists whom the toil of a day's hunting does not frighten. A good horse, strong in the legs, capable of galloping at a fast pace, and, above all, nimble in taking a fence or a ditch, is of absolute necessity. Without these requisites, this kind of hunt may prove fruitless or even dangerous.

About 12 miles S.W. from Tangiers, the wooded sand hills and plateaus of Hadjeriin, Agadir, Cherf el Akab and El Hawara contain numbers of wild boars. It appears that the right of hunting there is reserved for the diplomatic corps, the privilege having been granted by the Sultan a few years ago at the request of the English minister. Amusements for the members of the legations not being very varied at Tangiers, one must be grateful to Sir John Hay for having organised this exciting and picturesque sport. The wild boars, driven out of the almost impenetrable thickets by beaters and innumerable horrible mongrels from the Douars, are chased on horseback, lance in hand.

Directly the beast is in the open, the hunter gallops after it, and with a thrust of his weapon puts an end to its career. This is the theory, but the practice is otherwise. The boar doubles, gets into ground intersected by ravines, ditches, and fallen trees, and the hunt becomes a dangerous steeple-chase. But the greatest danger lies behind you in the crowd of Arabs or other lovers of the sport, who, in their mad excitement, may run you through with their poised weapons; and the facility with which the sharp head penetrates the thick hide of the boar, leaves an impression of uneasiness on your mind. I recollect having had my clothes pierced through by the lance of an effeminate young Moor who accompanied one of the hunters, an important religious personage. I need not add that the chastisement which at once followed gave the young fellow an idea of the disadvantages of running a lance through a Roumi's clothes.

Horses require early training for this kind of sport. I owned one, which, in addition to many other qualities, was able to follow the boar at sight, and, thanks to my nag, I seldom failed to return without something to show.

Shooting parties, organised by the diplomatic corps, sometimes resort to the mountainous regions of the Cape Spartel for their sport.

On such occasions, there exists a custom which it may behove the tourist to know. The sportsman, whose début it is, and who has occasion to congratulate himself on his success, is deprived of his gun or lance by the head of the beaters. The weapon is at once put up to auction, and the few douros obtained are transferred to the pockets of these worthies.

The wild boar is the only big game in the environs of

Tangiers. There are a few lions on the inaccessible mountains of the Riff or Atlas, but the last representative of the race in the province had his career cut short in the garden of the English minister, about forty years ago.

In the marshy district near the ocean, a good marksman equipped for conveniently wading in the mud may find a large bag of snipe in winter. These parts are hot-beds of fever in summer, a fact I learnt to my cost when encamping for a fortnight on the plateau of Cherf el Akab, where, at night, you may hear the short bark of jackals, and the dismal laugh of the hyena.

Thus the environs of Tangiers offer some interesting points not only to the sportsman, but to the lover of archæological researches. Outside the town lie many shady groves of orange trees, and gardens, which you reach by means of narrow footpaths winding across a mass of verdure and bordered by tall hedges of reeds. What delightful calm one finds in these charming spots! A small fee to the gardener and the gates fly open. These gardens are the property of wealthy Moors, and are full of trees which bear most delicious fruit. Here you can spend hours lazily strolling about. Should you wish to make a longer but exceedingly interesting excursion, you should go to Cape Spartel, the extreme point of Africa, where the waves of the ocean mingle with the waters of the Mediterranean.

Tourists who wish to go on a short journey with a caravan will find the route from Tangiers to Tetuan a most fertile one in picturesque impressions. A trip to Ceuta is hardly worth the trouble, especially as you will have to undertake a long day's journey in order to cross the copses of the Monkeys' Mountain, the only spot worthy of notice. Far more interesting than either of these places is Cape Spartel. There, the sight of the traditional resting-place of mythological heroes, the charm of the solitary coast, the silence of the country whence you have such a magnificent view of the Straits, and of the boundless ocean, will afford the traveller many sources of pleasant recollections when he returns to the misty north.

From the promontory to Tangiers the distance is about six miles, and the road is the best in the whole of Morocco. It has been partly paved by order of the committee of the Powers, as it is used for conveying provisions and stores to the light-house. At the very top of the town lies a vast plateau, called the plateau of the Marshân, which is used as a camping place for the caravans and horsemen sent here by the Sultan. From this spot may be discerned the whole of the inmost recesses of the bay where the range of downs spreads out in huge mounds of sand which the northeast wind has whirled up for centuries and accumulated in high masses. They are covered by a layer of vegetable mould, and that circumstance joined to a mild climate makes it possible to cultivate the greater portion of the downs. Close to the sea, the agave and squill are the only plants which relieve the monotony of these sandy tracts. The view from the road extends over the expanse of blue water from the rock of Gibraltar to Cape Trafalgar,[1] and you can discern the houses of Tarifa, and the minutest details of the Spanish Coast. On the land horizon are numerous hills covered with delightful gardens and orchards reached by paths bordered with fragrant flowers. At the extremity of the plateau a small deserted Arab cemetery

---

[1] Cape Trafalgar is the mountain of El Aghar mentioned by El Bekri who terms it also Tarf el Agher (Cape of El Agher) which has been corrupted into Trafalgar. When the wind blows in the right direction one may hear the reverberations of the guns of the fortress of Gibraltar.

with its sunken tombs and crumbling stones and tamarinds, palms, and a hundred other African plants, straggles up in tiers from the sea. Then you have to cross the stony bed of the little river of the Jews,[1]—an operation of some difficulty in winter, even for the boldest horseman. The river flows along a rocky valley, and effects its junction with the Straits at a few hundred yards distance. Here are to be seen small beaches of fine sand, most inviting bathing places. The banks are studded with flowers, and the remains of an old bridge, in the middle of some green meadows, make the scene quite a picturesque one. Altogether the spot is the most pleasant in the neighbourhood. After making the steep ascent on the reverse slope of the valley you reach the side of the mountain to which the diplomatic officials of Tangiers repair in the summer to inhale the pure and bracing breeze of the Straits and to forget the trouble and worry of modern politics while gazing from afar on the European shores. Everywhere are to be seen the eucalyptus, groves of orange trees, and sycamores beyond which rise the lofty summits clothed with dwarf palms, and broom and other shrubs. The road then crosses a grand and solitary landscape whose calm and majesty it is impossible to describe.

The light-house, of French construction, is not exactly at the point of the Cape, but a few hundred yards northwards near the Needles. This elegant structure has a small court with a Moorish arcade, and a fountain whose limpid and crystal-like waters served perhaps to quench the thirst of Hercules after his labours! We learn from Roman writers that the rocky point contained the tomb of Antæus and the grotto of

---

[1] This river was called the W. Boubara by Davidson, but the appellation seems to be unknown to the people of the country.

Hercules. Archæological researches have not brought to light any facts bearing on the matter. Mela supports the assertion concerning the tomb of Antæus, but M. Tissot has vainly looked for the spot mentioned by the Latin geographer, both in the environs of Tangiers and in the neighbourhood of El Araïsh. "Collis modicus resupini hominis imagine jacentis." It would need a mighty effort of the imagination to recognise in the solitary hillock of Ech-Cherf near Tangiers the tomb of the sons of Neptune and Earth. The destruction of the woods of the whole country, by radically modifying the climate, has removed the causes of those famous miracles of expiatory torrents "Unde ubi aliqua pars bruta est, solent imbres spargi, et, donec effosa repleantur, eveniunt."[1]

As for the celebrated grotto, it is difficult to come to any conclusion. The excavation shown by guides to travellers is nothing but an immense stone quarry. Certain authors assert that it is no other than the grotto described by Mela "in eo est specus Herculi sacer, et ultra specum Tinge . . ." but M. Tissot has proved that the words of the Latin writer can have no reference to that spot.

The remarkable promontory which forms the extremity of the African Shore of the Straits was called Ampelusia by the Greeks on account of its vineyards. It still yields excellent grapes, and when digging before laying the foundation of the new light-house, some years ago, enormous vine stalks were found in confirmation of the appropriateness of the name given to the place. The site of ancient Cotta, a Phenician town mentioned by Pliny as having been already in ruins at the time he wrote, has not been

[1] Mythologic memorials abound here. It would appear that it was in the Tingitane that Hercules laid low the Libyan giant.

discovered by modern explorers. Tissot is inclined to believe that it probably stood on the southern slopes of the chain of Cape Spartel in the neighbourhood of a small dchar of Mediouna.[1] These various memorials of antiquity should induce all tourists to make an excursion to Cape Spartel. The watchman at the light-house is an obliging old Austrian, who procures his visitors all facilities for luncheon, and who gladly shows them specimens of his skill in cabinet-making, at which he employs himself during his long lonely hours.

After a short ascent you reach the point of the rocks whence you obtain a fine view of the long sandy beach bordered towards the open by a belt of rocks marked by a white line of foam. The spot is much dreaded by mariners, there being no depth of water till far out at sea. Returning from the excursion to Cape Spartel you cross a charming wood of olive trees. The sun is sinking in the ocean and its rays, gliding over the wooden tops of the Djebel, paint them in roseate hue, and colour in the distance the mountain of the Rif with delightful half tints.

The bottom of the Valley is already in the shade, and the beautiful Eastern night has fallen, when in the midst of the perfume of orange trees, of laurels and myrtles, you return to Tandjah, where you hear the voice of the Mouedzenn calling the faithful to prayer in clear and melancholy accents.[2]

[1] *Mediouna* means small town in Arabic.
[2] The *ouzzenn* or *mouedzenn* is the crier who announces that it is the hour for prayer. The word comes from *oudzenn* or ear; whence *adzenn*, to announce the hour for prayer. The six obligatory prayers are, *el fedjer* or that of the break of day; *es cebaph* the morning prayer; *el dheher* or noon; *el acer* 3 o'clock; *el moghreb* setting sun, half-an-hour after the setting of the sun, and *el dcha* or 2 hours after the setting of the sun.

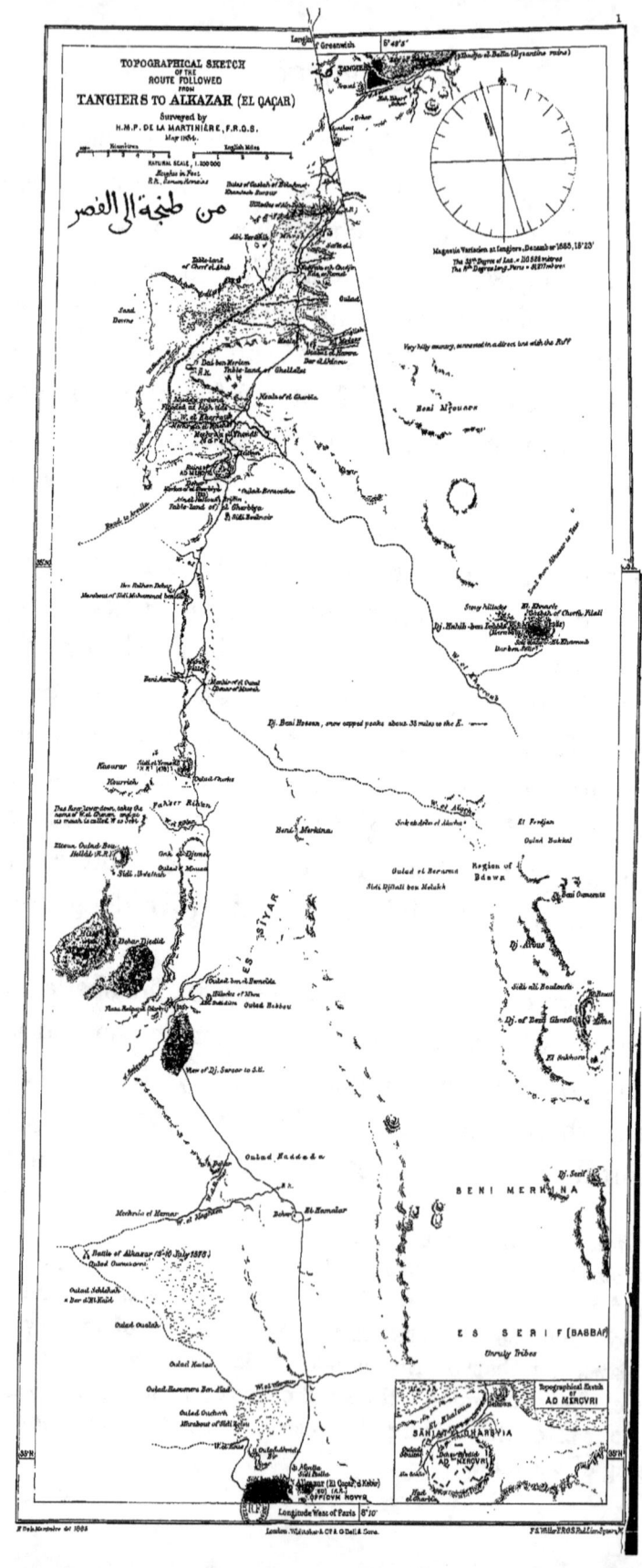

CHAPTER III.

Preparation for an Expedition—Purchase of Horses and Mules—Treatment of Beasts of Burden by the Arabs—Visit to the Sherif—the Sherif and His Household—the Start—Our Trouble with the Muleteers—The Marshy State of the Country on the Road to Alqaçar—Difficulties on the Way—The Site of Ad Mercuri and the Ruins—The Site well-chosen by the Romans—The Country People—Discovery by M. Tissot—Our Mule Bagatelle.

THE wintry rains had nearly ceased; a few cold showers still came down, but the intervals of fair weather heralded the approach of the African spring in all its splendour. It was then that we returned from France with my official letter and all the traps necessary for a long camping out. At the Legation where they had been expecting us for some time, we were welcomed by the French minister and our friends in the same affectionate and hospitable manner as of old. On the very evening of our arrival, whilst discussing our plans, we already imagined ourselves at Meknas, near the Sultan, and that our gallant steeds were carrying us away to the farthest limits of the desert. But a cloud was soon to darken our azure sky. Certain diplomatic difficulties had to be settled, and the Legation would not allow us to depart before that was done.

We were busy, for several days, packing, putting our apparatus straight, and manufacturing a quantity of cartridges sufficient to exterminate all living beings in Africa. We filled up an entire court of the Legation with our belongings, and even the whole of our friend G's. house was placed at our disposal. Everything in it was topsy-turvy; a barometer was stuck in a saucepan, a chest of medicine lay on a camp-bed, and a mule-saddle on the top of a photographic apparatus. It was no slight matter buying the animals necessary for the conveyance of all these things. We had to display in the Soko the sharpness of the horse-dealer combined with the deepest knowledge of veterinary art. We first gave all our attention to the choice of two steeds destined to carry us across the land of Moghreb. I was lucky enough to find an excellent animal, young and vigorous, whose qualities for pace and resistance I fully appreciated later on. My companion was less fortunate, and it was not till we had journeyed far inland that he found what he required. There is always a market held at Tangiers, on Thursdays and Sundays, when, if you only have some insight into Moorish methods of transacting business, you can pick up horses at very reasonable prices; numbers of mules and donkeys are also offered for sale. The prices vary considerably according to the cost of corn. A good winter, with just sufficient rain, and a promising spring are enough to cause a depression in the price of corn, and a rise in the value of the beasts. I believe, however, it may be taken for granted that there is no good travelling horse in Morocco worth more than a hundred douros. We instructed the "Metasseb"[1] to let us know as soon as any strong beast was offered for sale at the market; the "Dellah," a public auctioneer who walks about collecting the different bids, then brought us the quadruped, and we proceeded to

[1] An official appointed by the Sultan to keep order in the market.

make a minute inspection, as we had no faith in the "bittar" or local veterinary. It is always painful to see how the Arabs ill-treat their animals when finally put up for sale.

Some of the poor horses are dead-beat by the racing and mad careering which the public auctioneer thinks necessary to show off their vigour. The backs of most of the mules are covered with most horrible wounds, on account of the little care that is taken with their pack-saddle. It took us about two weeks to make all our purchases, at the end of which time we had not yet formed up the whole of our caravan, preferring to complete it in the interior, where finer horses can be procured. The start was fixed for the 4th of May, so as to give time to fatten up our poor animals which were quite starved and had been so ill-treated in every possible way that they presented a truly pitiable appearance. We first unshod them and led them every day to the sea in order to heal their skins damaged by the cudgels with which they had been belaboured, and we provided them with the most liberal fare that a Moghreb quadruped had ever set before him. Two weeks of such diet entirely changed their appearance; they were now sleek and fat, and their coat was of the shiniest gloss and most pleasant to look at. Having thus softened them down by gentle treatment, their temper was much improved, and the vilest mule had quite given up kicking. Altogether, we were highly pleased with our method.

My comrade busied himself with procuring the provisions, and soon finished his task, thanks to the assistance of Mr. John Ansaldo, the most courteous of hotel-keepers. The selection of servants gave us any amount of trouble, for laziness, lying, and stealing fall to the common lot of these amiable Mussulmans of Tangiers. As the successful issue of a journey inland partly depends on the men you take with you, I advise the tourist who cannot give up his European comforts to keep his former servants at Meknas and to pick up the rest of his attendants. We were compelled to dismiss all the servants we had engaged at Tangiers as we went along, and as the supposed dangers of the journey increased. These and other troubles experienced by us point to the fact that it is better to adopt the custom and manners of the Arabs at the very outset. Following the advice of the French Minister, M. Ordega, we decided before setting out to await at Wazzan the official letter which was to accredit us to the grand vizier at Meknas. We had, therefore, to procure a letter of introduction (a document similar to that I had obtained in my preceding journey with my friend Major Trotter), from the Sherif Sidi-abd-es-Selam to his sons, at that time staying at Wazzan, the holy city of Moghreb, as some writers pompously term it. There was no difficulty about this, for diplomatic communications had been opened between the Makhzen (*government*) and the French Legation through the petition of Sidi-abd-es-Selam for protection against the obnoxious proceedings and exactions of the Sultan. M. Ordega asked the Secretary and the head dragoman to accompany us into the sacred presence of the Sherif who had already appointed a time for our visit, and dressed in our best we entered the holy dwelling. We were graciously received and the fat Sherif, yielding to the eloquent prayer of our friends, acceded to our wishes. The interior of his house has a most vulgar appearance, and is quite in keeping with the ugliness of the exterior. It is filled with an extraordinary conglomeration of the most incongruous objects which no more bear the impress of Oriental workmanship than the building in which they are stored.

The Sherif being a great lover of fire-arms, is surrounded with weapons of all sorts, and at every visit you pay him most of the time is spent examining pistols and rifles. We were seated in straw chairs, facing the descendant of Mohammed, who was reclining in a large armchair of the First Empire style. His dress consisted of a suit of "dittoes" of brown cheviot, and on his head he had a cap of green card-board or something like it. We naturally addressed him only in the most deferential manner during the whole time of our stay. An enormous negress with pendulous breasts and oily skin, who had shown us in, came several times during the visit, and whispered mysteriously into his ear. So we took the hint and shortened our visit, tendering, as we left, our thanks to His Highness. At Tangiers, the neighbourhood of his house is always infested with ragged scamps, as bad a lot as ever was seen. He owns other houses in the suburbs, one of which is the residence of his latest wife, an amiable Englishwoman to whom I had the honour to be introduced a few years ago.

A glorious sun met our eyes on the morning appointed for the start. Our servants, quite contrary to their wont, were marvellously busy. At the last moment we were obliged to hire four mules to lighten the others whose burdens had attained extraordinary proportions.

It was decided that our first camping place should be at K'aa er R'mel (*sand bottom* in Arabic), about eleven miles from Tangiers, whither our luggage had already been sent. At four o'clock we got into the saddle, at the door of our friend the first Secretary of the Legation, who had insisted on giving us our last meal, and attended by his wishes for our success, we began our journey.

We rode swiftly on the road to Fez, accompanied by our soldier and by our faithful Diana whose strong English pointer legs created as much astonishment in Morocco, as in her journey from the Pyrenees to Gibraltar. Let not the word road evoke in the reader's mind any idea of comfortable travelling. In Morocco a road is simply ground which boasts no trees, and has not been ploughed. This does not, however, imply that you do not go across ploughed fields, for very often caravans will strike, without the slightest hesitation, right across the most splendidly cultivated country. Our route lay along a sandy path on both sides of which are little plots, tilled by shepherds who sell their vegetables at the Tangiers market. These fields are all enclosed by cactus hedges and impenetrable agaves. The scene grew more and more lovely as we got farther away from the town. We crossed the small stream of Souani and passed before a dchar[1] where we left the Tetuan road on our left. From time to time we saw in the distance one of these hamlets easily recognizable by their immense cactus hedges and numerous storks, which, protected by the inhabitants, as they are in certain parts of Europe, settle on the thatched roofs of the miserable buildings. The country is covered with hillocks. From the top of one of these, you have a beautiful view of the Straits and of the Spanish coast which fades farther and farther away on the horizon. Towards sunset all you can see are indistinct shades in which the colours, losing more and more of their brightness, change to the most delicate tints.

[1] The word dchar, plural dchour, means in the Morocco dialect, a fixed centre of population, while the douar is made up of tents and moves from place to place, always keeping, however, within a short radius. The former word is from the Berber tongue, the latter from the Arabic.

At this time of the year all the country we travel through resembles in its hue an immense meadow. The crops look promising enough. In the barley fields the light green shade predominates, and we should have formed a very incorrect idea of the East, if we had not previously seen the country covered with dust and the soil entirely burnt up by the glaring heat of long rainless months. The absence of trees is as prominent a characteristic here as it is in all other countries invaded by the Arabs. Here and there a meagre-looking olive tree stands out in its mournful greenish grey outline, whilst thousands of dwarf palms, more like hard, dark, tall grass, flourish in every piece of uncultivated soil.

The clayey ground is far from being hardened, for the rain has deeply soaked through the lower layers of earth. The muddy and swollen streams are still difficult to cross, and our horses continually stumble in the operation. We journey by the foot of the Bahreïn[1] hillock, which means in Arabic the hillock of the two Seas, and whence one catches a glimpse of the Ocean and the Straits. We soon reach the rocky acclivity which forms the northern boundary of the swampy region of the Hawara. The road winds between an endless number of pointed jagged rocks, and it is truly astonishing to see the clever manner in which the native horses manage to pick their way through the difficult passes.

From the top we have a fine view of the ocean, glistening in the last rays of the setting sun. Two small, white specks whose slightest details we can scan with the glass, reassure us as to the fate of our people, our animals, and camp material. We can even discern the row of mules attached to the stakes, and the movements of the busy servants.

[1] More correctly spelt B'hareïn.

The descent to the plain is a rapid one, and we push on our way amidst ferruginous springs which bubble between the stones lying on every side. We then skirt the W. el Mharhar[1] which we ford[2] before leaving the camp. Our horses have recognised their companions and are breaking the silence of this immense plain with their joyful neighing. Everywhere there is bustle and excitement in this our first encampment. Our attendants are serving their apprenticeship, and all of them are completely at sea, except the cook who had been in my service on several previous occasions, and my groom. Questions and high words are heard on all sides, and our appearance is barely sufficient to calm down the excited zeal of people who do nothing at all. The famous muleteers whom we engaged at Tangiers to go as far as Wazzan, now do exactly as they please, upsetting everything, and asking for fresh terms in the hope of awing us into acquiescence. We therefore inaugurate with pomp and

---

[1] The marshy hollow into which the Mharhar flows is bounded on the east by the Hills of Sáfet el Hamān (Stone of the Pigeons), by the heights of the Oulad Zian and of Seguelda; on the south by the rocky plateau of Daraklaou, a buttress of the great mass of the Beni Mçouars; on the north and north-west by the rocky ridge of Ain Dalïa which we have just crossed, and on the west by the sandy hill of Cherf el Akab (the hill of ruins, according to M. Tissot), and the great solitary downs of El Hawara and El Briedj. This low valley is nothing but a marsh, being flooded at each tide, and also in winter during the rainy season.

The sheet of water formed by the overflowing of the lower part of the river, is the lake near the valley of Pontion quoted by Scylax. In spite of the altered shape, caused either by the accumulation of mud, or by the sand brought from the ocean, it is easy to recognise by the contour and nature of the ground the lake Cephisias (lacum cephisiada quem Mauri vocant Electrum).

[2] Up stream from the ford where we crossed the river which is called Mechraat-ech-Chidjera (passage of the tree), the Mharhar is known to the natives by the name of Wad el Kebir.

ceremony an era of severity, and I threaten to have them taken back to Tangiers by the soldier to be dealt with by the Pacha.

As we do not possess as yet any official letter of the Sultan, we have to send our people for provisions. Barley, milk, chickens, and eggs are soon brought to us by some peasant women with wrinkled faces and senile appearance. These specimens of the fair sex of K'aa er R'mel do not inspire our servants with any desire to go and play the Don Giovannis. At night-fall a delicious supper gives us further proof of the talent of our cook, who does not rest on his laurels, and at dessert my jovial friend, carried away by enthusiasm, begins to sing the great air of the Huguenots. The astonished Arabs deem it to be the Roumis' prayer, and listen respectfully. But their reverence is changed into unbounded amazement when we set up the theodolite, a true wizard's instrument in the eyes of the superstitious natives. It is indeed a happy life, this life under canvas, and we feel much contempt for gilded palaces, and the hateful collar and necktie, which civilised communities compel its slaves to wear.

Having set up our thermometers for the night, we are apprised of the coming of the guards sent by the chief of the dchar, to protect us from any night attacks. These guards are poor devils who look more like brigands with their tattered clothes and rusty muskets. They certainly protect us against sleep, for, establishing themselves in a circle round the fire, they relate to one another some of those wondrously fantastic, and above all never-ending tales peculiar to Africa. But towards twelve o'clock my comrade, feeling annoyed, calls for silence, and soon everything is quiet. The barking of the dogs of some douars in the plain answering that of the jackals in the mountain, makes a weird sound, whilst the far off ocean accompanies it with a dull, monotonous murmur, which soon lulls us to slumber.

Next morning the sky was covered with huge clouds, dark and lowering. The pleasure we felt the previous day, all thinking that the rainy season had come to an end, was not now to be renewed. The clouds gathering over the ocean, and driven by a strong wind from the west, soon brought us some showers. We were compelled to strike our camp hastily, for, should the marshes of the valley or W. el Kharroub which we had yet to traverse that day be too much flooded, we should find ourselves in a most disagreeable fix. It is of common occurrence in this country for caravans surprised by the floods to have to wait for weeks without being able either to advance or retire. We quickly struck our tents and packed up, the men whom we had trained for this manœuvre acquitting themselves of their task in a fairly creditable manner. At length the animals are loaded, but not before three quarters of an hour have been spent in the operation. Let us hope that things will go off better to-morrow, because the ideal in these travels is a staff of servants capable of loading away in a twinkling. Mackintoshes are brought out, and the column sets off in a drizzling rain, which does not, however, lessen the enthusiasm of my companion, who enlivens the prosaic work of taking notes by most extravagant castle building. In these marshy meadows, the soil is soon soaked and our beasts slip at every step on the clayey and muddy ground; we direct our course straight for the rocky chain of the red mountain, called Akabat el Hamra, which we quickly ascend. From the top of this rocky spur, we descry several dried up lakes in the marsh basin which we have just crossed, whilst, at our feet, stretching to the south, lie the chain of hollows preceding the plateau of El Gharbïa, and traversed by the W. el Kharroub. The whole of the table-land and surrounding heights, scantily covered with stunted bushes, were at one time an immense forest, which has long since perished by fire. Game abounds there for an active sportsman whom the prospect of a night passed rolled up in his burnous, under a gourbi, does not frighten. A few years ago, some bands of marauders used to rob travellers who crossed the plateau. In consequence of this, the Makhzen established two outposts or nezla of men, taken from the neighbouring tribes. The one situated on the northern slope is the Nzala Mta A'amar, so named from its tribe, and the other, on the southern coast, is called Nezlah El Gharbïa, on account of the plateau of El Gharbïa, which lies opposite.

At the lower part of the small Eastern slope, a few pretty little meadows enliven the rather wild scene with their gay verdure. On reaching the W. el Kharroub which joins the Mharhar about three miles to the south to form the Tahaddar, we found it swollen by the rains, and its swift and turbid waters reminded me of the ford of Mechra'at[1] el Hechaf which I have so often crossed.

In the absence of our soldier who is always careful to remain behind in order to set to rights his trappings at critical moments, I have to venture first across the ford, an operation of some difficulty as the strong current threatens to carry away the horses. At last, thanks to my comrade, who superintends and organizes the crossing of the

---

[1] In Arabic, Mechra'at signifies *ford* and Mechra'at el Hachef is the ford of bottom rocks. A quarter of an hour's journey up stream will bring you to another ford practicable at all times.

animals, everything is brought over without any mishap or much discomfort except to our Arabs, who are forced to take a cold bath in the chilly weather and raging wind.

The plateau of El Gharbïa which we can discern at a distance of about 2½ miles rises more than 300 feet above the level of the sea. But to reach it we are obliged to cross a horrible marsh and to steer our course in a very zig-zag fashion, to avoid the pit-falls in which many an animal disappears during the winter. After a swift but cautious march of an hour and a half, we get clear of this dangerous spot. Behind us we espy a long train of heavily loaded camels floundering about. How long will it be before they reach the river? At every step they sink deep into the mud and seem to find a kind of pleasure in the change from the dry sands of the desert. The camel drivers, wielding enormous cudgels, belabour the unfortunate animals, but now and then a vicious roar shows that the chastisement is not always kindly received. A lusty little ass carries the smaller luggage of the drivers and proudly marches as leader at the head of the straggling caravan.

At length we reach a kind of narrow defile and at the end of it we suddenly catch a glimpse of the dchar djedid[1] situated at the entrance of the vast plateau which to-day will see the end of our troubles, for the soil is of a sandy nature and there our plucky mules will be able to march at a swift pace until the evening. Our road winds round a solitary hillock, the Djebel Zeïtoun, and ascends a steep slope, along which, on the right, we see a rocky ridge of remarkable appearance, called El Kalowa (the isolated).

At 12·15 we find ourselves in front of the site of Ad Mercuri on the right of the road. The mules which

[1] An appellation often met with and which means the new dchar.

THE RUINS OF AD MERCURI.

are coming up behind us are much out of breath, and our attendants show signs of fatigue after ascending the hill, and wading across the miry ground of the marsh. We give the order for a halt and at once proceed at a gallop towards the Roman ruins where we dismount.

The site has been well chosen; the table-land, which commands the lower ground, spreads in a northerly direction as far as the plateau of Ghellaïat and the hills of Hawara, exhibiting an immense cultivated surface, sprinkled with numerous dchours which are surrounded by waving corn and rich pasture lands. Two deep ravines, the Khandak el Hadjel in the north, and the Khandak el Djenanat in the south, descend towards the W. el Kharroub, constituting valuable natural defences which the Romans had completed by means of a large enclosure whose remains are yet visible.

Except some ruins and a few blocks of stone lying midst the corn, there is no memorial left of the past, for the plough has turned up the sod within the walls, and the untilled ground in the centre of a vast enclosure bears only a few shrubs and brambles. To judge from the extent of the traces of these ruins almost level with the ground, the Roman post must have been of great importance. Here was the junction, as the learned M. Tissot tells us, of the two ancient roads, one of which led towards the coast, and the other into Tocolosida in the neighbourhood of Meknas.

After ascending to the plateau we mount our horses and gallop to some dwellings which belong to the dchar of Had el Gharbïa. This hamlet lies to the south west at the bottom of a cool valley watered by a tiny brook, springing from an ancient fountain, which has defied as if by a miracle the ravages of centuries, and the spoliation of the natives.

We then encounter two Arab women bearing the classical amphora, who flee in terror at the unwonted sight. A young Arab, bolder than the rest, comes to us and offers to hold our horses in case we should like to shoot a few partridges. The firing attracts the inhabitants who curiously examine the trappings of our horses, and when we return we are escorted by all the male population of the place.

On our road we pass a cistern only four compartments of which have been respected by time and men. The extremely thick walls are still covered with a thick coating of that wonderful cement, the secret of which the Romans alone seem to have possessed. Close by we easily make out traces of buildings which must have been Roman baths. Not far from the spot M. Tissot discovered the foundations of a religious monument, most probably a shrine of Mercuri. Our beasts being rested and our men put in a good humour by the clearing of the sky, we resume our march.

The order of marching is picturesque. My friend, at times putting spurs to his horse, goes on, compass in hand, to reconnoitre from some lofty point, whilst I take charge of the scientific instruments with my barometer hung round my neck like some precious talisman. The mules take rank in Indian file according to the swiftness of their pace. One has already attracted our notice, a good beast that we bought at Tangiers half dead of fatigue and disease, now spruce and graceful, which, as if proud of being the bearer of our musketry store, always takes the lead of the convoy. Her obedience and intelligence in discerning the slightest dangers of the road have induced us to entrust her with the most fragile articles. She was christened Bagatelle and the name suits her exactly. The Moors take little care of their animals and content themselves with replacing them by others when no longer able to work. Thus, in consequence of the constant ill-usage to which they are subject, it is not of rare occurrence to see beasts of burden kick about, or bite the man who approaches with the load. As I had strictly prohibited any ill-treatment of my animals, they soon became perfectly docile and gentle.

CHAPTER IV.

On Our Way to Alqaçar—The Saint's Tomb—Our Soldier—All the Chatterboxes of the Country pay us a Visit—Our Cook and our Groom—A Group of Menhirs—Arthur Brooke's Opinion Concerning these—Origin of the Race of Inhabitants—The Roman Station of Ad Nonas—The Battle of the Three Kings—Arrival at a dchar—Pleasant Reception—The Cheik—Chaouch the Horse Dealer—The Town of Alqaçar—Its History—Horrible State of the Town, a Hot-Bed of Fever—Description of the Town.

BEFORE we resumed our journey, the barometer had risen, and the pleasant temperature (98°. F.) betokened more favourable weather, as the wind had quite fallen. After descending a succession of gentle slopes we soon arrived at a beautiful little plain, very well suited for cultivation, but quite deserted. Not a living soul was to be seen, and for two or three miles we could not discover any building. This was the valley of the W. el Aïacha, whose importance seems to have been exaggerated on various maps, for even after the continuous rains we found but little water there. Crossing the valley, we came to the chain of hills which forms the northern slopes of those heights, extending almost without interruption as far as the plain of Alqaçar. From the edge of the vast plateau we could see the small wood that surrounds the marabout of Sidi Mohammed Ben Ali, close to the dchar of the Beni Leiham, where I had encamped two years before. Like all consecrated spots, Sidi Mohammed Ben Ali (named after the Saint whose remains rest under the white qoubbah), has preserved its vegetation from the Arab's destructive hand, and lies in the midst of beautiful and luxuriant verdure. At the sight of those centenarian olive trees with hardy trunks, of the palm trees and arborescent ferns, it is easy to picture the appearance of the country when it served as a pasturage for innumerable elephants in the first century of our era; but all the forests have been destroyed since the Mussulman Conquest for the benefit of the wandering Arabs' flocks.

In this charming retreat we dismounted to await our people. It was a spot with a religious quietude about it, enlivened by the warbling of thousands of birds among the branches of the trees. The sky once more was blue, and its colour formed a striking contrast to that of the oasis, which two months hence would be completely scorched by the sun. The shouts of the muleteers roused us from our *far niente*, and recalled us to our duties. The dreadful soldier, with whom we had been encumbered ever since we left Tangiers, came up at a gallop, fearing, he said, that we might have been involved in some peril. This fear had indeed taken so firm a hold of our carabineer's mind, that he always rode in the rear of the column, and was the laughing stock of the caravan. The path on the plateau was very sandy, and the ground covered with broom and heather, reminded me of some French or English moorland. On the left, the peaks of the great mountains of the Rif and Beni Hassan soared in the distance above the cloudy vapours.

An hour and a quarter's march brought us at length on a level with Mzorah, where we struck off from the path followed by caravans, and descended the hill at the bottom of which we made a halt.

We tried to persuade our trooper to proceed to the dchar which loomed in the distance to seek information from the chief as to the best site for encamping, but in vain. The eccentric fellow was as obstinate as ever, and had it not been for the arrival of some natives, we should have been sorely embarrassed. The sight of our mules had excited these worthy people's curiosity. They took us at once to a very suitable turfy mound where the tents were promptly pitched; water was found about 200 yards from the encampment at the bottom of the hill. The luxuriant grass was much appreciated by our beasts, which began to graze at once with great gusto. Partridges were plentiful, and, thanks to our retriever, our meat safe was soon replete with game, while the numerous herds in a narrow valley through which a small tributary of the W. el Aïacha flows, gave promise of a good supply of milk in the evening.

After a hearty supper my friend inspected the neighbourhood and returned to inform me that no sleep was to be expected that night, as our people had collected all the jabberers of the tribe, who, warmly clad in their jellabas, were squatting around a large fire. They intended to talk of deeds of war and of love, and a little guitar was at hand on which to play in twangy tones an accompaniment to the general chanting. That was the great plague of our camp: these Moors could not make up their minds to sleep at night, so that in the day time they were dead-beat and scarcely able to set out on the march. Happily the forebodings of M. did not prove true that evening, as our energetic remonstrances showed them that we did not mean to stand any nonsense. The soldier, who had not done a bit of work, was already snoring in the corner of a tent wrapped up in at least a dozen burnouses, and reclining on a soft carpet which his fair one had no doubt embroidered for him, that he might, even in his slumbers, think of her gazelle-like eyes and jet black tresses.

Antonio the cook is a character worthy of an introduction to the reader. A bearded Andalusian, a great sportsman, and a pretty good cook, he was a fair representative of a certain class often met with at Tangiers, which unites the observance of Arab customs with European vices, and whose sole aim in life seems to be the plunder of travellers. He was always boasting of a courage which would have sufficed to conquer the whole dark continent. We were able to form an opinion of his bravery as we journeyed—not a very favourable one. Our groom Habmido was also a rather curious little fellow, "a boy with a melancholy voice" my friend T. used to call him. He seemed to be pretty influential with the other servants. As our personal attendant, he ordered all the others about, and initiated them with a certain degree of solemnity into the mysteries of furbishing bits and snaffles. A greater poltroon than any in Mauritania, he constantly exercised himself in the use of the Winchester rifle, and always carried about him a bag full of cartridges. During the march, perched on the top of a mule's load, and looking down on the remainder of the troop from an incredible height, he brandished now and then an old sabre with which he ran through some imaginary foe.

The night was cool, and in spite of the triple wall of our tent and the thick carpet, we suffered from that kind of shivering which is so well known to those who have lived under canvas. In the morning we found that the sky was as cloudy as on the previous day. The rainy season was not yet over, and our barometer indicated as much, for it fell persistently. The direction of the wind gave us indications of bad weather, so we hastened to pack up the tents lest they should be soaked, and prove too heavy a load for our beasts. The caravan hurried on in the direction of Tlata Raïçana where it was to await us before pitching our tents, which we intended to do at El Hamaïa, 28 miles from Mzorah. We then bade adieu to the worthy inhabitants who refused any payment for the milk they brought us, and directed our course towards the douar of El Outed, across the little valley below the camp. M. and the soldier went on in front, and I was obliged to follow their tracks as well as I could across the marsh, where my horse floundered about in such a way that I almost despaired of ever being able to extricate myself.

At last, covered with mud from head to foot, I succeeded by the greatest exertion in overtaking my friend and the soldier on a hill where stands the monolith of El Outed. Both of them were surrounded by a number of not very attractive women, who were much amused at my wretched appearance. In spite of the drizzling rain, I examined the curious monuments which consist of a group of cromlechs, the tallest of which is 6 metres high. The stones number about forty, but they are disappearing by degrees either through the destructive effects of time, or because the natives make use of them for their enclosures. This group seems to have been part of a series of more important monuments, for within an area of 500 yards I noticed about fifty of these cromlechs lying in the grass. They are very similar to those found in Great Britain. Arthur Brooke thinks they must have been erected by one and the same race, an hypothesis which is not without foundation considering that the inhabitants of the north of Morocco belong to a fair-haired race. In the Tingitane, fair-haired people number one-third of the population, and are fairer than the natives of Algeria. The Morisco Berber must then have been less modified by mixture with the native race than the Algerian Kabyle, and this supports the supposition of the English ethnologist; which, moreover, is borne out by the geographical situation. The north-west part of the African continent has been invaded from time immemorial by fair-skinned Europeans, so that now two-thirds of the Riffian colony is composed of fair or chestnut haired people, and the other third of a dark type which recalls that of the south-west of France. The Berber population of the province of Tangiers, which belongs to the great tribes of the Samhadja, and of the Betama, is similarly constituted; many of the women are fair, the greater number belong to the chestnut type, and those of the dark class are in character and features like the peasants of Burgundy, of Berry, or Limousin. The manners and customs of the entire Berber race are similar to those of the French, and strengthen the idea of a common origin with the latter.

We returned across the same valley to the plateau. The air, already very damp, had become cooler; the sky was covered with a mist, and the Rif, dimly discernible in the distance, had lost the enchanting aspect which it presented when flooded with the rays of the glorious African sun. The rain soon poured in torrents, and wrapped in our waterproof coats, we passed the qoubbah of Sidi el Yemani,[1] a

[1] When descending the declivities of the plateau of Sidi el Yemani, we perceived towards the west the hills of El Tourki, at the foot of which the town of Homar or Homara was built in the tenth century. Its fine walls are specially mentioned by Leo Africanus and Marmol, and some traces of this ancient place may perhaps be found in the large Berber dchar of H'oumar, and in the surrounding ruins.

celebrated marabout, whose remains lie in a verdant grove.

The Roman station of Ad Novas must—according to M. Tissot, who drew his conclusion from a calculation of distances—have stood at this spot, but no trace of it has as yet been discovered.

On descending the last declivities of the plateau, we had a fine view over the vast plain, watered by the little W. el Rihán, called by the natives Fah'ser Rih'an, "the plain of myrtles."

Numerous douars and some barley fields gave evidence of a rather thick population, but the greater part of the ground was uncultivated, though it seemed marvellously fertile and able to bear rich harvests. Towards noon the weather showed signs of improvement, and, protected from the west wind by a small marabout, we sat down with a keen appetite to lunch, with the necessaries for which the cook had furnished our saddle bags.

The saint whose tomb gave us shelter was perhaps a kinsman of his neighbour,[1] Sidi el Yemani, and may have played a part in the defence of Tangiers, when it was bombarded in 1844, for we saw an old cannon ball on the ground which encloses the remains of this respectable person.

Two hours later we reached the lower part of the plateau of Tlata Raïçana. All along the road, we met curious and interesting groups of people who were returning from the market held that day, in the same way that our peasantry at home return from the fair. There again the rich grass of the pastures gave ample evidence of the fertility of the

[1] According to a local tradition, Sidi el Yemani distinguished himself by catching in his hands the French cannon balls and then dropping them on the ground. This man, whose services must have proved invaluable during a siege, lived and died unknown to Europeans.

THE SURROUNDING COUNTRY.

soil. While awaiting the arrival of our mules we shot some wood-pigeons very much like those we see in Europe; they were perched in a grove of olive trees, at the foot of which our sheep were tied up.

The sky is now quite clear of the heavy clouds, and on the level plain we behold a scene which might tempt an artist by its succession of bright colours which are produced without any intermediate tones, and its curious effects of light playing on the white burnous-clad peasants on a green background. As we have no purchases to make, we avoid passing through the dense crowd, and so busy are all these country people, our passage remains unnoticed.

The plain here is terminated by a narrow valley forming, by a succession of gentle gradients from the W. el Rihán, the dividing line of the waters of the valley of the W. el Kouss.

In the west rises a succession of detached hills, towering one above the other, and beyond them lies a large plateau, at the extremity of which are to be seen other wooded heights in the direction of the ocean, with a small forest of cork trees, which are not sufficiently large to be put to any use. These are the remains of the immense forest which formerly covered the whole region. In the neighbourhood of El Araïsh (12 miles N.W. 85°) there are some more extensive woods.

We can easily make out the ridge of the Djebel Sarsar. The atmosphere is now exquisitely clear, so that we are able to see also all the details of the indentations of the Rif of which each mountain stands out on the coppery azure of a fine African evening. The air, after the long rain, is loaded with the most delicious perfumes, and all this added to the prospect of an hospitable welcome on the lands of the Sherif of Wazzan, makes us all bright and cheerful. The animals, urged on by their drivers, move on at a swift pace, whilst we remain behind to admire the beautiful country. Spirited Antonio is entrusted with the establishment of the camp under the protection of the valiant Moroccan warrior.

While slowly riding along we come up to a muddy rivulet, the W. el Hamar, a tributary of W. el Makhzen, and before 5 o'clock we cross that river, unknown before the "battle of the three kings," but which owes its celebrity to the disasters of the Christian army which put an end to Portuguese influence in the Moghreb.

It was our intention to skirt the banks up to the point of junction with the W. el Kouss, about 8 miles 74° S.E., probably the spot where the battle was fought, but we had to give up the little excursion on account of the bad state of the road.

This battle of Alqaçar is often termed the battle of the three kings, the three chiefs,[1] Mohammed, Sidi abd el Melek and Don Sebastian having fallen in the fight.

Instead of operating on El Araïsh, Don Sebastian, a young prince without any experience, meditating a great conquest in Africa, landed at Arzilla, and took at once the road to Fez on his way to Alqaçar after crossing the river Los Molenos, now El Rha. A few thousand Moors under the orders of Mohammed, a candidate to the Sherifian throne, reinforced the small Christian army, numbering 20,000 men,

[1] When Muley er Rechid had seized upon Fez in May, 1655, a number of chiefs revolted. One of the principal Keïlan had succeeded in subduing the Tingitane, but was beaten in 1666, by Muley er Rechid, and was besieged in Arcella, but he succeeded in escaping to Algiers. In 1673, on the death of his sovereign, he landed at Tetuan, but the new Sultan, Muley Ismaïl, marched rapidly to meet him, and came up with him early in July in the neighbourhood of El-K'sar (Alqaçar). In the ensuing bloody battle the Keïlan was killed.

among which were 12,000 Portuguese, the rest consisting of Germans, Spaniards, and Italians. The chronicles of that period state that the Mussulmans had 25,000 horse, 1,000 Turks, and 10,000 Arab irregulars, and 34 guns, to which the Portuguese could only oppose twelve pieces of cannon.

Abd el Melek, who was ill, was encamped below Alqaçar, awaiting his enemies. The battle began the 4th August, 1578, at noon. According to a plan given in Centellas' work, the Christian army was encamped about three miles from the W. el Kouss, not far from the junction of the W. el Makhzen. The battle was thus fought in that part of the plain comprised between the W. Makhzen and the W. Ouarour, a very inferior strategical position which, by forcing Sebastian on to a deep and swift river like the W. el Kouss, prevented his making any flank movement. The plateau Tlata Raïçana was occupied from the first by several thousand Arab irregulars, who very probably decided the day; as, taking advantage of a false manœuvre of the Portuguese light cavalry, they swooped down " with a fury difficult to realise." All retreat was, therefore, cut off, and the unfortunate Christian army was cut to pieces.

Mohammed's body was found in the W. el Kouss, Sebastian fell covered with wounds, and Abd el Melek, who had insisted upon being carried to the front in a litter, died the very same day from an attack of his malady. The field was covered with 15,000 corpses, which, according to the historians of the time, were buried a few days afterwards.

Whilst philosophically ruminating on the necessity of men killing one another in order to make their will prevail, we reached Hamaïa where, on seeing our tents already pitched, we had proof that our confidence in Antonio was not misplaced; meanwhile the soldier was watching the active movements of his busy companions with a drowsy eye, which did not exactly flash with the ardour of the ancient conquerors of Don Sebastian.

The region of El Hamaïa belongs to the Sherif of Wazzan, and the site of the dchar, where we had stopped, is truly charming. I really envy the inhabitants of this fine country, with such a beautiful view on the valley of the Kouss, whose vast stretch of verdure spreads itself out at the base of the plateaux, the fertile soil of which bears nourishment for thousands of cattle.

Everything looks pleasant here. Our people and the inhabitants seem to be already on very good terms. Our cattle are grazing among the green undulations of the plateau under the care of young herdsmen. Viewed by means of the glass, from the top of a hill, the sight gladdens one's heart and the arrival of the Chief of the dchar, who having been informed of our friendly relations with the Sherif, has come up to meet us with all the great men of the place, puts the finishing touch to this hospitable scene. "Es selam aleï koum" (Peace be unto you), says the Chief addressing us, draped in the flowing folds of his snow-white burnous. "Ou aleï koum es selam," we reply whilst we dismount, so as to cut short the interminable series of compliments which had already begun. All grasp our hands, and examine with an intelligent curiosity the different parts of our horses' trappings which to them are altogether novel.

But the Chief soon understands how troublesome this concourse of the inquisitive must be to us; he utters a few words, and accompanied by him alone we pass through the respectful throng with the calm bearing of a couple of pachas, whilst twenty eager hands take charge of our steeds.

As these country people wear no turbans, but have their heads uncovered and shaved, a few wearing a small lock on the temples, like the young Egyptians in the basso relievos, they have a decidedly biblical appearance. Their energetic bronzed features, slightly harsh, not very pleasing to behold, stand out well against their white garments. The tricolour flag, having been run up in the honour of the returning sun, waves gently in the evening breeze, our cook on this occasion making a grand Spanish speech of which the natives naturally understand not a word; but he is bent on showing us the extent of his varied accomplishments, for he sprinkles his effusions with more than extraordinary historical references. Provisions come up plentifully and joy reigns supreme; the soldier himself looks pleased! My companion astonishes the natives with his manipulation of the theodolite, and I receive under my tent the visit of the Chief who, through my servant who acts as interpreter, gives me information of this part of the country. He is only, he says, the chief farmer of the Sherif, but he assures us that his wish is that we should be provided with every necessary.

Night has come and M. is still at his astronomical observations.

The next morning we are up with the sun and shake our sleepy people. It seems really as if the disciples of Mohammed did not care to see the East reddening under the first rays of the glittering orb. The morning is splendid, but we have before us a long day's march before we reach Dchavénah on the other slope of the plain of Alqaçar, where it will be necessary to cross the W. el Kouss, one of the largest rivers in Morocco. Moreover, we contemplate visiting Chaouch to make a few purchases to complete our train of animals, and to enable us to dismiss the horrible muleteers whom we engaged at Tangiers. Chaouch is a well known man in the valley of Kouss. He for some time added to his business as a merchant the functions of French consular agent at Alqaçar, but a series of private misadventures having deprived him of his official post, he comforts himself by carrying on a most profitable business as a horse-dealer.

We decide to go ahead, leaving the care of the camp to Ahmet, the most intelligent of our servants, with orders to join us at the ford. The principal inhabitants again make their appearance, showering blessings on our heads and bidding us God speed.

Almost intoxicated with the enchanting scenes all along the road, and the delightful spring morning, we gleefully march on, doing in a short time the eleven miles and a half which separate us from Alqaçar, across a good deal of water and marshy ground, and at ten o'clock we ascend the last acclivities which hide from our gaze the famous town. The city was embellished and enlarged, according to tradition, by Jacoub el Mansour in the XIIth century.[1]

The origin of the town is very ancient; its position on the W. el Kouss, where it commands the river at the point where the tide flows in the midst of a rich valley, had certainly caused it to be chosen at the time of the Roman occupation as an important station on the road of Tangiers to Volubilis and Tocolosida.

[1] According to M. Tissot, the tradition recorded by Leo and Marmol concerning the building of the town by Jacoub (who, it would appear, had given it the name of Kasr-abd-el-Kerim), is reduced to nought by the assertions of Edrisi, who knew it already under the latter name. As for El Bekri, he calls it Souk Kotoma, terming it a great and magnificent city.

The buildings of the town are of brick, and still enclose a number of blocks of Roman origin. At the foot of the minaret of the great Mosque, M. Tissot discovered a Greek inscription, the only one as yet found in Morocco. The soil is there full of old relics such as are met with throughout Morocco.

Ruins of old buildings erected by the Portuguese moulder away in a marshy ground inhabited by frogs, which is a most pestilential source of disease. Alqaçar cannot reckon more than 5,000 inhabitants and does not seem to have an area equal to that of Tangiers. The unimportant commerce of the town is conducted by means of the neighbouring port of El Araïsh (Larache).

Vines, olive groves, and orange gardens, encircle Ksar-el-Kebir, (in Arabic the great castle), situated in the middle of a great marshy valley not far off from the W. el Kouss. The town is not surrounded by walls, notwithstanding its name. From a distance it appears to be a large, beautiful, and picturesque city, with its palm trees rising above a sea of roofs and the white storks flying about the minarets. Whilst admiring all the graceful details of this Eastern town, we reach the summit of a small hill on which a humble qoubbah is erected within a cemetery. Unfortunately, the air is redolent with the horrible odours of innumerable dunghills, which for years have been accumulating and rotting in the sun, and the unpleasant smell makes us forget the charms of the panorama. I do not know any town in Morocco—the traditional country of unwholesome odours —which could compete with Alqaçar in this respect. We enter the city between the huge heaps of refuse which have become quite respectable through age, (as they have been increasing there for several centuries), and skirt on the west old ditches half filled up. Some fine gardens, producing the most renowned figs of Northern Morocco, adorn the town; but how can you appreciate the shade they afford when the morning breeze, the heat of the mid-day sun, or the evening coolness, waft pestilential effluvia all around? I should not advise any traveller to encamp at this place, for, to the nuisances referred to, so offensive to the olfactory organs, must be added the ague and myriads of big mosquitoes which seem very fond of Nazarean blood.

We enter the town through a tumble-down gate and thread a maze of crooked lanes which lead to the market place. There we await the return of the soldier (whom we have sent to ascertain the whereabouts of Chaouch), surrounded by numbers gazing on us with uneasy curiosity, and who, at the slightest gesture, retreat into the throng.

The houses of the town not being whitewashed, the result is a greyish tint, which produces a wretched appearance in the bright light. The inhabitants' countenances bear evidence of the unwholesome climate; most have pale, haggard faces. Everything here savours of fever. But if the population does not make a good appearance, other inhabitants, the storks, look, on the contrary, wonderfully robust and active, the misfortune of the bipeds being the good luck of the winged race. On all sides we see their large nests well tenanted, and the colony seems prosperous enough. I never beheld anywhere else such a number of these storks, which seem as if the town belonged to them. Overhead fly the busy birds, bearing in their beaks dainty morsels, parts of which sometimes fall on the heads of the passers-by, to the great disappointment of the numerous broods.

The streets are lined with leafy trees and reeds which afford a pleasant shade and a picturesque chiaro oscuro.

At last here comes our soldier. We follow in the wake of his splendid burnous contrasting with the rags of the inhabitants, and we thus reach the dwelling of Chaouch, where innumerable cups of tea protract the conversation.

Escorted by a band of starving, half-naked beggars with bright feverish eyes and skinny bodies, we resume our march, and we reach the last houses on the road to the river. We then follow an old causeway whose pavement rings under our horses' feet.

CHAPTER V.

Roads from Alqaçar to Dcharchiera—Traces of the Portuguese Occupation—The W. el Kouss—We Cross the River—Change in the Temperature—Red Partridges Plentiful—Resemblance of this Region to Spain—The Orange Tree Garden of the Sherif of Wazzan—Dcharchiera—A Specimen in support of Darwin's Theory—Our First Night Encampment at Dcharchiera—Warlike Tendencies of the Berbers—Dolce Far Niente—Chimol Family.

THERE are two roads from Alqaçar to Wazzan, the shorter crosses in a northerly direction through Djebel Sarsar part of the marshy valley of the W. el Kouss, and beyond, it is impracticable from the beginning of the rainy season; the other (which I had already followed in 1882 with my friend T.) leaves the Djebel on the east and joins the first-named road at Dcharchiera after having wound round the mountain and crossed, in the south, the hills which on this side shut in the valley of the W. el Kouss. This river runs a little less than a mile south of Alqaçar. The road which takes you to the town is pretty well paved for three quarters of the way, but the remainder is, during the rainy season, a pestilential marsh where part of the garbage of the town is allowed to rot away. This causeway seems to date back to the time of the rule of the Portuguese (or Spaniards) in 1508, when they were masters of all the coast of Morocco as far as Mogador.

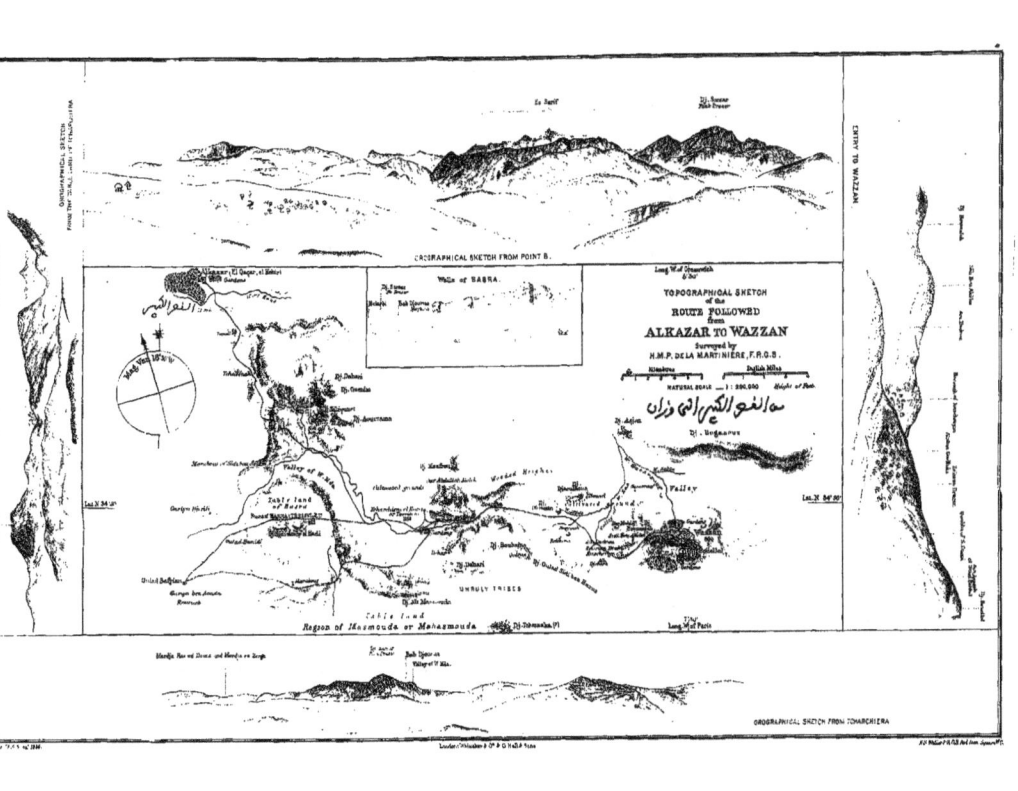

TRACES OF THE PORTUGUESE OCCUPATION.

It cannot be doubted that the proximity of El Araïsh, where they had established themselves, induced them to push on to this place, and that most of the bridges and other municipal works, which still exist, are due to their sojourn here, and to their influence over the country. When Marmol speaks of ancient Ezaguen, now in ruins, the site of which it would be rash to attempt to point out, he mentions the armaments which the pachas of the town were obliged to keep up in order to repel the incursions of the Portuguese who overran the country as far as fifteen or twenty leagues inland.

The W. el Kouss is about 70 yards broad at the ford where we crossed it; its swift, turbid waters have a depth which in summer hardly exceeds 16 inches. It must, however, be remembered, that when the slightest storm bursts on the Rif Mountains, it makes so much difference that often, even in summer, one finds the bed of the river suddenly swollen. You are then obliged to wait till the water subsides in order to cross it. In the winter the river is dangerous, and every year there are accounts of many accidents.

The vegetation on the banks is luxuriant, and one may at a distance easily distinguish the course of the river by the double line of trees, whose thick foliage indicate the windings of the river, hidden at the bottom of steep banks.

While waiting for the caravan, we watch the curious operations of some Arabs who take a flock of sheep across the river.[1]

---

[1] According to Joachim de Centellas it would appear that there once stood a bridge here, the remains of which seems to be the debris of that which was crossed by Abd el Melek before the battle of Alqaçar.

F

Some strong-looking negroes keep going from one bank to the other, on each occasion carrying one of the animals thrown across their shoulders. The whole scene is not devoid of interest, but it seems a tedious affair as a whole day is needed to effect the operation; but this is an odd country where time is of no account, and surely it is here that one must come to find the antithesis of the proverb: "Time is money."

The vegetation and cultivation of the plain are attended to more carefully on this side of the river than along the road to Tangiers. The road winds in and out across the marshes, and runs occasionally over old bridges, without which, winter or summer, it would be hazardous to wade through such a miry expanse.

The road which we follow is formed by the united tracks made by mules and other beasts of burden during the winter. To escape any misadventure travellers prefer to tramp across country; the result is great havoc to the fields; the unfortunate owners strive to check this by setting up barriers in the shape of stone walls or enclosures of bushes. This state of things is general in Morocco, and, in the end, one gets quite used to the sight of mules stopping from time to time in order to munch some tufts of barley or wheat. That which in Europe would be considered as absolutely illegal is tolerated and accepted in this country, the classic land of abuses.

The plain continues for two or three miles. When once the stream is crossed we pass large barley fields in a good state of cultivation, which promise an abundant harvest, and towards three o'clock we climb the first slopes of some rocky hills, which in some places are quite bare of verdure. On the right we see four tumuli with well-preserved outline, which do not seem to have been disturbed. It would be interesting to excavate them if the people of the country did not object. Five hundred metres further on, we cross a little stream of clear water, flowing from south-west to north-west, over a rocky soil. We then climb the last slopes to a vast plateau and reach the spot chosen for our encampment. At a short distance from the dchar of Dchavénah, there exists a small Zaouïa of the Sherif of Wazzan. The ruins of Basra, it seems, are at a three hours' march from this place. The region is absolutely devoid of trees, but it presents fine pasture land after the heavy rains. The scene reminds us of certain parts of the Pyrenees when the sun is sending forth its last beams from behind the hills, and when the bleating of the flocks alone breaks the awful silence of this mountainous country. In the evening which is of ideal loveliness, a south westerly breeze rises up cooling the atmosphere.

The thermometer which that night fell to 87°, stands now at seven o'clock, 96 degrees. The tents are almost soaked through with a heavy fall of dew, a general phenomenon throughout Morocco, and which is explained by the variation, often a considerable one, between diurnal and nocturnal temperatures. The sky, which remains bright until eleven o'clock, then loses its clearness by degrees; a damp cold is felt and a thickening fog adds a layer of condensed vapour. At daybreak, the mist rises, and towards seven o'clock in the morning it has wholly vanished, leaving only a few bright and flitting white clouds, which are wafted along in the high regions of the atmosphere, and soon disperse in the azure of the heavens. To this dampness are due the many cases of ophthalmic complaints, and of rheumatism, among the inhabitants.

At 9.30 we strike the tents, and at 10 the column resumes its march along the undulations of the plateau, of which certain portions bear evidence of cultivation; otherwise the remainder of the country is covered with the unavoidable and monotonous palmitos. The soil is thin, and in another month everything will be scorched by the sun.

From the camp we could, in the morning, distinctly perceive towards the east, the snowy profiles of the mountains of the Rif, whilst all the surrounding region with its numerous mamelons, limited our western horizon. The road runs along the prolongation of the Djebel Sarsar, which imposing mass rises to about two miles on the left. We can make out its minutest details, even to the denuded summit, full of chalky white rocks, whose edges stand out in the dazzling light on the crown of sombre verdure made by the copses which cling to its flanks.

A narrow steep footpath leads up nearly to the top of the mountain, which is inhabited by several fanatical tribes, the principal, the Oulad Migdoul, occupying the northern slope.

The country which we traverse is quite devoid of any habitation. It is a solitude with innumerable palms, which thickly stud the bottom of gorges as well as the tops of the hills, but at each step large partridges arise in pairs, and fly off at a short distance. Our cook cannot resist the longing to use his fowling-piece, but on this dry heated ground any wounded partridge is lost to the sportsman, as there is no scent for the dogs to trace the disabled bird.

Towards ten o'clock we allow our people to continue the journey, and taking a short cut we climb a height of about 400 feet, which commands the country, in order to sketch the profiles 1 and 2 (Itinerary No. 2). We are thus able to admire the magnificent panorama of the plain of Alqaçar. The early morning mist is now dispelled, and the minarets of the town stand out like white needles in the midst of gardens, whence issue the delicate forms of the palm trees. The course followed by the Kouss is perceptible down to the sea, and looks like a broad ribbon winding about the rich vegetation under a sky of so deep a blue, that it would appear unnatural in a picture. The extreme purity of the air allows of the most minute details being discernible without having recourse to our glasses, though we are at a distance of seven miles from the town.

It is in vain that we look around our observatory for any evidence of the presence of man among the innumerable hills which are like so many gigantic petrified waves. No dwelling meets the gaze, no sign of the presence of a human being. We only discover a white qoubbah in the north and another far away in the south, both being very convenient as landmarks.

We make our way back to the column, not without some difficulty, as we lose our way at the bottom of the furnace-like ravines where the air is so heated, and not the slightest whiff of the breeze can penetrate. The thermometer by eleven o'clock stands there at 94°. While surveying the surrounding country we cannot help recognising the felicity of the humorous remark of Alexandre Dumas who asserts that Africa begins at the Pyrenees. All this region is indeed very much like Sierra Morena, especially in the part comprised between Puertoleano and Marmolejo. It has the same kind of stunted vegetation, the same characteristics of the soil, the same hydrographic system of torrents dried up at the first summer heat, but which in winter form large rivers across all the valleys.

At half-past twelve, in our descent, we came up to a small brook which runs down from Djebel Sarsar, and on each side of which the valley expands. A few fields at that spot show both the superior quality of the soil and the proximity of a dchar. This brook has a welcome freshness, and some tall trees offer us a pleasant shelter from the heat of this the first day of an African summer. The water is nevertheless at 72° in the shade; but we must tear ourselves away from the pleasing repose, for our men are very keen on reaching the camp before sunset as the country has an indifferent reputation for safety. At a quarter to twelve we come in view of the ruins of Basra lying on our right half-way up the clayey hills, whose red colour can be seen from a distance. A small marabout, a short way off, and nearly on the same line, serves as a land-mark, for its white qoubbah can be discerned very clearly. The path leads up to the confluence of two brooks. We march up the course of one of these, which flows through the territory of the tribe where we shall encamp this evening. The temperature rises to 101° in the shade, and our beasts suffer visibly from the sudden change. Our plucky mules march on at a swinging steady pace; the horses are not so fresh, and the men are glad to stop now and then. We are obliged to encourage them, and renew their energy by promises of a week's rest to be enjoyed at our next encampment. The clayey valley which we are following must be very hard to cross in winter when the heavy and slippery earth is softened by the rains. Everything, however, is now dry, but the tracks of the winter paths are still there, and the animals are scarcely able at times to keep their balance in the holes made by the beasts of burden which have passed that way. At last, at half-past two o'clock, the olive trees of Dcharchiera are discernible. Our impatient men, giving way to their extreme fear of marauders, decided to make us travel at the hottest hours of the day, and we are reaching the goal long before nightfall. The prospect of being soon in camp makes them oblivious of their fatigue, and at twenty minutes past three we are in the orange gardens owned by the Sherif of Wazzan. This is a delightful spot. I stayed there in the previous year on my return from the excursion to Wazzan, which I made with Major Trotter. Unfortunately, the sojourn here is scarcely bearable on account of the strong perfume from the orange trees. In consequence, after a few minutes' consultation, we decide on the lofty hill which commands the whole valley up to Djebel Sarsar. There, we shall be in the midst of the great old olive woods, in the vicinity of a dchar, whose inhabitants are already running up to gaze on the Roumis who come to settle down on their lands. These people seem anything but friendly, and we are compelled to parley and show the letter of Sidi el Hadj Abd es Selam before we can obtain some convenient place for pitching our tents. The spot, luckily, is well chosen—the hill, 1050 feet high, is 150 feet at least above the whole valley. Water is plentiful, for close at hand are the sources of two brooks. The one, W. Mda, forms a small cascade, which has given its name to the dchar, which we perceive at a few yards from the camp; whilst the other one, springing from a dale in a more northerly direction, winds about in the plain before joining the first brook in the gardens of orange trees. The trees find there the necessary moisture and thrive wonderfully. This little stream forms part of the basin of the Sebou, which it joins near its mouth, after having traversed the vast system of the Merdja, close to the sea. M. Tissot has marked it in his excellent map, but not having seen its source, he only shows the lower course.

As for provisions, it is to be hoped that the dispositions of the worthy natives will improve at the sight of the white coin which our cook is about to exhibit. The fanaticism of the people is great; many fights are said to take place in the neighbourhood between different tribes, so that the natives, armed to the teeth, are constantly prowling in the country with long guns and large daggers. It is, therefore, not without some apprehension, that I see my companion beginning the preparations for topographic observations. But he assures me that the natives will be too much impressed with our mysterious operations to think of showing any hostility. And in fact, a number of bold and impudent urchins, whose inquisitiveness exercised itself on our property, fly in horror at the sight of the glass pointed to the horizon like a piece of ordnance.

Whilst our soldier, accompanied by the cook, is gone in quest of provisions, I enter into good-humoured conversation with one of the hill-men, whose new jellaba gives him an air of respectability. He is a kind of giant, whose anatomic conformation strongly reminds one of the chimpanzee. This evident specimen of Darwin's theory of the development of species gives us alarming information on the insecurity of the country, and the bad disposition of the natives. I am told also, that the principal owner of the neighbouring dchar is a certain Sherif on rather bad terms with the Grand Sherif of Wazzan, and that he is under German protection.

The question of protection in Morocco deserves special mention. I shall recur to the subject hereafter, but I may say at once that in this very dchar of Dcharchiera complete illusions were entertained by its inhabitants; some, indeed, went so far as to imagine they could claim the protection of the Legation simply because they had assisted our servants. Whilst in our service they fondly believed themselves freed from the shadow of authority which the Sultan exercises in this part of the country.

Our first night here was pretty full of incidents. The male portion of the population kept watch on their flocks and crops, while we, on our side, had to ensure the safety of our animals. We tied them between the tents, and each of the servants mounted guard for two hours. The palest of countenances would scarcely give an idea of the timid demeanour of all these poltroons. In order to give them courage, my companion promised them some gratuities, and was obliged to go the rounds himself now and then. The whole region was loyal to the Sherif, but not to the Sultan, so that the result was a kind of anarchy most pleasing to these hill-men. We had evidence of it during our sojourn here. The population has the characteristics of the Rifan type, and their territory forms the extreme eastern limit, where travellers may venture to penetrate out of the Wazzan track. Beyond that, special precautions, such as accompanying the Sherif himself in one of his journeys, are necessary in order not to run too much risk.

The region, the geography of which is but little known, forms the boundary of the independent and uneven zone of the Rif, inhabited by the Kebaïls, of the Berber race (which expanded as far as this region), the same as that of the mountain Kabyles of Djurdjura, which was subdued and absorbed in Algeria at the cost of so much effort and many lives, but which has already produced such interesting intellectual results.

The Berbers are, as is well known, very quarrelsome, and their social organisation into independent and often rival tribes, favours this natural disposition. At certain times in this pleasant district of Dcharchiera, in the gatherings on the occasion of fairs, you may witness bloody struggles; for the most trifling cause the natives will appeal to their guns. Their hostility is such that we could never prevail on a few men of the dchar to accompany us on an excursion to the hills of the southern slopes of the small valley below us, as they were occupied by an unfriendly tribe, and the consequence would have been a terrible revival of the fighting.[1]

As a natural consequence, our staff of attendants—bravery not being their *forte*—never left off quaking with fear. Every morning, one or other of their number would come and beseech us to hasten our departure from the plateau, so picturesque and so attractive, but for them, so full of terrors. We were even compelled to secure the cartridges which we had at first entrusted to their care, and to leave them a few only. They used to spend their days improving their marksmanship, under the skilful direction of Antonio, in order, our cook told us, to spread a wholesome terror among the Berbers.

The time went delightfully by under the shady boughs of the old olive trees. But even the sweetest *far niente* cannot last for ever, and we felt in duty bound, in common courtesy, while presenting our letters and our respects to the sons of the Sherif of Wazzan, to explain our intention of encamping for a few days at Dcharchiera before again accept-

---

[1] The Berbers of Dcharchiera only spoke the Arab tongue, and seemed to have lost all recollection of their native dialect, and only one of them could read and write Arabic, and that not well.

ing their cordial hospitality, which I had had occasion to appreciate the preceding year. My companion only knew of Wazzan from hearsay, and he rejoiced in advance, forming, I believe, certain illusions about the famous city, spoken of by some historians with a mysterious air, which suits neither its small dimensions nor its simple and good-humoured population.

CHAPTER VI.

Departure—The Start—The Deserted Aspect of the Country—Unexpected Meeting with an English Lady—Our Soldiers Terrified—The Sherif's Country House—Our Alarm—The Djebel Sarsar—We are not allowed to ascend the Mountain—Excursion to the Ruins of Basra—History of Basra—the Town of Barca—The Kaïd—We Lose our Way—The Marauders—Excursion to the Hill north of the Dchar—Features of the Surrounding Country—The Thaleb—Departure for Wazzan.

ONE fine evening we directed our soldier and the groom to dress themselves in their best, early next morning, and at day-break we were on our way to the Mecca of the Moghreb, with our high mettled steeds in handsome trappings.

Thanks to the coolness of the atmosphere, we were able, after three hours' march, to reach the town, about nine miles distant. On leaving the camp, we followed a path which winds along the sides of the hill and leads to a steep gorge at the bottom of which roars the W. Mda, a small torrent. The spot is picturesque enough, and its high, woody, steep hills are not devoid of a certain savage grandeur. After we had reached the sandy soil of the plain, we trotted briskly along on the undulating plateau which precedes the Djebel Wazzan. The horizon is limited on all sides by mountains rising in tiers, and enclosing some fine-looking fields, which, if well tilled, might bear rich crops. Such is not the case unfortunately, and with the exception of a few feeble attempts, the soil, barely scratched by rude and primitive ploughs, is nothing better than deserted moors.

The road crosses two small brooks, the abode of innumerable tortoises, and after having reached the bank of one of these, we passed within sight of the Douar, where the Sherif had formerly treated us to some coursing in which nothing was wanting but the hare. The path ascends the first undulations of the mountain of Wazzan, then it becomes stony and steep, till you reach the strong hedges of cacti, which at the bottom of Kuscherine or Kacheriyîn border the road leading to the market place. Certain rumours of revolt having been spread about, we might have naturally expected some unforeseen event, and the sudden appearance of an excited troop of armed men at the turning of the road, in so fanatical a country, could not but surprise us, and impress us as being the first dramatic incident of our travels.

I looked at my companion and saw him seize his rifle and place it across his saddle ready for use. The alert was unfortunately of short duration, and we were not long in discerning, in the first ranks of the troop, the English lady, the wife of the Sherif. Her presence among the descendants of Mohammed at once reassured us, and she was kind enough to inform us that it was in compliance with her husband's wishes that she returned to Tangiers. Two hundred horsemen of the Sultan having just arrived on the territory of Wazzan, an encounter with the population was to be feared, and we might expect to witness a great deal of bloodshed if we did not take her advice and follow her example by at once retracing our steps to Tangiers. She seemed much astonished, when, having thanked her, we informed her of our intention of pursuing our journey; my companion even expressed his gratification at the prospect of a little fighting, thus laying himself open to some suspicion as to the state of his mental faculties.

Our rifleman had taken advantage of the short halt to hold a lively conversation with some of the escort, and the information imparted to him seemed not very reassuring, as he came at once to beseech us to give up our rash project of entering the town. It was indeed a painful sight to see the fellow shaking with terror. But in spite of his entreaties we compelled him to walk in front. This was the only reply to his lamentations. Thus marching on, and looking as if we were dragging along some malefactor, we reached Sidi el Arbi's house.

I recognised the dwelling where Major Trotter and myself had found a lodging, and the young *secretaries*, who on a former occasion had proved to be great connoisseurs of claret, came up smiling as if in pleasant recollection of the bouquet of the wine which they had tasted, to acquaint us with the hour at which we should see their master.

In the Sherif's country-house, at the lower part of the town, we expected to find a merry gathering. From the noisy revelry which was taking place under the clumps of orange trees, we were able to convince ourselves that this city, on the point of being attacked, pillaged, and sacked, as we had been told, and which we had entered only for safety, still contained some merry souls. They were the families of Ben Chimol and Ben Assouli in *villégiature* here.

Thus we found some old friends from Tangiers. Coming up just as the dessert was being served, like two gloomy prophets, we tried to make a diversion by searching the depths of our throats for the most emotional accents, and depicting the volcano on which these unfortunate people were dancing, what horrible vistas of pillage and sacking was reserved for them by a detachment from the cavalry of the Makhzen just arrived from the interior with the most bloodthirsty orders and intentions.

But we did not find willing ears. The courage of the disciples of Moses put to shame the followers of Jesus and Mohammed, and incredulous laughter greeted our effusions, much to our mortification, and we had the cause of this artificial effervescence explained to us. We then easily realised the difficulties French policy would encounter if some degree of self-possession did not calm minds down. Whilst taking our share of a splendid feast, consisting of dainty Israelitish dishes, new to us, we recovered our equanimity, and we were then perfectly enlightened by our friends as to the importance of the difficulty between the Sultan and the Sherif who had just obtained the consular protection of the French Republic. The danger was that the local excitement should extend, and fanned into flame by fanaticism, should flare up into a general conflagration.

Having thus gathered information concerning the state of affairs, we were able to proceed to the house of the Sherif's son, with whose intentions it was important that we should be acquainted in the face of all this turmoil.

The reception was most gracious, and the entertainment was prolonged far into the day. My companion, finding that the dissertations were growing tedious, went into the town and purchased a magnificent horse, which the Sherif's people procured for him without much difficulty. When we had acquainted Sidi Mohammed with our resolution of prolonging our stay at Dcharchiera and making an attempt to ascend the Djebel Sarsar, the people of his suite endeavoured to dissuade us from our second project and kept enjoining on us the greatest prudence in our dealings with the natives of the place of encampment, pointing out to us how much to our advantage it would be to pitch our tents in the gardens of the plain, where we should be more secure.

We declined the offer of an escort, and, being desirous of returning to the camp the same evening, we took leave without having had to imbibe a frightful quantity of tea à la Marocaine.

On the way, thanks to the carelessness of our soldier, a true bird of ill omen, who kept us waiting as usual, we lost our way in the dark, and might have had an unpleasant time of it in the wooded and frightfully rocky hills, if the two horsemen of the Sherif, who were sent after us, had not galloped up and set us in the right way to the camp where strange rumours were afloat concerning our disappearance.

The Djebel Sarsar or Mountain of the Starlings was visible from our camp in all its huge proportions and details. We had decided to attempt its ascent in order to determine its exact position and to take from it a topographical sketch of the outlying country by means of the theodolite. Each day we arranged afresh our preparations for this little excursion on which we were to be attended only by our cook and the soldier, but on returning from a shooting expedition in the northern Valley of Dcharchiera we were surprised to hear of the arrival in camp of a delegation from the Oulad Migdoul; these worthy people having been informed of our intentions, hastened to assure us that they would do their utmost to hinder us from carrying out our plan. They considered it impious that we should attempt to ascend a mountain where two marabouts live in great odour of sanctity. Besides, we should come across an enormous excavation, our servants said, in which, as is firmly believed by the inhabitants, are hidden treasures which naturally must be protected against the researches of Christians. It would have been idle to endeavour to persuade the tribe of the purity of our intentions, for the mere sight of our instruments sufficed to arouse their suspicions and fears, and all our efforts would have been unavailing. Not being desirous of having recourse to violence and venturing on an unequal struggle, for our armed force only consisted of our valiant soldier who had turned as pale as a sheet at the mere idea, but, wishing to exhaust all legal means, we resolved to profit by the excursion which we had planned to the ruins of Basra to go to the Karia of Ben Aouda and ask the Kaïd of the Sefyian either for an escort to ascend the Sarsar or permission to undertake it. The celebrated traveller, Rohlfs, made the ascent in 1864, but not in very favourable circumstances, it would appear, as we have but scanty information concerning the mountain whose height is not even known with any degree of accuracy.

The distance from Dcharchiera to Ben Aouda may be estimated at about 12 miles. The road goes through Basra. We left the camp at half-past ten, and, having followed, for over an hour, the path which had brought us from Alqaçar, we immediately shaped our course straight for the Djebel Sidi Amor el Hadi, striking across the mountains, and then leaving the road at the spot whence one begins to discern, at a distance, the small qoubbahs (literally cupolas) of the marabout close to the ruins. We reached it at half-past two, without having hurried our horses.

The complete destruction of the city, the absence of historical documents relative to the incidents which attended the fall of this unhappy place—a small portion of its walls only having been left standing—are instances of the rapidity with which some towns of Morocco have disappeared, without leaving a trace in history, for little is known of the origin of the city, and still less of the events which brought about its fall.

M. Tissot, arguing from the respective distances of the station of Tremulae placed by the Antoninus' itinerary at 19 miles from Vopiscianæ, and 12 from Oppidum Novum (El Ksar el Kebir), comes to the conclusion that the present site is that of the Roman military post.

The topographical position, indeed, leads one to suppose that the Romans did not leave this plateau unoccupied, for it commands the valley which is traversed by a direct road to Sebou, and to the ancient towns of Volubilis and Tocolosida.[1]

But history is silent concerning the origin of the Arab city. Leo Africanus asserted that it was founded by Mohammed, son of Idris, and that at the time of its prosperity it reckoned about 2000 households; its decay seems then to have commenced only after the ruin of the descendants of the Mussulman religious apostle in Morocco who came there attracted only by the beauty of the site and charm of the surrounding country. The same writer tells us that the name of Basra had been given in remembrance of the antique *Basra*,[2] a town of Arabia where Idris's great-grandfather had been killed.

---

[1] Edrîsî, in his description of Africa and Spain, places the town of Al-Basra at a little less than a day's journey, on horseback, from Tochommoch, which was situated nearly a mile from the sea at the mouth of the W. el Kouss.

[2] It may be interesting to remark that El Bekri gives Basra the name of Basra-t-ed Dubban (Basra of flies) on account of its large produc-

The appearance of the ruins is now the same as in the time of Leo Africanus, for the description he gives of them corresponds pretty accurately to what I saw. The north west angle of the wall of enclosure is yet standing on a length of about 700 yards; but of this town which, according to Obeïd el Bekri, reckoned ten gates and a great mosque with seven naves and two baths, and which excelled all the surrounding locality on account of its pasture, and the number of its flocks, nothing whatever is left. A shapeless heap of stones, half hidden by vegetation, is all we are able to see of the city, whose inhabitants, according to Edrîsî, were noted for their politeness, their kindly and virtuous disposition—qualities, indeed, which do not appear to have borne luck to the unfortunate city.

As for the women, they were conspicuous by their great beauty and personal charms. El Bekri seems to have made a collection of a certain number of facts concerning this interesting subject, for he assures us that in no other part of the Moghreb was it possible to meet with such charming girls.

It is probable that the fair sex of the town, which seemed to possess the power of charming its adorers by the melodious accents of music, inspired the muse of Ahmet ibn Feth[1] who exclaims:

"Perish all other pleasures! give me the musician of Basra with a white and rosy face.

tion of *milk*. It had also been called Basra-t-el Killan or hemp Basra, because, when it became more populated, flax was used there in lieu of money. It deserves its surname of red "el Hamra" more than Venice, on account of the colour of the clayey soil of the mountain of Sidi Amor el Hadi on the sides of which the town is built.

[1] Poem in the honour of Abou-el-Aïchibn I. Brahim ibn el Cacem.

"Let her gaze, intoxicate (with love no doubt). Let the rose bloom on her cheeks; and let her slim waist remain supple," etc.

Alas! of all these gentle souvenirs there remains not even a trace, and I doubt whether one could find in the wretched huts of the dchar, some descendant of the divinities who inspired the enthusiastic poet. Some magnificent gardens which Leo Africanus mentions, and which were in full cultivation in his time, have not escaped the general destruction.

The weather was very unfavourable on the day of our visit, and large clouds hid the Sarsar from sight. We therefore made haste to determine the hygrometric altitude of the plateau, and set off at once in a south westerly direction to seek for the Karia of Ben Aouda which we reached at four o'clock.

A shapeless mass of ruined buildings surrounded by walls almost in ruins—such is the dwelling of the representative of the Makhzen. Lying in the middle of rich pastures, watered by a small brook, the Karia owes its importance to its weekly market. Wretched huts roofed with leaves, straw, or boughs, have sprung up under the shelter of the government residence. When we enter the court, we are still more impressed with the poverty and squalidness of the place; growling and starving dogs there are in plenty, digging for food in the never-failing heaps of refuse and dung of a Moroccan dwelling. The kind of kennel where the Kaïd was kind enough to receive us, and where, having been wakened up from his siesta, he soon made his appearance, is not much better than the other buildings. A few wretched-looking black soldiers form the guard of honour. They came prowling around us, whilst our canine friends never ceased

VISIT TO THE KAÏD OF BEN AOUDA.

to bark loudly during our conversation, making now and then a snap at our legs.

The fragrance of large heaps of refuse piled up in the yard did not seem to make the slightest impression on the nostrils of the great man. Our conversation was therefore brief, for, having confessed to us his lack of influence over the tribes of the Djebel Sarsar, we cut matters short, and being in a hurry to return to our camp, 15 miles distant from this place, we set out again at four o'clock. Our soldiers did not know the road, so we were compelled to depend entirely on the compass. Behold us now cutting across fields, and urging on our animals; for a storm which had been brewing since morning was threatening to break out. We returned to the plain, but this time we swerved towards the east, and passed the foot of a large hill which hid from us the ruins of Basra. On reaching the small marabout, which commands the road, we altered our course by inclining slightly towards the north. We crossed a small rivulet with steep banks, which we ascended northwards, then we returned to the east and, cutting straight across a mountain, we ascended the base of the big mass, allowing our good and sure-footed steeds to guide us through all this chaos.

Darkness comes upon us unawares, and as there is no moon, and the sky is cloudy, our situation becomes critical on account of our proximity to territories inhabited by unruly tribes not likely to receive us with much courtesy, especially at this time of night. Well, it seems as if fortune forsook us, twice losing our way at a few nights' interval. Surely some bad Moroccan fairy bears us a grudge.

We wander about at random, already anticipating the prospect of having to spend the night in this inextricable muddle when, happily, we perceive, in the distance northwards, a rocket flashing up in the dark sky, then another. This is a signal from our worthy cook, who, uneasy about our protracted absence, and fearing that we may have gone astray, follows our instructions by firing off the rockets. We joyously answer, and we march in the direction thus pointed out to us. After one hour's hurried march in the plain, we finally have the pleasure of finding ourselves once more under our cozy tent enjoying our hard earned supper.

The danger in this neighbourhood was still increased by our prolonged stay of three weeks, which further irritated the fanaticism of the surrounding tribes, and their jealousy at not being able to share the profits accruing to the people of Dcharchiera through the sale of provisions for our use.

The powerful tribe of Orghoma, which inhabits the region of Djebel Dorghona in the neighbourhood of Wazzan, came marauding quite close to our tents, and every night sentinels had to watch over the flocks and the fields as the robbers attempted to destroy the crops.

The life we led amongst these over excited populations, though interesting for a while, was now becoming very irritating. It was almost impossible to venture on the slightest excursion without having to expect some unpleasantness which at last would have compelled us to retaliate.

The disgust we felt at not having been able to ascend the Djebel Sarsar, induced us to climb a hill on the north of the dchar (marked A, in my itinerary).

I remember that the excursion took place amidst a great show of ridiculous precautions. Our friends of the dchar declared at the last moment that they were resolved not to give us the benefit of their company. It was impossible to get any explanation from them. Even our faithful friend tall Mahommed, who never left us, and wished to follow us as far as Meknas, forsook us and disappeared to escape giving any explanations. Thus, being reduced to our trio, we were obliged to fall back on our own resources.

On the road, half way, we heard some one calling out to us in Arabic, and Antonio acting as interpreter, informed us that some men of the famous fanatical tribe of the Beni Mçarra had been seen going in the same direction. Some of these in the preceding year had fired on the Sherif. Antonio added that it would be imprudent to continue, otherwise we might fully expect to hear bullets whistle about our ears directly we reached the plateau.

We held a short deliberation, but at last becoming furious at not being able to go anywhere, being put on our mettle, and wishing to show that fear has no hold upon the Roumis, we dismounted and marched in single file. But ill-luck clung to us. There was no danger to be encountered, and the fellows whom we saw at the bottom of the valley prudently retired behind the edge of the wood.

The scene was simply splendid from the narrow platform a few yards wide, on which we at last stood after an hour's arduous march up narrow paths and woody defiles in which no Roumi had ever set his profane foot.

Northwards are the mountains of Tetuan, and towards the east, the snowy summits which we saw from the encampment of Dchavénah.

According to every probability concerning their distance and position, we judge that these latter must form part of the hill-side chain of the Beni Hassan of the Rif whose principal peak bears, on 1711 and 1135, maps of the French Hydrography, the name of M^t. Anna with the figures 2210^m for an altitude.

At this spot in the Sarsar—the principal part of the mass whose last undulations spread as far as the hydrographic system—the main branch of the W. el Kouss takes its rise.

At the bottom of the plain of Alqaçar (the atmosphere of which the heat loads with a slight mist) and through an opening between two hills, we catch a glimpse of the windings of the capricious river, and we are able to come to the conclusion that the little brook of Dcharchiera does not empty itself into the Alqaçar river, as certain travellers seem to believe, but that it is a tributary of the basin of the Sebou. Towards the east, the view extends as far as the mountain and the town of Wazzan, which may be discerned at the limits of the vast plain which we had crossed some days before. At the extremity of the northern horizon which seems to extend farther than the eye can reach, stood out some great snowy peaks, which Antonio asserted to be the hills of Fez, but which in reality were some buttresses of the Atlas about 100 miles South of Sefrou. Towards the west a corner of the ocean or of a merdja glistened in the sun behind the downs. As for the Djebel Sarsar, its importance dwindles down when compared with these tall peaks of the Rif.

After gazing for a long time on this ever-varying scene lit up by floods of vivid light, and on the grand evidences of an approaching storm on the mountains south of Wazzan, we descended the heights and regained our camps without any incidents save the massacre of some partridges by Antonio.

In the tribe of Dcharchiera the spiritual authority seems to belong to the schoolmaster, if we may give this title to a person whom the natives pompously term Thaleb,[1] a savant à la Marocaine—the only one capable of laboriously deciphering Arabic writing. The Thaleb used often to come and spend an evening under the tent to have a chat with us, and his eagerness for acquiring knowledge much pleased us. The interest which he evinced when we were making use of our instruments, spoke highly in his favour; when we showed him some object new to him, he would shake his head, smile with an incredulous look, and, after listening with the utmost attention, say that the Roumis had invented everything save a means for escaping death. I often thought it a pity that such a philosophical disposition should have found no scope for development. But our conversation with the worthy pedagogue did not prevent us from finding the time hanging heavily on our hands, and as we could not prosecute our projected topographical operations in the face of the hostility of the inhabitants, we thought it much preferable to proceed without delay to Wazzan. So we gave orders in consequence, and our servants, overjoyed at leaving the brigands' den, to use the cook's expression, set to packing up everything with alacrity, and, on the 18th of May, at six o'clock in the evening we were in the holy town of the Moghreb.

[1] The name Thaleb, that is, scholar, — plural Tholba or Thoulbab — is accorded to those who, prosecuting the mnemotechnic study of the Koran, at last succeed in knowing it by heart. When they are acquainted also with the books on law, and write letters on legal matters, they then assume the much valued title of Fekhy or Feguih. These men are generally the secretaries to high officials. Such is, at Wazzan, our friend the secretary of Sidi Mohammed.

CHAPTER VII.

Wazzan—Antiquity of the Town—It is supposed to have been the Roman Military Post called Vopiscianæ—M. Tissot's opinion concerning Ancient Ezaguen—Leo Africanus—Marmol—A few Words on its History—Influence and Organisation of the Religious Brotherhood of Muley Taïeb, a National Order peculiar to Morocco—Its Chief the grand Sherif El Hadj Abd es Selam ben el Hadj el Arbi is in Favour of European Customs and Notions—Influence resulting from his Marriage with an English Lady.

THE history of Wazzan [1] is obscure, and it is not possible to frame any outline of it previous to the Mussulman invasion. Barth and M. Renou say that Wazzan was the Roman post of Vopiscianæ, and as it has not been ascertained with any degree of accuracy whether the Romans left any traces of their stay here, the supposition may be accepted. The name of Wazzan, it is true, appears to be of recent date, for no mention of it is to be found in the works of the geographers of the Middle Ages, but on account of its favourable situation, the Romans, so skilful in the choice of sites for their settlements, had thought it suitable as such. Tissot, whose name it is impossible not to quote whenever the question of Roman antiquity in the

[1] The English write it Wazzan, Wazan or Wazen, the French Ouezan or Ouezann, the German Vezan, and the Spanish Guazan.

Tingitane is raised, had been told by the grand Sherif El Hadj abd es Selam, that pottery and ancient coins are to be found here, and that a few years ago, three rows of tombs placed over one another had been dug out. It is then probable that at Wazzan, as at Basra, Roman constructions must have disappeared without leaving even nominal traces, and in case the military post should have been of little importance it is difficult to ascertain the spot where it stood, the more so as the Djebel Kourt at a short distance south of Wazzan on the road of W. Wargha, offers so important a strategic position that the Romans cannot possibly have failed to occupy it.

The question has become still more complicated through the desire of certain authors to assimilate Wazzan to another town now destroyed, and whose name, Ezaguen, has been transmitted to us by Leo Africanus and Marmol.[1] Leo places the town at 72 miles from Fez, and he states that it possessed 500 households. It was built on the side of a mountain about 22 miles distant from the river Guarga (now Wargha), measured across the plain. Marmol, who generally copies Leo with accuracy, adds a few details which tend to prove that he procured supplementary information. He tells us "that about three leagues from the river Erguille, on the slope of a mountain, there is an ancient town, built by the people of the country, surrounded by a fine plain stretching out as far as the river, with good land where much wheat is grown as well as on the mountain

[1] In the edition of 1555, translated from the Toscan by Temporal, the figure 2 must be the error of the copyist. I have corrected the distance in conformity with the geographical features of the country.

Marmol 3 Vol. "Africa" by Marmol. Translation of Nicolas Perrol, brother of Ablamont. Maps by M. Sanson, geographer to the King. MDCLXVII.

whose soil is excellent. It is at 23 leagues from Fez, possesses some 700 inhabitants, and has around it several hamlets which lie under the same jurisdiction. But the government is compelled to keep 500 horses for the protection of the province, on account of the Portuguese on the frontiers who make incursions of 15 or 30 leagues in the country. This place possesses strong, well-built walls, and the inhabitants are rich and dress generally like those of Fez though some have Berber costumes. The king allows them to make wine and drink it, therefore do they have excellent wine and large vineyards. The town possesses several fountains, flowing across the neighbouring fields, which, on this account, are fertile, and produce much wine and hemp. Every Tuesday a kind of fair or market is held here, where the Arabs and Berbers of the country do congregate with goods and provisions."

While we were staying at Wazzan, the state of excitement and revolt of the Berber tribes of the mountainous region of the N.E., caused by the dismissal of the pacha and diplomatic events due to the protection granted to the Sherif, would not allow of our carrying out our project of visiting certain ruins at the dchar of El Guzrouf described by M. Watson. It might be possible, perhaps, to discover a concordance between a few parts of the Djebel Darzaoun 22° N.E.N., or Dorghona, W., with the Rahoma Mountain, quoted by Leo Africanus and which was close to ancient Ezaguen.

But to continue, the true development of the town of Wazzan is only due to the influence and importance which the order of Muley Taïeb has assumed, concerning which I shall now say a few words.

Morocco being a country in which religion forms the

basis of the organisation of governing power, possessing an influence that is shown in the slightest actions of the people, we can therefore easily conceive the degree of importance attached to a brotherhood, such as the Muley Taïeb of which the sultan himself is only a Khouan (affiliated).[1]

In order to fully understand this exceptional state of affairs, it is necessary to glance at the history of the development of the order, and to enter into a few details of its organization.

The date of its formation is supposed to be 1678 or 1679 (1089 of the Hegyra), but a considerable number of Moors mix up the comparatively modern origin with the real sources of the Sherifian family of the Filali or Haceni, which, since the advent of Muley Ismaïl in 1672, has provided the Sultans of the Moghreb. This opinion would tend to show the conqueror of Morocco, Muley Idris[2] Ben Abdallah Ben Haam—founder of the house of Idrites—as a reformer and a kind of religious apostle rather than a warrior. Hence the title of founder of the brotherhood is ascribed to him by asserting that from the celebrated Zaouïa of Dar el Allim, at Fez, sprung a group of orthodox men or Djelala (picked men), forming among themselves an association which in the 16th century was split up into two branches; one, under the leadership of Muley Hamdan,

---

[1] The affiliated or brothers are also called Thouama of Sidi Thami, or Taïbin.

[2] Muley Hassan, the present Sultan, is the descendant of a brother of Muley Idris, and belongs to the family of Alaouïn. He therefore has for an ancestor Si Abdallah el Hamet, in common with the grand chief of Wazzan, but it is asserted that the Sultan's genealogy offers a blank. A very delicate question in truth.

gave rise to the order of Hamduchia, whilst it is contended that the second with Muley abd es Selam Ben Machich was only the embryo of the real brotherhood to which Muley[1] Taïeb gave his name and developed into prosperity.

But, as far as the study of the incomplete history of the Moghreb el Acsa can permit us to do so, we may say that the son of Idris, Idris Sérir, the founder of the town of Fez, was neither the promoter nor the forerunner of any religious order, and that the Djelala were only people of Sherifian origin whose incessant increase in distinct sects has produced in our days the whole of the numerous tribes of Sherifa Idrisi which are not much thought of on account of their numbers.

Nevertheless, the university of Fez or Dar el Amin produced in the 17th century a certain Muley Abdallah es Sherif, the probable creator of the Zaouïa of Wazzan. This person had a number of private conversations with the prophet who condescended, it is said, to make known to him his wishes.[2]

Having selected a little Berber dchar, situated on the northern slopes of Djebel Bouellol, he started the establishment of a Zaouia, whose extensive increase was to lead

---

[1] In Morocco the name of a chief is preceded by the appellation my master (Muley).

[2] Naturally, a series of extraordinary miracles thereupon occurred to encourage the zeal of the faithful. Of the different events—very disconcerting for modern science, and which were mentioned to us, by people of the country, with a triumphant look—I can only recollect that about some unfortunate cows of a certain village of Mitkal close to Wazzan. It appears these animals are refused the power of producing milk suitable for the making of butter and cheese, and this in order to punish a man of the place, who in the time of Abdallah had stolen a cow.

to the present Wazzan. Muley Abdallah having moreover succeeded in pacifying the country which fourteen Berber tribes had plunged into an utter state of anarchy received from the Makhzen some important grants of land which formed the nucleus of the immense property now owned by the brotherhood.

The first aim of Muley Abdallah seems to have been to sever the ties of the Moghreb Mussulmans, and the powerful order of the Quadrya which at this period was all powerful in the Sous, and whose main branch at Bagdad subjected all of the numerous adherents to foreign influence, proceeding from a rival district, and which was entirely beyond the control of Fez.[1]

This new group, which, to well-defined, political views, added firm religious ideas (without which it is impossible to do anything with the disciples of Mohammed), was, on the contrary, about to favour the power of the Chorfa Hassani or Saadiens who occupied the throne of Morocco before the Chorfa Filali or Haceni.

It was in 1554 that the Turks advanced as far as Fez, which they pillaged, and that the succession of continuous feuds with the Catholic nations, Spain and Portugal, nearly brought about a partition of Morocco. It is, therefore, quite natural that gratitude and interest should have induced the Makhzen to favour the religious development of Wazzan as being a kind of national church.[2]

[1] It is perhaps owing only to this rivalry with other religious foreign orders that Moors are conscious that they possess a fatherland; few of them save some among the most eminent in the land seem to have the slightest suspicion of the political bearing of their country, and would probably be surprised if they heard Europeans talking of a Moroccan empire.

[2] In 1860, when affairs with Spain were rather complicated on account of incursions of tribes on the borders of the praesidio of

Such is the explanation of the immense privileges conceded to this first Zaouïa and of the gifts intended to repay the grand masters for their interference.

The Sultans were not slow to understand the importance of favouring this religious association to assure the success of their policy, and from the time of Muley Abdallah they solicited their admission into the order as Khouan, thus becoming mere Thouama. The representative of temporal power bowed to the wishes of the head of the order; by appealing to him as an arbitrator, and seeking, on many occasions, his advice, which was always welcomed by the crowd as emanating from a holy source, a precedent was established which at the present day makes still more complicated the already delicate question as to the status of the Grand Sherif of Wazzan in the Empire.

Muley Taïeb was the first to shed the lustre of power on the influence which the brotherhood always enjoyed. We will pass lightly over the different local versions according to which he alone received the Dikr from the Prophet, now used among the faithful, while others assert, on the contrary, that Muley Abdallah had that signal honour. These religious puzzles gave rise to most curious disputes even among the high dignitaries of Wazzan.

It may be of service to note how Muley Taïeb[1] aided

Mellila, one Abd-el-Djebbar, Sherif of Wazzan, was sent to pacify these war-like mountaineers. At the same time the Grand Sherif, Abd-es-Selam himself, also showing an example by his piety, headed the troops sent to give battle to a chief who had risen against the Makhzen in the Gharb.

[1] Muley Taïeb, in reference to his Khouan and the Sultan of Fez, used to say: "he will not succeed by your means, and without you he will not succeed"; *i.e.*, the emperor cannot dispense with the aid of the Taïbya, but the latter do not entirely act at his bidding.

Muley Ismael, the most powerful sovereign of the Moghreb, and how far these enlightened and active men contributed to establish the modern power of Morocco, which, however, is much diminished nowadays. The Sultan was bound, therefore, to extend his special protection over the definite establishment of a religious order which his predecessors had already so much appreciated. But the moral union of these two men who personified the spirit of command and modern religious influence in the Moghreb, has, unfortunately, not left all the hoped-for results.

According to tradition, Muley Taïeb effectually aided the Sultan in the formation of the famous black body-guard called Bokharis[1] which, like the Mamelukes in Egypt, played an important part in the history of Morocco.

This Muley Taïeb seems to have been gifted with a prodigious power of will and a most vigorous disposition. On studying his life, of which Sidi el Debi at Wazzan was kind enough to relate the salient points, it is easy by giving one's attention to the support which he accorded to Muley Ismael, to find in it the explanation of the almost unique power of the Makhzen in the Moghreb. Very meritorious deeds are told of this holy man.

Living the most ascetic life and showing in his relations the most conciliatory spirit, the most exquisite tolerance, he did not, however, recoil from any act of violence which would promote the triumph of the religious principles of his work when gentle and persuasive arguments failed, then as a man of fertile imagination he knew how to draw from his brain all the necessary means, small or great. It is thus,

---

[1] Thus termed because they were placed under the protection of the celebrated theologian Bokhari, author of the Djami el Sahib (exact record).

it must be owned, that the most holy propagandas have been made on this poor earthly orb of ours.

Thanks to his felicitous mode of action, the number of Khouans rapidly increased. We are pretty often told of a prophecy of Muley Taïeb, which is, after all, only a variation of another of the 14th century, in which he advises his faithful to make no opposition to the possession of Africa by the Benouasfer (literally, children of yellow), that is the graceful appellation which Moors apply to us Frenchmen. He adds that these regions will fall again into the hands of the true believers to the great dismay of the infidels. This kind of political truth has begun to become a fact, thanks to the unprejudiced ways of the present grand Sherif.

After Muley Taïeb's death the order continued to prosper, and it took for good the name of the remarkable man. His successors offer little that can be interesting.

The father of the present Sherif was monstrously stout, and his son certainly takes somewhat after him in that respect. Sidi el Hadj el Arbi could only travel in a litter of really wonderful dimensions borne by eight mules, and the sanctity of this person was in direct proportion with the development of his fatty tissues. He enjoyed, indeed, an immense influence over the people who assembled in crowds to kiss one of the ends of the long cords attached to the litter, and which unwinding themselves among the concourse of the loyal, only allowed even those at a distance to imprint their lips upon those holy objects before placing their offerings in the alms boxes.

This question of collection deserves some attention, in order to show how the interests of the Sherif of Wazzan command him to live on good political terms with France.

They call Ziara[1] the offering which the faithful member of an association gives the Chaouch, sent by the Moqaddem to collect such due, when the strings of the faithful one's purse have not opened of themselves. The French government, justly moved with the abuses of all kinds to which the system gave rise, has, for a long time, restrained as much as possible the necessary authorization exacted from congregations by the military authorities since the first days of the conquest. But in these latter years, the governor of Algeria, M. A. Grévy, has established a new principle. Henceforth any Ziara is prohibited and considered as begging. Some exception will alone be accorded for services rendered. This measure has naturally much grieved the principal chief of religious orders, but it was really the only way to preserve the unhappy population from ruin. For the last six years the authorizations quoted by Rinn are: once to the Sherif of Wazzan on the request of M. Ordega, Minister at Tangiers, and only for himself and son. Once to the Grand-Master of the Zianin, as a reward for services during the insurrection. Twice to Tidjani and to Si Ali Ben Otsman. It can be understood then to what extent the chief of the order of Muley Taïeb, who has so many followers on the territories of Algeria and Tunis, ought to value the friendship of the French Republic—but here, in the Moghreb, in that country so full of bigotry, it is quite otherwise; and thanks to the inertness and the fatalism of the unhappy populations a perfect system of exaction is in full force. There is on the one hand the Makhzen, who is not to be trifled with, and on the other, the endless succession of Chorfa—God knows how numerous they are! those are the two curses of the country.

[1] Ziara, properly visit to a superior, and more especially to holy places. Hence the signification.

It is true that it is impossible for anybody, save the unfortunate Moors, to give even to their last sou. They will disgorge their all, thinking it will go to Allah, the wisest of the wise, the giver of all things. Truly, that is a beautiful creed, one easy to be played upon, and which ought to flood with delight and fat livings the practical hearts and big wigs of the association.[1] But alas! what is the result? One has only to walk in the fields to perceive that instead of enriching themselves with the treasures which might spring from the soil, numbers of men waste away, and starve, oppressed in every way, both physically and morally.

The gravest reproach which our modern society can make against religious brotherhoods is that they promote the development of a longing for a dreary, lazy life among people already so inactive. They thus arrive at a kind of cerebral atrophy, which confirms the Khouans in their sterility, the exact opposite of what Europe calls progress. This situation, made worse by the foolish pride of every Mussulman, who is fully persuaded, as soon as he has joined the brotherhood, that God can bestow on him power and fortune if so He wills it, taking no account of learning or personal worth, gives Morocco this peculiar aspect. The utmost contempt is shown for science, in one word, for all that is European; among the greatest persons of the Makhzen a great show of scholarship or of experience will always be met by some fine answer of this kind . . . It surely is very beautiful, but does that give you two stomachs or the power to double your life-time?

[1] The Mussulman religion in Algeria, according to the financial statistics of 1880, is, however, a cheap one. 310,000 Catholics cost 920,100 frs., or 293 each; 7,500 Protestants, 83,100 frs., or 1,108 frs.; 35,665 Jews, 26,100 frs., or 0,731 each; 2,842,497 Mussulmans 126,340 frs., or 0,076 frs.

The Moroccan Chorfa derive their influence from the strict observance of the law of the Koran, and of its principles expounded throughout the country, it must be owned in a singular fanatical narrow-mindedness, so that they may be accessible to an ignorant multitude.

Therefore, striving to bring about changes inspired by our own civilization in their vital organization, would amount to nothing less than reforming its very basis, and a struggle would ensue against the principles upon which the whole sacred fabric rests. It is well-known here in high quarters that the fanatical distrust so easy to inspire in a population whose ancestors have never had different ways of thinking, is the only prop for the old worm-eaten fabric. One should know these people very little indeed, to think them endowed with some power of imitation inducing them to alter their ways of thinking, and by imbibing our ideas, to act and live according to our notions; in one word, to place themselves in our dependence.

The one instance of the Grand Sherif, Si-abd-es-Selam-ben-El-Hadj-el-Arbi, a great admirer of European customs, ought not to interfere with the opinion expressed above. This man married an Englishwoman some few years back, having divorced his first wives, and surrounded himself with a certain pomp—a curious blending of European comfort and Oriental luxury. He even indulges in gastronomic eccentricities much enlarged upon by evil tongues, and yet it is not the less certain that the solidarity which bind all Mussulmans and fear of the unavoidable discredit which is thrown on those who adopt too freely our ways, will no doubt prevent the amiable chief of the Muley Taïeb brotherhood to indulge too far his whims, outside the Koran.

His popularity having suffered, in consequence, it is to

be wished for his sake that friendly advice should put some limit to his tendencies by enlightening him even on the theological results of his conduct.

From this special point of view his marriage has borne practical fruits compensating for the strangeness of the union. The Sherifa, a most amiable lady, having soon understood the part she had to play through a knowledge of both the language and requirements of her husband's congregation, is of great advantage to him when on his circuit. But if the Sherif is really sincere in his ideas, if by his intelligence and above all by that of his sons, (one of whom Sidi el Arbi from Wazzan appeared to us an enlightened man), he is enabled, thanks to this powerful brotherhood of Muley Taïeb, to throw a few rays of light on these regions darkened by fanaticism, then he must be pardoned the inconsistencies of his position.

It is easy to imagine to what extent all his actions have been turned to account by his detractors, especially in the entourage of Muley Hassan, who feels uneasy at the person of the religious chief being beyond his power owing to French protection.

For it cannot be ignored that the orthodox religious orders, however great their influence may be in Morocco, have in this country, as throughout Islam, numerous enemies; firstly the official clergy, then the scholars and all those who can have reason to fear that the services done by a brotherhood should not make up for the danger of an increasing influence like that of the Sherif of Wazzan. Moreover, assuming that each of these associations claims to be superior to its rivals, and thinks itself the only possessor of the "good path" (disclosed by the Angel Gabriel to the Prophet who has transmitted it to the founders of religious orders as well as obedience to the five commandments of Mohammed), the result is a competition, very amusing to witness, but which injures the prestige of each of the rivals.

It is true that the majority of Moors, totally unimpressed as they are by questions of religious philosophy in virtue of which certain scholars oppose the influence of the orders, are, on the other hand, attracted by the considerable strength and influence which union gives these Khouan. The grossest quackery, like the juggling of the Aïssaoua, for instance, finds much favour with the easily astounded vulgum. In this question of protection the Sherif could not have acted otherwise, and he found himself entangled in a painful perplexity. The representative kept by the Sultan in the territory of Wazzan, for the transaction of business, and especially to oppose the incursions of the Berber tribes of the Rif, was a Sherif of Muley Taïeb's family. Now, this official, Abd el Djebbar by name, filled at the same time the duties of the town's Zaouïas, for in certain districts the functionaries hold their appointment from the Sultan. This plurality of offices was dangerous and could not work without some hitch or other. Being in a position to thwart the grand Sherif's authority, this Pacha, an official of the Makhzen, had acquired a power most detrimental to the prestige of the chief of the order, being constantly in Tangiers, preferring, it was said, the society of the Roumis and the charms of his English consort, to his old Mussulman wives whom he repudiated, as we said before. The alarm was great in the religious sanctuary, and the situation could not endure longer in the face of the intrigues of the grand vizier, who, from Meknas, pulled the strings of the whole affair. In short, whilst soliciting the support of the French minister at Tangiers, Sidi el Hadj abd es Selam soon perceived on what side his interests should make him turn, and the Pacha of Wazzan, a true bug-bear for the descendant of Mohammed, was dismissed his office during our sojourn.[1]

Each Mussulman order having a special aim in view, a few like the Senousîya whose mission it is to oppose the progress of modern ideas among the Taïeb, veneration and devotion to the descendants of the prophet are aimed at, the consequence being that the Khouans to be faithful, must obey all the whims of their grand master, who it must be owned, sorely tries their orthodoxy.

It is one of the most characteristic signs of our age to see the most holy person of a Sherif of superior lineage—as being a descendant in a straight line of Mohammed—opening for Islam a new era of surprising prospects.

The initiation to the order of Muley Taïeb takes place with simple ceremonies which are not lacking in antique grandeur. The candidate goes to the Cheiks[2] or the Moqaddem of the neighbouring Zaouïa. When making his appli-

---

[1] The cause of the success of Mussulman brotherhood is to be sought for in the fact that Mohammetans are convinced that prayer said in common is more efficacious than otherwise. A more touching custom, a most exquisite one by its form, and which has no representative in our cold modern European society, is that all brothers of most orders, when some stroke of misfortune descends on a Khouan, and is brought to their knowledge, must congregate and recite during the day several chapters of the Koran or special prayers only known to them.

By making abstraction of the bigotry which mars these religious practices, we find here once more evidences of that solidarity, so beautiful, so lofty, of which the Mussulman religion offers so many instances. The religious brotherhoods spread throughout Islam now number 90, 21 of which are in the Moghreb el Acsa.

[2] Here the title of Cheik somewhat corresponds to the master of a lodge of freemasons, and the Moqaddem is a chief of more humble rank, who takes charge of practical duties, such as the tilling of the land and breeding of the cattle.

cation, the candidate puts down an offering, and requests the favour of receiving the Ouerd, that is the prayers which he must say at certain hours on his beads, as well as the religious duties which constitute the characteristics of the orders in the eyes of the vulgum, who very often cannot understand the political aim of the brotherhood.

This first stage of the proceedings gives the knowing Cheik an opportunity of exercising his skill. He acquaints the newcomer with all the responsibility which he is about to assume, and enlarges on all possible disadvantages. It is true, he adds, that a Taïbya has a reserved place in the delightful paradise of the Prophet, but he must feel certain of being able to remain true to his pledge.

The effect of this diplomacy on a Mussulman mind is a foregone conclusion. At each new obstacle the desire of the neophyte becomes more ardent, till at last he accepts every condition.

This happy psychological moment is at once turned to advantage to convoke an assembly (Djelala) of the most influential Khouans in the district, and after reading the Diar the candidate is requested to take an oath, which has nothing very novel about it—not to steal nor mix with revolutionists, nor with murderers—and he must promise to follow the "way"[1] till his death. Then he is to take an oath of absolute obedience to his chief, corresponding to that of the Jesuits: "Thou shalt be in the hands of thy Cheik, like a corpse in those of the washer of the dead" (it must be confessed the simile is not very pleasing); "thou shalt obey all his orders whatsoever, for it is the Lord Himself who commands through him, and

[1] The "way" is the Order's own peculiar doctrines, practices and prayers, taken as a whole.

to disobey him is to provoke the wrath of God; do not forget that thou art his slave and canst do nothing without his order. The Cheikh is a man beloved of God, he is superior to all other beings, and ranks next after the Prophets. Let therefore thine eyes never lose sight of him, have him present before thee everywhere, and dismiss from thy heart any thought other than that which refers to God and the Cheikh." The whole of Islam is in these precepts. How could one expect anything else but an absolute passiveness, a complete fatalism, and an entire lack of activity from men whose lives are regulated by such principles?

The set of prayers, which I was fortunate enough to be able to procure, is as follows:—

A. For good works which you shall do in your own interest, God will reward you. Pray to God that He may have mercy upon you, for He is merciful and magnanimous. —*Sourate* lxxiii., *verse* 73.

B. Glorify the name of God before the rising of the sun and before he sinks beneath the horizon.

C. Even will the Prophet himself and his Angels beseech God for your sake.

D. God and His angels honour the Prophet. O ye true believers, glorify His name and utter it with respect.— *Sourate* xxx., *verse* 56.

E. Know ye there is no other God but Allah.—*Sourate* xlvii., *verse* 51.

a. Implore the pardon of God, the ever just and ever merciful (*is repeated* 100 *times*).

b. Glorify God and praise Him for ever (*is repeated* 100 *times*).

c. O God, shower thy mercies upon our Lord Mohammed, his spouse, and his descendants (*is repeated* 50 *times*).

THE PRAYERS.

d. O God, be merciful unto our Lord Mohammed, thy prophet, unto his family and his friends, and may his name be uttered with respect (*is repeated* 100 *times*).

e. There is but one God Allah, and Mohammed is his prophet. May God shower His mercies unto him, and may he be saved (*is repeated* 100 *times*).

The genealogy of the chiefs of the brotherhood is the following :— Mohammed.—1, Fathma Zohra ; 2, Hocein-ben-Ali ; 3, Haçan ; 4, Abd-Allah (1) ; 5, Ali ; 6, Hoçain ; 7, Idris-el Kebir ; 8, Idris-Sur ; 9, Mohammed ; 10, Haidra ; 11, Mezouar ; 12, Sellam ; 13, Aïssa ; 14, Hormal ; 15, Ali ; 16, Ali Beker ; 17, El-Hechich ; 18, Imelah ; 19, Mohammed ; 20, Abd-el Djebbar ; 21, Ahmed ; 22, Amar ; 23, Brahim ; 24, Si Moussa ; 25, Si El Hassen ; 26, Moussa ; 27, Mouley Brahim ; 28, Mouley-Abd-Allah ; 29, Mouley Mohammed ; 30, Mouley Taïeb ; 31, Si Ahmed ; 32, Allaïl ; 33, Si-El-Hadj-el-Arbi ; 34, Si Abd-es-Selam.

The faithful add another lineage, admitted also by the Aïssaoua, which connects the doctrines of the Taïbja to those of Mohammed the Prophet.

The Angel Gabriel,—the Prophet.—1, Ali-ben-Abou-Taïeb ; 2, E. Haoussin ; 3, Abou-Abd-Allah-Djabir-ben-Abd-Allah-el-Ansari ; 4, Abou-Said-el-Razouani ; 5, Abou Mohammed-Fath-es-Saoud ; 6, Saâd ; 7, Abou-Mohammed-Saïd-el-Makhezoum ; 8, Abou-el-Kacem-el-Merouani ; 9, Abou-Isahak-Irahim-el-Bosri ; 10, Zin-Ced-Din-Mohammed-el-Kazuime ; 11, Chems-ed-Din-el-Turkomani ; 12, Tadj-ed-Din-Mohammed ; 13, Nour-ed-Din-Abou-Hassen-Ali ; 14, Fakhr-ed-Din ; 15, Taki-ed-Din-el-Faqir ; 16, Abou-zid-el-Madani ; 17, Abd-es-Selem-ben-Mechich ; 18, Abou-Hassen-ech-Chadeli ; 19, Abou-Abbas-el-Mourci ; 20, Tadj-ed-Din-ben-Atta-Allah ; 21, Abou-Abd-Allah-el-Mogherbi ; 22, Abou-Hassen-el-Harafi ; 23, Sid-Annous-el-Bedaoui ; 24, Abou-el-Fadel-el-Hindi ; 25, Abd-er-Rahman-er-Redjeradji ; 26, Abou-Osman-el-Hartani ; 27, Abou-Abd-Allah-Mohammed-Amrár-Sherif ; 28, Abou-Abd-Allah-Mohammed-ben-Abou-Beker-Seliman-el-Djazouli ; 29, Abd-el-Aziz-el-Tebbai ; 30, Abd-Allah-el-Razouani ; 31, Mahmed-el-Taleb ; 32, Aïssa-el-Hasjen-el-Messab ; 33, Ali-ben-Ahmed ; 34, Muley-Abd-Allah-ben-Brahim-ech-Sherif ; 35, Muley Mohammed ; 36, Muley Taïeb ; 37, Sid Ahmed ; 38, Allaïl ; 39, Sid-El-Hadj-el-Arbi ; 40, Sid-El-Hadj-Abd-es-Selam.

CHAPTER VIII.

Description of the Town of Wazzan—Climate—Population—Mosques—Tolerant Spirit of the Disciples of Muley Taïeb—Tomb of the Old Chiefs of the Brotherhood—Veneration of the Population—The Town and Part of the Rif Frontier Region—Incursion of the Berber Tribes—Dangers of an Excursion to the Orange Tree Gardens—the Sherif's Guard—Their Armament—Tragical Astronomical Surveys—Our House and its Discomforts—Wazzan, the Promised Land of Rheumatism—Dampness of the Tingitane again—A Cold Bath Interrupted—Feudal Life in Morocco—The Two Sons of the Sherif—Sidi el Arbi and Sidi Mohammed--Political Conversations—Tea à la Marocaine—The Tonkin at Wazzan—Our Host's Followers—The Sherif's Estates—Commonplace Appearance of the Architectural Style in the Town—Relations of the Order of the Taïeb with the Touat and the Oulad Sidi Cheik—Influence of the Senousîya—Hurried Departure of our Hosts—Once more the Fear of a *Coup de Main* on the Part of the Sultan—Our Preparations for Departure.

WAZZAN stands on the N.N.E. slope of the Djebel Bouellol, or Djebel Wazzan, and is built in three distinct circular tiers on the side of this mountain, which, at each extremity, has two high summits, visible from a great distance. The heights, entirely clothed with vegetation, offer a very picturesque scene, especially when you come up by the road to Alqaçar, and skirt the great centenarian woods of olive trees.

The altitude of the town accounts for the low temperature at that spot in winter.[1] It never falls enough, however, to injure the fine plantations of orange trees, which, though somewhat uncared for, yet form one of the principal attractions of this part of the country.

It is difficult to form very correct notions concerning the number of inhabitants, the more so as there is a floating population of the faithful who come here to perform a kind of religious pilgrimage. Nor can the size of the town give a clue in the matter, as it contains numerous mosques, houses in ruins, and gardens, which naturally are not occupied. We calculated the Mussulman population to be from 5,000 to 7,000, among which there were from 1,300 to 1,400 men capable of bearing arms, according to the information furnished us by the Sherif's people.

The tribe of Israel possesses no mellah, and occupies two or three foudouchs—(a kind of caravansary)—situated in the lower part of the town, in one of the streets leading up to the Soko.[2]

---

[1] The following details in respect to the geographical position and meteorological conditions of Wazzan will be of interest. These statistics have been corrected by observations with the theodolite and two watches verified during a period of several weeks at the French Naval Chart Depôt, and the figures given are kindly supplied by M. Bouquet de la Gyre, the chief hydrographic engineer. The altitude of the town is 1323 feet 52 ins. This was ascertained by fifteen hypsometric observations at our house on the lowest spot level with the market place. During the month of May the average minimum nocturnal temperature was 49° Fahr.; but at the beginning of June, after the rains, it was 58° Fahr. The average maximum temperature at two o'clock in the afternoon was 67° Fahr. The highest, 83° Fahr., was observed twice, that is, on the 30th May and 6th June, and the lowest at that hour 56° Fahr. on the 27th May.

[2] It may be interesting to give the chronological order of the succession of the first visitors. The question has lately been raised (though not very interesting), as there is no town in Morocco of more easy an

These dwellings are not remarkable for cleanliness, and the odours there are anything but pleasant. The Jews number about 1,500—thanks to the tolerating disposition of the last Sherif. A small hall serves them for a synagogue. They make their living, as everywhere else, by commercial transactions, which seem here pretty important on account of the anxiety of "the faithful" to take away with them some souvenirs of their visit. It is curious to see these worthy Moors purchase some piece of stuff or knick-knack manufactured at Manchester or Marseilles by "infidels," and brought here by bastard Jews. The principal market takes place on Thursdays in the great square, which you cross to enter the town. We purchased there an excellent mule for the sum of £11, others not so good for £6 and £7; also a pretty donkey for the small sum of £1.

The small suburbs of Kacheriyîn,[1] before which you pass

ccess, Wazzan having been, some five years since, the centre of a small gglomeration of Spanish, French, and German renegades. The European element has not, therefore, been lacking as much as some authors ssert. At any rate, Gherard Rohlfs, professing to be a Mussulman, nd passing himself off for a Turkish doctor, was, to our knowledge, he first European who sojourned for any length of time in the own. Nineteen years later, Count Chavagnac came there, dressed n European costume, and accompanied by his wife, but following in he train of the Sherif of Wazzan, then on a circuit. Then came Watson, in the native dress, Major Trotter, and myself, as mere tour-sts, without an escort, and entering at night the *famous Moroccan Mecqua*. Next, a secretary of embassy arrived here, accompanied y a drogman, to study the dispositions of the inhabitants, and finally, hole Jewish families from Tangiers, together with numerous travel-rs, visited the town.

[1] The name has generally been misspelt by travellers. According to e learned M. Duveyrier, the most correct way of writing it is El-

TOPOGRAPHICAL SKETCH
OF THE
TOWN OF WAZZAN

وزّان

Cultivated ground

Undulations of Dj: Boumeleh

Barley
OLIVE WOOD
Orange Gardens
Cemetery

Road to Kuscheryin

Market

Alcabat Ghetlida

Moulai Bou Selam

Ruins of Mishkal

Br Sidi Mou Thalt

DJEBEL BOUELLOU

Ain Akoudab of Oulai Bekri

Boroughs

W'or Lenia

W. Tagueno

Hillocks of Fejan Khala — Tagueno

Reference.

1. House of Sherif Sidi Mohamed's son.
2. „ where we lodged.
3. „ of Sidi el Arbi.
4. Pleasure-house of the Sherif.
5. Synagogue.
6. Mosque of Sidi el Hadj el Arbi.
7. Jewish Fondouk.
8. Great Mosque of Abdallah es Sherif.
9. Baths.
10. Prison.
11. House of Sidi Abd Jebbah.
12. „ Sidi Mohamed ben-Abdallah.
13. „ Sidi Mohamed ben-Mechi.
14. Mosque of the Beni Merins.
15. House of Sidi el Hadj Meh.
16. Mosque of Djenan Ali.
17. The highest house in Wazzan.
18. Remarkable House.
19. Qoubba Sidi Ali Ben Ahmed.

H. de la Martinière, del. 1886

London: Whittaker & Co. & G. Bell & Sons.

F.S.Weller, F.R.G.S. Red Lion Square, W.C.

when arriving at Wazzan, is partly deserted, and numbers of houses now in ruins give evidence of past splendour.

The mosques are naturally numerous in a city with such religious inhabitants. The principal most venerated was built by Muley Abdallah Sherif. It commands a view of the house wherein dwell the female household of the Grand Sherif, and its minaret is elegantly decorated with *azulejos*, but the brick walls are crumbling down, and are inhabited by innumerable hawks. The mosque of Sidi el Hadj Arbi is also a pretty large one, and in great odour of sanctity. By the side of these temples reserved for the disciples of Muley Taïeb stands another mosque used by the Aïssaoua. This would seem strange in a town almost entirely occupied by Taïbin, if it were not known that the branches of Sidi Aissa and that of Muley Taïeb have a common origin to be traced to Mohammed Ben Sliman-el-Djazouli, head of the Djazoulin, from which the Order founded at Meknas by Mohammed Ben Aïssa has sprung.

Numerous qoubbahs may be seen in the neighbourhood of Wazzan, some of which are very picturesque. Being the tombs of Sherifs, of glorious ancestors, grand-masters of the brotherhood, they are looked upon with superstitious respect by the inhabitants and by the faithful who visit the place.

The mountainous region of the Rif, whose high tops are crowned with snow till the spring, extending from the north of Wazzan to the shores of the Mediterranean, has not yet been visited by any European, at least not one in the garments of the Roumi. The vicinity of this wild and fanatical region makes the environs of the town unsafe. Even in ordinary times it would be scarcely prudent to venture into the hilly country[1] which precedes the

[1] Here dwell the Beni Mçara who fired on the Grand Sherif himself, and wounded his horse.

prolongation of the Djebel Chechawen and the Djebel Darzaoua.

Shortly after our arrival, the Pacha who had been recalled to Tangiers in consequence of the energetic action of the French Legation, had revenged himself in rather a curious way. He had found nothing better, according to what we heard from the people of one of the Sherif's sons, than to warn officially the neighbouring Berber tribes, notorious for their misdeeds, that they might, after his departure, make a raid on what they thought fit. It is needless to say that these worthy people fully availed themselves of the kind permission. The town and outlying country became most unsafe in consequence, and in all our excursions we were compelled to have the company of an escort of armed "ragamuffins," in order to guard against any surprise.

The very day after our arrival, we had been enabled to form an opinion on the state of affairs, when, having proceeded without any attendants on a shooting expedition, found on return all the people in a state of great alarm and excitement. They informed us that we had been in danger of losing our lives, and the head gardener, very wroth, locked us up in the house, explaining, by much expressive gesticulation, that the bad Berbers would have cut our heads off with the greatest pleasure, merely to do an ill turn to the Sherif whose guests we were. After this, to guard against such a mishap, we took care to have an escort. We then were able to fully realise all the disadvantages which attend notoriety, and the unpleasant necessity of a guard of honour composed of great skulking fellows, who proved to be for us just so many bores.

As the town does not possess any walls, and appears

never to have had any, it can be entered with great facility. The two worm-eaten gates, which, with great effort, are closed every evening, and which give access to the market-place, cannot be of any great defensive use; so that the population is at the mercy of any invader or marauders. The Sherif's guard does not suffice to protect the place; and the presence of a representative of the Makhzen is therefore of absolute necessity, for the departure of the latter had thrown the whole district into a state of the greatest anxiety.

Some days before our arrival, some Berbers who thought they had been swindled by a Jewish financier of the place, broke into the foudouch occupied by the offending Jew, and had begun to lynch him, when the intervention of the guard saved him from a dire fate.

This guard deserves to be described, for never was a police corps more strangely organised.

The dwellings of the head of Muley Taïeb's brotherhood being considered, like all important Zaouias, as inviolable sanctuaries,[1] Sidi el Hadj Abd es Selam takes advantage of this to recruit his bodyguard from repentant malefactors. This corps of protectors thus includes brigands, thieves, and murderers, one of the latter having cut his brother to pieces. Their repentance has procured mercy for them, but at the slightest sign of relapse, they are liable to be handed over to the tender mercies of the Sultan's dispensers of justice.

The municipal guard consists of about fifty individuals, armed in the most extraordinary manner, with nearly all the

[1] The act of seeking sanctuary, and imploring protection on the score of repentance, is termed Mzaoug. The supplicants are housed and fed for three days, after which they are free to dwell as long as they like on the estate of the Zaouïa, which enjoys this valuable privilege.

known types of rifles, among which are the Remington, the Martini, the Gras, and the Mauser, forming a most interesting collection for an armourer.

During the night, these guardians of the peace, clad in rather tattered burnouses, are supposed to watch over the safety of Wazzan, but in reality they go to sleep at the street corners, wrapped up in their rags.

Our dwelling, every evening, was surrounded by a number of these troublesome protectors, whom, to their great astonishment, I was obliged to dismiss, on account of the noise they made, and the unpleasant odours which were wafted from their persons. We were told that the Sherif could call together a small army, and recruit in a few days a body of some thousands of trustworthy horsemen. Though the assertion must be somewhat exaggerated, we were able to ascertain that each of the douars encamped in the plain west of the Djebel possesses several bands of well-mounted and well-armed horsemen, from whom we drew an escort on several occasions.

As regards the insecurity of the town, I may mention the following little adventure. I used to go out with my companion, when the weather permitted, to make a few polar observations with the theodolite. As the terrace of our house was very convenient for such observations, we made a kind of ladder, and having hoisted up our instrument, we began our operations; but we had not been five minutes so occupied when there was the report of a rifle a hundred yards off. We did not trouble ourselves about this, as in a Mussulman town they like to make the gunpowder "speak." But whilst we were busy gazing at the heavens, a bullet aimed at our lantern warned us that we had better desist and pack up our instruments, which we did with a certain amount of alacrity. This put a stop to our operations on the terrace.

Our cook was very indignant at what had happened, and wished to form an expedition against the miscreants—no doubt a second edition of the famous campaign of Tetuan—but as we did not feel disposed to renew such a fruitless attempt, we were compelled to calm the bellicose ardour of our Spaniard.

This event gave us matter for reflection, and a few days after, on the occasion of an excursion towards the east, in the valley where a Kaïd of the Sultan happened to be with a strong body of troopers, we were enabled to satisfy ourselves of the necessity of keeping on our guard, for we saw with what care they placed their lines of sentries. Besides, cattle were stolen every week, and even women were carried away by these Berber brigands, who are, it would appear, great admirers of the fair sex.

The house which we occupied, and which in Wazzan went by the pompous appellation of the Sherif's country house, would have proved a delightful dwelling for us if the damp climate had not treated us to a continuous succession of showers, unknown even to the inhabitants of the Zuyderzee. A ground floor with a solitary room forms the habitual "huerta." One would think that the taste of its owner for European comforts would have induced him to prefer his house at Tangiers. We lived here as if in an aquarium, the natural consequence being that on the fifth day after our arrival my friend was attacked with acute rheumatism, and could scarcely hobble along under the protection of a huge waterproof cloak. Our numerous assortment of such useful vestments had excited the mirth of our friends at Tangiers, but how thankful we were to have encumbered ourselves with them!

We could not reproach our worthy hosts for the deficient accommodation they had provided us with, for we received from them constant attention and the most hospitable treatment. The vicinity of the large gardens had induced us to insist on being billeted in this palace of rheumatism, as we hoped for a prompt return of the fine weather. But rarely was the end of May more suitable to the habits of the frogs; and I could scarcely recognise this town, which was so attractive under a beautiful sun, with its broad covering of verdure, as I had seen it the preceding year during my journey with Major Trotter.

Our cook established his larder in a half-ruined shed situated at the end of our garden. After some days, thanks to the not very commendable efforts of our Spanish *Vatel*, disorder reigned supreme there. To make things worse, the circle of local friends brought here by our servants gambolled about in the midst of our crockery and outfit every evening.

Our animals had better lodgings in a small neighbouring court, where it was even possible to put some into stables.

We had arrived in this charming abode on a magnificent evening, and the sight of the piece of water, the calm of neighbouring shades, and the tender cooing of the doves had given us a foretaste of the pleasures that we believed were in store for visitors who had so much respect for the brotherhood of Muley Taïeb. How different now!

Early the next morning we were taking a bath in the pond, but scarcely had we emerged from it, when lo! we saw at the end of the alley a numerous throng of people who were advancing with a slow and dignified step. Surely, thought I, Sidi Mohammed is coming—he must be one of our hosts. I do not yet know. The respect shown him by his attendants did not leave us long in doubt. Rather confused at being surprised in such deshabillé we bowed with a pleasant smile on our countenances, and his highness responded in most gracious style. We were much struck by the dignified bearing of these Moors, draped in their white flowing robes, and with a grave and earnest look. The impression seemed new to us—it was one that we had scarcely known in Tangiers, where the hideous European garb of the Jews is like a dark stain on a bright picture.

The more you see of Morocco, of the life of its inhabitants, and of their customs, the more you are struck with the similarity which they bear to those of European societies of the middle ages. The feudal system still flourishes here, and the Sherif of Wazzan being, after the Sultan, the most important man north of the Moghreb, we kept that impression during our stay, especially as insecurity was very rife. As a matter of fact, the existence of these two sons cooped up in a town away from the routes followed by the embassies and travellers in general, is more like the life which chieftains of old used to lead, and in the midst of these warlike Mussulman features we almost fancied we were living in some earlier century. This was certainly not the least of the interesting features of our travels through Morocco.

Sidi el Arbi and Sidi Mohammed are sons of the Mussulman women whom Hadj Abd es Selam divorced in order to taste the sweets of an European union, a marriage which has given him two children who were brought up at the College of Algiers. It might be asked, who will be his successor? His two sons, Sidi el Arbi and Sidi Mohammed, those who possess all the necessary qualifications for sanctity, always dwell at Wazzan. Nurtured in the mysteries of the brotherhood, they possess its secrets, and seem indeed to be the two real Khalifas of their father. The eldest, Sidi el Arbi, has devoted himself to religious questions, and the other to worldly interests and the superintendence of the estates.

Sidi el Arbi is about thirty-three years of age, and is blessed with two wives. He lives in homely fashion in a small house whose exterior has nothing remarkable, but which is arranged with a fair degree of comfort. It is full of clocks and musical boxes, which I had full leisure to examine, when that most amiable man offered me such a generous hospitality four years ago.

This Arab, with his olive complexion, large, black, fiery eyes, a sparse and silky beard, a semitic nose, and an aristocratic slimness of figure, seems to have come straight from the plains of Hedjaz, and has not the bloated and flabby look of the majority of Moroccan townspeople. All his gestures are graceful; his clothes, always of the most scrupulous whiteness, emit a sweet odour of I know not what Oriental perfume, but which I have always much admired. Besides all this, Sidi el Arbi is most courteous in manner, of the most exquisite bearing, and extremely hospitable; in short, he is a fair type of the Mussulman, with all his good qualities.

If M. Renan confesses the feeling of regret which he experiences at not being a disciple of Mohammed when he enters a mosque, we have likewise ourselves felt how Hadj el Arbi left us the impression of comparative superiority over the narrow forms of our prosaic, mechanical civilization with its scientific shams.

It is well known that Orientals doate on flowers, and our host seemed to have great affection for his garden, which he liked us to admire. How often, on the occasion of our frequent early visits, he received us in his garden, when the dew glistened on the bright flowers in the morning sun! He would pluck his finest carnations and offer them to us, his friendly guests, whilst paying us some gracious Arab metaphoric compliment. It was then I regretted having been born in our cold northern climes, where the history of the past is of so little account, whilst, thanks to this Mussulman life, the old Moghreb el Acsa, ringing yet with the remembrance of Idris the Conqueror, is now in its general aspect and features what it was in olden times.

I find that our host has some vague resemblance to the Sultan. The expression of his face is the same—that is, of one who forms no more illusions, but who still entertains kind and merciful sentiments for our poor human race. It was the same expression of condescending sympathy which he assumed when, armed with a whole collection of complicated scientific researches, we tried to explain to him the object of our travels, at the same time asking him for some advice, with the view of overcoming the fanaticism of the population.

If a lover of contrasts had wished to find a field for his observations, the summer-house in El Hadj el Arbi's garden would surely have been a fit place. Amid all these Eastern surroundings, we looked extremely awkward; for the operation of sitting down like a Mussulman—which apparently is so simple, but which really requires a great amount of study and complete practice, as regards the elasticity of the muscles—made us look ludicrously grotesque. On these embroidered carpets we never know what to do with our legs; and our feet being encased in boots must have seemed somewhat insulting according to Moroccan customs. I remember the alarm caused among a solemn party by my friend being suddenly seized with a very painful attack of cramp. He could not suppress it, and stretched out his booted leg right into a tea-tray loaded with the numerous utensils usually displayed on such occasions in Morocco. There was much shattering of china and a great commotion. The explanation we gave, coupled with our apologies, did not, I am afraid, altogether satisfy the high dignitaries.

The operations for the preparation of tea always seemed to me very complicated. They are the A B C of Moroccan hospitality, the obligatory accompaniment of all meetings, the never-failing ordeal which a traveller has to submit to directly he sets foot on the territories of his Sherifian majesty. A servant, or I should say, a slave, brings on a large silver or brass tray a number of tea-pots, a tea-caddy, and sugar-box. The cups are luckily of very small dimensions, and often of the finest and most ancient porcelain.[1]

This array of articles is placed in the centre of the circle of visitors, in front of the host, or before a kind of favourite or factotum, who then begins the complicated brewing. The required quantity of tea (generally green) having been measured with the utmost care, an attendant brings in a brass kettle which has been placed on a charcoal brazier in the court. The determination not to be poisoned is plainly shown by the way in which the tea-pot is washed out and the first decoction thrown away after it has been tasted by

[1] My friend P., when sent on a mission to Morocco by the French Government, has seen in many dwellings porcelain from China dating from the time when the Moorish pirates used to capture merchant vessels returning from Eastern India.

the tea-maker. An enormous quantity of huge pieces of sugar are then put into the mixture, thus forming a kind of syrup. After this decoction has been discussed by the guests, another brew is made with an addition of mint leaves, verbena, or ambergris, the latter being valued not so much on account of its aromatic properties as because it possesses aphrodisiac qualities.

A "tea" being composed of the regulation number of three cups for each of the party, and this being repeated at every visit, it is easy to calculate the quantity of this beverage one has to imbibe in Morocco.

During the long rainy days when showers were pouring on our "aquarium" we used to spend the long hours in visits to the son of the Sherif. It was there we were able to learn some details concerning the brotherhood of Muley Taïeb, whilst fully appreciating the remarkable intellectual parts of Hadj el Arbi. The latter often asked us (after much beating about the bush, as politeness requires in the country) for some information about European politics and especially about the expedition to Tonkin which at the time was engrossing the attention of France. The distance, the number of the soldiers, and above all, the enormous population of China astonished him greatly. We could see by the expression and change of countenance of the attendants the effect which each fresh detail produced. But it is almost certain that they were convinced we had told them a string of exaggerated and fabulous accounts—being accustomed to wondrous and exaggerated tales, they evidently judged us by their Mussulman standard and ideas.

The charm of these conversations was marred, however, on account of the necessity of our having recourse to an interpreter. Our cook, a Spanish *hableur*, translated our speeches, but exercised his imaginative powers, and I often perceived that he did not see the point of our discourses and launched out into endless dissertations to which we were entirely foreign. The circle of Hadj el Arbi's friends is composed of pious Thouamin whose principal occupation is commenting on holy books in the usual mysterious manner of Orientals. He, himself, with a strong sense of his duties, and finding that this kind of spiritual lieutenancy of the brotherhood gratifies his own tastes, keeps a strict observance of the precepts of Mohammed, but without any fanaticism.

Nevertheless, it was not without some difficulty that we obtained permission to photograph him, and we had to give him a kind of promise that we would destroy the plates after taking the first proof. As is the case with deeply religious persons of every nation, fear of public opinion seemed very apparent. I am convinced that the repugnance of Moroccans to being photographed rests, not only on their wish to follow Mohammed's advice concerning the reproduction of images, but also on the fear of some kind of witchcraft.

Hadj Muley Mohammed, Arbi's brother, is less reserved, and very much like his father whose comfortable obesity he already possesses, though only thirty years of age. He has a most open and kind countenance, and does not display the tranquil, solemn ways of his brother.

Hunting and long excursions on horseback seem to engross all his attention, and he is a great lover of fire-arms. He always received us in a large house, the garden of which is close to the town place, and has at one end a large gallery of primitive architecture intended for official receptions. It is not here that we must seek for specimens of

Eastern art. At Fez, at Meknas, or at Morocco, may be seen famous artistic knick-knacks, fine stuffs and embroideries, but in this house there is nothing but a number of modern Rabatt carpets of most vulgar design.

The floor is made of primitive tiles, and here and there may be seen some tin lanterns worthy of a booth at a fair or a stand of chassepot rifles which certainly do not impart any artistic features to the place.

On the whole, Wazzan is only remarkable for its situation, and none of its architectural productions deserve any notice. Thanks to a few German and Spanish renegades who made a stay here, some of the houses bear in certain respects the stamp of European tastes and customs, but the result is in no way favourable to the general aspect. The principal Zaouïa, the cradle of the powerful Order of Muley Taïeb, might awaken in imaginative minds the idea of a vast and marvellous Oriental palace, jealously guarded by fierce black slaves, whilst in the mysterious and silent courts, groups of solemn-looking Moors sit in a circle on the sandy ground, expounding with religious fervour the holy books. But such is not the case, unfortunately; and if to this, we add that the dwelling of Sidi Mohammed is adorned on the outside with horrible blue shutters, whilst the interior has the privilege of automatic pianos and plated tea-services, hailing from Cheapside, the lovers of Orientalism will indeed be grieved, whilst importers of European products will rejoice.

As Sidi Mohammed is entrusted with the functions of assistant manager of the business affairs of the Order, the house is always full of the faithful and overseers who attend to give an account of their transactions. His secretary might be taken for an European but for his Moorish costume.

The present head of the brotherhood is the proprietor of a goodly number of houses and foudouchs at Tangiers, Fez, and other places. He owns, also, some great salt mines which bring him in a large income. His private property is of course distinct from that of the Order, but the management of his estates does not seem very successful, and evil tongues do not fail to assert that the holy origin of the Grand Sherif does not preserve him from pecuniary embarrassment.

Among the numerous visitors at Sidi Mohammed's dwelling, were some curious-looking men in picturesque garb, who only made a short stay there and then set off again for distant lands. One of these, wrapped in one of those strange-looking black burnouses with red stripes, such as are worn in the Sahara, was a messenger from the Oulad ech Cheiks,[1] whose fanatical ideas seemed ill at ease in a place where Roumis were so hospitably welcomed, and the very next day this representative of the warlike tribe of South Oranese was replaced by a venerable old Moghrebin with flowing white beard, whom frequent journeys to Touat enabled to depict in most sombre hues the oasis of Tidikelt —that hot bed of religious doubt.

This person, who in no way seemed to be a fanatic, even allowed himself to be photographed, but the mere thought

[1] The whole tribe of the Oulad Sidi ech Cheiks is composed of Marabouts, though most are wholly ignorant, with the exception of a few who have preserved the traditions of knowledge and virtue of the direct descendants of their holy ancestor.

This great family whose chiefs have preserved, in spite of their vagaries, a considerable prestige and influence, is very hostile to French domination, and to it must be partly attributed the insurrectionary movements of the last few years. That is why Sidi Mohammed showed us laughingly the message in question, handing it to us as a hostile one.

of being compelled to return to Touat, after having tasted the sweets of Wazzan, he used to say, made him shudder.

Without making any precise statement about the amount, we were told that the taxes paid by the Zaïouas of Tidikelt had been very heavy in proportion to the scanty resources of the oasis.

From time immemorial the Sherifs of Wazzan seem to have had some partisans and to have enjoyed a certain amount of prestige at Touat, as Largeau in his work "The Country of Rirha" (Algerian Sahara), tells us that in July 1877, he learnt at Ouargla from one of the Sherif's relatives in Wazzan, that at that period Sidi Mohammed, son of the grand Sherif, was at Touat, and that he intended spending the Ramadan there. It is known, besides, that the German traveller, G. Rohlfs, was enabled to visit this part of the desert south of Tafilat, so little known to Europeans, only through the support of the Sherif. The most ardent fanaticism inspires the people there with feelings of deep distrust towards strangers, especially towards the French, owing to the belief that their Algerian forces are always preparing to annex the country. By cutting off the means of communication with the Soudan, they fancy that the sway of civilization will deprive them of the power of organizing those caravans which divide, when in the oasis, into two sections, one proceeding to Morocco through the Tafilat, the other reaching Khadames and the frontier districts of the Tripolitan by skirting the southern part of all the French possessions of Algeria and Tunisia.

Many maps show the Touat as forming part of the Moroccan Empire, but that is not at all correct, as these oases make up an independent confederation which acknowledges only the religious supremacy of the Moroccan emperor, and sends him presents of money somewhat similar to St. Peter's pence.

In a learned work, M. Duveyrier[1] tells us that as early as 1861 the famous fanatical sect of the Senousîya whose principles rest on the preaching of a holy and relentless war against the Christians and their civilization, reckoned many partisans among the people of Tidikelt. It would, at the present time, be very interesting to be able to study there the influence of Muley Taïeb's brotherhood, since its chief has shown so much favour to modern ideas, through his marriage and as a protégé of the French Government.

It is therefore hardly necessary to add that we perceived but few traces of fanaticism among the people and friends of the Sherif's sons. But their cordiality was not shown to us only, for the Ben-Chimol of Tangiers, who had settled down some time before, in the very same house, had received there in grand style their Israelitish friends in the town. The event would certainly have shocked the strict Mussulmans at the Sultan's court, but it may seem quite extraordinary for a traveller arriving at Wazzan to witness such a tolerant spirit in that town, which he is accustomed to consider, from numerous accounts, a most venerated sanctuary, a kind of Moroccan Mecqua, as it has been termed. To say the truth, the town loses day by day its renowned reputation for holiness. The blessing of Allah, and the protection of Mohammed, (being disgusted with so

---

[1] Duveyrier (Henri), "Exploration du Sahara," Paris, 1864. "Les Senoussi et les Tedjadjna divisent profondément les populations de la ville de Quaçar el-kebir." Regarding the Mussulman brotherhood of the Sidi-Mohammed-Ben-ali-es-Senousi, the same author says: " Dans la partie ouest du Sahara central le Gourara, un groupe serré d'oasis, le Touat proprement dit, et In-Calah ont chacun une Zaouiya de la confrérie de Sidi-es-Senousi."

many sacrifices to modern ideas) might forsake the accursed city, and seek refuge, say at Muley Idris, in that nest of Chorfa where no Christian or Jew has ever set foot, and which may be seen from the road of Meknas in a wild-looking gorge of the Djebel Zarhoun behind the Volubilis of the ancients.

If it were not for its large olive woods and numerous orange trees, its graceful amphitheatre of houses rising in tiers of white cubes, Wazzan would present a vulgar appearance. When the trade winds do not drive before them some heavy clouds which the tops of the Rif arrest in their progress and accumulate over the country, the neighbourhood of the town is exceedingly attractive. From the terraces one may enjoy a very fine view of the picturesque outlying country.

We were unduly protracting our sojourn, and the news from Tangiers concerning diplomatic events being no better, we thought it high time to leave this place where we had been enjoying the hospitality of the Sherif's sons, and to take leave of our kind hosts.

It was in June; the weather seemed to be improving, and we were making preparations for our departure, when, one morning, our servants burst into our room with a dismayed look, bringing us news of the impending destruction, not of the world, but of the city.

Sidi Mohammed, who had left some days before, in order to join his father at Tangiers, had entrusted Wazzan to the sole care of his brother. Now, the latter had just received an ominous and unexpected message, which compelled him to leave the town at once, and proceed to Tangiers, to place himself under the protection of Hadj Abd es Selam, as the Makhzen, it was rumoured, entertained anything but friendly feelings towards him, which might any day find expression in some unforeseen event, the consequences of which would prove highly disagreeable to our host.

We had, therefore, nothing to do but take our departure without delay, and our people, whose *forte* was not personal courage, did not fail to entreat us to join El Hadj el Arbi, in order to return in safety to the shores of the Straits under protection of his sanctity. Some astonishment, therefore, was caused, when, on taking leave of our hospitable, kind, and affectionate host, and expressing our respectful gratitude, we asked him for some letters of recommendation to the Moqaddems of the Zaouïas on the road to W. Wargha.

We witnessed the preparations for his hurried departure, and after the busy marching off of his numerous escort, we felt a strange sensation of loneliness in this town, forsaken, as it was, by all those capable of bearing arms, and who had insisted on accompanying their chief. Only half-a-dozen guards remained with us, and I could fully realise the anxiety of our followers during the last night spent here.

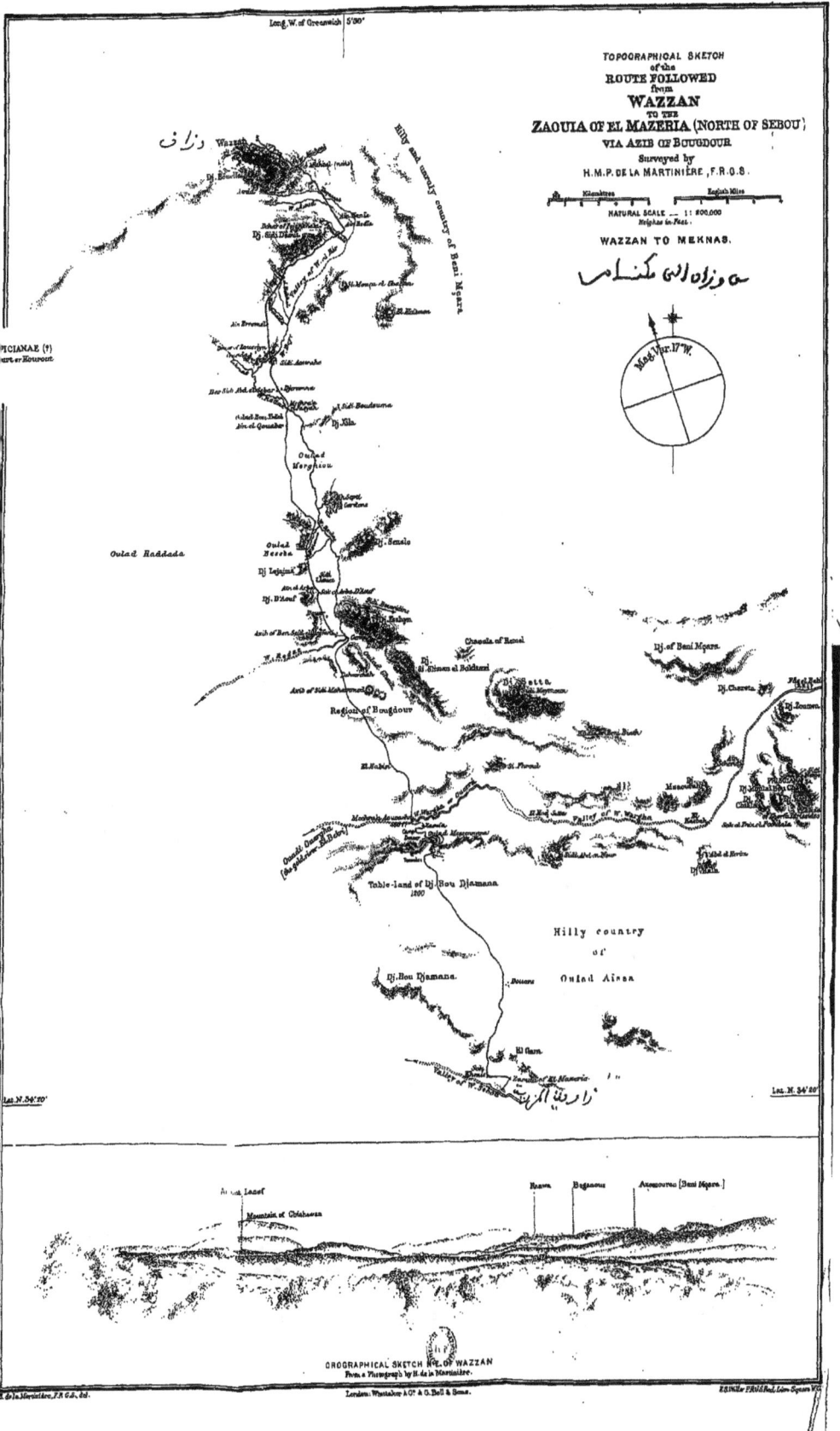

CHAPTER IX.

Route from Wazzan to W. Wargha—A Hydrographic Problem to Solve—The Shorif's Escort—A Runaway Mule—Camping at Sok el Arba d'Aouf—View of the Dj. Kourt—Numerous Remains of Antiquity—The W. Rdat—The Valley of the Wargha—Fertility—Comparative Geography—The Dj. Setta and the Roman Town of Assada—We Cross the River—Incidents—We Encamp among the Oulad Messenana—Disease in the Rural Districts.

THE distance, as the crow flies, between Wazzan and Meknas is about fifty-one miles. We were five days on the road. Having set out on a Friday at eleven o'clock in the morning, we entered Meknas on the following Tuesday at 5.30 P.M.; but the journey could very well be done in three days and a half.

On leaving Wazzan, you go round the Dj. Bouellol, so as to reach the plain, studded with hillocks, which spreads itself out at the bottom of the southern slope as far as the valley of the Wargha. Thus, you follow the narrow valley of the small W. el Beyt, a tributary of the Rdat, as far as the buttresses of the Dj. Bougdour. You cross the Rdat near the Sok el Arba d'Aouf, and the broad, undulating plateau, devoid of vegetation, which forms the northern boundary of the rich valley of the Wargha; you ford the latter river at Aoucacha, whence you have a good view of

K

the Dj. Setta, and you ascend some quite deserted and parched up hills, until, descending into the valley of the Sebou, you cross that river by means of a ferry near the douar of El Mazeria, where may be seen a Zaouïa which belongs to the Sherif of Wazzan.

After this you have to clamber up the massive Zarhoun and Tselfatz at the pass called Zeggotta, which leads into the old Roman road from Tingis to Volubilis and Tocolosida. From the site of this extreme post of the Roman occupation at the top of the hillside of El Arabi you have a good view of the plateau of Meknas and of the minarets of the Moorish Versailles.

The whole stretch of country from Wazzan to the Wargha is naturally very interesting, as it borders the extreme unexplored prolongation of the Rif, and it is little travelled over. Missions do not journey through it, and the travellers who have crossed it have furnished very scant information about it. That is why geographers scarcely know whether to place Wazzan in the valley of the Kouss or in that of the Sebou, and they prudently evade solving the question. No maps appear to throw any light on the subject, to which I will now devote a few lines.

The only brook which irrigates the lands at the bottom of the town is supplied by the overflow of the waters intercepted in the reservoir of the orange gardens of the Sherif, after streaming down the northern slopes of the Dj. Wazzan. From this reservoir issues another small stream, whose volume is very variable. It runs to the N.W. I was unable, unfortunately, to follow its course far enough for the object I had in view, on account of the hostile disposition of the tribes on my last visit. I believe, however, that it forms part of the system of the Kouss, and my reasons for this opinion are, that when you enter the sunken plain in front of Wazzan from the west, you notice two streams running from south to north, and which appear to spring from a succession of heights which must prevent any communication between other water courses and the brook I mentioned above.

I am, therefore, inclined to believe that the Dj. Wazzan or Bouellol (a pretty high peak of a range which connects the buttresses of the Rif with the Sarsar) forms the extreme southern line of separation of the waters of the basins of the Sebou and the Kouss, because the W. el Beyt—a tributary of the Rdat, as I was able to ascertain—takes its source in the southern side of this very mountain of Wazzan.

As for the brooks in the plain of Wazzan, none can possibly be mistaken for the little W. without a name in Tissot's map, as their direction is due north, though one of these brooks seems to issue from a valley intervening between the Dj. Masmouda and the Dj. Tchemakha.

Treating of the comparative geography of the Tingitane is generally a delicate matter, on account of the distortion of the Berber Arab words, the confusion being further increased by the Hispano-Jewish vocabulary introduced during the Middle Ages, after the expulsion of the Jews from Spain. The difficulties arising from this complication appeared to me the greater in the locality north of the Wargha, because only one Arab geographer, El Bekri, has left us any information about his journey from Ceuta to Fez, via Aftês.[1] As for Marmol, the only interesting information he gives us of the northern part of the valley of the Wargha is that furnished

---

[1] Written Afîch by M. Renou.

by the curious map of the French edition of the work.[1] It is possible that a certain river called "*Ador fl.*" corresponds to the present W. Rdat, but this is a mere conjecture, and it is scarcely necessary to add that the name is now unknown.

El Bekri speaks of a river called Souçac (Ouadi Souçac, translation of De Slane) which flowed between the Kouss and the Wargha and which was "as large as the river of Cordova." Now, though allowing for the statements of El Cortobi, full of truly Eastern exaggeration,[2] this stream cannot be mistaken for the Rdat whose name and position were known to El Bekri, since he mentions it in the relation of his journey to Basra. We have no means for clearing up the question, which must remain obscure, because it is quite possible that one of these two rivers—the Kouss and the Wargha—had received a different name at some point of its course, a circumstance of frequent occurrence in the case of other water courses.

After this lengthy tribute to the records of the Middle Ages, let us return to our journey.

In order to get round the Djebel Wazzan we had to traverse the town and skirt the sides of the mountain along a horrid path full of holes; but our exertions were rewarded by one of the most charming views one can imagine. From the heights, the orange groves seemed like a green

---

[1] Royaume de Fez divisé en Sept provinces. Tiré de Sanut, de Marmol, etc., par N. Sanson d'Abbeville. Géogr. du Roy. 1656.

[2] Abou Obeid el Bekri had lived many years at Cordova, hence his surname of El Cortobi. It may be interesting to record the fact that the general belief is that El Bekri did not actually explore the Moghreb, and that he drew his information from official documents, which his high position and family connections enabled him to procure. He died in 1094 (Chaoual 487).

velvet carpet with graceful folds bringing out the glaring whiteness of the houses. From the orange trees to the cultivated tracts of land, the eye glided along a well graduated scale of tints, and finally rested on the fine outline of the lofty mountains which contrasted on the horizon with the deep blue of the sky. The lands at the lower part of the Rif being in a state of cultivation, the result was that on each succeeding height the green tints of the foreground lost some of their intensity. Yellowish here, brownish there, all were blended in the distance into one undecided, all-pervading tint, which the most skilful painter would have been at a loss to reproduce; and in the full daylight, through the dry, clear atmosphere everything was seen as if in the midst of a brilliant illumination. I was, therefore, much taken up with this delightful scene; and as our sojourn at Wazzan had bereft us of the pleasures of the road, we joyfully experienced again the exhilarating sensation of travelling across the broad expanse, freed from all restraint, and camping out in the open.

The mountain of Wazzan, at a certain distance from its foot, is only covered with rose bay, and further up with vegetation, which, though sparse and stunted, gives the slopes an appearance of fertility which contrasts with the desolate nakedness of the peaks of the Dj. Kourt (or Kourout) and the undulations of the plateau of Tchemakha.

We were accompanied by an escort, which Sidi el Arbi had kindly left for us when taking his departure. This Sherifian soldiery, which presented a wretched enough appearance in the subdued light of the moon, when accomplishing their vigils, seemed still more ill-favoured when seen by the telltale rays of the fierce, glaring sun of June. These poor fellows had so little superfluous fat that they must have experienced no difficulty in running after the most agile malefactors. Their jellabas showed as many holes as patches, and compared to theirs, Don César de Bazan's cloak would have been deemed a comfortable and handsome garment. At the end of an hour, the men of the escort bade us God-speed and a propitious journey. No doubt their good wishes were not wholly disinterested, for I saw an expectant and ominous expression lurking in the twinkling orbs of the chief, so I thought it prudent to satisfy at once the requirements of this worthy commander and his followers, for I suspected them of being fully capable of imitating the Spanish custom-house officers, who, it is known, turn smugglers when they find that gratuities cease sufficiently to fill their pockets. The escort then took leave of us with many bows and expressions of gratitude. But after our caravan, swelled by the mules which we had bought in the town, had resumed its journey, and we were fairly on the way again, descending the last buttresses of the Dj. Bouellol in a long Indian file, we were joined by a negro, a member of the wretched troop which had just taken leave of us; induced, no doubt, by the recollection of the delights of our mess, this man, one of the leanest I ever saw, ran up, quite panting and out of breath, and begged for permission to accompany us.

One of the new mules of the column was then giving us some trouble. He seemed bent on accomplishing the journey on his forelegs, in imitation of circus-trained animals, and kept kicking out furiously with his hind legs. As our cook had conceived the happy idea of entrusting this unruly beast with the cooking paraphernalia, we were regaled with a deafening concert produced by saucepans and other utensils in violent collision. The mule, made lively by the horrible music, became furious, and breaking into a wild gallop drew us all after him in pursuit, in a most grotesque steeple-chase. Our new recruit, the Sherifian negro, swift of foot as a deer, had outstripped us at first, and I had to lay violent hands on him when I caught him up, just as he was preparing to take a shot at the recreant mule, saying that it was better to destroy it than to leave it to the Berbers with its valuable load. The rascal had recognised the cooking utensils and would not have seen them lost of all things in the world. At last my friend, by a daring and clever manœuvre, succeeded in catching the runaway animal, and order was restored among the caravan. After great loss of time, the loads were shifted, and we resumed our march towards the south. During this scene, which had much amused all our attendants who made various comments on the negro's conduct, one of them alone gazed on with unconcerned look, sitting immovable on his steed. This man was no other than our soldier who thought it prudent not to trespass on ground unknown to him and made dangerous, he said, by the proximity of rebel tribes.

When on the southern sides of the Dj. Bouellol, we had passed about 1600 yards from the small dchar of Asnid, which may contain some hundred houses; and before we had come across the ruins of a few hovels devoid of any picturesque features—the tops of the Dorghona were already hidden to us—and then, by degrees, the Darzaoua, the Tchaouan, and the snowy peaks of the northern districts of Beni Mçara had disappeared behind the hills, when we reached a plain where a rivulet was murmuring softly. At the extremity of this fairly regularly cultivated region, we arrived at the narrow but fertile valley of the W. el Beyt and W. Lekouas—a tortuous little river from nine to eleven yards wide. The whole country there is covered with numerous douars whose clusters of brown tents looked from a distance like large molehills. The district is well watered, and at any rate better cultivated than one would expect considering the insecurity and the raids perpetrated by the tribes of the Beni Mçara.

The direction followed was due south, and the outline of the Dj. Bougdour hills [1] marked the site of our evening encampment at the *huerta* [2] of the Sherif, lying at the base of these heights which connect themselves with the Dj. Setta. The horizon on the east is limited by some hills, the most remarkable of which on the southern extremity is the Dj. Kourt, the Kort of Tissot's map. The plateau there seems to be a waste, and the chalky ground remains uncultivated, and consists of a broad expanse of dreary steppes. It must be said that the whole ground is covered here and there with a species of saline efflorescence, which suffices to damage any vegetation. The temperature is very high here, and we were glad to reach, about 2.30 p.m., the sacred grove of the marabout of Sidi Aourao where we dismounted, whilst the train of mules continued the journey. The country showed nothing worth noticing; always the same succession of little valleys which would, I believe, prove very favourable for great agricultural undertakings, if there were any attempts at cultivation.

On the east, the orographic system is connected with the Rif mountains, but there must be some intermediate valleys which we could not get a sight of. One must be content with surmises, as no travellers have furnished us with any scientific information concerning that mysterious region.

A clump of fine palm trees, a little way from the W. el

[1] Dj. Senslo and Dj. Si Sliman el Boukhari.
[2] The Spanish orchard. This word is a remnant of the Hispano-Jewish Vocabulary imported here in the Middle Ages by the Israelites.

Beyt (whose capricious meanderings we had never ceased to cross or skirt), indicated that we were approaching the Sok el Arba d'Aouf where we were to encamp.

At four o'clock we turned eastwards, in order to get round a rocky spur of the Senslo, when suddenly Antonio broke out into a volley of awful imprecations, and stopped the whole column in order to relate his misfortunes. He had lost a tobacco-pouch, a cherished souvenir, and he assured us that he could never think for a moment of going on, if this "piece of his heart" were not found. We were weak enough to yield, for the dispute which had in consequence arisen between the cook and the soldier was taking an unpleasant turn, when luckily the object of our search was found; but meanwhile so much time had been wasted on this trivial affair, that we only arrived at 6 o'clock at the Sherifian huerta, distant about six miles north of the W. Rdat.

This huerta is a large grove of orange and fig trees, at the base of the Dj., and is surrounded with thick hedges of cactus, aloes, and other very thorny plants. A rickety worm-eaten structure, almost off its hinges, formed an apology for a gate.

The greenery at this place was luxuriant, but there were strong indications of dampness, so the tents had to be pitched on a small grassy hillock close by, a most pleasing spot. We spent the evening in a rather melancholy manner, that is, in tending the unlucky negro, who, having come into close contact with the high spirited mule so fond of circus-like performances, had received such a kick as would have smashed an artillery caisson; but a negro's jaw is proof against such accidents, as we could perceive next morning on seeing Sambo swallow an enormous heap of couscous.

This small territory of the Sok el Arba is occupied by a colony of Taïbin, and the news of our arrival having been promptly spread about, we received a most cordial greeting. The land is but sparsely cultivated, and with the exception of some light fields of barley, it bears nothing but palmitos; but the important market which is held every Wednesday in that locality draws a large concourse of people, and other commercial transactions compensate for the scarcity of agricultural productions. It is here that one can form an idea of the power of the religious organisation of Mussulman brotherhoods, and the influence enjoyed by the Sherif of Wazzan in this locality which lies in the vicinity of one of his estates, on lands belonging to the Order of Muley Taïeb, the power of whose Moqaddem is absolute.

Our camp was about six miles from the Dj. Kourt, and we could easily make out the configuration of this hill, which Tissot identified to a certain degree of probability with the Roman post of Vopiscianæ.

These appellations of Kourt, Kort, Kert or Kerdh are, in any case, of Berber origin, for they are met with in the geographical nomenclature of the Rif as names for rivers and mountains. The Dj. Kourt of this neighbourhood is a lofty hill, which commands on the north the valley of the Sebou and the road of the W. el Tynn valley. It may therefore be quite possible that the scarcely discernible Berber ruins at the summit, rest on the traces of Roman occupation. The qoubbah of a small but much venerated marabout, now occupies the highest point of the second mamelon and is discernible from a great distance. This mountainous group consists of slanting chalky layers which stand out with barren tops. The scanty population is Berber, and lives a wretched life on the dreary plateau, which extends as far as the ruins of Basra. The ground is cracked in every direction, and the crevices show the under strata of clay and slate. It is poor, and in many places it becomes sterile through saline efflorescence. The plateau ends at the valley which precedes the Dj. Sidi Hamor where the W. el Tynn has its source.

This range of heights bears the name of Dj. Tchemakha, then of Măsmoudă. Between these two ranges there is a small narrow valley. Further west the nature of the ground is altered, for Basra el Hamra was built, it will be remembered, on a rich ferruginous clay soil.

Towards the east our first horizon was limited by the chain of the Bougdour, the last buttresses of the Rif, and a small marabout stood out like a white spot on these absolutely barren heights, burnt during ages by a fierce sun. The W. Rdat has its source here. A few dchour, which are scattered far and wide, scarcely break the monotony of the landscape.

Far away in the south we could already see the mass of the Tselfatz, a lofty peak of the Zarhoun chain.

Next morning, at nine o'clock, we went to await the arrival of the column at the W. Rdat which runs less than a mile from the Sok; but we had to follow its course for a quarter of an hour before finding the ford, which at this time of the year was shallow and easy to cross. The river runs on a chalky bed, and is about thirty-five yards broad.

The country beyond this point was extremely monotonous, and consisted of a succession of undulating deserts covered with the everlasting palmitos. Now and then we could perceive a wider horizon from the top of a hill, and we took advantage of this to take the altitude of the Tselfatz and the heights of Wazzan. As for the Sarsar, it was concealed from our gaze by the heights of the plateau of Kourt. At noon we reached a kind of oasis consisting of rich lands bearing some slight evidences of cultivation; but here the camp formed by the horsemen of the Makhzen reminded the few and unhappy inhabitants that the best part of their harvests would become the prey of the tax-gatherer. A little further on we were greeted by an Arab with a *Bonjour messieurs*, given with a very correct pronunciation, to our great astonishment. Our astonishment, however, ceased when we were told that the tribe of the Habbisi (then encamped at a short distance off the Wargha) came from the district of the Oujdja, in the vicinity of French territory; they probably had been brought here, by order of the Sultan, in consequence of the disturbances on the frontier.

About 1.40 we began to perceive, through the misty vapours of a hot day, the bluish outline of the Zarhoun, stretching out behind the Tselfatz like a long train. At 2 o'clock we climbed the last hill, and we beheld beneath us the rich valley where the Wargha flows, in the middle of one of the finest districts of the Gharb, that inexhaustible granary, which, under more enlightened rule, would suffice to nourish large numbers of inhabitants.

The sight was well worth our halting. We had behind us the Bouellol, on the right the Kourt, and on the left, in the valley which we had just traversed, the chains of Bougdour; whilst in front the many peaks of the Tselfatz seemed to look down on the country like so many outpost sentinels.

The valley is narrow, being between $1\frac{1}{2}$ and $2\frac{1}{2}$ miles wide, but it expands more and more in a western direction. The rich soil is well tilled and is watered by the right tributary of the Sebou—the most important one. It would appear that the Wargha takes its source in the buttresses of the Rif, the Marnissa region, in the midst of that Berber population which is always in arms. Here, even, the tribes of the plains alone are loyal. The mountaineers do not pay any taxes, and at the time of our journey all the eastern district of the Oulad Aïssa, and that near the marabout of Sidi Mergo was in open revolt and even refused to accept the Sultan's Kaïd.[1] We crossed the river at the Mechráä Aoucacha in sight of the little marabout of Sidi Meymoun, perched on the southern slopes of the Dj. Setta. The Wargha has many fords, a fact which probably explains why the name of the one we crossed, and that given in Tissot's map, have not been mentioned by Arab geographers nor by succeeding authors. El Bekri speaks of the ford of the beam or Mechráä el Khachbä, an appellation now forgotten, as that of "the grey mountain," Djebel el Achhebeb, near which might yet be seen, in the Middle Ages, about 10 miles distant, the site of the Roman tower of Assada, on the road which travellers followed from Basra to cross the Wargha. The great altitude of that chain of the Setta prolonged towards the north, as has been seen, by the undulations of the Bougdour, would lead one to believe that the Romans did not neglect this advantageous site which commands, in the south, such a rich valley. M. Tissot, taking his cue from El Bekri, supposes the site of Assada[2] to have lain between the Wargha and the Sebou. The Arab text is, however, affirmative: the town of Assada, surrounded with trees and vines, stood six miles south from the Dj. el Achhebeb, and "the Ford of the Beam" was found further on.

[1] Kaïd, chief magistrate.

[2] Autant qu'on en peut juger par les indications très vagues d'El Bekri, elle devait être située non loin de El-Haliyn entre le Sebou et Ouargha. Tissot. "Recherches sur la Géographie comparée de la Maurétanie Tingitane," p. 295.

Long and patient researches, which are not possible in the disturbed state of the country, would alone enable one to clear up those interesting questions.

The W. Wargha[1] or Golden River, at the time of our journey in June, might have been about 100 yards broad, and the current being swift, we had an opportunity of witnessing the careless awkwardness of the Moors. We had to arrange a complicated system of transhipment, a not very pleasant occupation, to lighten the burden of the overloaded mules, whilst taking precautions in view of the risk of being carried away by the swift waters. At length, thanks to the Andalusian dash of Antonio who did not mind a ducking, everything went off in a satisfactory manner; and an unlucky mule, which we considered as already lost with her burden, was saved and brought to land. The crossing of a stream is always an operation of magnitude in Morocco, and I must add, a perilous one. It was particularly so on this occasion, when the animals would have sunk in the quicksand had it not been for an under layer of gravel of quaternary formation which acts as a support for the soft upper strata in the bed of the river.

After this we followed a narrow path which led us across

---

[1] The Berber word Ouyrghi, signifying gold, is spelt Ouargha by Tissot, who does not give the rendering of the word. The Roman denomination does not seem to have reached us as the French savant does not mention it. It must be remarked, however, that the mountainous region called Διούρ by Ptolemy, and which probably extended from Zarhoun to the Rif, was inhabited by part of the Οὐερμεῖς, the οὐολουβιλίανοι, and in the first of these words might be sought the root of the Wargha or Ouergha, for it is known that there still exists a district called Ouergha in the southern buttresses of the Rif. As for Marmol, he once gives the river the name of Guarga, then that of the river of Erguile, a town situated, according to him, in the east on the banks of the stream. Carte de M. Sanson. Geogr. du Roy. Tome ii., p. 137. MDCLXVII.

some fine barley fields to a half-ruined cabin, dirty enough to send a shudder through the most apathetic Africans. This wretched place went by the pompous appellation of Zaouïa of the Order of Muley Taïeb, and the servants of the Sherif did their best to induce us to establish ourselves there. A hideous-looking keeper escorted by a troop of howling children tried in vain to make us stop here. In spite of the disappointed look of all our attendants, we refused, and decided to pursue our journey till we reached an Arab camp which we had perceived from the hill top before crossing the river, and now half concealed from us by the high barley stalks. The dogs of the douars were not long in heralding our approach in the usual way, that is, by a loud concert of furious barks and howls, and the Arabs came at once to survey our preparations with much curiosity if not with friendliness. The place being thickly populated, we were quickly surrounded by a compact crowd which swarmed like ants out of the tents. Our soldier was even compelled to exert his influence in a rather forcible manner in order to keep the inquisitive at a respectful distance.

Although these people have some Berber blood in their veins in consequence of their mixing with the tribes of the neighbouring Rifan mountains, we saw among them a few Arabs whose easy manner formed a pleasant contrast with the heavy appearance of the northern Berber. The jellaba of the Tingitane coast gave way to the burnous which so faithfully recalls the old and majestic Roman toga. The majority of the races was, however, the result of numerous Berber intermarriages, and the Berber race being itself a mixed one on account of its affinities with the Vandals and other northern races, we had before us the representatives of all kinds of types, with here and there the pure Arab or Bedouin such as we are wont to depict them. It would be impossible for any one to describe accurately the Morisco type, which, as I said before, is formed from so many elements that it participates of all the specimens of the invading races in the country. By the side of fair-haired individuals which "make one think," says Hartmann, "of the fair Libu Tamhus of the old Egyptians, are found Kabyles with stout calves—" very few Arabs of pure descent being *built that way*. Some have fine extremities, well formed muscles, and their shaven crown, which is surmounted by a lock of hair, gives them some resemblance to the Sioux of Northern America. Their copper skins, which glisten strangely, would lead us almost to believe that the most varied of the human races have chosen this fine country as their place of sojourn.

It would, indeed, be difficult to imagine a more fertile country, and if the geographical denominations of the time of El Bekri have not reached us, the Valley of the Wargha has, nevertheless, preserved its former richness; but formerly this prosperity extended far beyond, and it would appear that in the southern part of this district a number of small, serried towns at one time existed, whereas now the country is deserted, save the parts on the banks of the stream.

We were in the midst of a douar of the Oulad Messenana (part of the Oulad Aïssa) and we were able to form an idea of the agricultural wealth and rustic comfort, strong evidences of which appeared here. The barley fields succeeded one another in endless expanse, and the evening breeze gently rippled the surface of this sea of barley. As the country appeared to yield everything in plenty and seemed so prosperous, Antonio promised us a royal feast for the evening. He, therefore, proceeded—as was his wont on the occasion of all memorable gastronomic events—on a diplomatic mission to the Sherif, escorted by the soldier, and preceded by the staff of attendants.

The Sherifian element we had in our train was far from being of the most brilliant description, for Idris was lying half dead from sunstroke, and the negro seemed, after the fatigue of the journey, to have less flesh on his bones than usual. But the holiness of Wazzan clung to us, and the greatest sympathy was therefore enlisted in our favour among the people of the district. So the culinary mission was not slow in making its reappearance, well loaded with victuals of the most varied kinds. The negro carried an enormous sheep, fat and fleshy, which he was lovingly ogling, while Antonio's person literally disappeared beneath multitudinous clusters of cackling fowls. In short, each member of the returning mission helped to complete the ensemble of a train worthy of Gargantua. The soldier himself, *admirabile dictu*, offered us a few delicious figs with which his highness had condescended to burden himself.

Whilst they thus busied themselves with the preparations of the wonderful feast, we had to withstand the onslaught of a whole troop of sick and lame people, the members of a regular "Cour des miracles" of the place, who came to seek the advice of the Roumi doctors. How careless and unmindful of the most elementary principles of hygiene these people must have been to allow of such a collection of various diseases in so fine and healthy a region!

The chilly and damp nights of Tingitane and the prolongation of the rainy season cause much rheumatism and disease of the eye. There is also another complaint—a venereal one—which is spread far and wide in the

Moghreb el Acsa. This dreadful malady assumes here a most repulsive form. The soldier, to give us an appetite I suppose, thought fit to bring for our inspection a poor wretch suffering from the above, and who had lost half of one of his jaws. We scarcely knew what prescription to make up for the unfortunate man. He had been suffering from sleeplessness for months and endured the most excruciating pain. We could only advise him to undertake the journey to Moulaï Jacoub where, near Fez in the Zarhoun, certain thermal waters are to be found, somewhat similar to those of Luchon, and which, with the aid of the prophet, somewhat alleviate the sufferings of ailing Arabs. A few opiate pills soothed the unfortunate man's sufferings, and the following morning we found at the door of our tent the grateful patient firmly bent on accompanying us, as he had formed the greatest confidence in the healing science of the Christians, and could not now think of leaving his benefactors.

CHAPTER X.

From the Wargha to the Sebou—Geographical Description of the Country—The Present Information Insufficient—Difficulty of Scientific Explorations—Hills which separate the Slopes—Travelling on Foot—Aspect of the Valley of the Sebou—The Basin of the Sebou—Commercial Roads in the Moghreb—The Moqaddem of the Zaouïa—A Moorish Fantasia—Gastronomic Achievements—The Passage of the River—Adieux to our Friend the Moqaddem—We Encamp—The Karia of the Kaïd Embarek ben Chleuch—The Zarhoun—Roman Roads in Morocco—Roman Antiquities—Volubilis and M. Tissot's Works—Muley Idris and the Fanaticism of its Population—Tocolosida—Environs of Meknas—Arrival in the Gardens—We enter the Moroccan Versailles.

THE valley of the Wargha is separated from the Sebou by a range of hills beginning at the Djebel Djamana, whose undulating prolongations command the intersection of the two rivers. These heights extend as far as the Djebel Muley Bouchta,[1] and are thus connected with the Sanhedja hills, and the orographic system of the Rif. The Djebel Muley Bouchta, which we could see from our camp, is celebrated on account of the marabout of Sidi Mergo, not far from which ought to be, in the south, the

[1] Spelt Busta and Basta by Rohlfs and Lenz. The ruins mentioned by El Bekri in his route from Sebta (Ceuta) to Fez, and which, to all appearance, were the remains of the old city of Assada, must have lain in the hills between the Sebou and the Wargha; but no traces of these are to be seen now.

site of Mergo, a town of Roman origin mentioned by Leo Africanus, and which, most probably, was built on the old Prisciania of Mela, one of the three important towns of the interior of Tingitane. We even find in the list of the bishops of that country, in the early times of the Christian era, an "episcopus Priscianiensis or Prisianiensis." All the region abounds in traces of the occupation preceding the Mussulman invasion, for the cheikh of the Oulad Messenana asserted that at a two days' march eastwards, some very important ruins[1] might be found.

It is, therefore, probable that the spot is not the same as that mentioned by M. Tissot when he identifies the site of Mergo with the region included between the marabout of Sidi Mergo, and that of Sidi Mohammed es Senousi, for, as far as we could judge, we were not at a distance of more than 24 miles from these two qoubbahs.

However, any intention of archæologic exploration in this region must be given up, and the reason is, that for a considerable time, the disturbed state of the Rifan district will prevent travellers from using instruments, or making any scientific researches. And, there being already great difficulties in the way of observations taken unopposed and without any danger, how cautiously one must receive the estimates and results of operations executed almost stealthily, under a disguise, and with risk to limb and life!

The upper part of the Wargha is not known. The stream must have its source in the Sanhedja, but the line of its

[1] It is quite possible that those ruins are those of the Beni-Tunde mentioned by Leo Africanus as existing in one of the plains of the Guarga (Wargha) and which was about 45 miles distant from Fez, in the vicinity of the Gumera Hills (El Ghomara).

THE VALLEY OF THE SEBOU. 165

basin and the outlines of the hills which bound the valley east of the point where we encamped, are imperfectly indicated in maps, or when they are, the indications proceed from native information. It has not been settled whether the streams flow north or south of the Dj. Bouchta, or, in other words, whether the main branch is not the stream which exists between this mountain and the Setta. The basin of the Wargha is narrow, for after leaving the camp we reached in half an hour the low hills of conglomerat, the plateau of which it is necessary to traverse before reaching the plain of Sebou. It is truly a parched-up desert, almost without any vegetation, where indeed we only came across a troop of wretched nomad Arabs and a tumulus. The monotony in the surrounding country, as may well be understood, was very great on account of the stony nature of the soil, from which the hoofs of our beasts struck up clouds of hot dust. I have not preserved a very pleasing recollection of the march, for my horse cast a shoe, and one of his pasterns was severely cut by a sharp flint, and all the mules being heavily laden I had to perform the rest of the journey on foot, taking a sort of pride in showing the Moors the extent of the walking powers of a Roumi.

It was with a genuine sigh of relief that at half-past one we saw the palmitos make their reappearance, and, shortly afterwards, we discerned some douars, heralding a more civilized district. The soil on these plateaus being of a slatey nature, is so poor that even the *doum* (the dwarf palm, *chamerops humilis*) cannot thrive here; but the Sebou valley, at the spot where we crossed it on the right side of the Tselfatz, is little cultivated; and in spite of its great richness—from the fertile alluvial soil accumulated by the ever-recurring and regular overflowing of the river—it is left to itself. The sea kale and the thistle reign there supreme. The Buridan ass would have found this place a real paradise, for never have I beheld such an array of thistles; it was like a sea which no breeze ever disturbed.

Gazing on this valley so marvellously favoured by nature. with a splendid climate, one cannot help lamenting that such fine resources should lie useless in the hands of people so apathetic. It must be deeply regretted that the fanatical interpretation of the precepts of their religion should lead men to live in such a sad state.

How many poor people, in our frigid European climate, are there, who, even by dint of severe labour, can scarcely draw from the frozen and comparatively barren soil enough sustenance for themselves and their children, while here, an endless expanse of agricultural richness is voluntarily left unproductive; the government meanwhile taking advantage of the mutual hostility of wretched tribes in order to put pressure upon them? Upon the whole the valley has a lonely appearance. Nothing moves within our view, and instead of large herds and flocks grazing in the fine pastures which might be artificially irrigated by the swift stream which flows yonder without being utilized—instead of luxuriant fields of corn, there is nothing but an endless stretch of grey, barren, parched-up ground. Here and there may be seen a tiny plot of pale verdure where some barley has been sown after the land has been only just scratched by a rude plough.

On proceeding up the valley, on a lonely hill which looks as if it had been thrust forward by the chain of buttresses of the range, our glance fell on a shapeless mass of hovels which I examined with my glass. Tall hedges of cacti guarded its approaches and nothing moved about the place;

for the heat was like that of a furnace. This spot, which belonged to the Zaouïa of the Sherif, was to be the site of our camp. The gaunt negro who accompanied us gave us all necessary details with a gleeful air, loudly praising meanwhile the gastronomic treat which awaited us.

But I was engrossed with the melancholy thoughts in which the desolate aspect of this otherwise richly endowed region had plunged me, and I was unable to share the joy of these ever-hungry Moors. After skirting the site of a very important market-place, which on that day was deserted, we suddenly found ourselves on the edge of the Sebou.

At the bottom of an enormous channel 25 or 30 feet in depth, with banks of red clay soil—such as is found in all lands where salt exists—a river flows, whose muddy waves during the floods, assume a very characteristic reddish hue due to the red clay bed. The breadth is not great, and the total absence of trees seemed to me at first extraordinary, for no leafy masses, such as may be seen on the banks of the W. el Kouss, warn the traveller that he is about to reach the banks of the largest stream in the Moghreb. The valley of the Sebou, near its mouth, offers a most complicated hydrography on account of the triple system of the Merdja which has deceived many geographers. But it may boldly be asserted that, thanks to the careful researches and conscientious labours of the learned M. Tissot, the matter has been cleared up.

Formed by the amphitheatre of the hills of Ain Felfel, the plateau of the Oulad Sefyan, the buttresses of the Sarsar, the plateau extending from the Dj. Sidi Amor el Hadi (the Basra mountain) to the Dj. Bouellol (the Wazzan mountain), and lastly, the unexplored buttresses of the

Rif; prolonged towards the south by the Beni Mtirs Hills which are connected with the Zemmours Chleuchs, the hydrographic system of the old Sebou,[1]—the most important of Northern Africa after that of the Nile,—is the most tranquil of Morocco, and that in which the Sultan can levy the heaviest taxation, which, as his troopers can easily penetrate into most parts of the valley, he fails not to do.

In the lower plain which is covered with ruins dating as far back as the period of the Roman occupation, the river attains a width of from 110 to 330 yards. The Romans, who were more provident than the Arabs, had built two bridges over the Sebvr, of which the remains are to be seen at Sidi Ali Bou Djenoūn in front of the site of old Banassa, and another at Sidi Ali Ben Ahmed at the mouth opposite Thamusida. No doubt, other bridges existed, traces of which a more searching investigation would enable one to discover. It is probable that another bridge had been built at the passage of the road of Aquæ Dacicæ at Gilda, a few miles south-west from our encampment, $9\frac{1}{4}$ miles south-east of the marabout of El Halïyn which M. Tissot thinks must have been the site of Gilda. The river is subject to sudden risings at the time of the thaws which cause it to overflow its high banks and flood the surrounding country. A mean depth of 9 feet would make it navigable during a great part of the year if the bar at the mouth were easier to cross, and if the constant hostility of the tribes along the sides of the river allowed of the establishment of a proper system of navigation, which would highly develop the agricultural as well as the commercial prosperity of the country as high as Fez—that is to say for a distance of about 205 miles. As

---

[1] The Sebou must not be mistaken for the old Sebous or Σοῦβους of the Greeks or Σουβοσ Ποταμοσ which is the W. el Sous.

matters stand now, the meagre traffic of the kingdom of Fez—between the latter town and the ports on the coast or with Tangiers—is carried on by means of camels or mules, through tracks which scarcely deserve the name of roads Thus, in winter, when a stream rises, or, at the slightest shower of rain, which turns the alluvion and clayey soil into marshes, all commercial movements are stopped, and the price of provisions in certain markets increases fourfold. The Jews drive a good trade on these occasions, for, possessing the coined wealth of the country, they can compete with advantage; but they thus contribute to perpetuate the fanatical hatred of the Mussulman against their race.

Though neglected by the Morocco government, the basin of the Sebou is, however, most important for the economy[1] of the Moghreb, and, from a strategical point of view, it is the natural communication between the Mediterranean hydrographic region of the Molouya and the coast of the Atlantic. The valley of the W. Yenahoum which stretches itself out near Téza may be considered as separating the prolongation of the Atlas from the buttresses of the chain of the Rif.

I then returned to the road which we followed when going up the river, and which enabled us to reach the spot chosen

[1] M. Ludovic de Campon seems to have studied the interesting question of a system of dykes for the Sebou formed by dams which whilst enlarging its bed would allow of the utilising of the considerable mass of rich alluvial soil which is carried away to sea.

Our observations of the width during the average risings are the following : near Fez at the bridge of the road to Oujdja, 90 yards and a few miles up the Djebel Tselfatz at the passage of Sidi el Hadj abd es Selam, 120 yards. At the Mechráá of Bel Ksiri, on the Tangiers Road before the Karia el Habbassi, 218 yards. The depth in June at the first of these places was $5\frac{1}{2}$ ft., at the second it was 10 ft. in April, and in September 2 ft.

for encamping about four o'clock. The temperature was almost unbearable,—certainly the highest since we had left Tangiers, 96° F. in open air, and 110° F. under the tent,—and gave promise of a very hot summer, as we were only in the first fortnight of June. The valley of the Sebou is a vast furnace, wherein the sunbeams are concentrated, and there is little ventilation when the west winds do not blow.

Whilst the usual deputation of servants had set out to search for the Moqaddem and the authorities of the place, I sat on the bank of the watercourse which M. Tissot has shown to have been the Krábis mentioned by Scyllax and the Phenician Sebou. Lenz gives the Arab etymology of es Seba (the lion). I own I fail to understand this, as the most ancient geographers give the river the name of Sebur or Soubour. I fancy that if Pliny had compiled his geography on the very banks of the Sebur, he would scarcely have given it the pompous appellation of Magnificus (*Amnis Subvr magnificus et navigabilis*). The epithet, I thought, was hardly appropriate, for *in winter* the river, hemmed in its narrow bed, flows along, its waters being muddy and of a dirty yellowish colour; whilst *in summer* it is so reduced that its many windings are often nothing but rivulets. But after a long journey on foot, all these historical considerations were barely sufficient to cool one, and the muddy nature of the banks and the swift current could not tempt me to plunge into its waters. Whilst my friend was attending with remarkable skill to the pitching of the tents, I mounted my horse and examined a mass of white rocks which from a distance looked very much like ruins.

Sidi Mohammed ben Ahmet, the Moqaddem of the Zaouïa, was a little old man with an intelligent face and quick eyes.

He was followed by a number of servants bearing plentiful provisions, and greeted us with much cordiality. We soon became fast friends. Whilst the preparations for supper made themselves apparent by the pleasant odour of a couscous made of the flesh of an unfortunate sheep, which had just been slain, we brought Sidi Mohammed into one of the tents where he furnished us with some details about the country. The inroads of the tribes[1] inhabiting the last buttresses of the mountains of Riata, he said, should be guarded against, for after the harvest the neighbouring country is scarcely safe. But in the excessive curiosity with which the worthy man examined our instruments and arms, he failed to satisfy us on many points. The smallest object, the merest trifle, he would seize hold of, and, willy-nilly, we had to explain its use to him. He was certainly a most amiable man of pleasant manners, but in this tropical heat rather wearisome. In all this display of arms, it is evident the Moorish blunderbusses did not cut a very great figure, and those were the only weapons known to our worthy friend. However, his face suddenly assumed an expression of triumph, and with a sly smile he declared that he was about to treat us to a wonderful sight. And the poor Moqaddem was right too, for never did we behold a more extraordinary scene than that of a "*fantasia*" (or equestrian performance) on the banks of the Sebou.

People have so often spoken of these performances and so

---

[1] The northern heights of the valley of Sebou are inhabited by the tribe of the Beni Mesgilda, and are visible under an angle of 240° from the camps which we had formed on the sides of Zegotta peak. This name Beni Mesgilda contains a repetition, for Mes in the old Lybian had the same signification as the Arab word Beni. It is curious, as has been remarked by M. Tissot, to find the same Roman name of the city, a proof that the Roman town stood at the same spot.

often praised the favourite pastime of the Arabs with such an abundance of glowing details, that I should feel I was not doing my duty to the reader for having brought him to this lonely plain on the banks of the muddy river, in order to give him merely a hackneyed description. But the whole thing was so quaint, so comic, so ludicrous, that I cannot refrain from mentioning those four horsemen each bestriding a broken-winded steed—the pride of the neighbourhood,—and performing a "fantasia" expressly designed for us. And in the same way that the cleverest Arab horsemen parade on fête days before some powerful and celebrated chieftain, so was the present grand ceremony got up in our honour! But if our pride of travellers thirsting for homage was thus gratified, I could not, nevertheless, help laughing, for it seemed to me I heard Tartarin de Tarascon when the worthy chief expatiated on the magnificence of his fantasia. Shades of Fromentin, you must have protested under the groves of the true believer's Paradise, for I wager that if you had seen our four Moors (even in the golden dust which the gallop of their "air devourers" threw up in the burning sunshine), never would you have painted those wondrous pictures full of marvellous Arabs, but merely drawn some amusing caricatures!

At length one of the horsemen made his appearance on a hill-top against the dusty and parched horizon. This Bedouin, perched on an enormous steed, with long grey hair which currycomb had never troubled (but whose emaciated and trembling frame seemed ready for the knacker), was probably aware of the sad figure he cut, for he seemed ashamed of himself. However, in order to give my narrative a tinge of picturesqueness, I should say that he looked like a savage scout of some barbarian vanguard, and his long gun, poised like a lance, completed the picture.

AN EQUESTRIAN PERFORMANCE. 173

Then came up three other heroes, who, standing in their broad stirrups and co-operating in a joint-movement, suddenly bore down upon us, charging like demons and uttering wild howls like infuriated Zulus. I must own that I felt rather anxious as some of our terrified beasts broke their tethers; my dog began howling and fled to the tent which these madmen would have upset in their wild charge had they not luckily pulled up their steeds just in time with a violent and savage tug at the bridles. The miserable animals which serve in such sports must certainly end their days with broken jaws or tendons; the Moors imagine themselves to be the best horsemen in the world, in reality, they are not worthy to sit a horse; the ass ought to be quite good enough for them.

To give an idea of the faded, tawdry garments, of the tattered and greasy rags of these fellows would be impossible without going into details of a very unpleasant description. The most ill-assorted colours seemed to be in great favour with them. One of them was dressed entirely in yellow, and with his head shaved and a plait on the top he looked like a Chinaman. But he was only an Amazigh (Berber), the disciples of Confucius having not yet made their appearance here.

After their more than abrupt arrival, the noble sons of the valley asked us, with a most gracious smile, for some powder to continue the performance. As we could not possibly spoil our metallic cartridges in order to comply with their demands, the performance was resumed without any firing. As this was not very interesting, we put a stop to it, thus abridging the sufferings of the poor plucky horses.

Our impression of the native cavalry would thus have

been very unfavourable had we not seen about the Sultan a few riders really worthy of the name.

However, it is customary to repeat that the Arab is a marvellous horseman, taking the most tender care of his steed. That may be the case in far-off regions, where the traveller who gives it as a fact does not risk being contradicted; but in the Moghreb, whether it be that the climate or some other circumstance has modified the faculties of the early conquerors, I have never seen the natives treat their horses otherwise than with the utmost negligence and brutality.[1]

The Arabian saddle is very comfortable, but to him who is established in such an arm-chair it is evident that his seat is so easy and so firm that good horsemanship becomes unnecessary. Their bit is a most cruel instrument of torture, and anyone riding in company of a native may behold him constantly tormenting his beast with it, grinding its jaws and lacerating its bleeding mouth. Their taste for mad galloping is so great that, I remember, when in the South, having seen the escort given us by the Sultan begin an equestrian performance after a forced march, when the poor nags were almost dead beat.

[1] The mode of shoeing their animals is most cruel. The shoes are very thin and almost always forged without being heated. The nails are bent so that they issue from the hoof very close to the shoe. The farriers, possessing only three sizes, all prepared in advance, the hoof is fitted to the shoe—not the shoe to the hoof. To procure this result they use an instrument in the shape of a small shovel with very sharp edges, a hammer, a knife, and rude pincers. This kind of shoeing is not durable in a country where even the best English or French steel shoes would soon be worn out on the sharp stones of the road. The native horses, with limbs covered with sores, have their hoofs frightfully mutilated, and one must not expect to find any but horse flesh much inferior to that of Algeria, and, *a fortiori*, to that of Hedjaz and Syria.

But the hours flitted by, and when we invited our friend the Moqaddem to share our supper, we had to swear by the shades of all our forefathers that neither grease nor hallouf (pork) formed part of the repast. This feast, whilst giving us an opportunity of making the gastronomic conquest of the place, gave the company a great idea of our sanctity. Whilst drinking milk and swallowing mountains of couscous, the two Roumis looked very much like men of Morocco, as Sidi Mohammed ben Ahmed remarked. At dessert he assured me again of his friendly sentiments and promised to take care of my maimed horse which I entrusted to his care; but his poor brain, in its efforts to try and understand the mysteries of European life, was quite exhausted, and the old gentleman soon fell asleep across the entrance of the tent, and there he remained till morning.

We had by this time become so accustomed to Morocco and its primitive ways, that we were almost surprised at the civilized means employed for crossing the Sebou in large boats. It is true that these skiffs are merely half-rotten, badly-built boats, and that the inhabitants of the Zaouïa go to work very awkwardly, armed with long poles with which they make an attempt at rowing. I am bound to state that we crossed the river really by the force of the current. We were lucky in being able to reach the bank safe and sound, and I was thankful for having escaped a ducking. The landing as well as the embarking takes place over stretches of mud and slime, in which you sink half-way up your legs.[1] We had made the animals swim across after having relieved them of their burdens and taken all the baggage in

[1] The place where we crossed the stream is the Mechráâ of Sidi el Hadj Abd-es-Selam. The Arab word can scarcely be rendered into our language otherwise than by ferry-passage. The transcription Mechráâ is M. Tissot's.

boats which were half full of water. This operation occupied fully two hours and a half. The Moqaddem looked on with a knowing air, and, thanks to him, the proceedings went on, if not swiftly, at least without any hindrance. The reception the worthy man gave us and his kindliness of manner were pleasing in the extreme, and after we had paid for all we had purchased, I presented him with a revolver and several cases of cartridges. He seemed deeply touched, and expressing his desire to see us again, promised to bring my new horse to Meknas. At last, mounted on a milk-white steed of a very meek disposition, I embraced Si Mohammed ben Ahmed, who, delighted to possess so superior a pistol, began firing a kind of *feu de joie* as a kind of adieu, making the bullets whiz about our ears in such a way that we thought it prudent to cut short this novel sort of God-speed and leave him to his balistic experiments.

The orographic system of the Moroccan Atlas may be connected by the Beni Mtirs Hills and the undulations of the table-land of Meknas to the Zarhoun,[1] of which the Tselfatz forms the northern end, thrown up by a geological convulsion like an enormous block commanding a view of the alluvial lands of the Sebou Valley. We had to skirt this mountain in order to go and encamp close to the Karia of a Kaïd of the Sultan, situate half-way up the Zegotta Hill top, and which keeps down the unruly Berber population of the neighbourhood. The height of the peak of Tselfatz is not very great. I nevertheless estimate it at 108

---

[1] This mountainous mass, a remarkable one, appears, however, to have been mentioned only by Ptolemy among ancient geographers.
According to the position of the Διούρ, long. 8° 30'; lat. 30°, doubtless the author of the Almageste gave this name to the chain of Zarhoun and the Tselfatz.

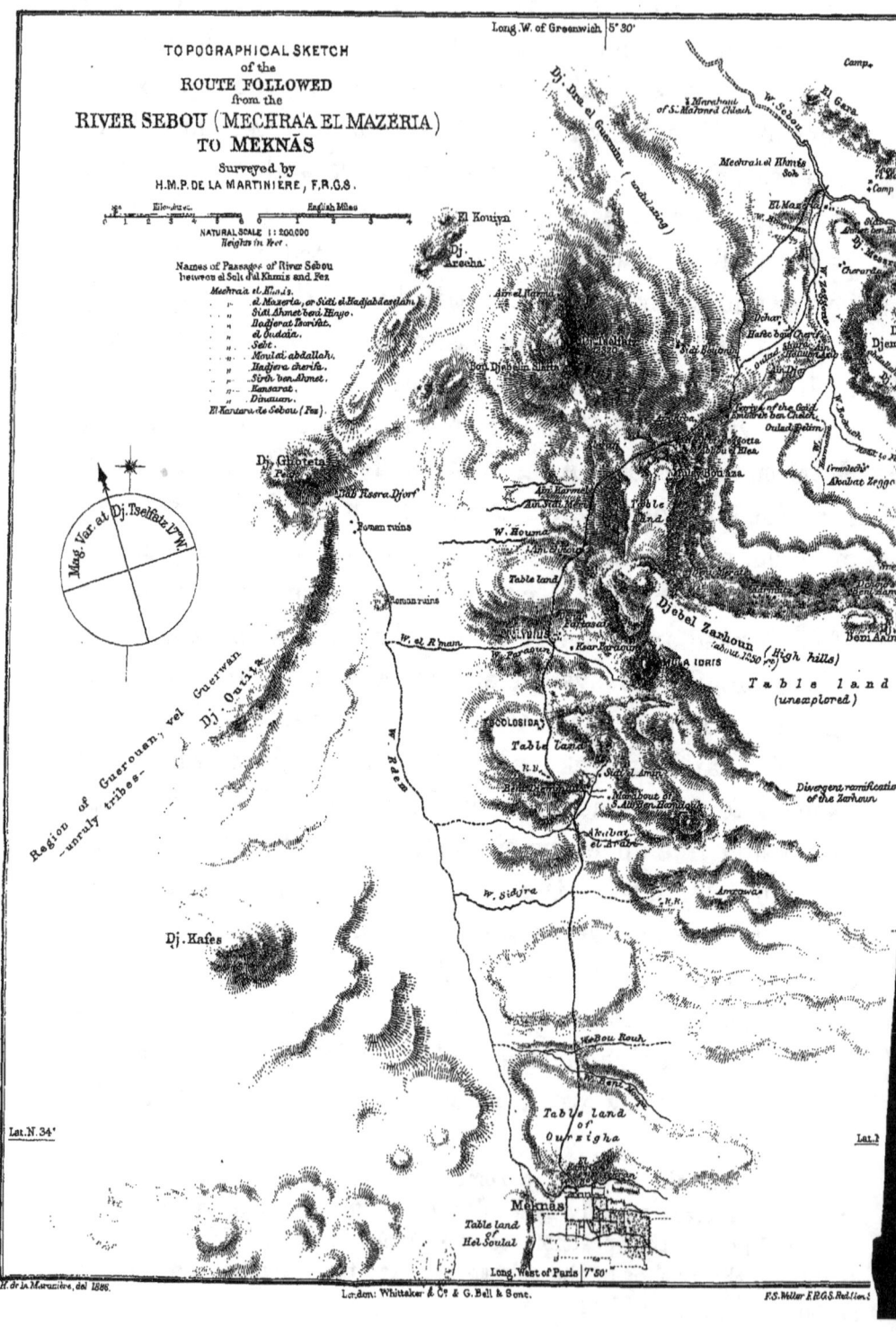

feet, and the hill top of Zegotta which we passed is about 140 feet. This orographic region not being always indicated on the maps in a satisfactory manner, can easily be depicted by means of a triangle whose apex pointing due north would represent the Tselfatz, the eastern side the Guerouans Mountains intersected in three places by deep indentations, Bab Tisra Djorf, Bab Tsiouka, and another which is without a name. The first of these breaks gives passage to the W. R'dem, the river of Meknas, and the last to the little W. of the Aïn Rebrit, both tributaries of the Sebou.

In these Guerouans heights the Dj. Outita abruptly marks the end of the valley of the river by an elevation of 1300 feet and $2\frac{1}{2}$ miles broad, whilst on the east of the other side of the triangle, the slopes of the Zarhoun project the undulations of the Dj. Torras traversed by three water courses, the largest of which is the W. Mikkés which joins the Sebou at the marabout of Si Malek ben Khadda. One may thus see that one of the chief characteristics of the Zarhoun is that it forms the side of a mountainous triangle with its plateau which has also a triangular form.

At noon we were on the road following a southerly direction, whilst we left the river [1] at about $1\frac{1}{2}$ miles on our left. The plain seemed to us in a better state of cultivation. After passing a village we immediately began to make out the prolongation of the Zarhoun and the flanks of the Beni Aamar mountains.

---

[1] This watercourse is probably the little Zegotta. I must say that from this place we could no longer see the course of the river which wound in and out of ravines and undulations which we avoided, so as to take a short cut. In my opinion, one of the disadvantages of making a survey in winter is, that you feel inclined when you visit the district for the first time, to exaggerate the importance of the smallest water-

At half-past one, after crossing a muddy brook, we came on the mountainous country, and the paths which in the plain were hardly visible on the alluvial soil where the tracks of a thousand animals crossed one another, now became quite lost among the rocks. The solar refraction which was very great in these clayey regions was very trying for all; the mules tailed off in a long file whilst slackening their pace to such an extent that we thought we should never be able to reach Karia that same day.

The musketeer provided by the Sultan began to roll his eyes in great terror, shaking at the very thought of having to pass the night in this, as he said, very dangerous place. What a tiresome fellow he was! He proved in reality to be nothing but an encumbrance, which I should willingly have given much to get rid of. I could scarcely refrain sometimes from wishing that one of the stout but much wronged Berbers should punish the Makhzen for its unjust taxation of the inhabitants in the person of this grotesque fellow his official representative.

The road was commanded by a platform of rock about 600 feet high, like an enormous wall, forming the eastern face of the Tselfatz, and above which on the hill side a small Berber dchar. The qoubbah of Sidi Bou Moutsen with a few stunted olives soon came in sight. This filled us with joy, for it became apparent that we were nearing the longed-for Karia. About four o'clock, having climbed a rocky plateau con-

course swelled out by the rains, which are particularly heavy in Morocco. We crossed some districts which were completely dried up, but which some maps give as being well watered. Thus the W. Zegotta, which has no name in M. Tissot's, would possess according to the way it is marked far more importance than it really has. From the month of June, after a rainy spring, its volume was insignificant.

sisting of granitic feldspath and of white, grey, and reddish orthose, we were shown on the far-off horizon a verdant oasis where, standing well out, was a square of white buildings, the dwelling of the Kaïd of Sidi Kacem and of the Kaïd Embarek ben Chleuch, and this we reached at half-past four.

We encamped on the side of the mountain at a spot whence we could glance along the whole valley with the Oulad Djemmah mountains facing us, and on the left the Berber villages of the Beni Aamars, Kermatz, Beni Merratz with a belt of olives; whilst at our feet were the houses of the Karia, of which the tall white walls bulged outwards; a shapeless mass of wretched huts stood against the government structure to ensure immunity from attacks of robbers in this insecure region. We had refused energetically the repeated but not very friendly offer of the Kaïd Embarek Ben Chleuch, who wished to induce us to spend the night in an interior court, full of anything but pleasant creatures. Our relations with him had, in consequence, become rather strained, and at last we ourselves made choice of an out-of-the-way site for encamping half-way up the hill and overlooking the country, but in this we were ill supported by our flurried soldier.

The view was remarkable, and the foreground of our surroundings was not less pleasant, as the younger of the feminine portion of the inhabitants had congregated at a fountain where clothes were washed. We quitted, regretfully, early next morning, this delightful spot; but we had yet to reach Meknas; the stage was a long one, and we were compelled to climb the Zarhoun in order to strike again across the old Roman road on the other side, a matter of no little toil for our animals. Here the mountain was quite barren; and the dchar placed almost at the top, and whose enclosures we skirted, had a very wretched aspect. The direct road from Tangiers to Fez passes close by, across the range, at the pass of Leggate which we left at a short distance on our left. (S.S.E.)

At an altitude of 1,300 feet, we could easily discern all the western slope and the great undulating plain which abruptly ends at the narrow ravine of Bab Tsiouka [1] opening like a veritable gate on to the plains of the Gharb, and the valley of the Sebou. We left behind us, winding down below the rocky descent (Akabat el M'ressa) leading to the dchour of the Beni Meratz, Kermatz and the Beni Aamars which we had perceived from the camps on the previous day, and whose details we could now survey.

In effect, the eastern slope of the Zarhoun forms a great curve which crosses almost at right angle the narrow plateau where we then stood, thus linking the chain of mountains to the mass of the buttresses of the Tselfatz. Now, the great dchar of the Beni Aamars with its large stone structures stands on the further and most salient extremity on a kind of cape far away in the East, and we could see at a shorter distance the Kermatz and the Beni Meratz with their fine groves of olives and oranges. These structures, which had a slight resemblance to European villages, seemed all the more pleasant to us, as, up till then, the Berber dwellings which we had seen were nothing better than heaps of earth or brown stones, presenting a most dismal appearance.

From the spot where we stood, we could survey almost the whole of this mountainous region presenting such abrupt features, similar to a geological irruption which had, all of

[1] The owl's gate, in Arabic.

a sudden, been solidified under some mysterious influence. We were at a distance of about six or seven miles from the principal peak of the Tselfatz, and the surrounding plateau presented a most dreary appearance. Though, on the one hand, the villages mentioned above with their white outlines gave an air of animation to the eastern side, on the other, the country which we were about to march through, appeared absolutely deserted.

Morocco is after all a dreary country, with large deserts; and during the winter, in the season of incessant rain and frequent fogs, it presents many features in common with Hungary or Russia. But at this time of the year, when the atmosphere is of an almost ideal purity which allows the eye to scan whole regions, these solitudes are so attractive that when the traveller has reached a town, after his curiosity has been satisfied, he longs to mount his horse again, to resume the long journeys in the hot sun.

If the top of the Zarhoun is now only a rocky and sterile table land, it was, at the time of Leo Africanus, a rich district covered with tall forests of oaks, beeches, and, above all, of olives. But these trees are only to be met now in the neighbourhood of certain Berber dchour of the eastern valley, on some of the southern stretches which stand opposite the plateau of Meknas, and in the gorge of Muley Idris. The celebrated traveller[1] and renegade, whom we can trust on this occasion since he was educated at Fez, describes rather minutely the whole of the region where, about the year 1540, it would have been a matter of difficulty to

[1] It is nevertheless worthy of notice that, in spite of the errors of copyists which possibly distorted the original text, Leo fell into a serious error on the geographical position and the respective distances of Volubilis (Oualily, Goualili), as will be seen hereafter.

discover an inch of untilled ground. Marmol, moreover, informs us that the country was full of lions, and he volunteers much childish advice for the benefit of travellers proceeding to the Wednesday fair of "Cazar Faraoun." Alack and alas! the country is now so bereft of inhabitants, both men and beasts, that "the king of the forest" has forsaken it a long time ago, and, to our great regret, we had no occasion to profit by the advice of the Spanish geographer. In ancient times, it even appears that the Sultans of Fez, when in quest of violent excitement, had some lion fights, the animals employed being those of Zarhoun renowned for their ferocity. These fights took place like the modern Spanish bull fights.

This mountainous mass is of considerable strategic importance, of which the Romans were fully aware, as one of their great roads[1] skirted the western slope and led to the town of Volubilis and then to the post of Tocolosida.

[1] This road led directly from Tingis la Colonia IVLIA TRADVCTA to OPPIDUM NOVUM (now el Ksar el Kebir) in a direction in conformity with the geological features of the ground, for, at the present day, the course is very nearly the same as that followed by caravans and travellers. At a certain point, the road branched off at the post of AD MERCVRI, and led in a western direction to the Colonia IVLIA CONSTANTIA ZILIS (now Alzila), of TABERNAE (Lella Djilaliya), of LIXVS (opposite El Araïsh), of BANASSA (on the Sebou at Sidi Ali Bou Djenoun); to THAMVSIDA (on the Sebou at Sidi Ali Ben Ahmed); and, lastly, to the SALA COLONIA (now Salé). But South of El Ksar, in the direction of the Roman way, which opened into Volubilis and Tocolosida, is not well known, as M. Tissot, unfortunately, had not time to survey the whole of the topography as he had done in the case of the regions on the coast. With the exception of Aïn Kibrit (Tissot), or Aïn Si' Yúsuf (Trotter), the Roman Aquae Dacicæ, at Volubilis, the sketch can now only be considered as hypothetic. We are acquainted with the probable site of the towns of Tremvlae (Basra), of Gilda (Sidi el Haniyn on the Sebou) through which the road passes, but we have no reliable information of the position of Vopiscianae, of

We followed exactly the end of this road, as far as the hill of El Arabi. The road from Tangiers to Meknas is partly commanded by these heights, and the same may be said as regards the ways of communication from Fez to Meknas. As for the capital of the kingdom of Fez, it is connected with the coast or the Straits only by the narrow valley of the W. Mikkés and by the pass of Zeggota. These northern roads which converge near the marabout of Sidi Gueddar on the right of the W. R'dem might be blocked at the narrow passes of the Dj. Outita, which we perceived from the plateau of Zarhoun, for these paths, used since the time of the Romans, are the only ones on which it is safe to venture in winter, or even at any time, on account of the turbulent propensities of the inhabitants. Finally, though the map of Morocco is still a thing of the future, and the task of drawing it up is a most arduous one by reason of the scanty stock of information at one's

Mergo and Gontiana, to mention only these three points of the medial line of Tingitane Mauritania. No doubt, the ancient geography of the country will be once more restored to its former state when archæologic explorations have completed our store of information in that respect. It is to be hoped that this result will be attained speedily—as the daily destruction of ruins, put to use by the inhabitants for the construction of their houses, or merely for the raising of walls—makes the undertaking more and more arduous on account of the despersion of the Roman remains. To quote one instance: the natives from the plain of Sebou, where no limestone is to be met with for miles and miles round, come here to provide themselves with stones, destroying all that remains of inscriptions, carvings, or interesting débris, whose gradual disappearance may be noted from year to year.

In his map of Roman "itinéraires" published in 1844, Colonel Lapie gives a sketch of the roads which probably connected the Tingitane Mauritania with the Cæsarian Mauritania and crossed the Rifan mass. It is useless to express any opinion on his surmises, since no geographical explorations in the region beyond the Rif, either in 1844 or at the present time, have made it possible to study the question.

disposal and the conflicting versions of explorers, it may be, however, safely asserted that the list of roads accessible for European travellers is indeed a very limited one.

The old Roman way is still recognisable through the debris of carved stones which we observed there. At about a quarter past one o'clock, after crossing the tiny W. Houma, we came up to a small spring in the cool shade of an old fig tree, where a few blocks of stones and some flag-stones half hidden under the tall grass formed a picturesque little picture. These remains of buildings which we discovered while searching about, show with what care the smallest streamlet of water—an invaluable boon in this country—was treasured up in olden times. But now this fountain, the Aïn Chkour of the Arabs, is left utterly uncared for; the cattle alone know the path leading to it, and on our arrival, an owl (who gave low expressions of his displeasure at being disturbed), was the only occupant of the secluded spot.

This is not the only spring in the district, since our mules, which shortly made their appearance, had slaked their thirst at the Aïn Taslat above which we had passed in following the mountain ridge.

The country was as monotonous in the plain as on the plateau. We skirted the Zarhoun whose dismal and barren outline still accompanied us. Of the forty large villages scattered about this mountain of which Marmol extols the splendour, very few traces indeed remain, and the population appears scanty. In the plain there is little cultivation, and the Arab douars do not pretend to anything like an air of prosperity. This would, besides, prove dangerous in the vicinity of an imperial residence.

At last, at two o'clock, we were in view of Muley

Idris,[1] the city blessed by all the Idriside Chorfas, when the qoubbah of the founder of the first Sherifian monarchy is the most venerated spot in all Morocco after Moghreb, and which no Christian or Jew has ever tainted with his presence.[2]

It was here that Idris, attracted by the beauty of the site, came to settle down after having induced the nations of Barbary to embrace the cause of Islam. He formed the project of rebuilding the Roman town whose ruins were, and still are scattered about the neighbourhood. His praiseworthy project was not however to be carried out, for the apostle of Mohammed died meanwhile, in rather inglorious circumstances, from poison or indigestion. Opinions are at variance on this point, but it may be thought that the holy man's digestive powers were not greater than the respect and love of his faithful disciples. Whatever the case may be, the body of Idris rests in a Zaouïa where every year thousands of Chorfa come as to a shrine. After the sudden death of Idris, his son (who does not seem to have been very proficient in the science of topography) abandoned the project, and proceeded to lay the foundations of Fez in the

---

[1] Captain D. E. Bonelli calls it Zerhon—6000 inhabitants—the little W. Faraoún is called the Muley Idris by the same explorer.

[2] In spite of the readiness with which G. Rohlfs professed the Mussulman faith, the traveller dared not enter the town, and latterly Dr. O. Lenz imitated his fellow-countryman's prudent reserve. In 1880, Captain P. D. Trotter, then a member of a diplomatic mission, risked the undertaking, but when he had reached the lower part of the high street, this gentleman was compelled to cut short his work of exploration, on account of the most threatening attitude of a crowd of Chorfas armed with muskets, who had hastened up to stop the progress of the Roumi. Captain Trotter's official character forbade him to raise any diplomatic complication and he was regretfully compelled to retrace his steps without having visited a place so curious and so fanatical.

funnel-like valley where the great town is smothered in heat and damp.

The view you obtain of Muley Idris, lying at the bottom of this wild and steep gorge [1] concealed under fine olive groves, is a most charming one, but unfortunately we were fain to be satisfied with gazing on it through our glasses, and to express our regret that such a beautiful spot should be the abode of such ferocious fanatics.

In this wild, hillock-dotted plain, which separated us from the mountain, we could discern the summit of the Basilica and triumphal arch of Volubilis, towering over a chaotic mass of broken stones, of shapeless blocks lying confusedly, and overthrown more by Moroccan Vandalism than by time. We were compelled to dismount in order to make our way over the broken pillars and enormous flagstones forming quaint heaps here and there, and to clamber up to the higher part of the plateau.

The site [2] of the Roman city occupies the undulating por-

[1] The Zarhoun consists here of a range with radiating branches. Two principal ones form a hollow at the bottom of which a rocky and barren hillock serves as a base for Muley Idris suspended, as it were, in the midst of verdure.

From this mountain gorge there seems to issue a system of valleys which, as already supposed by Captain (now Colonel) Trotter, must effect its connection with the eastern slope near the dchar of the Beni Aamars, or near the W. Mikkès.

[2] The Arab name of Oualily or Gualili quoted by Leo Africanus has for a long time been identified with the geographical position of Volubilis. Gräberg de Hemsö, Lapie, Maunert, and many others seem to have vied in making the most incorrect surmises, all based, as shown by M. Tissot, on Pliny's faulty indications, and on a most extraordinary mistake of Leo Africanus, who though brought up at Fez, curiously enough, says the site of these ruins is on the bank of the Sebu at a distance of thirty-five miles from Banassa, thus identifying it with Mamora in the neighbourhood of Mehdia. To add to the confusion, we may state that El Bekri gives Tangiers the name of Oulîli, which he asserts is of Berber origin.

tions of one of the buttresses of the Zarhoun and the natural defences consisted of a couple of ravines west and east, with the W. Faräoún in the south east. Three gates are still recognizable, and we perceive the remains of the outer walls of a round tower, whilst we have to judge of the shape of the fortification by the position of the stones which lie scattered about. Following the line formed by these stones we reach the remains of a bridge.

The scenery, with this chaos of debris, the evidences of past civilization in the now deserted country, is most impressive, and quite different from the fanatical Muley Idris with its narrow-minded inhabitants. Those grand forsaken ruins rise up, as if to attest the glorious past of that Roman race, so courageous, so enterprising, but whose traces unfortunately disappear day by day from the Tingitane.

It is only a few years ago that all doubts have been dispelled regarding the principal town of Mauritania. S.

Volubilis is called thus by Mela; Pliny terms it Volubile Oppidum; and Ptolemy, Ούολουβιλίς. The etymological analogy of appellation with Gualili is obvious. The obscurity concerning the town was all the greater before M. Tissot's observations, because Leo Africanus gives the village of Muley Idris the name of Gualili, assigning it a position at a distance of eight miles from Ksar Faräoún—a glaring error, since Muley Idris and Ksar Faräoún are only one and a-half miles apart, and since Muley Idris cannot be identified with any other Roman settlement, as several Thalba of Meknas who had visited the place told us no ruins were to be seen there.

The name of Ksar Pharaoun or Faräoún led astray many geographers who made remarks on the subject without having ever visited these parts, nor the ruins which they asserted to be those of a town existing at the time of the famous Egyptian dynasty. They are using a far-fetched origin for the word, since the name of the squill, which grows in great quantity in Northern Africa, is in Arabic Bsol Faräoún or Pharao's onion. It can therefore be surmised that this plant, which is so common on the plateau of Zarhoun, gave its name to a small unimportant dchar.

Windus proceeding to the Court of Meknas in 1720 to buy off some English prisoners, was the first to give a sketch of the triumphal arch of Volubilis, but no complete description was produced till 1874 by M. Tissot.

The custom of seeking among ruins for materials wherewith to errect their buildings is quite in keeping with the lazy habits of the Moors, and consequently they pillaged unfortunate Volubilis or Muley Israel in order to provide the palaces of Meknas with the necessary ornaments. The triumphal arch is now more than half in ruins. When we saw it last there only remained the square pillars and foundation-stone. The dispersion of the different parts of the monument since Windus made a sketch of it when the arch was yet in a comparatively perfect state, has caused the loss of two inscriptions of which he made a record. M. Tissot, notwithstanding, succeeded in finding the names of Caracalla and Julia Domna in whose honour the structure had been built. The inscriptions record the nationality of the *municipium* who erected the monument and the name of Germanicus is also mentioned, so that M. Tissot has been enabled to find the site of Volubilis and the date of the building of the arch,[1] posterior to 213.

[1] This learned and clever finding has been fully confirmed by the study of the inscription on the memorial stone of G. Cœcilius Domitianus which Sir J. D. Hay had already copied in 1842, but which escaped the notice of Windus and of the baron St. Augustine, and of which Tissot, I believe, gave for the first time a fac-simile in 1874. This inscription was found on the edge of the hillock on which stood the basilica, and it is perhaps the most important memorial existing of the Roman occupation in the Tingitane.

On comparing the inscription on the arch of Volubilis with those of the arch at Djemila erected also in honour of the blood-thirsty Domitian and his mother, we may come to the conclusion that the two monuments were built almost at the same time, most probably on the

At a distance of about one hundred paces from these ruins, stand more important and less defaced remains of the sole monument of the Roman town which local depredations have not caused to disappear. It must have been a fine piece of architecture built on a height whence you may scan part of the plain. Having a good view of all the ruins, it is easy, from that spot, to form an idea of the topography of the city. The structure seems to have occupied a space of the following dimensions, 48 yards measured from north to south, 27 yards from west to east. The west façade though much decayed is the only one which allows us to judge of the whole for an arcade, as both extremities of this façade and part of the corresponding inner portions are still standing. As for the middle part its remains are strewn on the ground, and the symmetrical order in which they lie allows of the hypothesis of the arch having been destroyed by an earthquake, probably the very one mentioned by Ali Bey which had such dire effect in the south of Spain and the north of Barbary.

Judging from the external ornaments, and the number and arrangement of the columns, pillars, and capitals which still remain, this vast building must have been a temple or rather a basilica. This fact being admitted, it is easy to make out the general plan of the *cella* and of the two *pronaos*, and the upper gallery whence idle people could view the business transactions below without hindering them—as we learn from complete archæological works published in Europe. Then the market was held on the lower

occasion of a journey of Caracalla in Africa. The belief may be further strengthened by the inscription of "Cinculitánia Colonia," in which he is designated as proconsul, and which M. Tissot thought right to insert in the inscription of Volubilis.

platform of the façade. Of all this, nothing unhappily remains, as the earthen columns must have been carried away before the others by Moorish architects, and a heap of débris is all that is left of the rest of the building. It is just barely possible to distinguish among these a few capitals of very simple workmanship.

The little W. Faräoún[1] which has its source in the Zarhoun at the springs of Aïn Chaneh and then effects its junction with the W. R'dem[2] (a tributary of the Sebou) separated the town from one of the suburbs whose extensive but much decayed ruins may still be seen on the left bank. A heap of debris, beyond a ravine which leads to the brook, seems to bear out the supposition that part of the suburbs extended as far as this spot. There are also a few traces of the bridge which connected the city with the suburbs. The remains of a similar structure which still existed in 1842 and which the Consul M. D. Hay alluded to in a note, have now disappeared. We were unable to find any signs of these remains, but we saw very distinct evidences of a large cistern, the destruction of which has brought to light a layer of fine cement.

We skirted the brook where Caracalla's horses had probably quenched their thirst. Our plucky beasts drank greedily for they were hot and parched after their exertions in winding in and out of the maze of ruins. The country on either side had a most picturesque aspect which was heightened by a number of oleanders growing between the

---

[1] The W. Faräoún, in its lower course, bears the name of W. el R'man, and skirts a great and rich valley whose slopes are well cultivated and covered with *douars* or villages.

[2] W. R'dem or Rdoum, River of the Ruins in Arabic.

stones with which the valley was studded, and we were loath to quit so attractive a spot.[1]

We soon came up with the train of mules, and the soldier, uneasy at our protracted stay in so fanatical a district, but becoming a little more bellicose as he drew nearer to the head quarters of his master, the Sultan, was already thinking of organizing a relief expedition with the aid of the cook and the attendants, but these brave men regained their composure when we made our appearance.

Resuming our journey, we came upon some flagstones nearly hidden by the tall grass near a barley field. It was necessary to be pretty well acquainted with the geography of Mauritania Tingitane, and to know that the Roman road was probably interrupted at that spot, to come to the conclusion that these humble remains must have been those of the advanced post [2] of the Romans, that is of Tocolosida.

---

[1] In the neighbourhood of a small dchar at a short distance from Fartassa, on the heights in front of Muley Idris, may still be seen, we were told, large quarries which provided the Romans with the fine hard, white stone which they used in the building of Volubilis.

[2] It was thought that the Roman occupation extended, in the interior, in a south easterly direction, farther than the post of Tocolosida, because no geographer of the Middle Ages speaks of any traces existing beyond this mountainous district. But there has been no corroboration of this surmise, by reason of the scanty knowledge of the country possessed by modern explorers.

All the region of Zarhoun, which forms a kind of advanced defences whose strategical importance we pointed out, must have been used by the Romans for the establishment of other military posts. An exploration of the whole surface of the plateau which now is known only by name to European travellers will no doubt result in the discovery of new traces of the Roman occupation.

Leo Africanus mentions Gualili as being on the top of the mountain, also the Palace of Pharao eight miles distant from this town, and he speaks also of Pietra Rossa and Maghilla. The first of these two towns is unknown to us, and as for the other, if we identify it with the

The choice of the strategical position commanding the whole plateau of Meknas had been most judicious, and even now, commanding, as it does, the communications of this town with the north, and west—since the road of Zemmours to Rabatt is impassable—an invader or an enemy could easily threaten the outlying country in the vicinity of the Imperial residence. In consequence of the facilities resulting from the proximity of the Imperial residence to the site of Tocolosida, the Moors have been enabled to make excursions here and have removed everything that was worth taking, leaving nothing standing among the ruins.

From the extremity of the plateau of Zarhoun [1] we had a view of the whole plain, on the right the mountainous country of the Guerouans with the high peak Kafés protecting an elongated hillock towards the N.E., on which Meknas is built, and we could already discern the grand but vague outline of the city; further on in the west the indomitable Zemmours, and still further in the south the lofty proud peak of the Beni Mtirs, the immediate buttresses of the prolongation of the Atlas mountains, finally in the east the denuded Zarhoun, whose sides now rough and steep, now rounded off into mounds, slope down as far as the plains of Fez.

At about four o'clock, under a fierce sun, and through a fine and hot dust, we rode swiftly down the hill of El Arabi

---

Maghaïla of Edrisi, we may consider its remains as being those on the road of Meknas to Fez, near the douar of Madhuma. Madhúm in Arabic signifies ruins.

[1] The geological nature of the Zarhoun seems complicated. In certain spots regular layers of Jurassic formation appear in very distinct tiers, whilst the northern buttresses which border the Tselfatz belong to tertiary formations hardened here and there into thick layers of sandstones. The upper parts are generally formed of miocene.

at seven miles distance from Meknas. In spite of the intense heat, we were in high spirits at the prospect of at last reaching our goal. As we proceeded, going at a good pace, we saw on the roadside a few stone columns, which had been abandoned by the slaves, who, about two centuries ago, were conveying them from Volubilis to Meknas, when they heard of the death of their master, the powerful, bloodthirsty, and much dreaded Muley Ismaïl.

The incline grew steeper, and the track became wider as we approached the town, whilst we often passed some government messengers, who, mounted on swift horses, were the bearers of despatches from the Sultan to some governors or Kaïds in the northern provinces of the Empire, perhaps with a command to share with His Majesty the profits of their lucrative offices, non-compliance with which would be met with disagreeable but efficient proceedings on the part of His Majesty.

We came across several brooks, but two only were not dried up. Bridges were thrown over them, a fact of rare occurrence in this country, and these bridges were in a good state of repair. This may be explained by their proximity to the residence of a sovereign, who, it is well known, has often to parade his artillery in order to impress his faithful subjects by a show of power, the said subjects being sometimes unreasonable enough to resist his arguments.

Meanwhile, however, passers-by became more numerous, and we passed women and children bearing to market the scanty produce of their gardens, also charcoal burners—a hateful race who pursue the silly work of destroying the woods—driving some lean asses laden with the produce of their manufacture. The proximity of the Imperial residence does not seem to benefit these poor people, for all of them presented a wretched appearance, and had scarcely enough rags on them to cover their nakedness. The women, especially, were anything but pleasant to look upon, so squalid and poverty-stricken did they appear, and at the same time heavily laden like mere beasts of burden. We threw a few *flouss* to these poor wretches who were proceeding at a kind of jog-trot on the hard road, the sharp stones of which made our horses stumble.

At length, from the top of the undulation which, in the north, commands the little W. Bou Rouh, Meknas burst into view, with its ranges of majestic minarets and numerous buildings. The gardens which covered the slopes and the bottoms of the ravines, appeared to be blended in an ocean of verdure and formed a most delightful scene. With its thousands of white buildings glistening in the fierce sun, and endless palace walls extending as far as the horizon in the background, Meknas bore the appearance of a city of great magnitude.

The grand looking ramparts are built of a kind of mud baked and gilded for centuries by the hot sun, and they wind round the city in snake-like folds. Meknas is not so extensive as Fez in point of the number of buildings, but its appearance and situation are far superior, since the one stands on a picturesque plateau, whilst the other is only seen by the traveller as he arrives at the very gates, the city being completely encircled by a range of heights.

The sun was slowly sinking on the copper-tinted horizon when, after having left behind us the last undulations of the plateau of el Hamrïa, through which flows the W. Bou Fekran, we crossed a fine bridge of a single arch, the work of Spanish renegades of the time of Sidi Mohammed. Then we followed a broad road bordered by some beautiful, leafy gardens which we appreciated the more as, since we left Wazzan, we had been entirely without shade. Some gigantic reeds, such as I had never before beheld, grew all around, and through these novel hedges, which waved gently in the soft evening breeze, came forth the perfume of hundreds of orange trees and pomegranates and groves of laurel; whilst a delicious coolness gave compensation for the heat we had endured during five days' journey through a hot and barren country.

But we were compelled to tear ourselves from these delights in order to resume our journey and reach the atrociously barren country which extends in front of the gates of the town. Here was much activity, as our arrival coincided with the conclusion of a fair held in the midst of an indescribable mass of refuse, as if purposely accumulated to stew in a thermometer standing at 120° F. The stench was frightful. But in Morocco a traveller must get used to such unpleasant details, and his sense of smell must get blunted if he would cross without nausea the belt of carrion surrounding every town, which nevertheless proves a source of great delight to prowling dogs and numerous wild animals.

As we had left our servants behind, the crowd, seeing us unattended, gazed curiously at us as we passed through a large monumental gate. We then found ourselves on an extensive boulevard with sun-scorched trees where dwelt a number of blacksmiths, and where the crowd was still thicker. We knew not which way to turn in order to find the house which had been retained for us. Our embarrassment became great, and, moreover, we knew that in our travel-stained garments, tired as we were with our long journey, our appearance could have been none of the best. But chance came to our succour in the form of a worthy Spanish renegade who, guessing the cause of our embarrassment, relieved it by taking us to the governor's dwelling through a long lane whose calm and silence contrasted strangely with the activity which we had so recently witnessed. The governor was a good-natured African who had been apprised of our arrival, and who seemed to understand that we stood in much need of repose, for, without any delay, he sent us with an escort of five soldiers to the house which his Majesty had been pleased to assign as a residence.

The entrance was extremely dark, and the passage which we had to follow was covered with an uninviting layer of filth. But, as the road to Paradise is said to be edged with thorns, so this passage opened into a small but very fine palace. We were able to keep our horses close at hand as there was a stable in the courtyard—a thing of rare occurrence in Morocco—and to our great joy, we discovered we were located close to the officers of the French military mission whose hospitable reception and obliging and most friendly treatment of us proved very gratifying during our sojourn.

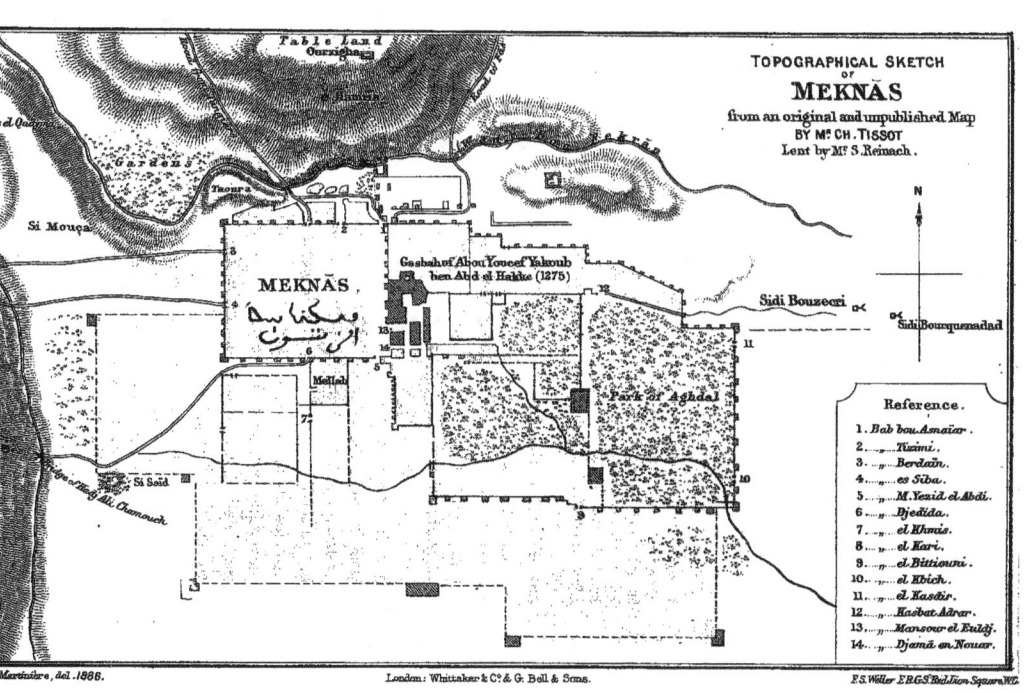

CHAPTER XI.

A Glance at the Origin and Historical Development of the City of Meknas—The Reign of the Sultan Muley Ismaïl, and the works undertaken by him—Treaties with the English—Antiquity of Relations with France—Want of Prosperity in Meknas—Insecurity of the Neighbourhood in the South—The Direct and Indirect Line of Communication between Meknas and the Atlantic littoral.

THOUGH Marakesch is the favourite residence of the Sultan in the South, Meknas is *the* town in Barbary in which Muley Hassan takes most delight when not traversing the Moghreb, in order to enforce, by royal military expeditions, his precarious authority over tribes always in revolt.[1]

Meknas, "the City of Olives," as it is described in the official documents of the Makhzen, is, in point of fact, a typical royal residence. The population, of comparatively small account in point of numbers (barely 20,000 souls), and devoid of all life, except that derived from the sojourn of the Court, exhibits a servility of character unknown in Fez, for example, where, on the death of one Sultan a rival has always been brought forward in opposition to the new

---

[1] The residences of the Sultan are Marakesch, Meknas, Fez; but the capital proper and the seat of Government being with the headquarters of his army. Rabatt, however, must also be mentioned, though the Sultan never resides there, and only uses it when on the march. The tower of Al Mansour is also the geographical key of the Sheriflan power in the Tingitane.

Emperor. Fezzians would think themselves lacking all loyalty if, on each change of Sovereign, they did not compel the new one to make some sort of military parade on entering the City of Idris the Young. Meknas, on the contrary, is submissive, and, in consequence, enjoys an amiable reputation as being the one town in the Moghreb most given up to pleasure and where woman is looked upon as an angel of grace and beauty!

Has the "City of Olives" always been what she now is? —without popular movements, or commerce, and occupying altogether so disproportionate an area that even the Court during its sojourn is unable wholly to animate it! Doubt is permissible when wandering, in imagination, through the wide corridors, the palatial courts now half in ruins, the posterns, and the noble porticos, brilliant with glazed azulejos, to which the sun of centuries has given an incomparable artistic stamp.

It is difficult to account off-hand for the complex topography of this pile of imperial structures, in which an absence of plan is the dominant feature. It would be impossible to attempt a detailed description, especially as certain portions are inaccessible during the Sultan's residence. This was the case at the time of our visit.

The works commenced by one Sherif are rarely completed, for the very good reason that death generally interrupts them. Perseverance is a virtue very little known in this happy land, and history furnishes many examples of the partiality of Arabs to a disturbed government. Therefore, in such a country, it is perhaps easy to understand the confused condition of a residence like the one at Meknas, where the Sovereign never stays more than five or six months in a couple of years.

The Spaniards have Europeanised the Arabic, or rather Berber form of Meknasa or Meknas, into Mequinez. The corruption now seems to be generally, though erroneously, used, for the appellation Meknaças was always of great note among the Berber nationalities. The Meknaças or Miknaças were known from the remotest times as a people of the greatest importance in the northern portion of the Barbary States. They occupied the region adjoining the towering heights of Mount Atlas and the eastern basin of the Molouïa, where indeed Roman historians and geographers seem to have located them. Even now-a-days the Miknaças are to be met with in the neighbourhood of Tlemcen on the approaches of the Aurés in the Zab, not far from Biskra and in fact in the very heart of the Algerian provinces.[1]

This renowned tribe must also be regarded as the founders of the present centre of population in the Oasis of Tafilalt. The learned researches of Walckenær, d'Avezac, and of Renou have identified the ancient Sidjilmasa[2] with the focus of Morisco influence at Chorfa Filali,[3] in other words, with the group of oases of which that at Abou Aam is the most important.

Returning, however, from a consideration of the question of the limits of the dispersion of this tribe, one learns, on consulting Ibn-Khaldoum, that there existed two towns[4]

---

[1] Consult on this subject Al Yacoub who wrote in the beginning of the 10th century, El-Bekri and Edrisi.

[2] One of the most conclusive arguments in favour of this question of identity which has engrossed the attention of savants is the work of "Aboulqâsem ben Ahmed Ezziâni," in which the names Tafilalet and Sidjilmasa are employed interchangeably by the author.

[3] Filal in Arabia, from whence came the ancestors of Muley Ali the Sherif-founder of the present dynasty, appears in the Berber Tafilelt or Tafilalet of Arabic authors.

[4] In the year 310 (922 A.D.) the Emir El Hassen secretly entered

named Meknas, or Miknaça, of which the one now under consideration was founded opposite the Zarhoun, and the other in the district in which rises the W. Yenahoum.[1]

The historical and geographical records cited by Leo Africanus and Marmol[2] possess but little value; more reliance may, however, be placed on the topographical description given by Edrisi on the subject of the plateau of Meknas, for some insight into the origin of the town.

It appears certain that when an offshoot of the Miknaças established themselves on this plateau they founded there several hamlets of which the Arabian geographer has given us a faithful account, his record showing an accuracy of detail little known in his day (1099-1164). The principal town on the plateau was named Tâgdert or Taguedart, but the appellation Meknas, of Berber origin, was also applied to it.

The situation of the plateau of El Hamria, opposite to the Zarhoun, and lying in the great geological depression between it and the mountains of Beni Mtirs has, without doubt, fostered the settlement of agricultural peoples by reason of the never-failing streams which water this favoured district. The original settlements were quickly multiplied; after Tacadart arose the neighbouring town of Beni-Ziad,

---

Fez .... caused himself to be proclaimed Sultan .... extended his rule over the towns of Louata (?), Sefra (Saforou?), Mediouna (Mehdoum), *the two Mekennés. Hist. des Berbères, trad. du Baron de Slane. Tome IV. p. 36.*

[1] M. d'Avezac identified Miknaça with the town of Théza, but our own information, which is confirmed by the statements of M. de Campou ("Un Empire qui Croule," Paris 1 vol. in 16. 1886) fixes the position of Théza some miles from the small town in question.

[2] Marmol identifies the town with the ancient "Gilda," but this supposition is from all points inadmissible, as we have already seen the probable position of the town mentioned in the itineraries of Autoninus. In all likelihood it is the same city as Ptolemy's "Silda."

flourishing and populous, possessing baths and buildings of note, the streets in the time of the Moravides being irrigated by numerous streams of running water.

These towns were each equidistant, by about one-fourth of a mile, from a third, Beni Tawra by name, which could likewise boast of a flourishing past. The name of its site is still preserved; it is situated at the N.W. angle of the walls of Meknas, on the rising ground which overlooks the W. Bou Fekran. There were also two other settlements between Tawra and Beni Ziad; one Alqaçar, the Castle, was situated on the road from Tacadart to Souk el Kadymé, the ancient market being at a distance of two arrow flights therefrom. This the Moravides surrounded with walls. The other was to the east of the latter, and bore the name of Beni a Touch; from thence, by following the course of a stream, the settlement of the Beni Bernous, a tribe dependent on the Miknaças, was reached. Edrisi further speaks of the Castle of Abou Mouça, to the north of which is found the old market where the Miknaças assembled every Thursday. The principal tribes of this district were the Beni Saïd and the Benou Mouça.

In all these localities only the name of the market has survived. This appears always to have been held at the same spot, a little to the north on the plateau Hel Soulal. As to the name Mouça, we came across it in the W. Beni Mouça, a small tributary of the Bou-Rouh, which is traversed when arriving at Meknas from the north. It is apparent, however, that but few vestiges could have survived. Owing to the works undertaken during the reign of Muley Ismaïl, the various centres of population were forced to coalesce, in a word, they became merged in the new and extensive improvements. This prince may, therefore, be regarded as the true founder of Meknas, which indeed he developed to such an extent as to make it almost unrecognisable, causing it to stand out with conspicuous lustre during his reign, contemporaneous with that of Louis XIV. Under the preceding dynasties, however, Meknas, as the seat of the Miknaça Emirs, who had reigned at Fez before the Maghraoua, elicited little remark in Arabic records.

About 1063, the inhabitants demanded a governor of Youssouf Ibn Tachefin, the real founder of the dynasty of the Almoravides. Then is recorded a journey made by Ibn Toumert, when Othman at the head of the Beni Merin revolted against the effeminate Youssouf [1] Mestancer (of the Almohades dynasty), compelling Fez and Meknas to pay him tribute.

From the earliest times the possession of Meknas has been indispensable to the rulers of the Moghreb, inasmuch as it is the key of the topographical situation as regards the Atlantic littoral, and without which communication therewith could be easily interrupted. This explains why Meknas has been besieged so often. Leo Africanus even mentions a blockade lasting seven years sustained against the Sultans of Fez. The author of the "Garden of Folios"[2] places the event 545 (A.D. 1150). In this year Meknas was carried by assault by the Almohades after a seven years' siege. They massacred the inhabitants, plundered the treasure, and invaded the harems.

---

[1] This Youssouf was the son of Mohammed en Nacer, who was defeated in the great battle of Navas de Tolosa.

[2] Roudh el Kartas, literally Garden of Folios, written at the Court of Fay in 1326 concerning the authenticated notes and documents of the Imaun Abou Mohammed Salah ben Abd el-Halim of Grenada. Many translations have been made, the most recent being by M. Beaumier. Paris, 1860.

It was at this period that ancient Meknas was abandoned, and the town of this name, as known to-day, built by the conquerors.

I quote here the text of the Arabic author. It will be seen that a divergence of opinion exists between him and Edrisi already cited. The performances in a "fantasia" brought dire misfortune to Muley Rechid, a prince who perished miserably at Marakesch (Morocco) on the second day of the fêtes of Aïd el Kebir held in the park of El Mesreb. His brother, Muley Ismaïl es Seman (the Fat), who was then Governor of Meknas, learned the news on the 3d April, 1673, and after crushing the revolt of Mohammed and Hadj Ebn-Abdallah in the country of the Chaouias towards the north, he returned to Meknas to busy himself with the construction of numerous palaces. This city, to the seductions of which he was very partial, had been given to him as an appanage by his brother the Sultan.[1] From the time of his accession to power he occupied himself in demolishing the houses adjoining the Kasbah, forcing the inhabitants to remove the debris.[2] All the eastern part of the town was completely destroyed, the site serving to develop the ancient Kasbah;[3] and in order to open up the approaches, the ramparts were also reconstructed, the new enclosure round about the Kasbah being at the same time isolated.

Detailed as this historical digression may appear, it is unavoidable, for the history of the development of Meknas is very closely interwoven with the annals of Muley Ismaïl.

[1] "Relation de la Captivité du Sr. Mouette," 1 vol. in 12mo. Paris, MDCLXXXIII.

[2] [Aboulqâsem Ben Ahmed Ezziâni.]

[3] The Kasbah thus became the most important citadel in Morocco. Its walls, built $\frac{2}{3}$ of sand and $\frac{1}{3}$ of lime, have in certain places a thickness of 27 feet. See Mouette, already quoted.

Some mention of the works and doings of this most illustrious prince of the present Filali[1] Sherif dynasty is, therefore, necessary.

Ever since Islam, driven into a corner of the Moghreb in its conflict with Christian powers, seemed to have lost all remembrance of the glories[2] of the Almoravides when the Koran reigned over Iberia, and when Youssouf ibn Tachefin, founder of the city of Morocco, and conqueror of Alfonso at Badajos, substituted the Crescent for Fetichism even in the extreme limits of the Sahara; or of the later days, when Abd-el-Moumen of the Almohades[3] took by conquest from the Normans the whole of the Tunisian coast, 1159, fortifying Gibraltar on his return, no power in this unassuming present age seems to have equalled the reign of Muley Ismaïl, who revived in a measure the exploits of the Sherif Ahmet el Mansour, sending his nephew, Muley Ahmed, to subdue that part of Sous which, since the death of el Mansour, had asserted its independence.

To continue, we see in Ismaïl the solitary grand figure among the modern rulers of the Moghreb. Although he possessed a fierce, bloodthirsty countenance, and was repulsive on account of excesses of all kinds, yet he was endowed with extraordinary administrative genius and unequalled energy. His diplomacy is revealed in the manner in which he conducted negotiations with various European powers. His efforts towards the consolidation of his rule even caused him to send a gallant ambassador, Ben Aïssa by name, to the court of "le Roi Soleil" to demand

---

[1] Haceni is also mentioned because they claim to have descended from Mohammed through Hacen, the second son of Ali and Fathma.

[2] The true name of this dynasty, which reigned from A.D. 1038 to 1145, is Morabethyn.

[3] The Almohades reigned from about 1130 to 1269 A.D.

in marriage the hand of Mdlle. de Blois, afterwards the princess of Condé.

The peace of Ryswik had undoubtedly placed Louis XIV above all his adversaries, and in the desire as the Sherif to establish relations with the Court of Versailles, concerning the redemption of some slaves, we can see proof of a due appreciation of foreign alliance, a lost, forgotten, or neglected factor in the narrow-minded policy which is nowadays pursued by the Maghzen. The presence of a Moroccan ambassador at the Court of Versailles excited the most lively curiosity in France at this period, and, in the "Mercure galant," the smart repartee and lively sayings of this Moghrebian, who certainly did not lack wit, have been preserved to us.

On his return to Meknas, the illustrious Cassini of the Paris Observatory sent letters to the Astronomers at Fez and Morocco. It is to be feared, however, that these epistles were unappreciated, since we do not hear that they were ever answered.

The offer of marriage, in particular, greatly amused the French wits of the period, and it is scarcely necessary to add that Louis XIV. refused the honour of this exotic alliance and replied in circumlocutory terms that the difference of customs and religion were unfavourable to such a union. And, when we read of the manner in which, nowadays, the Morocco monarch treats the fairer half of humanity[1] —how he causes the breasts of women who have displeased him to be placed under the lids of boxes, on the top of which

---

[1] It is stated that Muley Ismaïl had 528 sons by his 4000 wives. These figures would seem to be accurate for they correspond with the taxes levied on the Jews at the birth of each child of the Sherif. Later, under Sidi Mohammed ben Abdallah, the surviving male children occupied 500 houses (!) at Sidjilmassa, and a pension was assigned to them. See on this point Aboulqâsem ben Ahmed Ezziâni.

he afterwards executes a little dance of his own, in order to crush charms recommended by Mdme. de Sévigné to the care of her daughter as the most delicate of flowers—one anxiously asks herself what would have been the fate, in such a barbarous country, of the graceful damozelle, the daughter of Louis XIV, and Mdlle. de la Vallière.

All the additions to the ancient Kasbah of the Almohades (built by Abou Youssef Yacoub ben abd El Hakk in 1275, when a palace was erected in which he lived when the death of his mother raised him to power) as well as the formation of the Black Guard, and the general pacification of the country—indeed the buildings and institutions of Muley Ismaïl—bear the impress of a powerful dominant mind.

To carry out these extensive works, the magnificent remains of which are still, in spite of the carelessness of his descendants, preserved to us, this sultan brought together a large army of workmen. The prisons contained 25,000 Christian captives besides 30,000 criminals, such as thieves and bandits. During the day these prisoners were occupied on the numerous works and at night were confined under lock and key in frightful underground dungeons. Thus Mouette[1] estimates that 4000 Christian captives were engaged on the immense building alone, the ruins of which we have gone over. It is situated not far from the palace, and flanks a pond which he also caused to be dug, and on which one can row in boats. It is near to this piece of water that the gun practice, to which Muley Hassan is very partial, takes place.

These matamores[2] consisted of a long series of arches supporting extensive corridors, access to the surface being by

[1] An author already mentioned.
[2] This spanish word, which is to be found in works on Morocco of the fifteenth and sixteenth centuries, signifies *silo*, a pit or subterraneous store for grain.

means of a staircase. The slaves were divided into nationalities and slept in hammocks. One of the apartments served as a chapel, and this fact should be noted as indicative of greater tolerance than the accounts of the monks[1] of that period would lead one to imagine. It must be added, however, that when the Sherif found these unfortunate people were, by patience and industry, forming plans of their own, the building was evacuated. Of all this there only remain fragmentary portions, the walls, and the tottering vaults of arches under which it is risky to venture. These slaves were captured by the Barbary pirates, who were notorious for their audacity, and who in reality have only ceased to curse humanity since the taking of Algiers by the French. The surrender of Larache provided Muley Ismaïl with 1800 wretched christian captives whom he lost no time in setting to work. Considering the number of captives it is easy to understand why the work of redemption, nobly undertaken by certain associations and fraternities of the highest order (among whom must be mentioned the French "Pères de la Mercy") did not do much in amelioration. All these people worked with an uncommon assiduity.

The Sultan well understood how to supply his officers with very persuasive arguments for obtaining constant and economical labour. "Dogs of Moors!" said he to his officers, "do as the camels of my Empire. Serve me without asking why." For the unfortunate slaves he reserved a large variety of exquisite modes of torture, and the body of every prisoner who died was entombed in masonry to make the others think that it was a species of torture reserved for those who refused to embrace Islamism.

His artillery was drawn by Christians who had been

---

[1] Desmay. Relation nouvelle et particulière du voyage des R.R.P.P. de la Mercy aux royaumes de Fez et de Maroc. Paris, 1682, in 12.

captured on land and sea, and as at this time the government alone possessed fire-arms the Sultan was able to force the Berbers to bring on their backs all the necessary materials from the mountains.

Muley Ismaïl must indeed have been an extraordinary character if we are to believe all the stories told of him. Instead of imitating the example of would-be famous Moriscans, who regard the least movement as a sign of low breeding, finally arriving at a state when they never take a step, or doing so with extreme intentional awkwardness, he adopted a very different course. Sword in hand he stood over his workmen and, like a model architect, he made constant tours of inspection. He illtreated and unmercifully beat them, even massacring them with his own Sherifian hand if the work did not advance according to his royal taste and will. Consistency of purpose was sometimes lacking in this Moriscan brain, for many buildings were abandoned when half finished, and he had hardly completed one palace[1] before he started on another. The description of this Kasbah elicited the highest admiration from contemporary chronicles. It contained fifty palaces, each having its own mosque and baths—all being independent of the adjoining structures. These writers affirm that never was the like seen under any native or foreign government whether Pagan or Mussulman. The gates of the Kasbah were guarded by 1200 black Eunuch.

A gigantic stable, three miles long and capable of accommodating 12,000 horses, including store-rooms and granaries, all fringed by splendid trees, received the name of Aroua. Now, only a ruined heap is visible; about 1760, Gaddour lodged there, by order of Sidi Mohammed ben Abdallah ben Ismaïl, a party of rebels from Fez, who used the straw

[1] Aboulqâsem ben Ahmed el Ezziâni already quoted.

for mattresses and who ultimately became a prosperous colony.

The whole of the Imperial quarter, as some have called it, is a scattered mass of buildings, almost all in ruins. Even on horseback it takes hours to explore these vast deserted sites, connected by passages strewn with broken columns, and with fallen blocks of pisé in the roadways. The interminable walks flanked by high walls allow only a glimpse of the foliage of the mysterious parks. Here and there a palm tree rises to view, or the minaret of a mosque, or the roofs covered with glazed green tiles of some Sherifian dwelling-place are seen. At one turn, a porch; then a piece of dilapidated wall, and the silence of this ruined and forsaken town permit one to admire the deep shadows encircling the tombs and other objects of local veneration. Farther on are some stables and whole villages composed of the slaves' quarters—aqueducts, cupulas, and finally, when one would expect to have reached the open country, the fields lead to woods. Continuing farther on an enclosure is arrived at, and then a second wall before emerging from this extraordinary residence.

As far as the eye can reach nothing but walls can be seen to which the sun gives a delicately soft rosy tint. Here, they enclose olive woods with their greyish green foliage; there, they are connected with the enclosure of the town proper, after taking a devious line across the undulating slopes. Meknas might, therefore, justly be named the city of walls, for nowhere else can such a varied conglomeration be seen; and, as if the sum total of their measurement was not sufficient for Muley Ismaïl, this Sultan tainted with a kind of mania for architecture attempted a sort of second edition of the great wall of China in order to reach, it was said, the Tedla country. He was, however, none the less a man of parts. Having established his authority by almost superhuman efforts, menaced as he was by the warlike attitude of his family and subjects, he enjoyed a peace assured only by reason of the helplessness of the disaffected to rise in open revolt. Not knowing how otherwise to keep the Moghrebian population in hand, he gave a free rein to his mania for building; his jaded ministers and weary retinue had really no time for conspiracy. The country is still full of souvenirs of his sayings. One of a thousand will give an idea of the man. "If I had a number of rats in a basket no doubt these interesting animals would escape by gnawing away the wickerwork, if I did not constantly and vigorously shake the basket." This Sherifian illustration was, as may be seen, not wanting in point; its metaphor was very appropriate, and the Moriscan of to-day are not so changed as to be past recognition.

In other directions the holy war waged against the Christians appeared to him to have established his prestige, and the abandonment of Tangiers by the English in 1684, which he hastened to adduce as a proof of the weakness of European powers, conduced, to his heart's content, to his designs.

He took the citadel of Mamora from an insufficient garrison of Spaniards in 1681, captured el Araïsh (Larache) in 1689, and having entered Tangiers invested Ceuta with more than 40,000 men. Here his fortune changed. Ceuta was strongly entrenched and from this time a series of reverses cooled the ardour of the Sherifian. He was equally unsuccessful before Melilla which resisted the attacks directed by the Engineers that France, then at war with Spain, had placed at the disposal of the Moroccan government.

In his struggle against the Spanish influence he cleverly undermined it in the holy war by exciting the fanaticism of the Berber tribes, and Muley Ismaïl derived considerable support from these mountainous races. The name of Morabith was given to these defenders of the faith, but they are commonly called Modjahid. Religion, however, was ostensibly the least of the motives swaying these peoples in their Crusade against the Christians of the towns on the littoral; abundant pillage and booty very often fell to their share and was frequently the most powerful main-spring. It is necessary to point out this distinction, for the Berbers[1] have never at any period been very fervent Mohammedans, and the attraction of pillage would probably no longer tempt them in the event of the invasion of a modern European army, not only because it would through its superiority render a good account of itself, but also since in the colonial wars in North Africa the tendency is to eliminate baggage as much as possible.

But at the distant time of which we are speaking it was none the less a proof of Muley Ismaïl's clever administration; and it may boldly be asserted that had he not recaptured Larache and Mamora his effeminate and weak descendants would have permitted Spanish influence to play the same part in the west as it now does on the Mediterranean at Ceuta, Melilla, &c.

Extreme cordiality has never existed between the populations of the Algerian and Morisco frontiers, and one would be strangely deceived if the hostilities which now some-

---

[1] At the time of the taking of Mehdia or Mamora at the mouth of the Sebou (the ancient Thymiaterium or Ομματηρια of Punic origin) the booty was even exclusively reserved for the men of the Rif of the plains, specially enrolled for this holy war. Aboulqâsem's works, already quoted.

times take place were attributed to the occupation of Algerian territory by the French.

In the glorious period of the Almoravide, Ibn Tachefin made himself master of the Rif, Oudjda Tlemcen (where he founded the town of Tagraret), and Oran finally extending his conquest to Algiers. Tlemcen alone, however, received for a time the attention of the Almoravides, and of the Beni Merin, and to them must be debited the architectural and monumental splendours of which the Algerian Ediles have only left the ruins.

This unsettled state of affairs continued under Muley Ismaïl, and, even when this prince, at the height of his power, had established his authority over all the mountainous districts of the Moghreb El Acsa we do not cease to find, in the annals of his reign, accounts of hostilities continuing between Mussulmans, Turks, and Moroccans. His son, Zidan, after having chased the Turks at Tlemcen, was recalled by his father, and this transient success does not obliterate the memory of the notorious rout of 1701 when the famous Sherif himself was compelled to abandon his projects.

The Turkish intervention in the Moghreb, where, profiting by the dissension of the first Hassani, the Pacha of Algiers rushed to take Fez, had left a still lively remembrance in the minds of the Ottomans. But the power of Muley Ismaïl was too firmly established in Morocco for any reverses suffered by his armies on the frontier to cause him to fear the removal of such an adventure from that quarter.[1]

---

[1] Although the Sultans of Morocco have never recognised the Sultan of Constantinople as Iman, they feared the Porte, and it was by getting the latter to act that France was able to obtain the deliverance of a number of French residents who, about 1630, were unjustly imprisoned by Zidan.

The activity shown by this Sultan in pacifying the country was such that, towards the middle of his reign, there no longer remained in the tribes a single person possessing a horse excepting among the Zemmour, the men of the Rif, the Abids and the Oudaias. These last were a tribe of Arab origin, and formed, as we shall see, one of the bases of the military organisation. He had devoted 24 years to the pacification of the Moghreb, and in waging war against unsubdued tribes or those in revolt against his authority; and at the time of his death, at the age of 81, which occurred on the 4th April, 1727, the country was enjoying the most perfect security. A Jew or a female could travel from Oudjda to the W. Noun without running any risk of molestation; abundance prevailed everywhere; and cereals, provisions, and flocks were very cheap. Further, what was then an appreciable feature, but the which is unknown in these days, nowhere was a thief or a bandit to be found on Morisco soil.

The remains of this extraordinary monarch repose in the mausoleum of Elmedjdoub, and his tomb is placed by the side of that of his two sons, of whom one, Muley Mohammed, was a victim to paternal cruelty, having been thus deprived of both a hand and a foot. The spot is now a doubly revered one by the people in general and by criminals in particular, the latter finding there an inviolable sanctuary.

During his lifetime, Muley Ismaïl formed a library of 12,000 volumes—a considerable collection for such a country. Unfortunately, no trace of it can now be found, for about 1763 Sidi Mohammed Ben Abdallah Ben Ismaïl disposed of it by "hobons" or mortmain, dispersing it among all the Moghrebian mosques. These materials were thus scattered by an order as vandal as it was fanatical in character, and it furnishes another proof of the theocratical stupidity prevailing in the country.

The Jews also owe the establishment of their quarter at the gates of the town to Muley Ismaïl. The "Mellah" at Meknas is the most beautiful in all Morocco. A wide and open street traverses the whole of its length; a fine large gate encloses it every evening. It was in 1682 that the Sultan executed the measure of building a quarter to be specially reserved for the Israelitish race.

Only crumbling walls and cracked roofs now remain of the palace and series of one-storied buildings, where at that time the feminine army, formerly the harem of this monarch, was lodged. It now presents on all sides a lamentable aspect.

As to the highway leading to the spot where weekly the market was held, concerning the splendours of which contemporary Christian authors write in vaunting terms, saying that it was bordered with beautiful fountains: it now presents the aspect of a dusty boulevard of the Mazures allowed to go to ruin. We crossed it the day we entered the town, but as the foudoucks of the quarter converge towards this chief artery there is always considerable commotion about it.

The renowned treasure-house of the Sultan, which was guarded by a negro guard, who, according to tradition, never saw daylight after they had once entered this fabulous golden domain, does not appear to exist. Opinion is divided on this subject, and even the site of the building is problematical, for we were shown two or three towers elsewhere. It is, moreover, exceedingly likely that the Imperial treasure may have been removed for safety to Tafilalt for example. Sherifian prudence would have dictated such a course, as, in the event of war, the occupation of Meknas is an easy matter.

In 1665 England secured the renewal of certain commercial privileges first obtained in 1585. It should, however, be stated that the Treaty of Commerce only dated from 1721, in the reign of George I., and was not actually signed until the 14th Jan., 1728. M. John Russell, the English Consul-General, while detained at Tetouan experienced considerable difficulty [1] in negotiating this instrument which in reality ratifies that of 1721.

The first treaty [2] stipulated that each English colony should acquire a separate cemetery, and that they should be permitted to travel by land without let or hindrance. Further, that the Emperor alone should arbitrate in disputes between an Englishman and a Moor; and as England had taken possession of Gibraltar and Mahon, it was specified that any Spanish subject belonging to these two parts, travelling with passports under the English flag, should neither be molested nor disturbed. The treaty contained 15 articles bearing on many commercial matters. The treaty of 1721 contained, amongst others, two clauses of the highest importance. The first provided that in future every British subject should be surrendered, not to the Cadi, but to his Consul; this was, in fact, the genesis of the modern diplomatic system of protection. The second clause, one of the greatest value as regards the supremacy of the British flag at Gibraltar, secured the right to Great Britain to provision

---

[1] On the death of Ismaïl Morocco underwent a sharp revolutionary crisis.

[2] Treaty of Fez, Jan. 27. Subscribed to by Charles Stuart and Abboumazar. The narrative of this Embassy appeared in London in 1729. "History of the Revolution in the Empire of Morocco at the death of Muley Ismaïl."

the English fleet and draw the necessary supplies for victualling the garrison at "the kock" from Morisco ports free of export customs dues.

The following year additional articles still further enhanced this brilliant diplomatic success; for by its provisions an English subject, in cases of a dispute with a Moroccan, was only compelled to appear before the British Consul and the Governor of the town.

But the great strength of English influence thus established in the Moghreb should not cause us to lose sight of the fact that, since 1577, France had been officially represented in Morocco. In doing this, however, Henry III. only responded to the solicitations of the Sherif, and in view of the circumstances, the bold spirit of commercial enterprise displayed by the Marseillais should command our admiration. In spite of Morisco fanaticism, and political troubles at home connected with religious warfare and the campaigns of the League, they were able to achieve prosperity for their commerce with Morocco.

Mention has only been made of two or three aspects of diplomatic and commercial intercourse with the Moghreb, but it is well known that from the earliest period of the Middle Ages such relations were very consecutive, in every case much more frequent, and sometimes much more cordial than is generally supposed.[1]

But to return to the town of Meknas, mention should be made how later, in 1800, the famous treaty of the Peace of Meknas between Spain and Morocco, was signed there on the 1st March. After some preliminaries, philanthropic and

---

[1] See the capital account of Comte de Mas Latrie, "Relations et Commerce de l'Afrique Septentrionale avec les nations Chrétiennes au Moyen Age." Paris 1886.

a little platonic in character, concerning slavery, Spain secured the right of fishing on that Coast of Santa Cruz of Marpequeña which years of constant negotiation, even down to the present time, has not sufficed satisfactorily to define.

The prosperity of Meknas seems to have ceased all round with Muley Ismaïl. In 1732, his successor, Muley Abdallah, caused the Christians and the Châamba to destroy the pretty neighbouring environs of Erriâdh which had been at once the ornament and joy of Meknas. It is not known to what cause this stupid decree of spoliation is due, for Aboulqâsem informs us that this locality was the ornament and joy of the region enclosed by it, besides being the dwelling-place of the functionaries of the Oudaïas, and containing many beautiful monuments. Yet in the short space of ten days there only remained of all its splendour a heap of ruins. From this time the environs of the town were again rendered insecure, and many times the unfortunate city underwent terrible crises. This same Abdallah in 1740 subjected the inhabitants to a cruel system of molestation, imposing ruinous taxations upon them.

Even now-a-days, when the presence of the Sultan and his army does not suffice to overawe the tribes occupying the region of the Lesser Atlas to the south of the town, Meknas is sometimes besieged and has to be retaken. However, there has been no serious rising of the Beni Mtirs since 1879.[1] At the time of which I am speaking they blockaded the town, forcing the Sultan to come at the head of his entire army to re-establish order. These bold mountaineers did not, however, dare to attack the camp

---

[1] This orthography differs from that of M'Ters or Mters, or Mtirs as generally employed. The form used by Mgr. Houdas in his excellent translation of Aboulqâsem is Methirs.

temporarily entrenched with fortifications and provided with cannon. They pillaged the harvests as far as the Agouray region, a small district in the midst of mountains, about 17 miles to the south of Meknas. Even at the present time the country can hardly be considered secure.

It is difficult to conceive how it could be otherwise. The road from Meknas to Rabatt by the Zunmour, is 80 miles in length, and impracticable for travellers. It has but once been traversed by the Sultan, and only then at the head of his army, and finding the greatest difficulty in traversing the country, which abounds in unconquered and unconquerable tribes,

In order to reach the Atlantic littoral one is obliged, on leaving Meknas, to proceed north as far as the height of the Karia of Abdallah ben Chleub at the mouth of the pass called "Bab Tisra Djorf," and afterwards to cross the territory of the Beni Ahsen who, however, are not always quiet. A westerly direction is then followed till the peak of the ancient Thamusida is reached on the banks of the Sebou, and hastily striking to the south between the ocean and the forest of Mamora (a resort of robbers of tragic renown) Rabatt, at the mouth of Bou Regrag, is at length reached.

CHAPTER XII.

Evening on the Terraces—Scenes therefrom—Woman : her Condition and Life among the Mussulmans—Slavery in Morocco—The Influence of France on the Trade of the Sahara.

MEKNAS is built on a plateau in sight of the Zarhoun, and the prospect embraces even the remotest parts of these heights which fringe, on the N. and E., the beautiful winding and undulating valley of the Wad R'dem. The Dj. Kafès stand out in isolation, whilst the distant horizon is shut in, on the W., by the unexplored mountainous region inhabited by the turbulent Zemmours, who are a constant source of harassment and trouble to the Sherifian Government.

Before sundown we ascended to the terrace to get a breath of fresh air, and to enjoy the animated life which at that time is a characteristic of the roofs of an Arab town. The male portion of the population are in the Mosques at prayers, and the womenkind, clothed in their best,[1] show themselves without constraint in the natural outlines of their life.

When on the first evening, we suddenly appeared on the staircase, each like a Jack-in-the-box, armed with opera glasses, the commotion in the neighbourhood was extreme. There are no gardens in the interior of Meknas, and the houses, being only slightly elevated, the proximity of the

[1] Women are forbidden to enter the mosques, and their presence there would be looked upon very much as that of a dog in a European church.

terraces one to the other render them somewhat open to public gaze. However, our fair neighbours quickly regained self-possession, and, thanks to our semi-oriental costume, were readily assured that though inquisitive, we were none the less friends of the Mussulman and partial to his vestments.

In the clear atmosphere of a gorgeous sun, the last rays of which were casting a copper-coloured tinge over the sky, the effect of the blue, red, orange, and violet vestments of the women was most brilliant, emphasising the uniform whiteness of the houses as with so many bold touches of the brush. It should be borne in mind that the atmosphere in the extreme west of Morocco possesses the notable quality of rare transparency, most favourable to a clearer appreciation of colour than in the eastern districts (where the sun dazzles and darkens), leaving only tints so delicate as to surpass description. This truly African feature existed here to an extraordinary degree, forming a picture so marvellous that only a " Gérôme " or a " Benjamin " Constant could have produced it. There was indeed a great charm in going each evening on our terrace to admire under all its changing effects of colour, the panorama of the city of Muley Ismaïl.

At this time of the year the surrounding country had almost assumed the yellowish rural-red tint of the African summer, and, as most of the river-enclosed gardens situated in the valley were out of sight, the impression conveyed was of a town surrounded by a desert, the shades of the Sultan's palks being also concealed by the buildings of the Kasbah.

The sandy tableland of Hel Soulal, with its miniature mosque flanked by a solitary palm, was extremely picturesque. In the evening especially, this tree is of great beauty by reason of the scenic effects of its serrated leaves, which the clear atmosphere, distant though we were, permitted us to see in all their delicate tracery. A great variety of half tints were spread out in the west, and in the direction of the W. Beht, over earth and sky, separated only by a low horizon, and, when the sun in disappearing embraced the mountains of Guerouans, and, by reflection, threw with his last rays a tint of purple on the summits of Zarhoun whose regular silhouette, partly hidden by a wood of olives, seemed spread out like the folds of rich velvet in front of us, the contemplation of the outline grew upon all of us. It was the hour for revery, and a great calm fell upon us as the " Mouedzenn " in sonorous tones announced the hour of prayer in the Moghreb from the minaret of the neighbouring mosque.

And whilst we talked on and on about the influence such surroundings ought to have over the meditative Arab mind, contrasting it with the intellectual deterioration of the Moors stifled now by a narrow bigotry, the yet bluish sky became studded with brilliant constellations. Its height seemed to us so much the greater because its deep azure vault shone with the silvery whiteness of the stars, causing it almost to disappear under their pale light. Nor did the scene lose in vividness or become less conducive to meditation when the morn brilliantly illumined the whole of the city and its thousand terraces with an opal sheen, whilst the distant outline of the mountains in the background, and the peaks of the Atlas stood out in bold relief. There is nothing here to remind us of civilisation, or our former experiences,—in a word, of our native land and the past. The charm of our surroundings, however, would have dispelled any regrets which could perchance have troubled our serenity and enjoyment of the beautiful scene.

The time spent by women in Morocco on the terraces constitutes quite a feature in their existence. A special dress not being customary, we were enabled to witness this place of their miserably monotonous,—and, when dominated by masculine selfishness—abject existence in all its graceful freedom, untrammelled as it was by the eyes of their husbands and masters, one might almost say their tyrants. It may be contended that as they know no other life they can feel no loss; still, they ought none the less to have to endure it. I hold, indeed, that none have been created to lead such a secluded existence, interrupted only by short walks, when, disguised and shrouded in a thick uncomfortable veil, the fair sex wander about the street without other aim than that of escaping the eyes of the curious. It is thus easy to understand that the unhappy women, finding in these evenings on the terraces their only chance of freedom, profit by them to interchange visits among themselves by means of the innumerable stairways. Their joyous happiness is like that of birds escaped for a time from their cages, and at these moments one might doubtless be quickly initiated into the numberless secrets of their lives and toilettes, and, maybe, their love intrigues also. For the strict surveillance to which they are subjected by their husbands by no means prevents what the French call "coups de canif dans le contrat." In fact, these good ladies may be said to entirely "flock together;" they have much affection one for the other, thus differing somewhat from our own. They look upon man as a common enemy, whom they make a point of deceiving on the slightest provocation without any fear of being betrayed. How could it be otherwise? The condition assigned to them by the Koran is far from enviable: they cannot be blamed, for they are not accorded any moral responsibility. When no longer young, the husbands, according to their means, prefer to them adolescent negresses bought in the market. This is a stroke of far seeing economy, for, instead of contracting several marriages as allowed by Mohammed and running the risk of being burdened with four families at once, they purchase young and vigorous slaves, who, " utile dulce," will, while bearing children, help in domestic affairs.

Can anything more animal-like be imagined? The same gross and inexcusable morality is to be found in the towns from the highest to the lowest. The ease with which marriage is contracted facilitates the pathway for divorce. The rule is, that the smaller the means the more is the ceremony curtailed and its formalities glossed over. In no case does the prospective husband become acquainted with his intended. He places himself in the hands of his mother who, with the tact of a " mother-in-law," chooses her son's companion.

Such demoralising treatment of women is in truth neither chivalrous nor politic. If the history of the Moghreb el Acsa were more generally known among the Moriscos they would recall to mind that at one time there lived an accomplished woman, full of goodness and of extreme beauty, on whom her husband did not dare to impose the fatigue of a military expedition in the Sahara. Subsequently married to the famous Youssouf ben Tachefin she was instrumental in the conquest of the greater part of Morocco. History relates but few details concerning the physical charms of this distinguished woman, Zynebmas by name, but the author of Roudh el Kartas vaunts her wise and clever politics. She was the mainstay of the prosperity of the most notable of the Almoravides. It is, therefore, apparent that there have been exceptions to the inferior position to which Morisco women in general are reduced. Indeed, the marabout of the sainted Lallah Rahma el Ghazouania,[1] which we saw on our way from Basra to the Karia of ben Aouda bears witness to this.

The Mussulman Society of Morocco has often been the subject of rather sarcastic description, though few have thoroughly studied it. I shall not, however, in this place even attempt to sketch it, but having had the time and opportunity of penetrating the family life of Meknas we were enabled to make such observations on the condition of the female sex as will justify the following details. The beauty of Arab women has been much extolled, and the haïk which, in public, conceals them from the vulgar gaze, augments the mystery which, to the traveller, surrounds their life in the Mussulman world. It is, in fact, an additional allurement to the curious. In the Moghreb the Moorish women have retained the simplicity of the Arab. Their strange picturesque costume has here seen but few changes, although modern ideas have conceded certain modifications in the shape of patent leather shoes and white stockings, as in Algeria and Tunis.

Hard by, and located close to the leader of the mission, dwelt an agreeable family whom I wheedled out of their Mohammedan austerity by the attention shown to the husband, who was attacked by anthrax in the lumbar region. The distrustful jealousy of the master of the house was not long in giving way to an affectionate gratitude for the remedies we brought him. We were thus enabled to penetrate into the inner household life of a citizen of Meknas, a by no means easy task under ordinary circumstances, inasmuch as the stranger who seeks admittance to

---

[1] "Lallah" is the literal translation of "Madame."

a Moorish house generally finds himself left waiting in a damp and dark passage, so that the women may retire and seclude themselves from inquisitive gaze. The two wives of our invalid lived together in an amicable friendship, excluding any idea of rivalry, and the children, a little boy and girl, grew up together in approved Mohammedan fashion.

An extreme simplicity was apparent in the arrangement of the household furniture—rug-covered divans, some tapestries the length of the walls, together with the inevitable copper chafing dish mounted on a three-footed pedestal, constituting the whole of the decorative appointments. But few beyond those whom trade with the coast brings in contact with the outside world possess, with the exception of these chafing dishes, such uncommon pieces of furniture as the clocks and musical boxes which added to the comfort of our hosts at Wazzan. The arrangement common to all the houses, of a small inner court open to the sky, surrounded by a colonnade, on to which all the rooms open, is picturesque; and, owing to the resplendency of the "azulejos" pavement, the appointments, unlike as in other warm countries, need only to be of the soberest tints.

If, athirst with the spirit of romance, the traveller expects here to find the princesses of the 1001 nights as depicted in the marvels of the imagination, he runs a great risk of being completely disillusioned. The inner side of the singularly realistic Mussulman life should only be seen from a distance and with an artist's eye. Were one of Zola's disciples to wield his literary scalpel in depicting its scenes, he would no doubt present an analysis so delicately subtle that a disgust capable of driving away all travellers for the future would not be slow to follow.

Though in many respects the country is full of interest, I repeat that certain aspects of it will not bear close scrutiny, and without doubt a native " Pot Bouille " in all its nakedness would be very repugnant.

The whole existence of the women of Meknas consists in vegetating in dark, damp dwellings—eating, sleeping, and dressing forming their three chief occupations, in that respect placing them but little above the brute creation. By a curious perversion of taste, a woman's attractiveness is measured by her " embonpoint," and they resort to an ingenious method of cramming in order to increase the bulk. A most extraordinary ignorance dwells in their wooden-textured craniums; indeed, the brain is so little developed that the less said about its capacity the better. Their dress on occasions of ceremony is very costly, and is used at gatherings of friends at which each seeks to outvie the others. Void of all grace and character, it causes them to appear like some ethnographical dummy of a Mandchoux Tartar in his war paint from some museum. It is heavy and grotesque. A strange custom for so warm a climate makes the use of velvet in profusion an imperative necessity, and forming two gigantic sleeves, it falls in large and numerous folds over the bare skin. Through the slightly open bodice may be seen striped embroidery of many colours. The skirt is covered with common Manchester or Rouen muslin of a quality which with us would only be used for the commonest curtains. The head is enveloped in a head-dress formed of a brilliant silk handkerchief rather prettily arranged, and which, seen at a distance, bears some resemblance to the graceful national head-dress of Russia. This detail apart, all is ugly; the face is often marked with hieroglyphic arabesques traced in hennah;[1] and, in addition to the traditional tattoo marks, little crosses and marks appear all over the cheeks and chin. As to the hands, the treatment to which they have been subjected by means of this self-same pigment and cut-paper stencils is so elaborate that the first time I beheld them from a distance, I thought I was looking at a pair of embroidered gloves. This masterpiece of patient work is applied likewise to the ankles and feet, and requires two or three days to dry, during which the patient cannot walk or move, and food has to be administered by some friend or attendant. The ordinary costume is, on the contrary, pleasing and practical in its *négligé*. In its sash, often very rich and beautiful, is concentrated the coquetry of the woman, and the head handkerchief falling loosely over the dead whiteness of the dress, together with the scarlet of the babouches, causes the whole to present a pretty appearance. The arms are bare, and the open sleeves reveal to the gaze of the curious a kind of surplice over which a coloured waistcoat is worn. I should add that the hair is almost invariably black, and by a simple arrangement, the plait falling over the back is lengthened by the admixture with it of silk of the same colour. In the house both men and women go literally barefooted, their babouches being left upon the threshold.

At festivals the two sexes invariably amuse themselves separately. To Europeans this isolation of men and women even on the domestic hearth is one of the strangest features of Mussulman life. The result is not an absolute dearth of the social relations, but a real antipathy to them, and to

---

[1] The hennah is a shrub very common in North Africa. Its leaves, mixed with the juice of the citron, produces a brown paste, and from this a reddish-brown tincture is derived.

this may be attributed in part the absence of artistic genius. Thus the revelries at marriages last about a week, during which time the friends of the bridegroom do not leave him for an instant, whilst the females of the party give themselves up to their special amusements with closed doors. On the day of the final ceremony the bride, screened from view, is carried on the back of a mule, enclosed in a kind of very small conical-shaped casket, to the house of her future husband, who then opens this Pandora-like box.

The intellectual and moral status of these unfortunate women cannot, therefore, be very high, nor can much be said for their maternal instincts. The boys learn early to follow in the footsteps of their fathers as regards the treatment of women, and evince a strange facility for authority and command. The girls though receiving but little care, are for several years screened from the narrow influence of fanaticism and sometimes give signs in their early youth of a pleasing intellectual disposition. Our neighbour's little girl, six years of age, had learned in a few weeks to approach us and ask questions of us in French, thus exhibiting an intelligence superior to that of her brother, a young scapegrace whose overbearing manners already rendered him insupportable.

But one is strangely deceived if to modesty and dignity is attributed the submissive humility exhibited by the fair sex, or if the idea of being brought up for self sacrifice is associated with them. The stick alone rules the East and its cruel blows alone inspires them.

Inactivity and idleness characterising every family in easy circumstances, life in Morocco is terribly enervating. Exercise is totally neglected, field sports are unknown, and, in fact, unless compelled, one never stirs a step. Their highest happiness—indeed to them a divine pleasure inasmuch as it gives a foretaste of the Mohammedan Paradise—is to pass the day in a beautiful garden, full of secluded groves and there to sip the famous "thé à la menthe," whilst surrounded by a swarm of houris. This is not long in producing an atrophy of the mind and bodily vigour which ensures a train of maladies to precede their entry to the real "Paradise."

In such an existence,[1] the physiognomy of the women reflects an expression of beauty, perfect and regular, which possesses a great charm. The constant seclusion induces a delicate pallor, heightened by the voluptuous fire of the large black eyes. To borrow, however, a poetical metaphor, it is a flower that fades in the springtime of life. On African soil puberty is reached early; the girls marry at fourteen, at which age they attain full development; at twenty their beauty is rapidly declining, and at thirty they become old women with but few attractions.

When writing of such a subject and such a country one is compelled to omit much that a European code of morals does not recognise. Still, I must make mention of the extraordinary facility with which husbands can repudiate or divorce their spouses. If the average human heart is fickle what must then be said of the changeable passions of the Arab? It frequently happens that the young wife speedily finds herself supplanted by some rival or slave. As in such a case, it does not suit the whim of the husband to give the unfortunate woman her freedom, she descends to the rank of a servant and suffers great misery thereby, being compelled to live by the most shameful expedients.

[1] A woman of rank goes out but rarely and then only early in the morning, except to go to the Cemetery on Friday.

In the towns something of this misery rises to the surface, but what a heartrending chapter could be devoted to it as seen among the tribes! The friends of the Emancipation of women would find it a pitiable and burning question.

Life in the open-air quickly renders the frame robust and capable of sustaining fatigue, and, in such a case, the women are of great use as "beasts of burden." In among the Douars they are to be seen to a late hour of the day, footsore and weary, carrying often to a distance of several miles the water and wood required for culinary operations. Their limbs rapidly assume a very noticeable hardy appearance; a proof of this statement may be found even at the gates of Tangiers on market days by watching the transit of the caravans of women bearing provisions. Worn, wrinkled, and panting, the women and girls thus burdened proceed under a blazing sun, or in rain that drenches their thin rags, whilst the head of the family and leader of the caravan calmly and majestically issues his commands from the hairless back of some apocalyptic quadruped, whose species it is at first sight difficult to discover, horses, mules, and donkeys sharing alike with the women the same hard treatment.

In short, it may be taken for granted that if in Morocco the women in the towns are victims to a humiliating and abject servitude, Moorish cunning turning to advantage the slight restraint that the Koran imposes upon the animal passions of mankind, in the country districts and among the tribes the brutality of the husbands knows no bounds.

As a corollorary to this dark picture one can easily imagine that the evidence of women has very little value before the Kadi, especially as certain brilliant theologians very common in the Moghreb have taught that woman has no soul. In certain towns like Marakesch the female prison is also used as a dead-house, and it is customary for husbands to send their offending wives there to receive a conscientious bastinade until amendment occurs, or rather, as is more generally the case, they obtain the pardon of their lords and masters. The "Moulinn dor," a species of night police and guardians of the exits of the towns, keep a strict watch during the night and find a considerable source of profit in arresting ladies of easy virtue who venture out at a late hour.

Among the Berbers, however, the family life differs materially from that of the Arabs, women there enjoying a liberty and independence quite antagonistic to the spirit of the Koran, and which, while endowing them with a certain measure of authority, likewise creates points of similarity with European ideas. The Berber is monogamous as are the Touaregs (who are well-known to be directly allied to the Kabyles), and the advice of women and more especially the wife is asked, and she often takes part in the important decisions of the tribe. It must be added, however, that these customs show a tendency to disappear in proportion as the tribes are brought in contact with the Arab element, and whenever the means of the chiefs allows them to indulge in luxury they ever seek to conform to Arab ideas and surround themselves with a harem, thus assimilating their habits to those of their Mussulman masters.

To return, however, to the influence of women in these tribes of the wild and distant Atlas country, the famous part played there some years ago by a bold and daring heroine, whose weight of sixty years did not prevent her from equestrian pursuits, should not be forgotten. This Berber Joan of Arc roused and organised the powerful tribe of the

Aït Zedig, being for a long time a cause of much anxiety to the reigning Sultan, especially in the early part of his reign. Christianity, too, seems to have left some traces and traditions among the Berber population as seen in the invocations of the women to Mariah, and in the procession of dressed puppets called Mata.

Slavery has always flourished in the Moghreb el Acsa, and in the middle ages it was at once the pretext, support, and source of great profit to pirates who were well known to have infested all the coasts of Barbary. Though as late as the 14th century Mussulman slaves from the Moghreb were sold at Genoa, yet there is every reason to believe that the reciprocal sale of slaves as a regular traffic between Mussulmans and Christians was very rare[1] on the African coasts at that period. The influence of the Turks in fostering piracy was deplorable, and for a long time it served to perpetuate the proverbial insecurity of the Morisco littoral. Even to this day it is owing to these bold robbers of the sea that we find in the interior of the country the last vestiges of their marauding expeditions in the shape of objects of art, Japanese and Chinese porcelain, pillaged from the vessels which passed along the desert coasts of Morocco. The ransom of Christian captives was, as we have seen, effected in the reign of Muley Ismaïl, and as for those obtained by wreckers the last instance seems to have occurred in the early part of the present century in the case of the passengers on board the brig "La Sophie."

It is impossible now to estimate the number of slaves living in Morocco. Coming from the Soudan they arrive in caravans, forming in point of fact one of the chief imports,

[1] Cte. de Mas Latrie. "Relations et Commerce de l'Afrique Septentrionale."

although their introduction has sensibly diminished of late years. Some authorities estimate them at about 3000 yearly, and the Sultan collects therefrom a tax amounting to 5 % in kind. Young negroes, and above all young negresses, from 10 to 12 years of age, are purchased by preference. To efface the horrors of the desert passage, and at the same time to give them that plump condition so pleasing to the eyes of buyers and connoisseurs, the slave dealers fatten their gangs and allow them altogether to have quite an easy time. The principal slave markets are at Morocco, Mogador, and Fez, but they are also sold at the auctions in all the towns, and the vehement protestations of the Anti-Slavery Society may often be read in the European press at the news of the sale of slaves in the streets of Tangiers in sight of European coasts.

It would be hard to find another kind of merchandise to yield such enormous returns. Originally purchased, by an exchange of salt, in Central Africa, and especially in the basin of the Niger, the prices of slaves go up in direct proportion to the enormous duty which the caravans must pay for each journey with new gangs. Going, they carry salt, and returning they bring back human flesh. In the Moghreb the purchase price of a slave varies from £2 to £20. The last figure is that fetched by a choice young negress possessing a fair number of charms, including youth and intactness.

But it is sometimes expedient to include white slaves with black ones. These are unfortunate young girls whom wretchedness and bad treatment have caused to flee from their tribes, and who seek refuge in the towns with people who at once sell them as slaves, generally obtaining a very high price for them.

The docility of the slaves is greater than might be expected, considering the precepts and laws regulating the treatment of women, an idea of which we have already given. As a matter of fact, once sold, and fairly installed at the house of the purchaser, the black slaves experience no worse a fate than that of a servant. On the contrary, they are treated with the same care and solicitude which a careful proprietor in this country extends to other costly commodities and animals, and if neglected in this respect, the precepts of the Koran which enjoin the good treatment of slaves enable her to demand to be resold or exchanged with another master. For the rest, the fact that it frees the son of a slave and a master, is sufficient evidence as to the spirit of Mohammedanism in this respect. It is, indeed, regrettable that similar usages[1] did not prevail among Christian nations in times of slavery, and particularly among those notorious Spanish and Portuguese colonies whose infamy never could plead ignorance in excuse, as could African populations.

But, if the condition of the slave is a comparatively easy one, their treatment at the hands of the dealer is frightful and abominable. It is this phase of the evil trade afflicting the dark Continent that constitutes the gist of the question. Its suppression can only be effected by attacking the evil at the roots and not by the thunderings of pathetic tirades of exaggerated horrors at slavery in Morocco. The deputations of members of the European Anti-Slavery Societies to the Court of the Sultan will never achieve much good: they

---

[1] The ceremony of freeing a slave has some resemblance to the old Roman custom. Sometimes, when about to die, the master gives liberty and a certain sum of money to his slave, who then follows the funeral procession, bearing the letter of enfranchisement aloft on a stick.

offend and wound Mussulman ideas by demanding the suppression of customs sanctioned by the Mohammedan faith. In short, in view of this fact the Morisco officials can do little, since it is certain that the cruel treatment of slaves and the cause of slavery is practiced by, and is to be found, in the caravans and their Central African raids. It is in this direction, therefore, that protection should be extended to the unhappy down-trodden populations against the rapacity of those who organise these manhunting expeditions. For, to speak only of the heart of the Western Soudan—the region in which Morisco trade is alone interested—it has been shown that the Arab merchants reduce to slavery not only the pagan negresses, but also those professing the religion of Mohammed. Although the Koran forbids the sale of Mussulmans,[1] it adds that if he who was an idolate when made a slave afterwards embraces Mohammedanism, he is not entitled to emancipation if his master pleases otherwise. To sum up, no one may force an idolatrous slave to embrace Islamism, but it is incumbent on masters to inculcate its principles into young slaves.

This traffic is still carried on with full force, and the Sahara is even yet tracked by long caravans of captives. The only power capable of entirely suppressing it by its civilizing influence in the north of Africa, is France. Unfortunately, to the material difficulties which her admirable troops in the extreme South of Algeria encounter, must be added the paltry diplomatic mistrust of certain European powers whose defective constitutions, confused finances, as well as, from an intellectual point of view, their antiquated armies, prevent them from undertaking remedial measures

[1] Langeau, "Le pays de Rirha."

from outside. Moreover, France has not been able to extend her political influence to the Fidikelt routes at Rhadamès. In this connection should be read the remarkable study published under the direction of M. Ch. Féraud,[1] whose picturesque notes were furnished on his returning from an expedition to El Goleah.

Previous to the occupation of Algeria, communication with the Soudan was very active, and the slave trade enjoyed a prosperity unknown at the present time. France very soon undertook to oppose the traffic, an action which was all the more meritorious seeing that Algerian commerce thereby received a blow from which it has never recovered. The caravans, therefore, made their way direct to Tripolitane or proceeded circuitously by way of the Toucat on the Cyrenaique to the Moriscan side of the frontiers, thus avoiding by a wide detour, the extreme limit of French rule and influence in the southern portions of the neighbouring territories, afterwards reaching Rhadamès, the great Saharian market, from which radiate five chief routes. The evil would have been lessened if the mainstay of the commercial currents uniting the Soudan with the Southern Mediterranean Coasts had been confined to the traffic in slaves, but they also embraced the thousand and one other valuable products of the Soudan. It should be added that slave merchants now inspire their merchandise with terror at the name of

---

[1] Revue Politique et Litteraire, Paris 1873. M. Féraud speaking from his deep knowledge of African affairs, strongly recommends the substitution of black agricultural labour for the Arab element from the Tell. It would then be suitable to institute in Algeria a system analagous to that employed by the missionaries, and buy all the slaves, making them serve an apprenticeship at remunerative work before giving them their liberty. This, while bringing back the disbursement, would also serve the cause of civilization. This system, however, requires a strict surveillance to prevent abuse.

France, persuading them that the French will devour them[1] if they succeed in escaping to Algeria.

In order effectually to suppress the slave trade it would be necessary to strike a decisive blow by means of vigorous repressive measures in Central Africa, which, under existing circumstances, would be a colossal undertaking. It means nothing less than preventing the supply and disposal of the slaves. At present they can be bought in Tripoli and in Morocco, a condition of things which bids fair to continue, since French influence is, unhappily, too circumscribed.

The stream of slaves arrives at Fez by way of Tafilalt and Gourarat; but mention should not be omitted of the route, recently described by Dr. Lenz, from Sous through the country of Sidi Hechan el Howara, which supplies Mogador, Morocco, and all the Southern districts of the country.

[1] Le Pays de Rirha par Langeau.

CHAPTER XIII.

The ever-recurring Ambassadorial Ceremonies—The Manner of Living in Morocco—Our Quarters—First Visit to the Sultan—His Personality and Pursuits—A Morisco School—The Morisco Politicians of the Future—Education in the Moghreb: the Narrowing Influence of Mussulman Bigotry and Fanaticism—Manner of Bringing up Children—Pitiful Influence of Residence in Europe on Morisco—Science in the Moghreb—The Sultan as a Chemist and Photographer—A Morisco Disguised as a Spanish General—Beauty of Arab Ornamentation—Good Quality of Morisco Goods.

WHEN an Embassy is announced, and this generally takes place several weeks, if not months in advance, the streets in the towns and the roads in the country assume, although very vaguely, an almost presentable aspect. The Chiefs of the Quarters, or Metasseb, set a thorough cleansing process on foot, and either expel the fanatical members of the community, putting them under lock and key, or charitably warning them if they cannot show friendly sentiments at all events to keep within bounds, to observe a silence as prudent as it is absolute.

All the mounts in the district are requisitioned, and these are sent forward, together with many horsemen, on the road by which the Embassy will subsequently follow, to be in readiness for the entry. In a word the aim is to gather, by all the available means an autocratic Government has at its disposal, what we should call an immense crowd of sympathetic and orderly people.

The same ceremony, I was nearly saying the same comedy, is re-enacted with each important Embassy, and from the enthusiastic correspondence published, and the stereotyped despatches spread abroad, it would appear that, in every case, never in the memory of man was such a reception given or could such a sympathetic concourse be remembered. The old Moghrebians who, in the course of their life, have been able to take part in a number of these wearisome ceremonies, would laugh uproariously if they read the comments which we in Europe make on such occasions.

Ours was not a diplomatic mission so we could hardly aspire to the prodigal honours extended to the Embassies. We did not expect to receive any official visit at our residence, and so could not hope to rejoice in the extraordinary barbaric festivities which have already been so minutely and so often described, and which the Sultan and certain of his ministers inflict on the unfortunate diplomatic service. Ours was a very quiet life spent in examining and exploring the town, and in attempting to give an account, unprejudiced, calm, and without depreciation, of a veritable curiosity of the middle ages in which, in the midst of the nineteenth century, is seen a dash of the thousand and one rights—the Government of the Sultan.

It must, however, be remarked that when a European arrives in an inland town, failing official letters of some acquaintance with the Government, he has no other resource than to seek lodgings in the Foudouks of the Israelitish quarter, where dirt and every kind of filth in creation seem to have found an abiding place. We have, therefore, cause for thankfulness that we are not precisely so placed, for according to the importance of a traveller in the eyes of a Pacha, that person without much ceremony expels the residents of some house where he installs the visitors in lieu and place of the proprietors, obliged to take themselves off to other shelter—it does not matter where. This proceeding may appear barbarous, but it must be admitted that it is singularly practical, effective, and expeditious in a country where there is not yet a branch establishment of the Hotel Continental in the interior.

When one is ever so little accustomed to life under canvas, town life becomes sufficiently easy and simple to the new-comer. We therefore very rapidly extemporised a comfortable and practical home in the dwelling which His Majesty had reserved for our use. The owner, an influential Kadi, who appeared to be in favour at Court, was absent on an expedition to the Atlas, a fact profited by to send his family to some retreat, to put the movables in a room, and to prepare for our use his dwelling, which was one of the finest and most handsomely decorated I have seen in the Moghreb. Our servants were installed on the ground floor, and we—proh prudor!—quickly transformed the women's apartment into an excellent bedroom. I must confess that we forthwith smoked in it as readily as if we were at home.

The ceiling was delicately traced with ornaments of painted wood,—miniature triangles, lozenge moulding of a thousand colours and gilded arrises—such as constitute the well-known features of Moorish architecture, and which are so much admired in the remains still extant at Grenada. A sort of cupola, similarly decorated, produced, above our heads, a very charming effect of light and shade. A single window diffused the pale light of the mysterious harem. We were thus housed after our own hearts—quietude and coolness being never wanting, and one felt tempted to dream away the long summer days within sound of the pellucid murmuring of the fountain in the court which flowed ceaselessly. The fountain is an embellishment always to be found in the dwellings of those of any social standing.

We took our repasts on the ground floor, one apartment having been transformed into a kitchen by the lively Antonio who feasted his eyes on the marvellous azulejos. A plethora of rats, however, was a set off against all these conveniences; advancing in battalions, coming out of all the corners, allured by the culinary odours and not in any way despising European products, they became a veritable scourge. Each morning my dog vainly essayed to build up a bloody hetacomb: the tribe of rodents multiplied, and we were obliged to suspend all our stores from the ceiling, thus completely giving the house the appearance of an old clothes shop. Boots and breeches the length of the walls replaced the rich tapestries, and our saddles swung from the centre of the old harem, together with other incongruous articles.

We much regretted the absence of a gardener, but in Meknas few houses possess one. We wished, on the night of our arrival, to ascend to the terrace, but the door was carefully nailed up and padlocked in order that the Roumis might not profane the view from the house tops of the town, which is held sacred as the domain of the women.[1]

I confess that we did not pay much attention to this prohibition, and though taking it for granted that H.M. would certainly not wish to deprive us of such innocent pastimes as the contemplation of the heavens in general and in particular the female stars of Meknas, the city of pretty women as they say in the Moghreb, it is to be feared that we were

[1] Mussulman prudery, by common consent arising out of centuries of custom, has reserved the horizon of the house tops for women, so that jealousy so easily awakened in African latitudes may not be excited.

guilty of a clear breach in forcing the threshold of the paradise. These drawbacks were, however, largely compensated by the proximity of our dwelling to that of the Commandant Le Valois, the good natured chief of the French military embassy. We were thus able to take advantage of the knowledge of this distinguished officer, and, in every sense of the word, to explore with him the town and its environs, collecting a thousand curious facts concerning the heterogeneous and really extraordinary surroundings of Muley Hassan, pompously dignified in Europe with the title of "Le Gouvernement Marocain."

As M. Ordéga had sent me an official letter for the grand Vizier since my departure from Tangiers, it was imperatively necessary that I should be received by this exalted personage who, rightly or wrongly, is supposed to exert a very powerful influence over the Sultan, from whom we hoped to obtain a special permit for prosecuting our travels among certain tribes. This worthy having deigned to intimate that he would receive us some morning on his return from the palace, we arrived one day at nine o'clock at the house of the Moroccan Richelieu accompanied by a "spahi" of the military embassy as an interpreter. The sun was powerful and we had to wait a long time; for the minister, like other dignitaries of note, gave us leisure to reflect upon what to say while contemplating the entrance to his residence, the doors of which were covered with sheets of white iron of an exceedingly hideous appearance. Our situation in the narrow street, incessantly jostled as we were by the crowd, had nothing attractive in it; and I was nearly driven to despair when a small band, hastening along at a swift pace, came round a corner of the road. It surrounded, preceded, accompanied, and protected an enormous and richly caparisoned mule bearing a gigantic pile of obesity half hidden under a heap of fine haiks, and who we were told was Si Mohammed ben Arbi himself. This pillar of the government hardly deigned to cast a glance at the Roumis who were awaiting him half baked by the sun. The process of alighting was particularly painful to the obese Moroccan, but, thanks to a swarm of assiduous slaves, he accomplished the feat without mishap, and disappeared in a large, newly-built vestibule. We only got a mere glimpse of the interior as the obsequious valets who had for an instant thrown open the two folding doors of the large gateway, slammed them in our faces much to our discomfiture. At last, just as our stock of patience was beginning to be exhausted, we were ceremoniously introduced into a kind of long lobby at the end of which was a fountain, giving one the idea of a bathing establishment, but in place of the usual inner door there was a kind of platform on which stood a large and old gilt arm chair, hailing most likely from some European old curiosity shop. There, mopping his face, sat the person of the chief minister of the Empire of Morocco. He was, in all conscience, one of the finest specimens of a human mastodon I have ever seen. The type of face crowning this edifice of fatty tissue had nothing attractive in it, and it would have been an easy matter for the most inexperienced physiognomist to have read in the features a clear witness to unnatural passions such as it would not be easy to detail to ears polite. Moreover, the reputation borne by this government official was an execrable one, and his morals were said to be extremely lax. The expression and the nose were quite a poem, and indicated a mixture of Hebrew miserliness and African obscenity. The position on the arm chair,—his legs crossed, and his monstrous calves coiled up—must have been a severe trial to this victim of punctilious decorum. As for ourselves, two very small low chairs were placed at our service at the foot of the dias. They were very ricketty and insignificant looking, no doubt in order to indicate the respectful distance at which the infidel should be kept in this function of diplomacy.

After some customary commonplaces, in the course of which His Excellency over and over again assured us that he loved and cherished us as the apple of his eye—a statement which nearly caused my companion to burst out into laughter at once the most hilarious, incredulous, and disrespectful—the difficulties which we should encounter in our projected travels to Tafilalt were discussed, and the superior advantages of going to Moulouia and Ksabi were urged. This spun-out Oriental trickery caused us to conjecture how long we should have to wait before the Sultan would give us authority to carry on our explorations under his permit. That really was the root of the whole matter, as the entire region is only nominally in subjection to the Sultan.

The vizier also specified clearly that we must remain at Meknas pending a reply to a special communication which would have to be sent to the legation at Tangiers, subsequently to which alone would the Sultan be willing to give his signature.

Later on, we understood the manœuvre. It was in order that as much time as possible might be taken up, and by dilatorilary spinning out every formality, at last to cause us to miss the opportunity which at this time of the year offered itself. The conference over, a tray bearing the instruments of torture for the inevitable tea was brought in, but we cut the audience short, as it was dragging and degenerating on the part of His Excellency into a series of irksome and circumstantial inquiries concerning European society.

Si Mohammed el Arbi is possessed of an immense fortune, and we were informed that he manages it with a rare ability, uniting the science of a Colbert with the craftiness of a Mazarin. This Moroccan would be perfect if the autocratic form of government that he serves did not make him continually tremble for the safety of his dollars, and may be his head also. All administration, properly so called, to which we shall enter into detail later on, is carried on under his orders, or to speak more correctly, under his supervision, for (and this is the one redeeming feature of the Sherifian government), the Sultan holds all the reins of power. The vizier is, therefore, a very busy man, and his post is far from being a sinecure; in truth the fibres of his adipose tissue are essential in order that in such a country, and leading such a life, he may not succumb!

The rising of Phœbus witnesses his arrival at the Dar Makhzen,[1] preceding even his secretaries. He does not return till rather late, and, in our ignorance, we were not half grateful enough for his prompt return to receive us at his residence. After the enforced mid-day siesta he again returns for the despatch of business, often remaining till nightfall. Night and day he is at the beck and call of the Sultan—a veritable political factotum to his master.

On returning from this reception, which very disrespectfully I shall call a bore, we had the inexpressible pleasure of feeling more at ease, and were quite overjoyed to experience the quiet and cool repose of our pretty house. But each morning at break of day, and each afternoon until

[1] The generic name of the seat of government.

sunset, we heard, at the entrance of the semi-subterranean passage which led to this princely dwelling, the most comical discords. These sounds were echoed, increased, and swollen by the acoustic properties of the arched lobby, and the sonorous waves were singularly intense. First came some deeply modulated elocution in a powerful bass, and the last note of this melancholy lament was hardly started than immediately a strange concert of flute-like voices burst forth as from blackbirds, young cats, and chickens just flayed alive. The discord made us gnash our teeth, but the first blush of hilarious wonderment over we went to inquire the cause of the hubbub. Our astonishment reached its height when we discovered it to be a school frequented, we were told, by the youthful aristocrats of the locality. The decoration and furniture were, however, in every particular, such as Lycurgas himself would have approved. On a spread mat squatted the scholars, listening all agog to verses of the Koran that a grave professor-like personage, with an uncultivated air and questionable style, was intoning to them. Afterwards they all repeated at the top of their voices the theological teachings of the divine prophet.

It was a remarkable exercise for the lungs, and the young rascals acquitted themselves with such vigour as to drive us to despair. They all swayed comically to and fro like those grotesque Chinese porcelain figures which are to be seen in bazaars. Quietude was banished from the whole neighbourhood. I do not know if this instruction was gratuitous, but it appeared to us to be strongly compulsory, inasmuch as the concert was often interlarded with dolorous yells by which we understood that the Moroccan ferule had caressed the hide of a coming philosopher. We were at our wits end, and already dreamed of changing our habitation and abandoning the palace, when the commander of the military mission, very anxious to mitigate our position, procured a decree of expulsion against the unfortunate assembly. Two Mokhazni of the Sultan came to put it summarily into effect. Next day the offenders were removed to the end of a neighbouring street to a disused stable, at which we had a look in passing, when the prescribed course for the dissemination of the blessings of education in the Moghreb had been resumed.

I will touch lightly on this topic, as thereby the cause of moral decrepitude and of the insuperable difficulties which stand in the way of the country being brought into touch with modern ideas will be more quickly appreciated.

The backward condition of Mussulman countries is, now-a-days, pretty generally recognised; but in no other quarter is the lack of intellectuality, brought about by the decay of Islamism, so apparent as in Morocco. Mussulman pietism, when the warlike movement of foreign conquest was exhausted, led to a relapse into barbarism. Indeed, though the nomad Arab[1] is the most learned of men, and of all the least mystical and the least given to meditation, yet these civilising tendencies were quickly destroyed when the people left to themselves, and dissociated with the Spanish races, for example, were stifled by the theocracy of the Soudanese black element. That at first it was hardly brought about by those acts of Vandalism of which humanity thinks only with shame is clear from the anxiety shown by Jacoub, inasmuch as he caused the manuscripts ceded by the king of Seville, Don Sanche, in the treaty of 1198, to be transferred to Fez, whilst the downfall of Averroes was one of the clearest examples of that narrow-minded bigotry which was afterwards to sway the Moghreb. Since the year 1200 there has not been a single Arab philosopher of renown.

[1] Renan.

But Islamism alone must not be held responsible for this arrest of civilisation; and if the Moghrebians were not to-day stagnating in the blankest of ignorance it would be an easy matter to demonstrate the baneful influence which black blood has exercised over the proud and noble descendants of their ancestors of the Hedjaz.[1]

The Koran is heavy feeding and the indigestion resulting therefrom leaves the understanding in a singularly crippled state, admitting that it still holds sway over the Moghrebian brain. Being firmly persuaded that fortune and power can only be possessed by favour of Allah, and, not even dreaming that God helps those that help themselves, the Moroccan vegetates in a stupidity from which only greed of gold or other disgraceful passions can allure him. It can, therefore, be understood how centuries of such reasonings have produced a result which, in the name of humanity, is to be deeply deplored. No parallel can be drawn between the existing narrow and degrading bigotry and the pure religious tenets of Mohammed to which innumerable peoples have owed their glory, fame, and future.

I do not think there is a definite age at which children in Morocco are sent to school; for we came across them of all sizes, and the young scapegrace of four or five elbowed the Thaleb candidate of twelve or thirteen already independent in his ways. Let it be well understood, however, that in this respect we speak only of the inhabitants of the towns and the Arabs of conquered dis-

---

[1] The name Hedjaz signifies, literally, "elevated" or "raised," uneven and stony country. The admixture of two mountain races therefore guarantees certain strongly marked intellectual qualities, especially as the Berber element is composed of many ethnological divergencies.

tricts, the Chleuhs mountaineers having other roles in view for their sons than Tholbaship.

The school which would most nearly correspond to the last of our primary schools is called Mekteb or Maktab,—*i.e.* if comparison at all were not an insult to European institutions. To each mosque of any note is attached a Medarsah or College, and from these having attained the title of Thaleb and already believing themselves to be paragons of knowledge, the Moroccan elite gravitate to the pale of wisdom and the centre of learning in the Moghreb—I mean the University of Fez. It is possible that the gross Moroccan ignorance exaggerates the learning of the Tholba, but the impression produced on a European by even a superficial study of these individuals is, I hold, proof absolute that ignorance engenders an infatuated pride.

Though education, as we have often both seen and heard, is compulsory, and is only rendered effective by the grace born of a conscientious application of the stick, it is on the other hand cheap, and good value is given for one's money. The poor pay nothing, whilst the rich contibute sums ranging from seven to fifteen centimes a-week. After learning the Koran on the lines aforesaid the young men study Commentaries and other religious books, and attain the degree of Tholba. They then appear to give themselves up to ceremonious promenades in order to receive the admiration and deference of the people. The Feguih or Fky and the Kadi are recruited from their ranks, and, previous to an appointment in the Government service, they go to Fez to complete their intellectual training! The schools of Fez are nowadays considered in the Mussulman world to be the most famous, and the Moroccan artists to possess an incontestable superiority over those of Tripoli, Tunis, and Algeria.

This was stated recently by one of *the most erudite of our Arabic scholars*.[1]

Physics, chemistry, and other natural sciences are regarded as "Haranis," that is to say, from a religious point of view they are forbidden subjects. It is therefore readily conceivable that, viewed in combination with Moorish indolence, the Moroccans possess little beyond the rudimentary elements of knowledge. As a set off, Alchemy flourishes; and the rogues who trade upon the credulity of the public are numerous. With regard to astronomy the descendants of Aboul Hassan Hali no longer know even the first principles. Beyond the ability to determine the time of the passing of the sun across the meridian to ascertain the true noon, their science stops short. Yet they keenly cultivate astrology and cast complex horoscopes of the heavens.

However, during the last few years the Sultan (probably through caprice) has dabbled in chemistry and photography. We were informed that his instructor in the science of Berthollet and the art of Daguerre was Capt. E——, the first chief of the military mission. It is, however, difficult to picture the Sherifian descendant of Mohammed shut up in a laboratory, and being initiated into the mysteries of precipitates and developing solutions. As usual, nothing came of this zealous freak, and the same may be said of many others. The Moroccans are like big, overgrown children, and possess all their changeable whims, want of perseverance, and defective understanding. Muley Hassan's mania for photography recurs periodically; for, during our stay in the mountains to the south of Fez a special courier was sent after us with instructions at all hazards to overtake us as soon as possible. He bore an official letter and

---

[1] Henri Duveyrier.

reached us in the Beni Mtirs chain, and our natural emotion in opening the missive will be well understood. The first of it was that the Sultan, to satisfy one of his imperial whims, wished immediately to possess a photographic apparatus similar to ours of which he had heard a great deal. He applied to the chief of the military mission so that a model might at once be made. That officer, in despair at having such a delicate order to execute, and not even dreaming of the possibility of making the sovereign understand the unsurmountable difficulties in the way, obtained from us such information as would enable him to order a set from France.

To sum up, it may be taken for granted that the few Moroccans who possess any notion of science owe their knowledge to contact with Europeans and such educated renegades who have lived or now reside in the country. It is to be hoped that this state of things will change—perhaps in consequence of the praiseworthy work of the military mission. Beyond this, however, the Sultan who is full of good intentions, has made several attempts during the past few years to send young men to Europe, there to study its civilisation and science.

The results have not been promising; indeed, if it were not for damping the ardour of such praiseworthy efforts they might be said to be pitiable.

Such a method of procedure will never produce practical results, and not in this way will the root of the evil be destroyed. Although the task of the regeneration of the Moroccan nation—if such a title can be given to the tottering power of the Filali Sherifs—may be very arduous, we can, *ex abrupto*, glance at the round of experience favoured by these Moroccans who visit our country.

We have just stated that practical instruction is entirely absent from the Moroccan Curriculum, and the same may be said of education generally. If the mind of a young man is ill fitted in consequence of the paucity of the former to assimilate our knowledge, it is, on the other hand, rendered extremely liable, by reason of the failings of the latter, to appropriate all our vices. Brought up in an Eastern seclusion, where women are of no account, and in the most dissolute of society, children from their earliest days are accustomed to the strangest talk. The promiscuity of which they are constant witnesses is a painful example for them, and naturally results in an undue precocity in everything. As to the girls, the less said the better. They are very lax, and for fear of accidents, they are married as soon as possible.

What, then, in all sincerity can these young men learn from the surroundings of European barracks, industrial schools, and manufactories? In addition to this the country is so overrun with theocracy and fanaticism that all advanced thought or synthetical intelligence is very dogmatically condemned *à priori*. Thus it is easy to understand the mistrust and antagonism engendered if the young Moghrebian returns with even the very thinnest varnish of a superficial training as acquired in some Continental manufacturing town.

We were one day very surprised to encounter a gorgeous Spanish general in one of the Courts of the palace. He was wandering alone, with a melancholy look, and his gilded trappings sparkled and blazed in their glory under the Sherifian sun. A Castilian patriot, foreseeing the time when the Spanish flag would wave over the ruins of Meknas, had once prophesied such an apparition. Alas! close proximity to the swarthy complexion of this dusky and woeful pedestrian soon undeceived us, and revealed the fact that he had but a very slight kinsmanship to the successor of Prim. He turned out to be only a common Moghrebian, who, having been sent to Spain, had returned from some second-rate workshop or school with a fancy for the stripes of a pretty officer. Like a nigger king of the Congo, he had attempted to impose on the credulity of his countrymen by making a triumphal entry in the plumes of a Captain-General bought of some Andalusian dealer in old clothes. The indifference and universal contempt meted out to him soon taught him a severe lesson, but we were assured that the return from Europe of such youthful prodigies was often marked with the same characteristics.

Some hold that it would be otherwise if the Sultan, instead of sending students of low birth to Europe, were to encourage the youth of the highest families of the empire to seek similar training; but then the Government would run the risk of grave dangers when the elite of the nation—the aristocracy, if such an expression be permissible, of Mussulman Society—became imbued with our habits of thought, customs, and learning. The Makhzen of to-day would then have run its course, and would come to grief amidst hopeless dissensions. This is quite outside the consideration whether the country would gain by a too violent attempt to free assimilation to European principles. Is not the memory of the scandalous administration of the Bey of Tunis previous to the French intervention a forcible warning in this connection?

There is, however, one point on which we must be undeceived. We generally flatter ourselves that a demonstration of modern progress would result in a wonderfully radical and lasting change in the dense and narrow fanaticism of the Moroccan intellect. This is a very grave error, for if their journeying is, above all, no other than a means to increase the sum total of sensual and grovelling enjoyments, and to borrow what is the least worthy of imitation, and which only serves to intensify the unmentionable native debauchery, it must be acknowledged that the result of the analysis of our civilisation of which we are so proud is singularly discouraging when the last of the Thaleb gives his impression of men and things. Though the argument may be specious, it is none the less appropriate to a society the foundation of whose character is that philosophy which each day in its modern aspect is making for national ruin. As yet perfectly happy in their very modest material requirements, they see no reason for revolutionising both their country and their daily life by the introduction of a civilisation which creates so many artificial wants.

Seeing that the sight and use of railways and telegraphs does not arouse their covetousness, that they cannot understand the necessity for such costly and complex inventions to men who, trusting in God, do not seek to thus increase the pace of life, and that the old beaten tracks of the Moghreb have sufficed them for centuries, it would be extremely idle even to discuss the introduction of new methods of communication, which after all would only bring crowds of infidel strangers—a result to be avoided at all hazards.

In a word, they would rather pay to be left alone than to receive the blessings of the nineteenth century. This is the men of the great majority, and even the exceptions who think otherwise avoid speaking of their opinions—and with good reason. Capital punishment was the cruel reward of that other intelligent race of Berbers. Indeed, nothing can foreshadow the far-reaching results that such assimilation would have produced. Such a change will yet come, since the mountain races of the Tingitane and the Atlas are more independent now than at the time of the advent of the Romans. Idris perceived the value of this fact, whilst in every Morisco are to be found palpable traces of an intermingling with the licentious negro. All this would lead us to believe that it is too late to look for amelioration, that the debasement and degeneration have been going on too long. Moorish citizens may be regarded as a striking example of a weak effeminate race, as produced by repeated crossing with the Soudanese element, and by the enervating influence of town life. On the other hand the Berber so well endowed intellectually (*i.e.*, if we judge him by his brethren of the Algerian Kabyles) has never renewed its contact with the impoverished blood of the early Arab conquerors.

However, from the time of Idris the Apostle, no foreign power has subdued the interior of the country, in the same manner as, for example, in Tunis and Algeria Turkish rule has crushed everything. The Moors, after their expulsion from Spain, where their rule produced all that is yet the most beautiful in the peninsula, were thrown back upon themselves, and retired to the Moghreb el Acsa,—to a theocracy and dogmatism which produced, as we shall see later on, such disastrous regnant results. It is necessary to lay due stress upon this paralysing influence, for the Moroccans, standing in the light of their history, cannot attribute their lack of a philosophic and scientific spirit to Turkish supremacy, because, I repeat, they have never endured it. To the last Saadien and Filali Sherifs must this extinction of intellectuality be imputed. It is, however, true that the Arabic language, though it lends itself so readily to poetry, and an eloquent imagery, is yet a very inconvenient medium for the expression of metaphysical ideas and the facts of science. It further appears that the great Arab thinkers were all of foreign origin; still, it is deplorable that the later Moroccan dynasties have done nothing to keep it alive in the same manner as did their glorious predecessors.

As to Mussulman intolerance, so frequently quoted as a deterrent influence, history furnishes many proofs to the contrary. It is often more imaginary than real. Those who are so strenuously antagonistic to Islamism might study with advantage the religious persecutions which have also victimised the Occidental world, so true is it that the human mind is everywhere shaped in the same mould. May not Spain, who at one period lost all scientific spirit in consequence of terrible oppression, be quoted as an example? What at first sight is most striking, as it has been well put by one of the greatest minds of the nineteenth century,[1] is the Mussulman's vice of indomitable pride: it is, in fact, his radical vice, and like a band of iron it encircles the head of the faithful from the age of ten or twelve years. How then could things be different, and what other result could be expected from a training which merely stupifies the mind and banishes every intellectual tendency from the youthful mind?

This picture might appear to do the black an injustice were I not to add, what is indeed well-known, that the Arabs have ever been clever architects, possessing the most refined taste. Even now, amongst the shallow-minded Moors of Morocco, in a country of which I have just written in terms of strong disparagement, may be found an innate

[1] Renan.

simplicity of taste which shows itself in industrial products often very coarse and primitive in design, and unskilfully wrought, but exhibiting the most ingenious and delicate decorative taste and appreciation of colour. The pavements and ceilings of the houses, and even the inner doors, reveal a most marvellous instructive blending and grouping of thousands of exceedingly graceful designs.

The art of matching colours is innate to the Arab artist, and it necessitates genuine talent to blend as they do a dazzling red with a brilliant green, a violet and orange, and so on, making use of the most daring combinations without any knowledge of the art of mezzotints, they boldly group the whole together without any loss of effect as regards a play of colour agreeable to the eye.

Their costume presents many features of a patriarchal character, and without being suspected of Arabomania or narrow prejudice, we challenge criticism. The dress bears all the marks of antiquity, and they cannot endure our hideous but necessary garb, and consider, not altogether without reason, that black is an accursed colour. Under their sun they are in all respects clothed with a majesty of drapery of which, alas, we have little conception, and which we can only realise by means of ethnological collections.

CHAPTER XIV.

The Makhzen—Military Resources of the Sherifian Government—The Tribes of the Makhzen—Their History and Organization—The Moroccan Cavalry—How Recruited and Mounted—The Degeneracy of the Moghrebian Races—The Armament and Equipment of the Service—Military Tactics—Want of Homogeneity.

THE foundation of the military resources lies with the tribes of the Makhzen, that is to say, on those furnishing the Government with a number of fighting men who in return enjoy certain privileges as to the payment of taxes, some even being altogether exempt. They also receive a monthly money payment called "rateb," its amount being fixed in an inverse ratio to the wealth of the tribe.

This unique system of military centres ought to prove a source of considerable strength to the Government, inasmuch as all the tribes find their means of subsistence in the subsidies they receive from the Sherifian authorities. This fact should necessarily ensure their devotion to the Sultan and provide him with an unfailing recruiting ground of tried warriors. Liability to service is hereditary, descending from father to son, and in some of the tribes the land is the absolute property of the Crown.

This organization, though so well adapted to sustain military prestige in a country composed of such rival ethnographical elements, is, however, subject to horrible abuses on the part of the Sultan's entourage.

The soldiers sent by these tribes form the "Guichs," and they are nearly all mounted. Their total effective in the time of peace rarely exceeds 12,000 men, but it must be stated that for every contingent on service there is a counterpart which never leaves the tribe or town, a feature which bears some analogy to European regimental depots. Certain tribes must also be mentioned who furnish mounted troops called "Nouaïb," but these only join the army in case of need, and may, therefore, be looked upon more in the light of a reserve force.

These "Guichs" of the Makhzen possess many privileges. Besides their allowance, partially or wholly, from taxation, and their excellent pay, they are employed by the Governors and Kaïds in the provinces to collect the special taxes or contributions levied by them. Their remuneration then varies, and, in point of fact, the regimental pay forms the least of their emoluments,—the principal being rather the pickings they appropriate to their own use. This is a feature inseparable from the collection of taxes in a Mussulman country. In Morocco the victimised taxpayers are, by custom, expected to deal generously with the official agents, and it is easy to imagine the train of abuses which follow in the wake of such a system. The officers, likewise, are subsequently not at all backward in claiming a share of their subordinates' plunder.

The tribes of the Makhzen constitute the following corps, some of which have a sufficiently interesting past to warrant a few details. These are

> The Mechaouari.
> The Abids Bou Khari.
> The Oudaïa.
> The Cherarda.
> The Cheraga and the Oulad Djama.

The Mechaouari or soldiers of the Mechaouar may be compared to the troops of the imperial or royal guards of Europe. They form the body guards, the household troops of the Mechaour or imperial council chamber and the palace, being in fact its guardians. They serve on foot or horse according to circumstances; sometimes they are fully equipped as in time of war, and at others they carry only a long pole to be used in dispersing a crowd. They wear the red-tipped chechia, and are dressed in a kind of dark blue or red tunic surmounted by a white cloak.

The Sultan's umbrella-bearer is chosen from among these men, as also are the bearers of the fly nets for the horses and the lancers and musketeers who surround the sovereign on all state occasions.

Their number is unknown but it may be estimated at about 2000. They accompany the court on all its expeditions, and are in attendance at all four of the Sherifian Palaces, viz., Morocco, Rabatt, Meknas, and Fez.

The Grand Vizier, the Ministers, and the high functionaries and dignitaries of the Government are preceded by the Mechaouari. Dexterously plying their courbaches, they scatter any crowd which may surround the palfrey of their chief. They seem to have adopted a racing pace as a distinguishing characteristic, and I have ever admired the expeditious way in which they always penetrate even the densest and most stubborn crowds of people.

As troops of the palace guard the Mechaouari merit first mention, but in reality they are picked men drawn from the most famous of the old regiments which are still in existence, and who have played such an important part in the history of modern Morocco. I have also mentioned the Abids Bou Khari, or Slaves of Bou Khari, who regard themselves as under the protection of the celebrated theologian, commentator of the Koran, and author of the Djami-el-Sahi, a man who is universally revered amongst the Moroccans.[1]

Like the Turkish janissaries, this Moroccan troop is under religious patronage, and each new recruit is required to swear fidelity to his chief on the sacred book of the Saint. Nowadays, a copy, preserved with much respect and superstition, accompanies the Kaïd of the blacks in all expeditions, being religiously placed under a special tent. To this talisman is attributed the success attending the warlike valour of the corps.

The renown of the most famous of the Almohades fired the ambition of Muley Ismaïl, and in his efforts to organise the Moroccan power, he aimed at restoring to the Moghreb the eclat of the glorious reigns of Abd el Moumeïn and his son. In pursuance of this object he conceived the idea of organising a special body of troops which should constitute an unquestioning and direct vehicle for the execution of his will, and in the blind devotion of which to him as its chief he would find a sure means of enhancing the range of his power. At all events, the idea of thus bringing, by such means, all the scattered elements of an energetic and vigorous black race to a common focus was a happy one, while it also served to further his principal aim in pacifying and bringing into subjection the restless and unsubdued Berbers. The Government thus acquired a blind force, the value of

[1] Mohammed el Bokhari was born at Boukhara and died near Samarcande. In his work the Djami-el-Sahi or "Complete Collection," he enumerates 16,000 traditions, sentences, and words of Mohammed, which in Mussulman eyes are so much the more true inasmuch as the committal to writing of each was always preceded by the author performing his ablutions in the well of Zemzem.

whose services would only increase in proportion as it excited the antipathy of the aboriginal races.

The nucleus of the corps was not, as is generally stated, recruited solely from the blacks of the Soudan, though Muley Ismaïl, had he desired, could easily have obtained a full complement from that quarter. Though on his return from the expedition to the Sous in 1678 he brought back 2000 mulattoes with their children, whom clothing and arming he sent to the Mechra'a Erremel,[1] it must be remembered that for some years previously he had been collecting a not inconsiderable army of negroes from the same quarter. In this he exhibited an unequalled assiduity and care, thus furnishing proofs of a capacity for organisation very rare at all times among Arab races, and more especially so at the present time.

One day, Muley Ismaïl being in Morocco, and a taleb of the city having placed before him a list of all the negroes who had composed the army of El Mansour, the Sultan immediately enquired if any of these slaves were still living. The reply being in the affirmative, the Sherif sent his secretary, Mohammed El Ayyâchi, to all the accessible tribes, among the Beni Hassen, &c., with injunctions to bring back all the negroes to be found there. Further, the Sultan's deputies in the tribes received instructions to purchase any slaves owned by the latter. No time was lost in carrying out these orders, and at length not a black man or woman, not even a freeman, was to be found throughout the Moghreb either in the towns or in the country.

The Sultan then caused clothing and arms to be distribu-

[1] That is, the ford of the Remel, a small stream which rises in the mountain chain of the Zemmours and flows thence across the marshes of the O. Beh't to join the Sebou.
Mechra'a Erremel thus becomes abridged to Erremla.

ted, and set officers over them. Then having provided building materials, he sent them to Mechra'a Erremel. Arriving on the banks of the W. Felfela they built houses and cultivated the land, living there until their children arrived at the age of puberty. The Sultan then ordered all these negroes to bring their children, whether boys or girls, of the age of ten years to him. Some of the children were apprenticed for a year to masons, carpenters, and other craftsmen, whilst the others were employed in other ways. During the second year they were trained to lead the mules, and in the third learned to puddle or ram and make pisé. In the fourth year they were entrusted with the care of horses. These they had to mount barebacked, holding on by the manes. In the fifth year they mounted saddled horses and generally perfected themselves in horsemanship, at the same time learning to shoot on horseback. When these children attained the age of sixteen years they were enrolled in the army under the control of picked officers. They were then married to the young negresses who had been distributed in the palaces of the Sovereign and taught the arts of cooking, housekeeping and washing.

Those of the young girls who possessed good looks were placed with mistresses who taught them music. Their musical education finished they were each given a dress and a dowry and assigned to a husband who took possession, the couple having first had their names inscribed in a register. These married couples had to devote their children to the service of the Sultan; the boys going to the army, and the girls entering the domestic service of the palaces. This system of recruiting lasted to the end of Ismaïl's reign, the Sultan going each year to the camp of Mechra'a Erremel and bringing the children back with him.

It is quite impossible to imagine a more practically conceived system. The roll-call of this black army numbered as many as 150,000 men, 70,000 of whom were at Mechra'a Erremel, 25,000 at Ouedjh Arous at Meknas, the rest being scattered in the various fortresses which the Sultan had built in the Moghreb of Ouedja to the O. Noun and which were 76 in number.

In addition to the natural and practical difficulties contingent on such a vast organisation, Muley Ismaïl encountered great opposition from the theoretical spirit of the country. Thus, the possession of the lands given to these negro slaves brought about a conflict in May 1697 between the Sultan and the Ulemas of Fez, the latter refusing to recognise the power of the registered slaves of the Makhzen to exercise the right of proprietorship. It was necessary for the Sherif in the following year to send an edict to Fez to be read from the pulpits which assured this right to the Abids. Now as Mussulman law does not recognise the right of a slave to possess property, the importance to the Sultan of this modification in favour of the black colony will be sufficiently apparent. It was the only military force on which he could depend to support his sovereignty and to curb the independent fault-finding spirit evinced by the upper clergy and the citizens of Fez.

To sum up, the importance and influence of the Bou Khari, modified in proportion to the power of the Sultans, has been felt even to the present day. At times, turbulent and invincible they present a complete analogy to the Mamelukes of Egypt. At other periods in Moroccan history certain Sherifs found themselves in open hostility to this army of slaves. For example, Muley Abdallah was not able to subdue them even by exciting the Berber tribes in the neighbourhood of Meknas against them. Their decline dates from the reign of Sidi Mohammed (1747-1789), who assiduously destroyed the work of his ancestor who had annihilated the power of all the Arab tribes of the Makhzen. This was a fatal mistake, and every succeeding Sultan has in consequence suffered by a complete disorganisation of power. Ismaïl's successors were unable to continue on the lines prescribed by him, nor could they command the troops he left at his death. They were consequently reduced in strength and dispersed, some even going so far as to plunder their camp. Then the Abids and Oudaïas sided with Elyezid in his revolt against his father, and the latter expelled them to Tangiers, Larache, and Rabatt. But so indispensable was their presence to maintain the Sherifian prestige that this same Sidi Mohammed, after having commenced to undermine their strength, was forced to write that celebrated letter to them in which he fixed upon Meknas as their residence, and four years later he pardoned those who still remained in the Sous, being only too glad at last to load them with presents in order to have at command a force on which he could rely; but insurrection had spread throughout the tribes and the irremediable crumbling of the Empire of Ismaïl was the first sign of the decline of the power of the Sherifs in the Moghreb.

The Bou Khari have played a part analagous to that of the Pretorian guard of the Cæsars, but now their influence is considerably weakened and their numbers diminished. They still, however, occupy almost all the posts of importance about the court. Owing to their dispersion over Moroccan territory, but more especially to the sanguinary struggles that Sidi Mohammed caused them to undertake against the Berbers, the numbers of the Abids and Bou Khari have been actually reduced from 100,000 to 5 or 6000 men on a peace footing, and to 15,000 to 20,000 in times of war.

We have seen that their increase was so much the more rapid because under Muley Ismaïl they, their wives and children being the property of the Sultan had been safe from persecution and revolutions, which in Morocco are the ever recurring experience of the masses of the people. Their colour has become very mixed, for, besides the crossing with white women, Berbers, and others given them by the Sultan which has taken place resulting in a modification of the ebony type, it must be remembered that a certain number of Arabs have always gained admittance to the ranks of the Bou Khari, at first by favour, but once included in their ranks they and their descendants become the inviolable property of the Makhzen.

An Abid Bou Khari may be enfranchised in return for service, but the majority remain in their condition of servitude whilst attaining to the rank of Kaïd Mia and Kaïd Rahel. In reality, however, they are only slaves for they are employed on the most varied kinds of work. There were Bou Kharis who a few years ago constructed the walls enclosing the entrenched camp and the earthworks in front of the Sultan's palace at Fez.

The history of the Guichs of the Oudaïas [1] or the third regular cavalry corps of Morocco is rather singular. At first the Oudaïas were a tribe of from 100 to 300 horsemen (opinions vary on this point) of Arab origin and were always regarded as one of the principal integral parts of the regular army. The Sultan Muley Ismaïl attached them to his

---

[1] European authors write Ludaya, Ludayres, but as a matter of fact the appellation of "the Black Guard" has been given to this corps in contradistinction to the Abids Bou Khari.

person at the same time that he organised the Abids Bou Khari. They, together with the Aït Zemmours and certain tribes of the Rif, were alone allowed, after a lapse of the first 24 years of the reign of the contemporary of Louis XIV., to retain their horses, and formed the only force on which the government could then depend. Located in the first instance at Rouali near Meknas they subsequently were installed at Fez, and in recognition of their fidelity the Sherifian Court gave them a large tract of land from the Sâïs[1] to the Valley of the Sebou. The Oudaïas multiplied in number so rapidly that they could in time easily furnish 25,000 to 30,000 mounted troops, and, owing to this powerful force, the Sultans succeeding Muley Ismaïl were able to reduce numerous Arab and Berber tribes to submission. The Viziers, Kaïds, and Governors of provinces appear then to have been selected from among the Oudaïas, for local tradition has preserved the memory of these personages who seem to distinguish themselves in their offices.

In this way, the Oudaïas played a part similar to that of the Abids Bou Khari, and they began to exercise a preponderating influence in the conduct of State affairs, on many occasions overruling the will of the Sultan. They are often mentioned by Aboulqâsem, who gives an accurate detailed account of their wars and revolts. They rendered themselves obnoxious to the inhabitants of the large towns of Fez and Meknas, plundering the suburbs, sacking all the houses, thus laying waste the whole country, and on many occasions they came into conflict with the Abids Bou Khari. These dissensions resulted in the most deplorable anarchy. Muley Ismaïl dead, there was no power to restrain these

[1] *i.e.*, the plain in which Fez is situated. The word is often written Essâïs.

factious troops, and the only way in which the Sultan Abdallah could keep his regular army in check was by stirring up the most belligerent of the Berber tribes against them. They robbed all the troops, and destroyed all the crops. This was effected all the more easily because the "Mechta" or cattle farms of the Oudaïas were situated in the plain of Fez and in the valley of the W. Mikkès, both of them exceedingly easy of access.

The Oudaïas were at that time all the more powerful as they had entered into open alliance with the warlike tribe of Guerouans.[1] Later, in 1758, Sultan Mohammed decapitated the principal Oudaïas who were guilty of having encouraged the selfsame Guerouans in revolt.

The most serious insurrection on the part of the Oudaïas has, however, occurred in the present century. It arose out of a most inadequate pretext, the carrying off of young girls to Fez, but the circumstance, in the light of subsequent events, assumed the utmost gravity. The population became engaged in civil war and desolated the two largest quarters of the town, viz., Andalous and Adoua. The authority of the government was also at length set at nought in this popular outbreak, and Sultan Abd. er Rhaman, dismayed and frightened at the probable results of this revolution, fled by night to Meknas with a few faithful followers. There he spent two long months in reorganising his army of Abids Bou Khari and other contingents. Then when he had collected 100,000 men he marched on the rebel town which the inhabitants had proclaimed as a Republic under the control of a Djemâa or Assembly of

[1] The Guerouans inhabit the little known district of the Zemmour mountains, and especially the valley of the W. Beht. The continuation of the highlands extending to the Bab Tissra Djorf goes by the name of Dj. Guerouan.

Notables. About half way at Mehdouma the Sultan met 30,000 mounted Oudaïas, but by the aid of his artillery officered by renegade Spaniards he completely routed them.[1]

The Oudaïas took refuge in Fez, and the siege lasted for more than a year. The Sultan engaged all the neighbouring tribes in this arduous undertaking, thus completely blockading the place. Famine alone compelled it to surrender, and then ensued all the usual concomitants to the entry of a Sultan into a conquered city, that is to say the leaders lost their heads and their possessions were confiscated, whilst the Oudaïas dispossessed of their ancient rights were despersed to

> Taza (the Kasbah.)
> El Araish (a town.)
> Azerer (among the Beni Ahsen.)[2]
> Rabatt (a town.)
> Sekirt el Krounfel (a Kasbah near Rabatt.)
> Morocco (a town.)

A group however still remain on a part of their ancient lands near the W. Mikkès not far from Fez.

---

[1] In 1748, the inhabitants of Fez had already sustained a siege of 27 months' duration, and this insurrection seems to have exhausted itself amongst the Oudaïas, for in making peace with the Fezzians the Sultan Abdallah assured them that he bore them no ill will, and that all the misunderstanding arose with the Oudaïas who devastated the country. Peace was subsequently made with them on the tomb of Muley Idris.

[2] The Beni Ahsen are located in the region of the plain situated between the W. Rdem and the W. Beht. The latter rises in the heights of the Guerouan at the Dj. Kafes, and forms vast swamps at its confluence with the Sebou bounding the forest of Mamoura on the north.

It will save confusion to use the spelling Ahsen to distinguish this tribe from the Beni Hassen, a tribe of the Rif to the south of Tetuan and of which the limit in the Tingitane is the mountain marked Anna in French maritime charts, situated on the coast, and 2210 metres or 6630 feet high.

On the eve of the battle of Isly in 1844, Muley Abd. er Rhaman provided his son Sidi Mohammed, then in command of the Moroccan army, with all the troops there at his disposal together with the contingents from the tribes. On this occasion he supplied arms to each of the companies of Oudaïas of which we have just spoken. After his defeat by France, however, he recognised the necessity of reconstituting his forces. From that time each of the groups of Oudaïas, although still separated one from the other in consequence of their warlike tendencies, was incorporated in the Makhzen and thus became entitled to the privileges granted to similar tribes.

A corps of 600 cavalry is always encamped at Sidi Jacoub el Mansour close to Fez to await the will of the Sultan. The Oudaïas of to-day are submissive and humble, but at the bottom of their hearts they cherish the consoling hope that their present humiliation is only to be regarded as transitory. They believe that the prediction made about them by a holy marabout will yet be realised. This marabout prophesied that after a political revolution all the scattered groups of Oudaïas would be reunited and once more regain their independence, that they would again be masters of the situation and for a long period exert a dominating influence greater than that exercised by them previous to the events which led to their dispersion.

But the reverse of the shield of this dazzling future is tarnished in the eyes of the Oudaïas; their coming splendour will be succeeded by a period when beaten and defeated a second time they will be finally driven from the neighbourhood of Fez. Then transplanted to the district surrounding the town of Oudjda on the Algerian frontier they will dwell in peace and oblivion.

The Cheragas[1] inhabit a part of the rich plain watered by the W. Sebou, being located on the left bank between the confluence of the W. el Liben and the Mechra'a at Hadjerat el Kahila on the government lands or Azibes Soultans. They constitute with the Oulad Djama a powerful centre of population and influence. Always faithful to the Sultan they have become strong and numerous chiefly through the generosity of the Sovereign. Their loyalty, however, has not invariably been so thorough, for in the time of the Sultan Errechid, his brother Ismaïl then governor of Meknas and the representative of the Sultan at Fez, had cause to put sixty bandits of the Oulad Djama to the torture. The bodies of these malefactors were suspended at Bordj Eldjedid.

These two tribes are charged with the maintenance of law and order in the extensive valley of the Sebou from the suburbs of Fez to the sea littoral. They bear arms when required by the Sultan, but in ordinary times they only furnish a thousand mounted troops for the disposal of the Sovereign. They are encamped partly at the gates of Fez, and partly outside its walls. Since the year 1680, a cavalry corps of 500 Cheragas has been commissioned to guard the road from Saïs to Mehdouma. They are stationed at Fort Elkhenies. When speaking of the Cheragas and the Oulad Djama, a passing mention must be made of the powerful tribe of the Hayâïna, the lands of which are also contiguous, and who have played such an important part in the modern history of the Moghreb being almost constantly allied with their neighbours. They do not, however, belong to the Makhzen, and, therefore, their fidelity to the Chorfa Filali dynasty is so much the more meritorious.

Finally, to complete the list of tribes forming the military

[1] Also spelled Cherâga.

power of the government, the Cherardas must be mentioned. Coming originally from the Sous, a province from which has proceeded the best soldiery of the empire, they have been constituted into two distinct battalions, the new company taking the name of Soussi. At the beginning of the century, the Cherardas were settled in the fertile district of the Laouïa Cherardi, adjacent to the city of Morocco, but in the reign of Abd er Rhaman in consequence of a long standing dispute between the Makhzen, the tribe then was transplanted *en masse* to the territory of the Aït Imour[1] to the north of Bab Tisra Djorf in the plains of the O. Rdem, whilst the Aït Imours were transferred to the neighbourhood of Morocco.

The new geographical situation of the Cheragas added to their importance from a political point of view. Encamped at the outlet of the defiles of Bab Tisra Djorf and Bab Tsiouka where the two roads meet which communicate between the capitals of the Tingitane, Fez, and Meknas, and the northern seaboard and littoral, they were responsible for the security of the frontiers of the territory adjoining that of the Beni Ahsen who were notorious as incorrigible thieves. Indeed, the whole of the region lying between the Sebou and the W. Rdem belongs to this almost unsubdued tribe, the source of whose power lies in the anarchy of the district. The region is also subject to the depredations of the Zemmours, another gang of notorious thieves who are allied to the Beni Ahsen by ties of interest and plunder, and when the Sultan seeks to exact too severe a reckoning for their depredations they seek refuge in the neighbouring

---

[1] These Aït Imour or Immour are the Chelleuh, or Berbers of unmixed blood and are indomitable in character. They originally inhabited the district of the Zarhroun, and proved themselves insurmountable obstacles to traffic.

mountains. Savage and unhospitable, the Beni Ahsen never permit strangers to penetrate their territory. The road which passes from Sidi Kacem to Mehdiâ by way of the W. Beht is the only one which by tacit consent is open to the officers and troops of the Emperor. Still the agreement is often violated, and the importance of having the cavalry of the Cherardas near at hand in such a region may be well conceived. In such circumstances they constitute a trusty and efficacious source of assistance and fill a role similar to that taken by the Algerian Spahis.

While on this subject, it must be mentioned that a certain number of mounted soldiers drawn indiscriminately from the tribes of Makhzen, constitute a special corps called Mosakkherin[1] or native gendarmerie. Outwardly they bear no distinctive feature to mark them from the rest of the Moroccan Cavalry.[2] It is supposed that they, conjointly with their other duties, exercise functions which are sufficiently remunerative, being entrusted with the administration of justice in Morocco.

Of all the tribes of the Makhzen the Mechaouari and the Bou Khari are alone equipped, clothed, and mounted by the State. The Oudaïas, Cherardas and others supply their own accoutrements, from their horses to their guns, only receiving their ammunition. On ceremonial occasions, and in the field in order to distinguish them from the other troops, all the cavalry of the Makhzen are uniformly dressed, that is to say in the red pointed skull cap with two tufts of hair peeping out down

[1] Houdas gives the orthography as Mosakhkharin.

[2] One fact must not however be overlooked. This corps seems to be regarded as a very crack one, for the Kaïds agha of the Mosakkherin carry a velvet cartridge box, embroidered with gold. It is the only sumptuous mark of rank to be found in the army.

to the temples, a white jellaba over a sort of gandoura in coloured cloth, the whole secured at the waist by a leathern girdle to which is suspended a dagger often very handsomely engraved or inlaid with silver. The traditional "Soulham" or large burnous of dark blue cloth, covers the whole, sometimes gathered in large folds and sometimes flowing in the wind.

The pliable red or yellow leather boots or "temmag" of the Arab horse soldier are rarely met with in the Moghreb. Simple babouches are generally worn and the Sultan forms no exception to the rule. They also rarely carry spurs, as the points of the Moorish stirrup advantageously serve the same purpose.

This uniformity of appearance has caused many travellers to suppose that they all formed part of the same corps, and as the common herd of the sea-ports speak of all of them under the generic title of Mokhazni or troops of the Makhzen, the mistake has gained currency, more especially as the soldiers who serve as guards to the Consulates, Legations, and all resident foreigners demanding such protection, are drawn from the ranks of the cavalry and principally from the Abid Bou Khari, in the sea-ports and at Tangiers.

It is customary also for the hotels to employ a soldier as concierge. When these Mokhazni speak Spanish or French they prove very useful servants in fetching letters and accompanying their masters. It is considered to be exceedingly good form to be preceded by a soldier, and they are invaluable on market days as the dense crowds respectfully give way before the representative of Sherifian authority.

The legations at Tangiers possess guards varying in number from two to six. Seated on low round cushions, their only occupation is to act as doorkeepers and to rise and salute the secretaries and other officials. This gives them a somewhat important bearing which loses none of its significance from the point of view of Mussulman prestige.

Among the surroundings of the court the picturesqueness of the Makhzen cavalry and their costume always produces a marked impression. The military life of the mountains and plains has given them a ferocious warlike appearance, which the soldier valets and porters of Tangiers have entirely lost. Their black or copper-coloured faces, quite oriental in type, are artistically set off by their brilliantly coloured chechia and the white haik which envelopes in large folds their features bronzed with long service in the field under a fierce Morocco sun. A troop of Makhzen cavalry in the immense courts of the palace at Meknas is a sight not to be easily forgotten.

The various regiments of which we have now given a short account constitute the cavalry of the Moroccan army. It is at the entire disposal of the Sultan, who can count on its fidelity, and, with the artillery, it forms the most effective nucleus of his power. Their number varies, and it is very difficult to estimate it on account of the prevailing abuses. The Sultan himself is ignorant of the exact number of his horse soldiers, as the system of "paper regiments" is widely practised in the muster rolls and in reviews.

We were assured that in the event of a general levy the cavalry of the Makhzen could furnish about 30,000 men; but these figures, very excessive for the size of the country, are far from being reached on ordinary occasions, for of late years the total effective of the Moroccan army has not exceeded 25,000 men. However, to these must be added a large number of volunteer horse and foot-soldiers, drawn from among all the able-bodied men of the subdued and unsubdued tribes. All these, whether horse or foot, are armed with guns, and are keen to fight, especially in prospect of booty. However, though the tribes of the Rif shared the plunder in the time of Muley Ismaïl, now-a-days the tactics and solicitude of the Sultan's advisers lie rather in the direction of an intimate acquaintance with the resources of their enemies. The imperial troops are managed thus, and the hope of plunder fills the neighbouring tribes with courage and ardour to such a degree that the army visibly is growing into a vast and clamorous rabble.

Quite recently, in June 1886, the result of the Sous campaign redounded to the credit of this political foresight of the Sultan; thanks to his understanding with the principal Chiefs of this province, and especially with some neighbouring Berber tribes, the insurgents laid down their arms to the Sherifian army without striking a blow.[1]

But in this respect it is doubtful in the event of the advance of an European army into Morocco whether the same expectations would attract so many combatants. It is already well known in the Moghreb that the amount of baggage is now reduced, and that an European army engaged in African warfare only carries absolute necessaries. This fact has been recognised since the Spanish campaign of 1860, and especially in consequence of their proximity to the Southern Oranese, the Moroccans have been witnesses of the tactics of the famous French columns, and have convinced themselves that the impedimenta of an army tends to grow

[1] However, it was of the utmost importance for the maintenance of the Sultan's authority in this region; for certain powers, Germany, for example, were suspected of having some intention of occupying the littoral of this rich southern province, which for some years had enjoyed a kind of semi-independence.

less and less. The chances of booty, therefore, disappear, and it is no longer possible to dazzle the eyes of the Berbers with such a bait.

Further, as these Berber mountaineers are very indifferent Mussulmans, the question arises, how the Sultan could raise the army of 300,000 men spoken of by some authors. Without taking into account the fact of their fantastic armament forming the sum total of their discipline, and the incessant advance of European military tactics, as well as the increasing topographical knowledge of the country, it would be easy to deal with these masses. A few salvoes from a great distance alone would at the commencement have an enormous moral effect on a population so utterly ignorant of the superiority of our armaments.

The command in chief of the cavalry is confided to the Kaïd el Mechouar Dris ben el Alam (the standard bearer), whilst the Sultan reserves to himself that of the artillery. The direction of the infantry devolves on the Minister of War, the present one being the brother of the Grand Vizier.

It only remains for us in concluding this rapid survey of the Moroccan cavalry to touch upon the quality of the horses, and the care bestowed upon them, finally dealing with the tactics of warfare practised by these troops.

Horses in Morocco vary in quality according to the places from which they are drawn. In the district situated between the W. Sebou and the Tensif they are vigorous and substantial in character, and would even be suitable as mounts for cavalry of the line.[1] To the north of the river

---

[1] In Morocco the maximum height of a horse rarely exceeds, on an average, $16\frac{1}{2}$ hands, and the price ranges from £25 to £30 for a superior animal. £12 is the average price paid in the North of the

they run smaller in size, but possess more sagacity and endurance than the former.

The most valued horses in the Moghreb are to be found in the fertile province of Dukkala, to the south of Mazaghan, but it must also be mentioned that the Sous and the valleys situated between the Atlas, and in the Atlas itself, produce animals a little inferior in outline, but still very handsome. They approach very closely to the Arab type, with graceful neck and shoulders, fine silky hair, and symmetrical limbs; the type, however, degenerates in the north of the Tingitane. These latter have indeed retained very little of the Barb. The want of care exercised upon them when young, their narrow rumps, and their puffy limbs, make them ugly-looking beasts, though they are well able to endure fatigue. Arab stallions must not be sought for in Morocco; indeed, the breeding of horses is attended with considerable difficulty and disadvantage on account of the rapacity of the armies or governors of provinces who never rest until they have acquired any horse with at all good points. This degeneracy is also attributable to the fact that the distinguished personages in the immediate entourage of the government rarely ride on horseback; they all, except the Sultan, prefer the prosaic mule, which in Morocco is a very fine beast. This animal allows of rapid circulation through the crowded streets without fear of accidents, and for travelling its indefatigability and sure footedness, together with its rapid pace, render it a really agreeable means of locomotion.

Even the Sultan's stables contain no thoroughbred Tingitane. Their exportation is strictly forbidden, as also is that of mules. The price of the latter is always proportionately higher than that of horses. Thus some large mules are worth £40, but these are magnificent animals.

animals, and only big puffy and fat horses are regarded as of value. It is evident that such animals have not been stinted of their corn. The present of Normandy breeding mares given by Louis Philippe, King of France, has not produced all the expected results. Moorish indifference and want of care, even of the human race itself, so characteristic a feature of the Moghreb, have not been able to make a judicious selection, and the heaviness of type has only been intensified. As to the gift of several mares of excessive beauty[1] which quite recently M. Féraud offered in the name of the French Government, it was a veritable sacrilege to give such beautiful creatures to men so ignorant of the art of horse breeding. This recalled to mind " Margarita ante porcos." However, the points of beauty in a horse are not regarded from the same standard as with us, for defects in its limbs do not detract from the value of a horse. The deplorable state of the hoofs of the Sultan's horses is a sufficient indication of this. Tightly tethered, they all, even the stallions reserved for breeding, are compelled constantly to occupy a cramped position; their hoofs become badly deformed and their fetlocks get cracked and cut to the quick.

If this is the case in the stable of Moroccans of high rank, it is easy to imagine what care and food would be bestowed on their mounts by the poor and simple Abids Bou Khari. All the army horses present a most miserable appearance, and they have much to gain in the way of suitable treatment. The government frequently pays the cavalry in kind, but for the most part the money which

[1] As for the animals sent by the Sultan to the heads of European States it will show what they are worth if it is stated that a horse dealer, a connoisseur in one of the principal cities of Europe, offered £20 apiece for them.

should be devoted to the keep of the horses is unblushingly pocketed by the soldiers who content themselves by giving their mounts a little straw, or, when the season permits, green forage. They allow the animals to sleep on the bare ground in the open air, a harmless proceeding in so temperate a climate, but they never groom them. From time to time they wash them, but allow them to roll in the dust when bringing them back from the water.

The harness consists of an Arab saddle of even more comfortable make than in other Mussulman countries, for its usually very high cantle is lowered a little and is more yielding, giving the illusion of the back of an armchair. Fastened by a single girth and placed on a considerable thickness of packing it is most comfortable. No crupper is used, but there is a free breast strap which is generally ornamented with a silver buckle, the large knob of which is artistically wrought.

The large Moorish stirrups, silvered and sometimes gilded, are in the making adjusted very short by a number of small woven leather cords. The bridle is similarly constructed, necessitating each horse to have its own. The Arab bit is provided with a fixed curb, the shank of which bent at right angles leaves the tongue free, but it often breaks the horses' teeth.

As Moors are ignorant of suitable methods of preparing ox-hides, and only tan the skins of dogs, which though pleasing to the eye by reason of their rutilant colours have no durability, the horsemen in consequence are constantly employed in repairing their harness.

Two large cloth pockets often superbly embroidered, and kept in position by the cantle, serves to store the provender.

CAVALRY TACTICS.

The Moroccan cavalry cannot boast of any regular tactics; they follow the first inspiration, and it would be difficult to make a Moor understand that the duties of cavalry are complicated. Of reconnoitring and scouting they understand nothing; in their eyes every engagement of the army appears to be a kind of military parade attended by more than usual excitement. So few are killed that they regard it as a species of "fantasia," a little more animated than usual.

Relying on the trite maxim that speed is the surest means of avoiding bullets, the Moroccan cavalry dash forward at a wild galop, fire when passing before the enemy, at the same time scampering away, then returning and so on. Besides the absolute impossibility of taking a true aim by such methods, one can easily understand how these brilliant horsemen come pitiably to grief when brought in contact with the smallest company of marksmen armed and trained in Europe.

The result is that this primitive organization so defective in armament,[1] (a bad flint gun into which the bullets fit loosely being wound round with palm tow, and a short sabre) does not give the cavalry, so remarkable otherwise for the endurance of its horses, the power of resisting trained troops and still less of attacking them. Its chief duty in the ad-

[1] In an escort of Bou Khari that the Sultan had entrusted with the protection of our caravan, we had horsemen whose flint guns had been repaired with numerous pieces of string. As to the sabre called Koummyah it is generally much too short to be of any service; in the improbable event of a conflict with white troops these unfortunate horsemen would be annihilated long before they could arrive at the infantry lines.

The Sultan recently having contracted for the supply of 5000 Winchester rifles and several million rounds of cartridges it is possible that he is thinking of more effectively arming his cavalry.

ministration of the Empire is the collection of the taxes, and though they unceasingly harass the tribes of the plains they become useless in the mountains where the smallest Berber ambush demolishes a whole column with the same ease as they would a cardboard castle.

Thus though these cavalry corps were in the first instance recruited and almost entirely composed of picked men, yet in times of war they would no longer be of much service for they would be swamped by a crowd of entirely untrained volunteers, and perhaps would be more detrimental than useful in consequence of the confusion that they would cause in the ranks on the final reverse.

As to a system of concentration it may well be doubted if such a thing exists in a country where a commissariat and the least idea of orderly administration is unknown. All depends upon the good will and competence of the provincial governors, who are very dishonest and crassly ignorant. If they obeyed the orders of the Makhzen, they should liberally supply the volunteers with the powder and shot which is sent to them for distribution, but it is clear that these honourable governors rarely hurry themselves in obeying these instructions, which they interpret as enjoining them to tighten their purse strings. To this drawback must yet be added the state of the roads and the difficulties which in the rainy season prevents intercommunication. The conclusion must also be drawn in respect to all branches of the service that the lack of cohesion in the Moroccan army makes it an instrument difficult to oppose to a body of European troops.

CHAPTER XV.

The Sherifian artillery; Its Composition—Armament, Material and Instruction—The Infantry—The Prevailing Disorder—The Wretched Accoutrements—Mode of Recruiting—The Harrabas Battalion and the Kaïd Maclean—The French Military Mission—Its Diplomatic Object—History of the Christians in the Moroccan service.

THE artillery is Muley Hassan's favourite hobby; upon it he concentrates all his thoughts, it being with him in fact a matter of prestige. He quickly perceived that cannon would[1] prove very weighty arguments indeed with the ignorant tribes of the Empire who were entirely without the means of defence against such arms. He carefully supervises all matters of drill, laying and organization connected with it, while to him also belongs the credit of having created an arm of the service, which, developing year by year under the intelligent and judicious instruction of the French Military Mission, is calculated to shield the

---

[1] The effect in the expedition to the Sous undertaken by the Sultan some years ago was singularly odd. The natives of Farroudant had never before seen either a cannon or its carriage, and they brought a load of provisions to propitiate an infernal monster capable of blowing everything to pieces!

The artillery is regarded with such fascination by the Moroccans, that, oftentime, wretched culprits about to be arrested throw themselves upon, and cling to the wheels of the field pieces, in the belief that thereby they place themselves under a protection which always claims respect in the Mzaoug.

focus of power in the Moghreb as represented by the Makhzen from surprise at the hands of rebel tribes.[1]

It is evident that if comparison between the Moroccan army and European troops generally is out of the question, still less reasonably can any parallel be established in respect to the artillery armaments of His Sherifian Majesty, and those of continental powers. Although the guns, ammunition and stores are, comparatively speaking, in good condition, it cannot be denied that the evolutions are executed with extreme carelessness, amidst a confusion which it would be impossible to eradicate without shaking the theocracy of the government to its very foundations.

The result of the instruction of the last few years is, however, none the less surprising and admirable—scarcely ten years ago and prior to the arrival of the French mission of which we shall speak later on. This was the old-fashioned artillery and its material was under the care of a body of renegades, mostly Spaniards, whose incontestable bravery did not, however, compensate for their ignorance and want of discipline. The Sultan was not long in realising the futility of such supervision, for, his defective artillery having been surrounded and captured in a rebellion on the Rifian frontier at the beginning of his reign, he only owed his safety to extreme coolness and subsequent good luck. The present Sultan is not singular in his partiality for artillery, since one of his ancestors, Sidi Mohammed, the father of Muley Yezid, endeavoured to establish an arsenal, bringing artillerymen and artificers from Constantinople for

---

[1] The artillery, however, is recruited from the elite of the army, from among the Guichs of the Makhzen tribes. It generally comprises two battalions, each commanded by a Kaïd agha. These are divided into 15 mia or companies of 100 men, but the total effective on paper is rarely reached.

the purpose; this zealous activity merely ended in a shot foundry at Tetuan which did not long remain in active working. Nevertheless, it cannot be said that the Moroccans are destitute of ordnance. In the shape of presents from European Powers, gifts by Ambassadors[1] or pieces wrung and extorted from traders anxious to dispose of their worthless wares, specimens of field pieces dating and hailing from every period and nationality may be seen in all the ports, but, however, such a thing as an arsenal is unknown in the Moghreb; all this warlike show is for the most part of no value, and the coatings of rust are clear proofs of extreme neglect. Still the strength and quantity of the artillery is always eulogised before the ignorant and constantly deceived Sultan. At the time of the Tetuan war, in particular, Morocco entered into contracts in England and on the Continent for the purchase of a large quantity of ordnance and ammunition.

The French officers charged with the instruction of the artillery corps found it, therefore, no easy matter to make a serviceable selection from among ordnance so old fashioned and varied in type.[2]

[1] These gifts of artillery have not been confined to recent years, for the Ottoman Sultan Mustapha sent in 1767 by El Hadji abd el Kerim Arghoum, a magnificent offering consisting of a ship loaded with cannon, mortars and ammunition.

[2] The available force comprises :—
- 3 Mountain batteries of four pounders of six pieces each of French origin and muzzle-loading.
- Wall pieces.
- 2 Whitworth mountain batteries.
- 4 Field pieces (smooth-bored).
- Gatling Guns.
- 1 Hodgkiss mitrailleuse.
- 2 Mortars, fifteen pounders.
- 1 Battery of large Krupp, field pieces.

The introduction of breech-loaders, as advised by the French officers, is delayed as much as possible, and consequently this diversity of type forms one difficulty the more in training recruits. Although this duty is undertaken by the most intelligent of the natives, the somewhat complicated mechanism of the ordnance requires management and care incompatible with the defective instruction and inadequate practice of the Sherifian artillerymen, especially when the natural ingrained indolence and heedlessness of their characters are borne in mind. At the time of our sojourn in Meknas we actually saw a piece of ordnance the moveable breech of which had been fixed in order to allow the gun to be charged from the muzzle. The tables were thus somewhat turned; for at each volley the breech threatened to burst, and kill the gunners.

The battery exercises are performed with the French and Spanish field pieces (smooth-bored) presented by Louis Philippe and Queen Isabella after the peace of 1844.

The words of command are given in French, Arabic not readily lending itself to the exigencies of European manœuvring. It is easy, therefore, to apprehend the obstacles in the way, and the time as well as the patience required to impart the traditional course of study, tedious enough in the

4. Belgian mitrailleuses.
5. Small mortars.
6. Spanish mountain batteries, (smooth-bored).
1. Armstrong shifting gun.

The difficulty of effectively organising these armaments will be readily understood, but such, with slight exception, is the composition and strength of the Sultan's artillery. It should be remembered that outside the Krupp ordnance and the cannon presented by the French Government or by the Ambassadors of the Republic, it is all of very inferior quality, dishonest agents having supplied very worthless articles.

case of European recruits, to the Moghrebian mind. It is therefore useless to expect much more than a mere travesty of artillery manœuvrings, though in such a fanatical country they are at first sight none the less a matter for surprise. It seems odd indeed to have all the minutiæ of European drill reproduced before one's eyes. The practice takes place every morning except on Fridays which is a *fête* day, and on Mondays the Sultan himself attends the gunnery drill. It was one of our principal diversions at Meknas to go and see the evolutions of the Tobjyah, as artillerymen are designated in the Moghreb.

The skill of the Morisco artillerymen is certainly not to be despised. Exercises of this nature seem congenial to the race, and from His Majesty downwards all the gunners display a skill which for a long time impressed the officers of the French Military Mission. It is, however, entirely mechanical, and we might add, without fear of contradiction, that intelligent knowledge of these matters on the part of Muley Hassan—even indeed, to his lowest kind—is very limited. The use of the backsight is a great mystery to them, and it is impossible to induce them to adopt it. When a redoubt fortified by some of the Berber mountaineers has to be attacked the foolish Moroccans insist on efficient artillerymen placing their ordnance in batteries at a distance of only some hundreds of yards, and they refuse to believe that the destructive effect would be greater at a longer range, or that they would run less risk to their own lives. Such courage is indeed foolhardy and useless!

The target practice, that each Monday the Sultan presides over with Sherifian competence, takes place at the gates of the palace, the butts, which are fixed, being at 250 yards range! Shooting continues until all the targets have been smashed by His Majesty! The Sultan is very fairly successful at this operation—which in view of the short range is somewhat childish—and Moroccan enthusiasm manifests itself in protracted shouts of triumph at each battered target. It scarcely needs to be recorded that the same balls are used over and over again, and when a supply is required, they are hunted for in the rising sandy ground behind the range. It would not be altogether incredible if these projectiles were found capable in the long run of finding their way unassisted to their billets!

As to the enthusiasm displayed by the Sherifian entourage, I fancy it is mainly due to royal command. At any rate it seems to know no bounds, and Muley Hassan in the eyes of his faithful followers is apparently at once the most skilful cavalier and most expert gunner in the Mussulman world! But then, should not a descendant of Mohammed be superior to all, in all?[1]

On active service the artillery generally carries three mountain batteries on the backs of mules, and two mounted batteries, the rest of the supplies being transported by camels. These animals are very numerous in the country, and are extremely serviceable for this duty as thereby the total absence of roads forms no obstacle to the transport of heavy ordnance. A litter is fastened to the backs of two or four camels and the cortege proceeds slowly and with difficulty. Should one of the beasts lie down the burden tilts, and the cannon falls to the ground carrying everything before it. This, however, is a mishap common to all animal transports. It may generally be computed that a

---

[1] This naturally, of course, only refers to those expeditions in which the Sultan takes part. Beyond that, smaller sections are often allotted to the corps entrusted with the everlasting collection of taxes.

camel can easily carry a cannon of 9 cwts., but in the rainy season on slippery ground the difficulty these animals experience in retaining their footing is notorious.

The ammunition, packed in cases as it arrives from Europe, is easily transported by means of mules, which, as previously stated, are numerous in Morocco, and are of a fine breed similar to that indigenous to the north of Spain.

The mounted batteries are horsed with native animals, the trappings being of French make. Contrary to expectation, the drivers quickly get accustomed to their novel saddles,[1] and the horses are sufficiently drilled in a few weeks to enable them to execute the most complicated movements on all manner of ground. This fortunate and surprising result is due to Capt. Erckman, the first chief of the French Military Mission.

It only remains for us to mention a corps of young "savants" or Thalba, called Mohendezz. They are engineers and have a smattering of arithmetic and geometry. These young Moroccan prodigies are attached to the artillery in the event of detachments being sent to this arm of the service, and are employed in reading the tangent scales, in calculating distances, and in laying batteries, &c., for the majority of the Kaïds are unable to read. The officers of the military mission are expected to turn them into storehouses of knowledge, a thankless task were the circumstances other than we have been stating all along.

The corps of artillery are under the superintendence and direction of a Miralaï (a Turkish title equivalent to the

---

[1] This particular circumstance has lately given rise to the idea of forming a cavalry corps equipped and harnessed in the European fashion. Report also speaks of important purchases of harness in England. Up to the present, however, no confirmation of the rumour has transpired.

Colonel in rank). At present this office is filled by Muley Ahmed Souari (*i.e.*, originally of Mogador) a sympathetic and intelligent man educated by the famous French renegade Abd-er-Rahman.

As to the artillery stationed on the coast, the remarks in connection with the defence of Tangiers are also applicable to it. Rabatt alone possesses batteries which are better cared for, the Sultan from time to time putting in an appearance when going from Morocco to Meknas and Fez.

The service of engineers is unknown in Morocco in spite of the absence of roads, and the fact that a simple muddy stream will often delay an army corps for many hours. Excellent sappers are, however, to be found among the Berbers of the Rif, but in the army itself the use of the pick and shovel is unknown. In consequence, therefore, Major de Vallois, the second chief of the military mission, has organised a company of sappers and miners. The Sultan was highly interested in some mining experiments made at the time. Some dynamite and electrical discharging apparatus having been obtained from France, experiments took place during our sojourn at Meknas, which fairly astounded His Majesty. About this time an unfortunate Berber tribe in the vicinity of Ksaba el Chourfa had rebelled, and sought refuge in an inaccessible rocky Dchar, and the Sultan was glad of an opportunity of experimentalising with the new explosive on these wretched creatures. Shortly afterwards some dozens of disfigured heads ornamented the pediment of the palace gates forming a kind of object lesson for the populace.

Those of the rising Moroccan Thalba [1] who have evinced

---

[1] Treated with consideration and treated as non-commissioned officers, these young men bid fair to give satisfactory results.

a decided taste for Vauban's art have been sent to France, to the corps of engineers stationed at Montpellier. They should there be able to acquire the elements of the science of fortification, and, in time, form the nucleus of a company of engineers capable of rendering valuable service to the Sultan.

In addition to having improved his artillery and developing the instruction of this section of his army, he has likewise attempted to infuse a little spirit into the battalions of infantry created by Sultan Abd-er-Rahman on the Turkish model. He served his first campaign in this corps under the auspices of a notorious English renegade bearing the name of Ingliz Pacha.

It must, however, be confessed that in spite of the efforts of the Sovereign the infantry is undubitably in a most pitiable condition. The dress is incongruous and its composition grotesque. Old men of seventy clothed in tatters, some in black and some in blue, are to be seen side by side with lads of fifteen absurdly decked out in tinsel. This want of uniformity is universal, even in parade, when the words of command are given in French or English according as the sergeants have been trained in schools of one or the other nationality. Gross confusion is prevalent, and the evolutions tend to remind one of the Tower of Babel, for they all seem to inspire an ideal of carelessness which is apparent even in the shouldering of arms. Consequently, a Moroccan infantry review has always to my mind borne a comic aspect, and these concessions to modern ideas and the introduction of the features of modern warfare amidst surroundings which if picturesque are still oriental and savage in their nature, seem to border on the burlesque. Lacking[1]

[1] Although the facilities of instruction have sensibly increased in the artillery as a set off, they are said to have suffered material dimin

a martial bearing the soldiers are mere caricatures, and the assumption of extreme dignity by the officers, supported by the dangling of a huge old-fashioned sabre by their side, puts the finishing touch to a gigantic parody. The discipline is very lax, and as the state of health appears to me to be likewise very precarious, the execution of manœuvres is proportionately deficient. The guns are varied in pattern; the age, size, and even the bearing of the men are odd. Some burly fellows—musketeers of the old type— execute a movement to the left, whilst their neighbours wheel about in an opposite direction; and striplings of fifteen break down under the weight of clumsy muskets, with bayonets fixed, all patched up and abundantly tuckered with string.

When the scabbards are lost the bayonets are carelessly suspended on the back or in the lining of the tatters which do duty as a uniform. This only serves to intensify the odd appearance of the troops, and at some distance they look like so many unfortunate wretches impaled. There is greater confusion and disorder in the infantry than in any other arm of the service; for the officers of the military mission have the care of the artillery, and the cavalry, possessing the penchant of all Moroccans for fantasias and the ceremonial parades, consequently perform their evolutions so much the better; but in the infantry all is in a state of confusion except perhaps the battalion commanded by Maclean and a small detachment stationed

ution in the cavalry. The infantry is far from brilliant, and the contemporaries of Abd-er-Rhaman allowed it to be generally understood that the cavalry was then more numerous and much better disciplined, and they praise up the old organization, and the mobility of the troops which then allowed of the boldest strategetic movements without the sacrifice of picturesque and dignified effects.

at Rabatt officered by French Zouaves. When on the march the "mud-crushers" may be seen to disburden themselves of their muskets and securing them in bundles load the baggage camels with them.[1] The sight of these tattered cohorts forcibly reminds one of a masquerade, and furnishes abundant scope for amusing comparisons. Thus in a defile it is difficult to distinguish whether one is not encountering a troop of cavalry, each individual being mounted on either a mule, an ass, or an emaciated broken-winded jade. The column stretches itself out indefinitely and offers innumerable facilities for a flank attack in spite of the care taken by the Sultan in clearing the road by means of the numerous bodies of cavalry who hold the surrounding heights. Barracks properly so-called do not exist, and, when in garrison, the soldiers who belong to a crack corps, as for example the Harrabas, are billeted upon the inhabitants, or in lieu of that they are quartered in the camp which always accompanies the Sultan and his retinue. This town life gives the soldiery an opportunity of making money, opportunities which are enhanced by the complicity of the officers who are only too ready to share the spoils in order to increase their own slender resources. The Moghreb is the land of low wages: the head of a battalion receives one shilling a day, and this, moreover, but rarely. It falls only to the share of a privileged few who possess influence at court.

Everything else runs on a similar footing, and abuses would appear to rank among the necessaries of life with these poor wretches in spite of the genuine and almost absurd cheapness of all commodities.[2] Discipline is a very

[1] It should be said that these poor devils have very little baggage.

[2] The strangest familiarity exists between the soldiers and their superior officers. The latter, lacking all prestige and dignity, are often

secondary consideration in all this, and soldiers and officers alike follow the most arduous vocations. All occasionally sell their belongings, even to their weapons. I have in mind one battalion in particular who were notorious in this respect, and to which muskets were only served out when about to be drilled. At harvest time the ranks get thinned to the extent of 80%.

After the conquest of Algeria by the French, Muley Abd-er-Rahman wished to create an infantry[1] corps modelled on the prototype of the Turkish troops. For this purpose he had in view El Hadj abd el Kader of the regulars and summoned to his aid a certain Tunisian Kaïd and a Turkish officer. The semi-European uniform of this troop brought it, however, into discredit, especially among the upper Chorfas. The hideous blue cotton checked trousers and small tight jacket, in which this wretched corps is dressed, are likewise displeasing to the orthodox Sherifian, averse to the introduction of modern ideas. It gives them a mock Albanian brigand appearance and this repugnance redounds to their good taste.

At first it was proposed to confine this new corps solely to volunteers, but the result fell far short of expectation, and now the contingent is drawn from all the provinces in proportion to population, the various governors being charged with the duty of recruiting for the Askars. At this moment Muley Hassan has nine battalions of this kind, but the custom of compulsory service, besides

subjected to the bastinado and other degrading methods of punishment inflicted on the rank and file. The petty officers, whose numbers are small, are called Mokaddem, an expression which has lately become so common that muleteers apply the appellation to one another.

[1] Under the vague denomination of Askars, *i.e.*, soldiers.

giving worthless soldiers, is also productive of the gravest abuses. No faith is put in the tempting offers of an increased pay, or the other advantages held out to those who enlist voluntarily. Recruiting is carried on with such difficulty that the wretched conscripts have to be chained together, and I have been assured that many of them have been branded on the hand. What fidelity, therefore, can under the circumstances be expected of such troops; besides which the love of freedom and the independent life of the noble Berber races are not qualities to incline the mountaineers to submit to the restraints of town life. It is true that as far as recruiting is concerned there is never any serious obstacle to overcome in the towns, and when recruits are scarce, bodies of conscripts are obtained by way of fines and penalties. These remarks are clearly not applicable to the Makhzen tribes who living under the ægis of the government cordially support it. Amongst them recruiting goes on exactly in proportion as the fighting is near home. Elsewhere the greed of the Kaïds is an important factor, as they find recruiting a facile and inexhaustible source of revenue. The contingents are in point of fact raised only from amongst the indigent, and the poor wretches are chained together to prevent their escape. Those possessed of means can always effect an arrangement, so while money forms the sinews of war it is also in this case the surest antidote to the inconveniences of military service.

Theoretically the infantry are only liable to serve three years, at the end of which time they are supposed to be at liberty to return to their homes, forming then part of the reserve and only being called out again in case of need. As a matter of fact it is far different, for, owing to the iniquitous prevalent system of prevarication—which has made

Morocco a gigantic nest of swindlers[1]—the actual duration of service is lifelong, a state of affairs which would doubtless delight the hearts of European ministers of war. The longevity of Arab races is well known, and consequently the venerable beards of patriarchs of upwards of seventy summers may be seen in the ranks fulfilling the modest duties of gunners of the second grade. Some tribes not caring to part with the able-bodied send children of ten in place of their young men. We have seen such in the train of some battalions looking more like troopers' children. Or, in lieu of these the old and infirm are sent, who impart such strange features to the already odd appearance of the imperial army.

It would be difficult to form very brilliant soldiers of such materials, and the blame, moreover, does not rest with the present Sultan, who, indeed, has neglected no opportunity of improving the instruction of the army. He is, however, surrounded by apathetic and narrow-minded courtiers whose fanaticism renders all reform well-nigh impossible.

It has been Muley Hassan's aim to bring up the effective of the Askars to 15,000, and it was at the head of the first of these regiments that he served his initial campaign in the Sous. When he mounted the throne the regular infantry numbered 10,000 men divided into battalions. Their chief, invested with the rank of Sari Askar or general, was Hadj Mennou, a native of Sous, whence nearly all the rank and file were drawn. El Hadj Mennou was a very brave man and was much liked by the troops. He had served in many campaigns undertaken by the Sultan Muley

---

[1] Substitutes may be had for a money payment. Thus when the native "John Atkins" becomes possessed of means he can always buy himself out.

Mohammed and was much appreciated by the latter. But the exposure of his intrigues with the reigning Grand Vizier Si Mouça made him notorious, and, in spite of signal services rendered to Muley Hassan at the siege of Fez, he was dismissed from office and cast into prison at Tetuan.[1] After the incarceration of Mennou and the subsequent almost complete desertion of the troops from the Sous, his Sherifian Majesty made fresh levies in order to reconstitute the infantry. Each tribe was forced to furnish a certain number of men, and each town its battalion, so that at the present time the Moroccan regular infantry consists of about 25 tabous or battalions of from 400 to 1000 men each, the latter figures, however, being rarely reached.[2]

Kaïd Maclean, an old British officer now in the service of the Makhzen, has specially under his care the command and organization of a certain battalion called the Harrabas which is infinitely better equipped than the rest of the army, and in every respect well trained as the regularity and perfection of their movements amply testify. From this regiment a good number of instructors are drawn and placed over other battalions which are then designated either by the name of their chief or by that of the province from whence the men were recruited. The Harrabas number about 800 men, and were originally composed of subordinates who had been sent to Gibraltar to learn European drill. It is a well disciplined and trustworthy guard

[1] The present Grand Vizier (1886) Si Mohammed El Arbi El Djemaï (of the tribe of Oulad Djema) was formerly at the head of the infantry occupying the place of Mennou. This Grand Vizier is the maternal uncle of the Sultan.

[2] Besides these must be mentioned three battalions stationed in eschelons between Fez and Morocco: on the road passing through Rabatt avoiding the chain of the Zaïr—the imperial road *par excellence*. These three battalions are said to have an effective of 500 men each.

to the Sultan, and in case of need, would render him great service. During our sojourn at Meknas, drill succeeded drill, without interruption, in the evening, taking place on the plateau of Hel Soutal, and the target practice in the morning completing an effective military education. This guard takes part in all ceremonials, and at each ambassadorial reception it puts in an appearance decked out for the occasion in their most dazzling uniforms, their heads dressed in new tarboucks, and with lemon coloured babouches on their feet. They thus accompany, both going and returning, the *personnel* of the Embassy.

If the whole army were judged by this regiment, the verdict would be an exceedingly favourable one.

Their armament is satisfactory—Martini Henrys—and their trappings bear the motto, "Dieu et mon droit," thus giving them a spurious resemblance to Indian troops. But the rest of the infantry is far removed from this corps in point of appearance and quality, although there is every reason to believe that the impetus given by the Zouave officers and subalterns of the mission at Rabatt bear the palm as producing better results during recent years. Yet one effective battalion isolated at Rabatt is of little service as a leaven for the infantry as a whole.

Next to the Harrabas, whose marching is indubitably remarkable, rank the Cherarda foot soldiers, 600 strong, and resident permanently at Morocco. Latterly a company of about 200 natives of the Oudaïas has also been formed.

As a rule the equipment verges on the ridiculous. The cartridge pouches, among other things, are rarely forthcoming, and when they do, are used to stow away the soldier's "flouss"[1] or his petty comestibles.

[1] Copper money of the smallest decimal value.

The cartridges are carried in a kind of handkerchief knotted by the four corners, the slightest movement upsetting its unstable equilibrium. As to the armament itself, we have already explained that all are of an antiquated type. It is difficult to conceive what the commissariat of such a cohort in action can be. Up to the present all arms and ammunition have been obtained abroad,[1] but the reigning Sultan has established manufactories at Tetuan, where a pretence of turning out Martini Henry rifles is made. The Tetuan artificers have always been celebrated in the Arab world for their skill in the manufacture of firearms, but as this famous arsenal has up to now been unvisited by any specialist capable of pronouncing an opinion, judgment must be suspended as to its capacity for turning out in the Moghreb such delicate pieces of arms as the one mentioned.

Whilst the command of the cavalry is confided to the Kaïd el Mechouar and that of the artillery is undertaken by the Sultan, the nominal chief is the Minister of war, the brother of the present Grand Vizier.

Officers have no distinguishing uniform costume in the Moroccan army, nor are there such decorations which would by the regulations distinguish them from the rest. All is a matter of caprice, scions of good family richly dressed and smothered in gold braid, rub shoulder to shoulder, even in the cavalry, with their superior officers and comrades whose attire is in a pitiable condition. An officer decked out in sky blue, yellow or green may be seen marching at the head of a band of swaggerers whose incongruous tatters,

---

[1] The Sultan has lately contracted for the purchase of 5000 repeating rifles of the Winchester pattern, and subsequently others of the Martini and Weider type.

though of the gayish hues, give the finishing touches to a discordant picture.

The chiefs of the Mokhazni are distinguished by a white turban, which, ball-shaped, surmounts the red fez. The only regulation ranks are:—

The Kaïd Mia commanding 100 men.

The Kaïd Rahal, chief of several squadrons of battalions to the number of 1000 men, the rank of general not being bestowed by reason of the fear of the Makhzen to create too influential an office, especially since the Mennou affair.

What might be designated the army administrative service consists of,

(1.) El Hallaf or Chief of the Commissariat. During active service he levies the contributions in kind on the inhabitants, and distributes them among the troops. This office in a country like Morocco may readily be supposed to be one of the most lucrative, and one which speedily enriches its occupant.

(2.) The Kaïd El Ferraya, who has charge of the camping material. He is chief of the muleteers, who convey the Sultan's huge tent, a kind of palace, with a harem, mosque, &c.

(3.) The Kaïd El Sckhara or Chief of the Muleteers employed among the tribes for the transport of provisions, tents and munitions. It is to be observed that the simplicity which characterises the administration of the Moroccan army does not allow of an ambulance service. This, indeed, is represented by a few barbers whose forte is blood-letting, and who subsequently tend their patients' needs; whilst some bone-setters, whose skill is very indifferent, follow in the wake of the army.

It is impossible to treat of the Sultan's army, even in the cursory fashion I have adopted, without mentioning the

French Military Mission, and without making some reference to its organization and history, and above all to the remarkable work undertaken by it. The object of this mission being of the noblest character, it is fitting that all idea of petty diplomatic and international jealousy should be put on one side. It is well to recognise the fact that if the idea were eventually a barbarous invasion of the country, thereby entailing the loss of much time, treasure, and life, such is hardly consistent with the humane co-operation it affords a Sultan who, though worthy of all sympathy on account of his good intentions, is, alas, crippled in all his efforts by a fanatic and theocratic entourage. Viewed in this light, both England and France[1] can join hands in this respect and be inspired with the same ideas since we have seen that the nucleus of the crack Infantry Corps received their military training at Gibraltar. In that may be found a similitude of diplomatic action which it would be well to develope, but it is none the less incumbent that the work already achieved and the services rendered by the worthy officers of the French mission should be recognised. Their lives are bereft of all charm and are essentially of the nature of self-sacrifice as we can personally testify.

The very fact that the French government has put a certain number of its best officers at the service of the Sultan is a sufficient proof that it has no such end in view as the immediate conquest of the country. Such a line of conduct would indeed be a curious method of procedure, and in any case it would be sheer folly to initiate a people, whose territory it was eventually intended to invade, into the mysteries of military science. Moreover, it would appear that the powers most jealous of this action have never very

[1] England even more than France.

energetically opposed the formation of this mission, a clear proof that the political and geographical claims of Algerian France on the Moghreb El Acsa are recognised and respected, and even assuming the truth of the supposition her rivals would watch with malicious pleasure the forging of weapons which would then be turned against herself.

Later on it will become apparent how circumstances at the beginning of Muley Hassan's reign compelled him to seek aid of foreign officers as instructors for his troops. The *personnel* of the mission was first organised [1] in 1877, and a little later the command fell to Captain Erckman. Since then a change in the administration has twice occurred. In 1884, the direction of affairs was confided to Major Le Vallois, who had under his orders a captain of artillery, an officer drawn from the Zouaves at Rabatt, several subalterns, and last but not least, the learned and sympathetic Dr. Linarès.

The name of Kaïd Maclean has already been mentioned, but although his duties likewise have in view the raising of the standard of the Sherifian [2] army, it is important to remember that a radical difference exists between the official position of this old English officer who is absolutely retained by the Sultan and who is not in any way subject to European interference, and the French Military Mission. The members of the latter are in a way lent by

[1] Originally located at Oujdja, the mission was subsequently divided into two sections. One, under the direction of the commander-in-chief, accompanies the Sultan everywhere, occupying itself with the parades and the up-keep of the artillery; the other is stationed at Rabatt, and its duty is to train the depot of infantry stationed there.

[2] It might perhaps be said that Maclean is merely an imitator of the famous Alphonse de Gusman, Lord of San Lucar, who, when he became embroiled with the Castilian Court, retired to Morocco and became general of the army of Abou Yousouf, in which office he achieved fame by reason of his bravery.

the permission of the French Minister of War at Paris for an undefined period. As a matter of right they retain the national uniform of France, or, to speak more correctly, that of the Algerian troops of the Republic. Maclean on the contrary has adopted a uniform which, though practical as far as serviceability is concerned, is elegant and picturesque, and is yet oriental in character, consisting of the burnous, turban, and other Eastern vestments.

The presence of Europeans at a court so fanatical, and their employment by the government of the country would appear very extraordinary, were it not remembered that the adoption of such a course does not date from yesterday. Almost from time immemorial the sovereigns of the Moghreb have had Christians in their service. Leaving renegades out of count altogether, many instances of the troops in the service of the Chorfas may be encountered in Moroccan history.

The Almohades dynasty even went so far as to employ the Kurd militia, and these Asiatic soldiers fought side by side with the mercenaries, the whole constituting a singular conglomeration of divergent races. Under the Almoravides we see the Chorfas of Morocco employing soldiers to take part in the struggle of Abd el Moumeïn against Tachefin ibn Ali between the Moulouïa, Tlemcen and Oran. At this time especially, Christians occupied a singularly curious position, for it was then that a terrible and bloody struggle was in progress in the peninsula, where the Crescent and the Cross were standing face to face. Reading the history of the Moghreb in the light of the materials which have come to our hand, we conclude that at certain periods the Christians enjoyed a substantial political influence. By suring the punctual payment of their wages, El Mamoun succeeded after the capture of Morocco in retaining in his service a corps of 12,000 Spaniards whom he had brought from Andalusia.[1] Following the example of the Almoravide Sultans, he thus instituted a regular corps of free auxiliaries in his army, and his sons kept up their numbers by successful enrolments, the Merinides in their turn following the example thus set them.

In another instance a certain Francyl, a commander of the militia, on the death of El Mamoun (in 1332), assisted the other generals of the Empire in proclaiming the new Sultan Emir el Moumeïn under the walls of Ceuta. It is noteworthy that the free militia were subsequently officered by men of their own faith. Later on it fell to the lot of these contingents to render as good service to El Reshid and El Saïd as that which had previously won the confidence of their father, El Mamoun.

These troops, brave and disciplined, faithfully serving the government, from whom they punctually received their pay, formed one of the most powerful defences of the Makhzen against the unsubdued Beni Zian in the struggles which took place in the region of Tlemcen, and sometimes also against the Merinides when the latter were masters of the region of the south west.

In short these free auxiliaries crop up so frequently in detailing the history of the incessant struggles, in the course of which the dynasty and Empire of Abd el Moumeïn degenerated, that citation must perforce be curtailed if this narrative is to be kept within reasonable bounds. It is imperative, however, that some mention be made of the fact, that under the government of El Saïd the sum

---

[1] The author of Roudh el Kartas describes this as the first occasion on which Christian troops entered and served in the Moghreb.

total of Christian warriors was indubitably very numerous, inasmuch as the letter addressed by Pope[1] Innocent IV. to this Sultan was chiefly written to secure increased protection for the sacred buildings, and the persons of Christian soldiers then located in the Moghreb El Acsa, as well as to obtain control of some strongholds on the littoral for these Christian auxiliaries, so that they could protect the country from surprise by an enemy—in a word *to confide to them the protection of the sea ports, so that in case of need they might depart and return with reinforcements to the succour of the Sultan.*

These strongholds, in the Pope's mind, would none the less have remained part of the Sultan's possessions, still it was certain that placing them under the protection of the auxiliaries would have assured the security of troops, the fidelity of which both he and his ancestor had fully appreciated. But the idea of making over whole towns such as Tangiers or Ceuta to a body of men composed entirely of Roumis or infidels did not in the least commend itself to that theocratic influence which has always had full sway in Morocco, and no response was ever made to this insiduous political demand.

This fact has only been cited in support of our statement that the number of Christians in Morocco was at one time very considerable, and had they been guided by an energetic and strong leader they would have formed a stable element in the country. As it was they seem to have missed such a destiny.

[1] Dated from Lyons, Oct. 31, 1246, and addressed to the "Illustrious Sovereign of Morocco." The beginning of the text is to be found in the celebrated work of the Cte. de Mas Latrie.

CHAPTER XVI.

A Moroccan Court of Appeal and Justice—Taxation—Presents to the Sultan—The Government Budget and the Emperor's Fortune—The Expenditure—The Harem and how Recruited—The Europeans who figure in it—Administrative Disorder—The Influence of Renegades—History of two such Celebrities—Our Andalusian Servant, a hoary old Renegade Assassin.

THE very name even of the Moroccan "Office of Complaints" or Court of Appeal is significant. Its chief is one of the most influential personages in the Government; he enjoys the confidence of, and advises the Sultan, as seated each morning at one of the entrances to the palace he is supposed to examine the claims of the unfortunate wretches who crowd there seeking redress or other official recognition. Each applicant for "God's justice from the Sultan" is cross-examined by this dignitary before being allowed to penetrate further into the administrative sanctum. Analytical examination of this kind, of a summary and yet only preliminary nature, is naturally very lucrative as may be imagined, and it would, moreover, be a difficult matter to control it in any way. The post is in consequence much sought after. A commission, or "Sokhra," often a very substantial one, is paid by the miserable applicants; indeed, it is impossible to move a step without submitting to this tax, which forms a ready means of spoliation. In Mussulman countries it is rarely possible to obtain a definite legal settlement, and in consequence the palace is crowded each morning by a concourse of applicants, who effectually block up the approaches to the Imperial residence, all anxious to seize a favourable opportunity of presenting their petitions for reinstalment.

Justice, as based on the tenets of the Koran, is called Cherâa. The most widely used books expounding the law are the Commentaries of Sidi Khelil and the works of Ibn Selmoun (Abdallah ben Abdallah ben Ali who died in 741), (1340-1) the author of the most approved modes of procedure amongst the Mussulmans of Northern Africa. As a rule everything in the first instance goes before the Kadi, and then to the Adoul a kind of notary. Plaintiffs are allowed the assistance of an Oukil or advocate, but suits generally end in an oath called the "hack Allah" taken at the Zaïoua, the possibility of false swearing not being dreamt of. In addition to all this must be mentioned the innumerable wiseacres who pretend to sift and examine difficult cases for plaintiffs as a last resource.

On the whole, therefore, it may safely be affirmed that the administration of justice in Morocco is one of the chief sources of the Imperial Revenue. The Sultan is inspired with a sincere belief in his absolute proprietorship over not only the territory, but likewise over the chattels and persons of his subjects. This fosters an internal administration, having nothing in common with Thebaïde, and which can only be compared with a winepress, of which the whole hierarchy of officials form the screw and the sovereign the motor. Tax-payers of every kind are squeezed, and it is a matter of careful arrangement that the operation is capable of repetition, and that more than once. In a word they never kill the goose that lays the golden eggs, the collection of taxes forming the all in all of Moroccan officialism—the one object which inspires the powers that be with an intelligent mission in life.

From high to low—Kaïd and magistrate alike—all shamelessly prostitute the privileges of their office; moreover, every industry is saddled with exorbitant taxation; notably shoemakers, saddlers, and tanners—all the workers in leather which represents the principal commercial product of the country. As to import dues they are very high, even on necessaries.

Strictly speaking, the only taxes authorised by the Koran are the Achour[1] or tithe of the grain, olive, and other harvests, and the Zekkat or 2% on the value of animals, but frightful abuses exist in the method of collection adopted.

There is a regular body of officials who scour the provinces, their duties consisting in making valuations. Hence, another fruitful source of profit, spoliation and undue favouritism, for no hesitation is shown in making exaggerated estimates, so that by the payment of a bonus by the poor Arabs, a juster assessment may later on be arrived at. Verily, the system is a convenient one! At all events the husbandmen can console themselves with the thought that the agents on their return will in turn be dispossessed by their superiors of a large portion of the ill-gotten gains.

Consequently, when the country people see the burnouses of the Mokhazni from afar, together with the inevitable

[1] This tithe is one of the five fundamental obligations imposed upon the faithful, and which form the pillars of the Mussulman faith. (1) Professing the religion of Mohammed; (2) Prayer; (3) Observing the Fast of Ramadhan; (4) The payment of tithes; (5) The Pilgrimage to Mecca; (6) Taking part in a Holy War—Al Djihad—or to take the word in its milder sense, to prosecute religious propaganda is regarded with prayer on Fridays as the sacred duty of all good Mussulmans.

Chechia, they lose no time in concealing their valuables. Once, when we crossed a deserted and abandoned tract of country our muleteers were at no loss to explain the cause of the devastation, putting it down to the Mokhazni or "the locusts" as they were satirically designated.

With regard to the tax on cattle, the Kaïd of the district acts as he sees fit, appropriating everything upon which it pleases him to lay an embargo. This state of things is alone sufficient to explain the inferiority and stagnation in Moroccan horse-breeding.

In addition, on the occasion of every fete day,[1] and whenever a birth or marriage occurs in the Sultan's household or in those of his Viziers, Pachas and other officials, every shop and house in the city, and every trade guild, is called upon to give a present commensurate with their means, the greedy and avaricious functionaries enforcing compliance if necessary. No pretext, whether of a religious nature or whether simply based on official whims is neglected, and it needs no saying that in the matter of finding excuses for further taxation their powers of inven-

---

[1] Among compulsory acts of charity is El Fythrâ consisting of grain, dates, fruits, and generally of portions of the customary food of the donor and his family, all of which is given to the poor. The celebrated commentator, Sidi Khalil, says, "it is proper to entrust these alms in the hands of the Iman;" but bearing in mind the notorious morality of these religious functionaries, this would only serve as a means of diverting the gift from its proper channel, and the Moroccans of to-day, both rich and poor, fully appreciate the action of the Emir Jacoub in abolishing in the year 1236 A.D., the custom of confiding such contributions to the appointed officials, and in leaving the discharge of the duty to individual good faith. It must be added that the sense of honour respecting religious matters in the Moghreb has always ensured the observance of the moral duty.

Alas! for the abuse remedied, many still flourish, and under a myriad forms impede all national progress.

tion are most lively and fertile. Disaffection is, therefore, pretty general, and there is no legal redress, the caprice of despotic power alone governing the situation.

However, I must not unduly exaggerate the dark picture, for this, according to European ideas, vicious method of collecting taxes is common to all Mussulman countries. The Pachas and Kaïds[1] imprison delinquents on the most frivolous pretexts, and the unfortunate victim is then kept under lock and key until he has disgorged an amount more or less exorbitant. These functionaries are not too sparing of such delicate attentions, for they do not fail to remember that they themselves are at the mercy of their superiors and the Sultan, who are always quick to pounce down and make them disgorge when the money bags get well filled. When summoned to court the representative of Sherifian authority disburses the round sum demanded from him with commendable alacrity, when other means having failed, the gentle persuasion of the stick or fear of being cast into prison are brought into play. He is then generally sent on his way loaded with honour and reinstated in his office with all its prerogatives. He is not in these circumstances very likely to be slow to display constantly increasing ardour, in the future, in taking care that his own personal interests do not suffer.

Some attempt to put off the day of reckoning by making voluntary substantial presents[2] to the Sultan, whilst others

[1] It must be remembered that the word Pacha is of Turkish and not of Arabic origin. It has become naturalised in Morocco through the Mecca pilgrimages having brought about contact with Ottoman officials in Egypt. Amil is the native title of a governor of a province, and Ouali that of the chief magistrate of a large town.

[2] These presents are known as Ferd. Three times a year at the Grand Hedias or ceremonial receptions of the Great Mohammedan festivals the Kaïds levy the most incredibly fabulous sums under

having a profound belief in fate, await the falling of the sword of Damocles without troubling themselves about means of escape.

In the event of the Sultan imposing an ordinary tax of 2000 piastres, the Amil forthwith multiplying this sum by the number of Kaïds under him, and, these latter following suit, the result is a most curious and iniquitous fiscal system.

One would suppose that the natives, living under such social conditions, subject to incessant spoliation, having no security for the future, and oppressed by the most absolute administrative tyranny would welcome[1] a government analogous to that which prevails in Algeria.

I have already spoken of the hideous aspect of the prison and its occupants; at Tangiers, matters are much worse in the interior of the country, and the kind-hearted Europeans who in the towns of the Tingitane and in the sea ports can,

this pretext. The Mouna must also be mentioned as one of the crying evils to which the population is subjected. This tax is imposed to defray the hospitality extended to dignitaries and guests of the Makhzen.

Only some very privileged Zaouïa are exempt from taxation. These are then designated horra or harra (free). At the same time this very rarely occurs in Morocco and is only applicable to the lands in the neighbourhood called habas.

[1] My good friend, Vist. Ch. de Foucauld, speaks of having seen during his famous expedition in 1883 the whole population of Taza weary with the oppression endured at the hands of the pillaging tribes of the Riata, and having no hope of intervention on the part of the Sultan, longing for the fortunate day when the French would appear on the scene. As the town has an important trade with the Rif coast, with the market town of Tafersit and with Mellila, Fez and the villages in the valley of the Molouya, the negligence and impotence of the Makhzen is very manifest. It lies also on the road from Fez to Oudjda and the neighbouring town of Meknas, and its fortified Kasbah is the only halting place for the Imperial troops.

in a measure, mitigate the arbitrary aristocracy of the Government, have no opportunity of doing so inland where the one object seems to be the steady squeezing of the people.

As it is alleged that the taxes do not suffice to satisfy the requirements of the Government, it may be asked why the Sultan is not tempted to grant concessions for working the mines, quarries, forests and other sources of revenue which European companies have often offered to purchase. The very pronounced spirits of defiant fanaticism so prevalent in the country is really responsible for this policy. Such proposals awaken the suspicion that it would lead to a general immigration of Christians into the country, whereas they would rather drive all those now in it beyond the frontiers. Although many Moroccans who have travelled in Europe or worked in Algeria are not altogether opposed to a more liberal policy, yet the Sherifian Government, fearful of awakening the jealousy of the Powers, opposes any alteration in the *Status quo*. Besides, nothing would convince the Sultan's advisers that in a thousand ways the adoption of such measures for augmenting the revenues of the empire, would tend to diminish the taxation which crushes and discourages agriculture.

Taxation—incessant taxation—without the least show of justice, forms the basis of the State, and the caprice which presides over its administration is felt even in the customs dues. The right of exportation has ever been in force, but all the same a prohibition exists against sending certain products out of the country. The Customs Houses are each administered by two oumana, one being drawn from Fez and the other being selected from among the notables of the district, each receiving respectively three and two douros a day. These posts, very lucrative for Morocco, are much sought after.

Since the wiping out of the debt contracted with a group of London bankers for the payment of the Spanish war indemnity of 1859-60,[1] the revenue from Customs had again been lodged in the Imperial Treasury which is considerably augmented by the innumerable taxes, the fines and the various exports and import dues. The first alone is subject to the provisions of treaties of commerce; imports bear an ad valorem duty of 10%, whilst the duty on the export of merchandise varies according to the fancy of the Makhzen.

All these circumstances, added to the exceptional benefits accruing from the guarantees of the European powers, make Morocco one of the most curious countries of the world, in that she not only possesses no national debt, but on the other hand, has assets more than sufficient to defray the cost of public works, which, however, she does not carry out.

The army is paid on a low scale; and the 25,000 to 30,000 men who compose it do not cost much—they invariably live on the populace, at least according to common report. As to the Moroccan marine, it has for several years

---

[1] The result of the Tetuan Campaign was that Morocco had to pay to Spain an indemnity of one hundred million francs ostensibly for the purchase of the town of Tetuan. England, however, to avoid every pretext for a military occupation by Spain, favoured the lending of this sum to the Sherifian Government by a syndicate of bankers. With a view of guaranteeing and reimbursing this advance certain maritime dues were for several years collected by European agents assisted by Moroccans. Now, all having been liquidated, the intervention of foreigners has disappeared. Under this arrangement, however, the Sultan still received one fourth of the dues, but strange to say, this fourth part exceeded the sum total produced before the war—a striking proof of the integrity of European surveillance.

been non-existent, and only a single trader now carries the Sherifian standard in the bay of Tangiers. It is a miserable turn out, although the Government paid dearly enough for it. Originally manned by an English, Danish, and Belgian crew, who were wholly corrupted by the inactive life, it is now worked by Spaniards, which the home Government by a clever stroke of policy has lent to the Sultan.

The budget,[1] therefore, is in reality nothing more or less than the private fortune of the Sultan, composing in addition to the proceeds accruing from his immense possessions presents of all kinds which come literally in shoals, and the so-called legal taxation.

The most onerous charge incumbent on the Sultan is to a moral certainty the support of his numerous family—his father's wives,[2] and those who compose his own harem.

Setting aside the bigotry which we have spoken of as enveloping the Sultan, the most enervating influence of Muley Hassan's domestic life is that of his harem. Next to his devotions, his wives occupy the first place in his life. They wait upon him at his toilet; even on his expeditions they precede him in a mysteriously secluded tent, which no one may approach, and they receive him when he alights from horseback. A group of favourites, indeed, invariably accompany this martial hero on the most insignificant ex-

[1] This is generally estimated to yield about £520,000 annually to the Sultan, whilst his expenditure rarely exceeds £198,000. The yearly surplus is therefore readily ascertainable. In this connection it must also be remembered that many important administrative offices which in Europe absorb enormous sums of money cost absolutely nothing, whilst some are here altogether wanting, such as public works, agriculture, manufactures, navigation, police, &c.

[2] The women of the former Sultan are lodged in immense barracks, a kind of cloisters, at Tafilalt, or in the Sous. It is a kind of living death, which they resignedly and patiently await.

cursions. Carefully veiled, closely muffled, and perched on strong quick-trotting mules, they often even precede the escort so that they may be at hand to receive the thrice blessed Sultan in their arms on arrival!

It is affirmed that the Sultan has a considerable number of women—some say six thousand—in each of his capitals—all being organised on well defined lines. More order is discernible in this respect than in any other branch of the Moroccan regime. Recruiting for this prodigious army proceeds apace, and none of the officials, or Kaïds, or indeed the most influential families of the country, enjoy any real security unless they can claim relationship with the imperial harem. No hesitation is ever shown in compassing such a tie. The demand for place and power greatly exceeds the supply. The Sultan never intervenes when candidates are being selected, for the chiefs of this army of women which is organised and divided into distinct companies, possess a rare judgment in such matters, the outcome of experience. Their practised eyes and admirable tact easily enable them to judge whether the budding charms of the young aspirants warrant the extension of special inducements.

The overseers of these troops of women are called Arifas, and their influence in the palace is naturally very great.

The life led by the women in the Sultan's harem is of the most debasing description—personal adornment, sleep, and the exercise of the carnal appetite, rounds of an existence which can only be compared to that of the brute creation. It may, therefore, be readily conceived that such a life is productive of the most rampant corruption. Petty jealousies are inevitable; these form a hotbed of intrigue, and the end is that the favourite Oriental warrant of poison is brought into play in order to terminate them.

Friday is devoted by the Sultan to the society of his womenkind. Entirely screened from the gaze of the inquisitive, he walks in his gardens, surrounded by a bevy of his wives; and, one must charitably assume, that his days are times of refreshing indeed! At Meknas his chief amusement lay in getting astride of a tricycle which was then pushed along by his consorts who thus voluptuously desported themselves amid the groves of orange trees.

European women have always been found among the slaves of the Sultan's harem. Even in the time of El Mamoun, in 1227, the imperial harem contained Christian women, who, like the free soldiers, were allowed their religious freedom. One of them, Habiba by name, a woman of superior intellectual qualities, was the mother of the celebrated Caliph el Reschid. More recently there have been no less than thirteen French women in the harems of Muley Abd er Rhaman, Muley Mohammed, and Muley Hassan respectively, most of whom have borne children to the three emperors. Here then might have lain an opportunity for elevating the standard of Sherifian intelligence. All the women have seemed contented with their lot, and have never sought to avail themselves of means of returning to their native land. One of them, named Fanchette, a very beautiful woman, was originally carried off by some of the Emir abd el Kader's horsemen from a farm of the Mitidja, and was presented by him to the Sultan Abd er Rhaman. Two sons were born to him of her, who were brought up like other princes of his family. On arriving at the age of twenty, however, their French blood asserted itself, and their impetuosity having given umbrage to other members of the royal lineage, they were put to death by being poisoned.

I have already stated that the recruiting of the harem proceeds without intermission. To the young girls hailing from the provinces and towns must be added the Armenian, Georgian, and Circassian beauties generally, whom the Sultan purchases in Turkey. The introduction of fresh blood to the various ranks of his establishment is provided for by the gift of concubines to some of the more favoured functionaries. This is indeed the highest mark of honour the Moroccan sovereign can bestow. This favour, together with the gift of a burnous, takes the place of the honorary decorations customary in Europe, but which in Morocco are unknown.[1]

From time to time the Sultan marries some of his wives to favourite officers, ostensibly as a mark of esteem, though cynics assert that he has tired of them. Nothing, however, can be more repugnant to European ideas of morality than his practice of lending one of his wives to a favourite courtier. When we were at Meknas the harem of the Grand Vizier possessed one of the Sultan's wives—the hidden motive being that she might act as a spy, and later on, when returning to the palace, bring back a report of all she had seen, heard, and learnt concerning the domestic life, tribes, and plans of the prime minister. This kind of spying prostitution is, verily, doubly repugnant. Eunuchs are, however, very rare, and I have only seen them in the Sultan's palace—great burly fellows of the most fashionable ebony hue, but minus all distinguishing attributes of

[1] Morocco possesses no orders, the Sultan having hitherto ignored the numerous suggestions and projects for the establishment of such decorations. Quite recently a proposal for the creation of an order of the Sherifian Sun was submitted to him. It bore the modest device "The sun never sets on the empire of the Moroccan Chorfas!"

sex. Their chief, called El Kaïd, as though he were the superior *par excellence*, totters along most feebly; his face is like that of an old woman, whilst his harsh voice gives the finishing touch to a ludicrous picture.

But the chief shame of the country lies in the practice of unmentionable vices. The Grand Vizier at the time of our sojourn had a most extraordinary reputation in this wise—indeed, the Sultan alone seemed sheltered from slander of the kind.

A profound acquaintance with the Arab world is necessary in order that the erroneous conception of Morocco being on the eve of total ruin and dismemberment may not be entertained as is the case with many diplomats and writers. Far from the last vestiges of her independence being about to disappear, the semi-disorder characterising the government, and which is only curbed and kept within bounds by the diplomacy of the Powers, has always found favour in the Arab mind. The history of this incurably nomadic race is sufficient evidence of that fact, and though certain geographical considerations have alone brought about a semblance of organisation, yet it has never yet attained to stable political power. The Moroccans have long been accustomed to a condition of things bordering on anarchy by reason of the absence of an established succession.

The lack of an administrative service in the country is surely not a matter of surprise, and above all, it is rather premature to predict the sudden collapse of a government machine set in motion by the religious sentiment and the moral authority of a sovereign pontiff just at a time when it retains some hold on the people.

Thinking minds being rarely met with in Morocco, it is somewhat difficult to account for results already apparent accruing from an imitation of European institutions, as for example, army organisation, if the not inconsiderable influence of renegades were not taken into account, setting aside the special work of the French Military Mission in that connection. It is, however, well known as already stated that the Christians in office at court during the middle ages[1] were very numerous, as also were those who entered the Sultan's service as mercenaries; renegades, however, are few enough in number now-a-days. Those employed by the Makhzen are engaged in very secondary occupations, as for instance, in the bands and armouries, whereas a few years ago there were some whose names, past history, and above all whose public services are especially worthy of record.

One, whose real name is unknown, but whose nationality is sufficiently well attested by popular report I have already mentioned—Ingliz Pacha. He may be regarded as the real founder of the Moroccan infantry corps. He was a British officer, and coming to the Moghreb for reasons which are not apparent, and taking a liking to Mussulman life he subsequently became an invaluable servant of the Sultan in the matter of military organisation.

Muley Hassan served his first campaign in the Sous with

[1] It must be specially remembered, however, that Morocco on the death of the last of the Edrisdides became subject to Mehdy ben Ismael through the famous Djouhar el Roumy who at the head of 20,000 cavalry left Kairouan in 957 A.D., and took Sidjilmassa and Fez completely routing the Omnyades. Now with Djouhar was a slave of Greek nationality, who having been freed by El Mansour, Calif of the Fathimides in Africa, rose stage by stage in military rank until he became general of the army. He it was who conquered Egypt for Mouaz Ledyn Illah, but his chief claim to remembrance at the hands of posterity lies in the fact of his having founded Cairo which is ruled in its horoscope by the planet Mars. It is called El Kaher by the Arabs.

him, and developing while there, it would appear, the warlike qualities for which he is famous.

Another, Abd er Rhaman, was always a most mysterious character. He died at Fez a short time ago, in the month of March 1881. Feeling his end was approaching, "the Engineer," as he was called, asked for one of his old compatriots[1] then in the Franco-African flying column in order that he might confide to him his dying behests in the event of his family making enquiries whether from interest or sympathy concerning him.

This hero of romance, a detailed account of whose life would prove a curious and enthralling narrative, merits a few lines of notice at our hands. When young, and with his future all before him, being at the time lieutenant in a corps of engineers, Count Joseph de Saulty, a native of the Pas de Calais, was in garrison in Algiers. He became enamoured of the wife of one of his superior officers, with whom he subsequently eloped. Taking refuge in Tunis, he lived there for some time in retirement until his companion died; then, the unhappy man, realising the gravity of his position, branded as he was a deserter to the enemy, and being thus unable to return to France, proceeded to Morocco where carrying out different engineering operations he speedily found consolation in work. It was then that the Sultan Abd er Rhaman attached him to his person, and, having persuaded him to make a profession of the Mussulman faith, married him to two Moroccan girls of noble birth, one of whom, the daughter of the Kaïd Mahdjoub the superintendent of the gates of Morocco, gave him a son now 32 years of age, and who holds an important appointment in the palace of the Sultan.

[1] Abd Allah Latapie.

Abd er Rhaman was the commander of artillery and instructor of what are called here the engineers. On the eve of the battle of Isly he did all he could to avert war with France, and when he boldly declared the powerlessness of Morocco, and predicted their defeat, he was nearly killed by some of the fanatical party. The Sultan, quick to see the justice of his prognostications, and regretting not having taken his protégé's advice, held him in still higher esteem, and gave him a most splendid palace in Morocco.

This act of justice and wisdom brought its own reward to the Sherif, who found in Abd er Rhaman one of the most enlightened of his councillors.

Then in 1846 the Emir Abd el Kader driven from Algeria and hemmed in on the Moroccan frontier, took refuge in the Moghreb. Taking advantage of the unsettled condition of the country he rallied round him some malcontents, and marching at their head, he threatened the route to Fez. He wished to be proclaimed Emperor, but thanks to the skill of Abd er Rhaman, the Sherifian army succeeded in checking his progress. The Emir thought to emulate the old strategetic move of the Carthagenians by sending camels loaded with inflammable resinous torches into the Moroccan camp; but the ex-French officer was quick to circumvent him by clever ambuscade, and the camels checked by the grapeshot, returned to set the Emir's own camp in a blaze. Abd el Kader was then forced to return to Algeria and give himself up as a prisoner to General La Moricière.

On the death of the Sultan, his brother, Muley Mohammed, fully recognised the debt of gratitude his predecessor had incurred of the French refugee. He loaded him with honours, and retained him near his person in order to screen him from the fanatical malice and hatred arising from jealousy of his exalted position, and the ascendency he exercised at Court.

In 1877 the members of the French Military Mission who accompanied M. de Vernouillet to Fez, remember to have seen an old man supported by two attendants silently contemplating the uniforms of a country which awoke in his mind memories of such an unhappy past. The French Military Mission, however, did not at that time penetrate his identity, but his grief was none the less respected, and no one felt any curious desire to add to it by indiscreet questioning.

Up to the last the present Sultan retained for him the same lively regard and affection as had been previously bestowed by his father and grandfather.

The Count de Saulty lies buried at the gates of Fez in the cemetery of the Marabout Sidi[1] Bou Becker el Arbi. His son, Sidi Mohammed, is entirely ignorant of the French language.

But side by side with these two Europeans of well-earned celebrity, who became Mussulmans, there are ranged many refugees from Ceuta and Spanish prisons, together with fugitives from Algeria, whose reputation is more than doubtful. Nevertheless, the number of Spaniards has sensibly diminished since a treaty was concluded between His Catholic Majesty and the Makhzen, in which it was provided that escaped fugitives from justice are to be given up at Ceuta and Melitta.

We had a certain native of Seville in our service who, to Andalusian shortcomings, added Mussulman roguery. With

---

[1] This spot is the burial place of other persons of note, for in 1763 the Kaïd of Kaïds, Sidi Mohammed ben Haddou Eddouk Kali was also interred there.

a frankness that was truly charming he acknowledged to having assassinated his brother and mother, for which exploits he had been compelled to quit the banks of the Guadalquivir. He managed to exist very comfortably as a Mussulman, and had married the daughter of another renegade who was also a fugitive from Ceuta, condemned for murder. Such marriages are frequent, and it is strange if their progeny have not some very curious instincts. At any rate our servant was very eclectic in his religious sentiments, for I surprised him one day making the sign of the Cross under his turban. He was engaged in the timber trade, and every year scoured the region of the Atlas in following his avocation. He ought in consequence to have been an invaluable guide if his exploits in the south of Spain did not awaken too uneasy a feeling of unpleasant apprehension.

CHAPTER XVII.

The Sultan at the Mosque on Fridays—The Ceremonial—His drives—His Carriage—Muley Hassan on horseback—Various customs of the Moroccan Army—The Sultan a man of war—His good intentions—The procrastination displayed by his orthodox Entourage—The deplorable influence on the destiny of Barbary of the black Soudanese element—The probable effects of the Derkaoua and the Senousyia—Incessant political and religious rivalry—The intellectual pabulum of a Moroccan Sultan in the 16th century—Ignorance of the Court—The real capital and camp of the Emperor—Want of prestige on the part of the Government—The abuses arising out of the insufficiency of the salaries—Military supplies—— The story of a gun battery—Imperial favour obtained by means of a watch.

LIKE Louis XIV., Muley Hassan might say, "L'Etat, c'est moi," (The State? I am the State). Even in a greater degree than "Le roi Soleil" he is the incarnation of despotic power. Ruling on the lines laid down by the Koran, his subjects look upon him as a direct descendant of Mohammed, and his autocracy is rounded off by the exercise of spiritual power in which he plays the part of a sovereign pontiff.

Before, however, entering into a detailed description of the cranky old government machine of the Chorfas, it may be as well to give a bird's eye view at once of the country, its government and its extraordinary court, as seen in the weekly procession of the Sultan every Friday to the Mosque for prayers. It is a spectacle which recalls in many particulars the ceremonial observances of the past.

The Turkish Sultan reigning at Constantinople, whom,

however, Moroccans hold in little esteem,[1] has completely transformed the life, manners, and customs of his court and suit by large concessions to modern ideas. In the Moghreb, however, a frockcoat has not yet gained a footing in Muley Ismaïl's ancient palace where the conservative turban and burnouse still reign supreme.

I felt very eager to visit the Sherifian Court and to awaken the echoes of the magnificent ruins of the Moroccan Versailles. The gate through which the Sultan would pass had been pointed out to us as well as that by which he would enter the Mosque. I had already attempted to picture the scene in my mind, for the first Friday of our arrival at Meknas we had, full of curiosity, visited the imposing portico of the renegade Mansour[2] to take our stand amongst the silent crowd, who in the early morning awaited the coming of the chief of the State.

High walls, rose-tinted by the sun's rays, with lozenged-shaped macheconlations[3] stood out against the deep azure of a cloudless sky, and enclosed us on all sides. At one of the extremities of the courtyard was the Mosque attached to the palace. The picturesqueness of the whole structure was only intensified by the completeness of decay stamped

---

[1] The Moroccans, indeed, accuse the Turks of becoming Christianised, and if any question arises as to the adoption of the European customs in vogue at Stamboul they immediately reply that the Sultan on the Bosphorus is no Sherif (*i.e.* no descendant of Mahomet and Fatima. *Tr.*)

[2] Bab Mansour el Eudj. This gate which is a very remarkable one was completed in 1732 under Muley Abdallah ben Ismaïl. It is now, however, very much dilapidated by the rapid action of the weather on the worthless materials used, and its appearance is further deteriorated by the Vandalism which covered the original beautiful arabesques with plaster.

[3] Balconies or parapets with openings from which one looks down on passers by. *Tr.*

upon it. Being constructed of moulded blocks of clay, dried in the sun, the wear and tear was all the more apparent—indeed everything was in a crumbling state of ruin. In Morocco it would be deemed a crime to touch or repair the work of a former Sultan, and as, moreover, custom prohibits the Sovereign dwelling in the palaces occupied by his ancestors, the result is incessant building. The surface of the ground is blocked and choked by ruined foundations and sub-structures, and half-buried rubbish; grass grows rankly in the shady corners, footpaths being beaten out in the more frequented places.

The crowd became more and more dense, and I was very glad that we had retained our horses, enabling us to see over the heads of the multitude. A body of infantry, drawn up in a square, left three-fourths of the ground clear, through which space the cortege could advance, and its accompanying crowd of attendants move freely. Punctuality, the crowning grace of kings, is here an unknown factor, and we were thus afforded an opportunity of exercising the virtue of patience. We occupied ourselves in noting down the details of the accoutrement and grotesque appearance of the Sherifian soldiery. At length the band struck up, followed by the irregular beating of drums. Words of command, perfectly unintelligible to us, literally clashed with one another in every sense of the word. We then saw emerging from one end of the court a kind of vanguard bearing lances and marching in a somewhat disorderly fashion. These were followed by a compact group, whose gait and bearing was stiffer and more presentable. In their midst was seen from time to time a rhythmical waving of handkerchiefs—a proceeding intended to ward off the flies from a wheeled vehicle, a chariot of the 1830 type, drawn

A GROTESQUE PAGEANT. 327

by a white ambling steed whose paces were somewhat shaky. This rattletrap contained His Majesty, who was saluted by the troops and crowd with lusty cries of "Allah y barek Amer Sidi."[1]

Remarking that the coachman's seat had been removed from this vehicle, we were informed the reason was that no one should be placed higher than the Sovereign. The horse, harnessed with trappings much too big and ill matched, causing unevenness of locomotion, was led by hand. As to the carriage, its antiquity was evidenced by the scratched paint and its wheels and springs holding together only by a miracle; the comic melancholy of the whole echoing as it were the burlesque music of the troops. The Sultan seemed very ill at ease, and the narrow limits of the cranky machine were not sufficient for his turban, haik, and the majestic voluminous folds of his Oriental costume. The whole bore a delicious stamp of masquerading, the attendant functionaries in their piled up turbans completing the ludicrousness of the scene.

I had so often been led to expect an imposing ceremonial with the inevitable picturesque umbrella scene, the interest centring in a potentate of ideal majesty, that my annoyance at having waited so long under a burning sun merely to witness the parade of an antiquated coach[2] roughly jolted through a courtyard full of rubbish was only equalled by

---

[1] "May Allah protect the life of our Lord." This salutation appears only to be used by the artillery and cavalry, being a privilege reserved for the flower of the army.

[2] We were gravely assured that there was a similar carriage at each of the principal imperial residences, viz., Morocco, Fez, and Meknas. The Sultan takes a most childish delight in them, but history does not record to whom the Empire of Morocco is indebted for the introduction of these chef d'œuvres of coach building.

my contempt for the whole spectacle. The music, or to speak more correctly the clashing din of European instruments, indifferently manipulated under the direction of a Spanish renegade, never ceased. Several airs were vigorously and simultaneously executed, the procession being brought up in the rear by some fine horses richly caparisoned and with beautiful flowing manes. This, however, following close upon the unfavourable impression produced by a chariot worthy of Mdme. Tussaud, only served to intensify the drollery of what was nothing more than a parody of a travelling raree-show.

Immediately the Sultan had entered the Mosque, attended by a portion of his suite, the procession broke up to await his departure. As the devotions of the Dhor[1] only last half an hour we decided to remain to the end, and it was well we did so, for, in proportion as I had previously been disappointed, so I was delighted when Muley Hassan reappeared on a splendid charger which he rode with the skill of a practised horseman, his steed by rhythmical evolutions producing quite a scenic effect upon the crowd who were deep in contemplative admiration.

This time nothing was wanting in the scene that the imagination had conjured up—even to the traditional umbrella, which purple, gold embroidered and open, cast a soft shade over the snowy whiteness of the Imperial burnouse. The Moul Mouddall ran behind his master, who, with the majesty of an opera bouffe potentate, thus returned to his palace. He was also accompanied by the Moul Choukat,

---

[1] On Fridays, during the progress of prayers, the gates of the town are closed. It is curious to note that this custom dates from the year 1184 A.D., when the town of Bougie was surprised by El Mayorky, who took advantage of the moment when the entire male population were in the Mosques.

the keeper of the spurs, in momentary readiness should the Sultan wish to perform some feat of equestrian prowess. Close at hand were the Moul Stroumbia bearing the small cushion upon which His Majesty reclines, and the master of the Babouches.[1] Preceding all these strode a giant negro, the Moul Zerbyah, master of the carpet, stout of limb, with head adorned by a turban proportionately tall, towering above the rest of the crowd. This anthropological specimen—a veritable Soudanese drum major—brandished a pole of the dimensions of a telegraph post, and, in a stentorian voice, gave the signals for acclamation. This was the Kaïd el Mechouar; he was followed by his deputy, a second or sub Kaïd el Mechouar, also a negro, but whose thin face and inferior stature rightly placed him in the second rank. This group, preceded by some foot lancers, was the outward incarnation of the Sherifian government. Further on we noticed the Grand Vizier, the Minister of War, and other officials. All slowly wended their way, surrounded by a swarm of Mechouari, who with their pointed chechia headgear and dazzling burnouses, partly concealed by a kind of white tunic, were of sufficient interest to the crowd to keep them standing to witness their progress.

The Sultan alone wore the hood of his burnouse raised, it being one of the royal prerogatives. No one else was to be seen on horseback, for all had dismounted in the Imperial presence. We followed suit in order to avoid committing an act of supreme indecorum in being seated higher than the monarch. We followed the cortege through the

---

[1] The Moul Belgha or Moul Baboudj—the keeper of the Royal footgear, sometimes spoken of in the native historical records—(Houdas—Translation of Aboulqâsem, p. 96).

blinding dust, scorched by an already torrid sun. It was a striking sight to see these people—the representatives of a regime perfectly strange to us—escorting their sovereign in the great avenues of the palace, such scenes being utterly unknown in Europe.

On arrival we expressed our admiration to the Grand Vizier, who had ridden up upon his elephantine mule. He informed the Sultan of our presence, and a most gracious smile from Muley Hassan terminated the ceremony as far as we were concerned.

It would be almost superfluous to add that we were treated throughout with the utmost courtesy, were it not that the fanaticism of the people will not allow the presence of Jews, who are "radically unclean," on the route on such occasions.

According to those who have surrounded the Sultan since his infancy Muley Hassan should now be 47 years of age. Tall of stature, bronzed complexion, his hair growing grey, his beard black and flowing. He possesses a most sympathetic face; and whilst betraying all the characteristics of his negro origin has a distinguished and noble bearing. He enters ardently and personally into all matters pertaining to the army, but without any special qualification in this respect, unless a taste for making expeditions, and a fondness for calling in the arrears of taxation can be so regarded. The army plays an important part in all Moroccan affairs, taking the place even in the most trivial respects, of civil administration. Here, more than elsewhere, might is right, and the taxes are literally collected at the point of the bayonet, shells also being used as a notification to the people that they have an account to settle. It must also be added that not the least distinguishing feature of the country is that the army is organised for maintaining the Imperial power over the tribes and peoples of the interior, and not with a view to carrying on war with foreign powers. This would indeed be an onerous task in face of the jealousy of the powers and the entire absence of any national sentiment. No such idea as that of patriotism has dawned on the Moroccan mind; they are ruled by the religious instincts alone, and they are carefully fostered within the narrow limits of a mistrustful fanaticism.

Having described the army, which in point of fact will not bear comparison with even the worst of European armaments, it only remains for us to deal with the Sherifian Court as far as that is possible in such a *terra incognita*.

In spite of all his failings,[1] and the grotesque eccentricities of his army, Muley Hassan is a typical warrior Sovereign. In this respect he differs from his father and grandfather, who were devotees of Venus rather than worshippers at the Shrine of Mars. The absolute impossibility of collecting the taxes throughout two thirds of his dominions in consequence of repeated failures and defeat in his attempts to subdue the tribes had long exercised the mind of Muley Hassan. Perceiving the necessity of organising his army on a sounder footing he secured as a means to this end the co-operation of the French Military Mission. Unhappily the perseverance without which difficulties are never surmounted, has never constituted a strongly marked characteristic of the Sherifian brain, and the so much vaunted bravery[2]

[1] However, it must not be forgotten that the Moroccan army is noted for its capacity of endurance and power to resist fatigue under all circumstances.

[2] I use the expression advisedly, for the custom which provides for four mounted soldiers whose habiliments are counterparts of those of the Sultan has always seemed to me an incongruity in reference to the bravery so persistently ascribed to the Sultan.

which he displayed in the course of the Moulouia insurrection, and in the Sous Campaign does not supply its place. The compass of the Sultan's intellectual capacity is shown in the puerile gunnery practice of knocking down targets at 200 yards' range, with which he periodically amuses himself. He completely ignores the only effective method of creating and organising an efficient army; if he desires such a result he certainly does not understand how to arrive at it. Thus it has been impossible to get His Majesty to recognise the necessity of sappers and miners, and the advantage of opening up roads to the mountainous fastnesses inhabited by refractory tribes.

It is only just, however, that some of the Sultan's good qualities should be placed on record. Only, when he manages to shake[1] off the narrow bigotry of his surroundings will his genuine desire to improve the condition of his empire have full sway. But it is certain that he fully appreciated the happy results accruing from the financial reform carried out by a syndicate of Paris and Brussels[2] bankers, by means of which the most complicated monetary system in the world was simplified.

If Muley Hassan had not received a military training, making him a kind of bold guerilla chief, going incessantly to and fro ransoming the tribes of his empire, Morocco would in all likelihood have passed through a prolonged revolutionary crisis, in which her independence would have been

---

[1] It is seldom that the teaching of the commentators of the Koran is able to institute such useful reforms, as for example the recent prohibition of the sale of Kiff—(Kiff or Kif is a species of hemp, the leaves of which are used like tobacco. It produces temporary intoxication and has a very demoralising effect upon its votaries). (*Translator's Note.*)

[2] Seilliere, de Machy, Allard.

extinguished. This danger is to a certain extent diminished by taking the Moghreb for what it is, as a very decided improvement in the army, brought about by the Sultan's efforts, and constituting it an armed force capable of coping with all haphazard insurrectionary movements on the part of the Berber tribes. Touching this matter, it must be remembered to the Sultan's credit, that he knew how to use his army to the best advantage to conserve the supremacy of his authority in the west of his dominions where it was hotly contested. But in every direction he is cramped by the conservative instincts of an orthodox entourage, especially when the impetus of reform proceeds from that Christian influence which attracts the detested Roumi to the Moghreb, and acclimatises him there. It takes years of patient diplomatic efforts to obtain the least result, and in spite of all the fine talk to the contrary, this state of things will continue; for on the one hand jealousy causes the powers to view with suspicion every advance or attempt to open up the country made by a rival government, while on the other, the bigotry of religious orthodoxy—the curse of Morocco—already so probably acute, tends to incurability, save perhaps by measures so radical in their nature that were they attempted an outcry would be raised throughout Europe. Theocracy is rampant on all sides, whilst the element of barbarism, constantly fed by an influx of black Soudanese blood, completes the decrepitude of the people.

In the eyes of all devout Moroccans—and Allah knows that the country, if anything, is religious—Muley Hassan is pictured as a living reflection of Deity—a unique personality, and directly descended from the prophet Mohammed. He cannot be compared with any European potentate, not even the Pope. Uniting as he does, in his own person, such attributes of spiritual power, leading him to assume the modest title of Commander of the Faithful—Emir el Moumenin—[1] it is but natural that he should endeavour to surround himself with an atmosphere and an entourage which enhances his authority—a fact which in our idea militates against all progress. This theocracy, absolute as it appears, is not, however, so dormant as to preclude blame being cast at the Sultan, for besides the brotherhood of the Der Raoua the leaders of the Senousyia [2] most certainly reproach him for the smallest concession to what they regard as the accursed influence of Europeans.

The aim of these brotherhoods is notoriously political; and peculiarity of precept and discipline give them immense power. All Mohammedan sovereigns recognise this fact; and but few of them have regarded such formidable combinations with any favour, but they are well aware that hostility on their part would shake their power to its foundations; and even in Morocco, where tyranny knows no bounds, all attempts to break them up have proved futile. Mohammedan potentates have no choice, therefore, but to submit to the existence of these menacing brotherhoods side by side with their own governments, and, being unable to suppress them, they seek by the characteristically

---

[1] This title of Prince or Commander of the Faithful was first borne by the Almoravides who reigned for 78 years at Morocco and Cordova simultaneously.

[2] According to the accounts of those who have lived at court the most influential factors there are the representatives of the Muley Taieb, Tedjini and Sidi Moktar. On the other hand, it is known that the teachings of Senousyia, the founder of a powerful sect who oppose modern European tendencies, lean to Pan-Islamism. (See Etude de M. H. Duveyrier). As to the Derkaoua we were assured that they can back up their fanaticism by having at command important depôts of arms secreted in Morocco.

tortuous ways of Oriental diplomacy either to checkmate their machinations, when it is possible to foresee them, or, on the other hand, they seemingly join themselves to them in order the more effectively to weaken their influence by all the means at command. The struggle between the Sherif of Wazzan and the present Sultan, as yet far from a decisive termination, is an instance of this half religious, half political strife for ascendency. Moreover, all this secret religious plotting might suddenly terminate in a state of anarchy, for it is well understood that though the Sultan above all claims to rule by virtue of the Koran, yet that authority contains no precept giving him a monopoly to the right of succession. There is, therefore, absolutely nothing to guarantee the country from a lamentable return to revolutionary struggles.

From the day that Muley Hassan ascended the throne, or rather from the time that he was officially recognised as Sultan by the representative of foreign military power,[1] and subsequently at Fez by the High Council of the Ulemas, he has sunk into the same bigoted condition from which nothing seems able to arouse him. He has become in fact one of the many examples which Morocco afford of the prevailing gross and universal stagnation.

I have already stated that the infusion of black blood has borne its legitimate fruit; indeed, while it has produced no sensible effect on the Soudan, the bestial, brutal, fanatical, narrow-minded and stupid characteristics of the negro have utterly ruined the comparatively noble nature of the Arab, and likewise the Berber, cramping literature and art to such a degree that the Morocco of to-day has entirely lost sight of

[1] M. Ch. Tissot, a French plenipotentiary, made a special journey to Tangiers and Meknas for this purpose.

her ancient glorious civilisation. Those who claim an equality for the black man with the white should study the history of Morocco, even though superficially, and they would speedily discover the enormous deterioration that has taken place in those arts and sciences, and that literature which once for a time shone with brilliant resplendency in the annals of Europe, and made her famous. The numberless uncivilised though strictly orthodox Marabouts from the banks of the Niger and the heart of the Soudan whose advent followed the Ahmet expedition, have completed the work of barbaric ruin. As the religion of Mohammed attaches no social stigma to the negro, the Chfa or Filali have been so Catholic in their religious instincts in this connection that to-day the simple result is rampant and irremediable brutishness and decay. The Soudan has indeed proved a source perennial and close at hand from which the spirit of barbarism has been enabled constantly to draw fresh elements of vitality.

It is, therefore, no matter for surprise that Muley Hassan, like his Court, is exceedingly ignorant, or that his judgment concerning latter day topics is not altogether unreliable, or indeed, that he should be incapable of distinguishing between the serious and the puerile. He has been known to devote whole days to the consideration of what is childish, or worse, obscene, matters, shamelessly brought under his notice by those who seek favour at this extraordinary Court. The Sultan, however, must not be altogether condemned, for his sympathetic personality is nevertheless very remarkable, and his intentions very praiseworthy. The religious life he leads does not, as may be imagined, lend itself to scientific pursuits, while the diplomacy of the powers jealously perpetuates this state of childish vacillation.

On waking, which occurs some time before the tadera, (the prayers offered an hour and a half before dawn) Mulai Hassan appears to be lost in contemplative study of Sidi el Boukhari's tedious commentary of the Koran, which, as already stated, is greatly revered in the Moghreb. The Qadi of Meknas,[1] a holy personage of considerable theological renown, is charged with the special office of reading this indigestible mass of nonsense to the Sultan, it forming his sole intellectual pabulum. One quickly understands how the governmental stupidity of Morocco must be attributed to narrow-minded theocracy, rather than to the seductive pleasures of the harem.

When a code of morals, so diverse as those of the Koran, forms the sole basis of national government, or rather, what is worse, when it is founded upon commentaries of that code, one cannot wonder at the negligence which characterises its head. Remembering this fact in conjunction with a recognition of the extreme partiality of the Arab race for confusion of this kind, the conviction forces itself upon us that it would be possible to regenerate Morocco without violent conquest, by acquiring an experience and knowledge of the race, its customs, and history alone.

Mulai Hassan's manner of life, worthy of a hero of the middle ages, only follows in the traditions of those of his ancestors who had warlike tastes. The real capital of the court is the Sultan's camp,[2] and I would strenuously recommend European diplomatists who zealously impress upon their colleagues at Tangiers the necessity of residence

---

[1] The present Qadi is Si Ahmet ben Souda, chief spiritual adviser, a sort of chaplain. He naturally possesses very great influence over the mind of Mulai Hassan.

[2] Thus one of the highest dignitaries in the Empire is the chief of the Sultan's encampment. He is called the Qaïd a Ferreghy.

in proximity to the Sultan, occasionally to visit the encampment of the Sherifian army. A more extraordinary scene of confusion cannot be imagined; grosser pestilential exhalations, a more horrible lack of all sanitation, or a state of things more like what one pictures the camp of the Huns or barbarians in the middle ages as having been, could not be conceived.

The visits of the Court to the towns are of brief duration, and the exodus from life in camp is effected very rapidly with hardly any preparation, the functions of the government being carried on in the meanwhile without intermission, and always with an extraordinary simplicity of detail.

For instance, the Grand Vizier generally holds his audiences in the open air, very early in the morning, and in close proximity to His Majesty. When the first Minister of State is discovered squatting on the ground, seated on a small strip of carpet, surrounded by about ten secretaries, and behind him a small wooden despatch box, it is difficult to realise that there is to be seen the highest Councillor of the Makhzen. The surroundings of all the other officials are, however, in keeping, and at Meknas we were shown the Minister of War, a brother of the Grand Vizier, and the commander-in-chief of the infantry,[1] transacting the business of his department in a low booth, which was nothing more than a wooden packing case!

One advantage attaching to such a primitive method of administration is that emoluments are low. Thus the Minister of War only gets a salary equal to that of six

---

[1] This Minister is the brother of the Grand Vizier Si Mohammed el Arbi el Djemaï. The latter is the maternal uncle of the Sultan, but by reason of an attack of general paralysis he has not been in office for several months. (Sep. 1887.)

cavalry officers. In principle, this may be all very well, and no doubt many European ultra-Radical partizans of financial reform would find the system to their heart's delight. But the expensive tastes and the cost of the harems of the pillars of the State of Morocco[1] necessitate a regime of bribery and corruption, and consequently these flourish in full force to allow them to meet the large demands upon their purses. The Minister of War realises a profit on the commissariat consulting only his own personal interest in the matter, and he has clothed the army in the cast-off garments sold to him wholesale by traders.

Napoleon I. caused fraudulent commissaries to be shot. Mulai Hassan has no commissariat officers, but I imagine if he were to exercise such a salutary deterrent on such ministers as he possesses, he would soon stand alone, minus and destitute of officials of any kind, so rampant are abuses in his entourage amongst whom bribery and corruption mitigate the inconveniences of inadequate salaries, or indeed in some cases the entire lack of remuneration whatsoever.

If cannon are required they are paid for out of the Imperial Treasury to the extent of seven or eight times their actual value, commission after commission running up their cost; and before even a single one of His Majesty's rebellious subjects shall have been taught to respect their authority they will have enriched a long list of unscrupulous ministers and officials. The son of one of these functionaries, well versed in European matters, was once, through

[1] I may mention without comment that the Grand Vizier is in possession of a large fortune. He dwells at Fez in a veritable palace, on the declivity of a hill, where skilfully arranged terraces give an effect like to the hanging gardens of ancient Babylon. The green foliage gracefully predominates over the surrounding scenery. Other dignitaries emulate this luxury.

the influence of his father's position, sent to Europe to place some orders. A certain incident relating to large ordnance is worth relating here as it well illustrates the usual course of affairs.

This young 'Moghrebian went to the most celebrated manufactory of war material in Europe. He there requested specimens to be shown him, desiring especially to see the largest field pieces made. In vain the experts told him that the absence of roads in such a mountainous country as Morocco would render the transport of such ordnance a matter of sheer impossibility. The Moroccan perfectly understood matters, but nevertheless insisted on having the largest and heaviest pieces possible, so that in proportion to the cost a larger commission might be squeezed out of the purchase; and as the Sultan in the first instance had only given an order for a certain number of cannon he tenaciously adhered to his resolution.

To cut the story short, the battery was paid for and sent to Rabat. Thence, as foreseen in Europe, it took an infinite time and an enormous amount of trouble to convey it to the Sultan at Meknas. Special waggons had to be constructed, and to get it up the Sebou, even boats with flat bottoms were rendered necessary. Meanwhile the poor Sultan, who was all anxious to see the cannon whose power and splendour had been so often lauded to him and who dreamed betimes of the enhanced efficacy to be derived from his gigantic artillery, often enquired for news of them. He was reassured by being assured that the winter had been an exceptional one, and that the ground was abnormally heavy from the torrential rains. However, the cannon at length reached their destination, but by the time of their arrival the general enthusiasm had cooled down, the Moroccans being in this respect like overgrown children, and they completely forgot how much before seeing the ordnance they had admired its good points. It was in short a caprice which long since had had its day.

During our sojourn at Meknas the pieces were lying neglected in a sort of shed with but little chance of ever being removed. It must not, however, be imagined that such experiences are confined to purchases so badly chosen as was the case in this instance. The agents of the manufacturer in question afterwards appeared on the scene, and thanks to the good offices of the father of the official, who had already distinguished himself in the matter, they carried away another order from the Sultan for a battery on similar lines—an excellent arrangement no doubt from every point of view for the pockets of the officials. A moment's reflection concerning commercial tactics of this kind will throw a flood of light on the morals of administration in the Makhzen, and to the numerous defects already mentioned must be added the excessive ignorance and unreasoning mistrust born of notorious narrow-mindedness and want of judgment. This state of things favours the operative efforts of the most egregious sharpers who reap abundant harvests from the heads of the government for the most outrageous chicanery. Were all to be told that could be said on this subject, I should risk the recital of things little edifying to civilised ears. Let it suffice to be known that even certain officials connected with the Legations have been beguiled from good faith and have lent their influence to such transactions. The remembrance is still lively in the country—anyone would be able to supply the details—of a certain drogman who, profiting by the blind confidence reposed in him by his chief, amassed an enormous fortune in cheating the Sultan in a most radical fashion. He it was who sold the government of a country possessing no practicable roads a whole series of transport carriages for the army, and powder-making machines at five times their value, and finally dared to threaten the Sultan with diplomatic complications if he would not bestow some superb jewels upon him.

Let me, however, hasten to add that such glaringly flagrant abuses as this one have for some time been conspicuously absent, but unfortunately they are always possible of occurrence in a country *sans* morals, *sans* order, or indeed mental culture of any kind.

Mulai Hassan's favour and friendship were won by this individual cunningly taking advantage of the Sultan's proclivities, presenting him with a superb watch the mechanism of which put in motion a revoltingly obscene toy. The European press and certain diplomatists persist in treating the Makhzen as a civilised power, but a true and edifying appreciation of its moral worth may be gleaned from a consideration of such facts as these. While on this subject it is a matter of regret that our ambassadors who in presenting their credentials bear also costly gifts to the Sultan[1] are not oftener better inspired in making their choice of presents. Imagine the wonder of the Sovereign at presents of quite a different stamp to the famous watch, Sevres ware, solar telegraphs and other objects whose artistic worth or scientific value entirely escapes him at present. The first

[1] It should be remembered that gifts from the European embassies are regarded by the Sultan as humbly offered tribute, more especially as the Moroccan vulgar herd ignore the fact that the Sultan sometimes sends presents of native jades and hacks to the heads of European powers.

are now relegated to an isolated storehouse[1] which must by this time contain a mine of artistic treasures of every period, and the rest are made use of as it pleases the fancy of the moment. I have heard of the solar telegraph mirrors being given up to the denizens of the Sherifian harem for the purposes of personal adornment.

[1] In the storehouse of the palace at Meknas, shut up for a considerable period, have recently been discovered superb specimens of ancient armoury presented at the time of the Portuguese rule in Tangiers.

CHAPTER XVIII.

The excessive Fanaticism of Meknas—Our perfect security—Tranquillity assured by the system of Collective Responsibility—The Aïssawa—Their practices—History of the Confraternity—Our projected journey to Tafilalt rendered uncertain—Departure for Fez—The Route—Mehedouma—The Adventure of the Sultan's Musician—Insecurity of the Country—Arrival at Fez.

THE fanaticism of the town of Meknas has often been the subject of comment. It has been supposed that the presence of the Zaouia, the mother of the Aïssawa, and the proximity of the sacred mountain of Zarhoun have had the effect of enfuriating the easily excitable populace against strangers. Now, our stay was sufficiently protracted—differing in this from that of the generality of travellers, and embracing also the period of the Ramadan, when the Mahommetans are in an abnormally excited state—to enable me to rehabilitate to some extent the city of Mula Ismaël. I spent two months there in absolute quietude, and except for the confounded trumpets of the Muezzins nightly reminding the faithful of the dinner hour, during this season of gladness, and the nocturnal feasts of the Ramadan, I could have lived there perfectly happy.

In the streets, even in the densest crowds, both in our own quarter and at the extremities of the town, on fête days, as well as on those when certain streets are deserted, not a shadow of anything disagreeable ever came near us, whether we were attired in an English travelling suit or in a comfortable "djellaba." I maintain therefore that in this respect the education of the towns of the Tingitane has commenced, as is proved by the indifference of the populace to strangers, for I have been able, alone, and without any escort, to photograph all the most interesting nooks and corners. Besides, in order still more to reassure the general run of tourists, I may add that it is rare for a Christian to find himself in any difficulty, for the Government wishing above everything to avoid all cause of diplomatic differences in native affairs, have on the one hand made the "Homa," or chiefs of the different districts, responsible for whatever may occur in the quarter under their jurisdiction, while on the other hand, especially if the traveller be good-natured and easy-going, they do everything they can to make life as disagreeable as possible by a thousand petty but irritating vexations. If any difficulty arises matters are sure to turn out to the advantage of the Moroccan officials, who levy a considerable fine on behalf of the Government and annex the greater portion of it for themselves.

The streets are larger and more airy than those of any other town in the country, but the population is inconsiderable, not exceeding 20,000. It is, however, difficult to make any accurate estimate, for during the time of our stay circumstances were modified by the presence of the Court, which greatly increased the general activity, though not sufficiently so as to enliven the enormous area covered by the town.

Everyone has heard of the confraternity of the Aïssawa, and their frantic practices— borrowed from some demoniacal repertory, and from those hysterical scenes which some two hundred years ago caused Urbain Grandier to be burnt alive—are so well known that we can dispense with any description of their habit of swallowing whole sheep, chewing iron and stones, and putting live coals into their mouths. Some of them have even organised themselves into a sort of perambulating company which has travelled all over Europe, and has exhibited before some of our elegant and astonished clubmen, and other select audiences, their paroxysms of religious mania.

Their practices are at once grotesque and frightful, and when they dance about with wild bounds and dishevelled hair, uttering invocations the rapid rhythm of which is sustained by a continued crescendo of tambourines, a physical excitement and intoxication is produced which is really only a horrible delirium. On these occasions they devour whole animals, or, to be more exact, they cut them up as it were into mincemeat. Besides these coarse methods, which are intended to appeal to the imagination of the lower orders, the Aïssawa have certain other charlatanic practices, like jugglers and showmen of serpents, which procure them an extraordinary reputation among the narrow-minded low-class Africans. It is only fair, however, to add that the chiefs of the order disapprove of these practices, and even advise the faithful not to believe all those who, though calling themselves Aïssawa, are only vulgar clowns. But it is to be feared that the current cannot be quite stayed, and we must admit that it is precisely these coarse practices of bestial delirium which attract the people from the lower orders, from which the greater portion of the most fervent disciples are recruited.

This frenzy is seldom seen except at their meetings, and though at a reunion of the Aïssawa the most sanguinary practices may be indulged in, the fiercest among them have been known to be of a gentle and kindly nature. Such was a famous Krimo—formerly in the service of Bompard, then in that of Benjamin Constant—who, like an honest sailor when out of work, most prosaically turned his hand to cleaning, brushing, and polishing for his master.

The history of the confraternity of Si Mahned Aïssa is little known, but as it was at Meknas that the latter accomplished the series of great deeds on which his reputation is founded, and as we believe that it is at the present day the home of the grand master and the mother Zaouia, we will say a few words about it.

Certain legends tell us that a poor inhabitant of the town, by name Ben Aïssa,[1] unable to procure the means of living for his family, but full of confidence in God, had that rare happiness in this world to be fed by divine providence, which constantly renewed his provisions, whilst he was enriched by his wife one fine morning drawing from the well a bucket full of gold pieces. Aïssa, like a practical man, hastened to profit by a profession for which he felt a very natural vocation, and which seemed to promise so brilliantly. He then had a vision, in which God appeared to him, and ordered him to establish a confraternity according to certain special rules. He hesitated no longer, and the legend goes on to tell us of a certain mystical comedy, in which, having proved the faith of 40 disciples, he instituted a council of 40 believers, who remained with him until his death, and formed a kind of general chapter, or "hadra," of the order, which has been kept up until the present time. But his fame increasing he soon incurred the jealousy of the Sultan of Meknas, at that time Mula Ismaïl el Merinide,

[1] The tomb of Ben Aïssa is situated at Meknas, near the new gate Bab Djedid.

whom we must distinguish from Mula Ismael the Great who reigned a century later. The unfortunate Ben Aïssa was banished,[1] but his departure produced such a void in the town that the Sultan himself could not get any labourers for certain works in course of erection, and the saint's popularity increasing in consequence of the miracles which he wrought and his triumphant struggle with the Sultan, the latter was obliged to compromise and to allow the Marabout to return to Meknas, where, in order to conciliate the rising order, numerous favours were bestowed upon it. The fact of the whole population of the town following the founder of the order into banishment shows the difficulty—always followed by defeat—which has been experienced by the followers of Mohammed when they have tried to attack these confraternities. At Constantinople, as at Moghreb, the sultans have been obliged to permit the existence of these dangerous societies, and even to conciliate them later on. Thus in order to lessen the effect of the public complaints which Aïssa addressed to the Sultan Merinide for not having aided the moors of Spain in their endeavours to drive the Christians out of Andalusia, the Sherif bestowed upon him large buildings and vast lands, which served as a foundation for the mother Zaouia of the order at Meknas.

At Meknas the Aïssawa are exempt from nearly every tax, and from all statute labour, and as they compose about the entire population, I expect the revenues of the sultan there must be very small.

In Algeria, during the time of the Turkish rule, the Ouzera, descendants of Aïssa, were exempted in the same manner. It is to these facts we must look for an explana-

---

[1] The place of exile was not, however, very far off, Aïssa having established himself on the plateau of El-Hamrïa.

tion of the great repute of the order as well as of the custom of the disciples holding seances of prayers and practices at the houses of those who are ill.

Here we find again the ancient theory, which obtains in India, of the innocent person who for love of God offers to expiate the sins of others.

The curious point is that for the most part the noisy din we hear is intended to cure some unfortunate sick person, in whose house the nocturnal revels are held. So we see that underneath this grotesque layer lies a pious and charitable foundation, a view which has escaped the notice of superficial observers, who, calling themselves free-thinkers, condemn at once as jugglery ceremonies of which they understand very little. It is only fair to clear the character of a confraternity which strives for a nearer approach to God by sobriety and abstinence, and in one word, the absorption of the divine essence, in such a manner as to be insensible to all corporeal sufferings and afflictions. As moral subjects, the Aïssawa are advised to fear nothing and only to recognise the authority of God and his saints, and only to obey those who allow the practice of the doctrines of the Koran, so that the independent tendencies of the order are likely to render it dangerous to the government. Therefore in Algeria, although they have never given an opportunity for any justifiable indictment, and have held aloof since 1842 from any insurrection, the French administration consider it prudent to keep a watch over them. In Morocco the order is not so dangerous to the Sherifian authority as the Derkawa, the Taïbïya, and above all the Wiziriin of Fez, of whose rules and regulations scarcely anything is known, and where members are supposed to carry on their operations in the most profound secrecy.

There does not seem to be any connection, or rather any alliance, between this confraternity of Aïssawa and the Oulad Aïssa who inhabit the district to the south of Wargha and Sebou, although there exists in Algeria in the district of Aumale, a tribe which considers itself to be the issue of Si Mohammed ben Aïssa, and which is called Oulad Aïssa, but which is only a group of "shorfa" rather than a portion of the order.

It has not as yet been found possible to connect the Aïssawa with the dangerous sect of the Senousïya, although Si Senousi calls them Djazouliya of whom the Aïssawa are the successors.

The feast of Ramadan was just over, we had had time to take part in the nocturnal feasts and other *fêtes* which the disciples of Mohammed go through as a penance for a month, under the specious pretext of fasting during the day; when our departure was settled the Sultan in giving us permission, was good enough to point out by the Grand Vizier, the escort which was to accompany us. We had been delayed until the hot season by diplomatic differences and doubts and by the secret opposition and fanaticism of some high personages at court, and finally our project of reaching Tafilalt was rendered very uncertain. We were also very unfortunate in missing a last splendid opportunity in the departure of a Kaid for Qçabi[1] at the head of a hundred Boukhari.

After having done everything we could to get permission to accompany this individual, and thus traverse rapidly

---

[1] Qçabi ech Shorfa, inhabited as its name indicates by the holy descendants of the prophet, lies in a plain where the upper branches of the Moulouïa unite. The Sultan maintains a post there in order to keep up communication with the oasis of Tafilalt.

the upper region of the Moulouia, we were obliged to abandon our project, and one morning, our escort being in waiting for us, we set out for Fez intending afterwards to go on to Safrou, a little town at the foot of the mountains, and there wait for a favourable opportunity to go amongst the revolted tribes. The immense geological depression on which the plain of Meknas is situated extends to the west as far as the valley of the river Sebou, which in its upper course flows, as we know, not far from the town of Fez. This plain of Meknas is, in short, only one of the undulations of the unexplored thicket of the mountains of Zaïanes, a direct extension of the Great Atlas, which begin to decrease at Zarhoun, ending suddenly as we have seen to the north of the valley of Sebou at the Dj Tselfatz.

To the west of the road to Fez the plateau forms a sharp ravine, at W. Djedida nearly on or level with the Pic de Kannoufa, or Qannoufa, and then comes the long plain which opens on to the valley of the Sebou by the *funnel* on which is built the town of Fez.

The whole southern horizon of this district is bounded by the high ridges of the lesser chains of the Atlas, which hide from view the peaks of the principal range, and as the north is also bounded by the Zarhoun and the narrow valley of the Mikkès, which in the distance appears insensibly to join with the Dj Terat and the Dj Zalah, the result is, that the country which separates the two imperial residences of the Tingitane looks like one vast passage. The plateau of Meknas tapers gently towards the W.N.W. and the town belongs to the hydrographic system of W. Rdem. The water-shed of this secondary basin and the chief basin of the Sebou is situated about six miles to the east of the town, on the rocky elevation which overlooks the ravine of the W. Djedida, an affluent of the W. Mehdouma and consequently of the Mikkès.

This situation is extremely favourable for irrigation, and the Moors are shamefully careless in neglecting the treasures which flow from the rivers of the Mounts Beni Methirs. The population of the Mount Zarhoun, although very fanatical, is in a state of subjection, but that of the south, the Ait Youssi and the Beni Methirs, are more often in a state of revolt than of obedience, so that even during the stay of the Sultan at Fez or at Meknas the safeness of the route is doubtful,[1] in spite of the presence of a number of tribes brought there to act as road police and to resist any attack of the mountaineers. As to the *state* of the roads, that is as primitive as in any other part of the country. However, there are some bridges, and although to speak the truth some are half in ruins, still they are evidences of extreme good will very rare in Barbary, and show also the anxiety of the sovereign to be able to move his army quickly. The mounted artillery, however, would encounter some serious obstacles, especially in the ravine of Mehdouma going down to Djedida.

On leaving Meknas by the Bou Asnaïar gate, after having crossed the W. Bou Fekran,[2] we came immediately to a kind of large park, planted regularly with olive trees, with a good system of irrigation, being intersected by numerous trenches; the whole, however, is now-a-days miserably neglected. We then skirted the sides of the plateau of

---

[1] For all the names of this part of Morocco I have adopted the orthography of Houdas in the translation of the fine work of Aboul Qassem, for no one knew this region better than the latter, who spent the whole of his life there in an important post at the coast.

[2] The source of Bou Fekrân rises at a little distance south, it is called l'aïn Magrafa.

Ourzigha which extends as far as the two ravines and in which flows the little brook called Harina, a tributary of W. Islem. At the time of our journey all this ground was burnt up by the sun, and the poor olive trees which, we were told, had been planted by Mula Ismael, seemed to be regretting the days of their youth, for their bark was like charcoal and their foliage dried up. The park is immense, for it took us half-an-hour to reach the last enclosure. We had already crossed the foundations of a wall when we came to a large breach apparently made to shorten the road.

On the eastern declivity of the plateau of El Hamria the earth is of a curious red colour, and the contrast between the blue of the heavens, the slatey grey of the dusty olive leaves and the bright red of the soil makes a pretty picture.

Our escort was extraordinarily zealous, and if our clownish carbineer from Tangiers had been still with us, he would either have died with shame, or what is more likely would have hidden himself in some corner out of sight of these fierce Boukhari whom His Majesty had condescended to send for our protection. Their appearance was as imposing as it was picturesque, and as we rode in the midst of them we were never tired of admiring the warlike aspect of this troop of old soldiers grown grey in the service. We had decided to encamp at Dchar de Mehdouma about 15 miles off, thus dividing the distance between Meknas and Fez, which is about 31 miles as the crow flies. A great deal has been written concerning this distance, but the question may now be considered as settled by the astronomical observations of Messrs. Desportes[1] and François of the French navy, which have fixed the positions of the two towns.

[1] At the beginning of the century Ali Bey put the position of Fez

On our left was the straight crest of Zarhoun, the sides of which are densely populated with people whose principal occupation is the cultivation of olives. The little (!) marabouts which we had passed in coming from Meknas by the Volubilis route enliven by their white peaks the dark tints of the mountain, dried up by the fierce rays of the sun. From the plateau which we had now reached, and which overlooks the W. Islem, we could easily discern the topography of the district, and the Zarhoun appeared to sink gradually, and at last to expire at the foot of the Dj. Kafés, an isolated peak detached from the Guerwau chain: we were at too great a distance to be able to see the narrow valley through which passes the W. Rdem.

Our little column soon crossed the W. Islem over a bridge in tolerable repair, but approached by the most atrociously stony ascents, which must, in their present condition, prevent any carriage properly hung from even attempting to cross it. It was at this bridge that, in 1758, the Oudaïa and the Guerouan were defeated by the Beni Idrassen, and 500 of the Makhzen were massacred. When the news of the combat reached the then Sultan, Sidi Mohammed, he was so irritated at this fresh insult on the part of the Oudaïa, that, on their return to Meknas, he beheaded the chief amongst them and hung their heads on the new gate, Bab Djedid.

The Chief of the Military Mission, who had very graciously made a point of accompanying us, now took leave, and his last piece of advice was as full of affectionate care

at 7° 18' 30" Long O. Paris, and 34° 6' 3" Lat. N. MM. Desportes and François in 1877 gave it as 7° 15' Long. and 34° 6' 2" Lat. N. But none of the travellers mention the exact position of the house they happened to occupy, and as Fez is built over a considerable area this would certainly make some difference.

as had been the services which this distinguished officer and devoted friend had continually lavished upon us. After leaving the suburbs of the town, we next came to an extremely bare and most monotonous plain, and glancing at the far-off imposing mass of minarets of the Morocco Versailles, we pushed our horses on rapidly, raising thick clouds of dust, but the heat being moderate, and a pleasant breeze springing up, the journey was delightful, and we soon resolved to take our way leisurely, sending on the greater part of the troop to find an encampment. We alighted about noon at a fountain shaded by dwarf fig-trees in order to take our lunch comfortably. The chief of our escort, a sort of antidiluvian qaïd, whose shaking head could hardly bear the weight of his turban, which was as big as a tower, looked on curiously at our repast. We invited him to share with us the impure food of the "roumis," which he did with very great gusto. He stopped short, however, at the claret, a present from the chief of the mission at Meknas, but he appeared to regret that, not being alone, he could not infringe the holy precept of Mohammed by tasting of the divine juice of the grape.

A great deal too much has been said of the fertility of this plain and table-land, for the ground is only a very poor and sterile conglomerate. We remarked, however, some deep geological channels, caused by the streams which flow northwards, whose argillaceous soil, rich in vegetable mould and abundantly watered, is, on the contrary, extremely fertile. Having set out again, we soon reached the ravine of the W. Djedida, which, by a rather deep descent, brought us into the plain of Fez.[1] We had previ-

---

[1] This is probably the place where we must look for the plain or district of palms spoken of by El Bekri.

ously noticed to the south the "marabouts" of Sidi Ismaïl.

The high peak of the plateau of Kannoufa, of which we had hitherto only discerned the outline overhanging the plateau of Zarhoun, now stood out in all its grandeur. It was at the foot of this mountain that we intended to encamp, and on the right, at the extreme south, the summit of Kandar indicated the road to Tafilalt, and the last spurs of the Atlas overlooking the valley of the Sebou.

The little W. Djedida affords an example of those fertile valleys hollowed out of this conglomerate, where we suddenly reach the bare banks, and at the bottom we find the river running, bordered by a rich and lovely verdure. We then took a more southerly direction, hardly a mile from the sides of the Zarhoun, and at four o'clock we arrived at the ravine of Mehdouma, whose name in Arabi means *ruins*. All our investigations have not enabled us to identify this river with the W. Sanat quoted by Edrisi, but perhaps we may find it in the course of the Djedida.

A half ruined bridge crossed the rivulet of Mehdouma, with its rapid torrent; the ravine is very deep, and its sides of clayey schist have curious gaps (or cracks) caused by the sun. The depth is about 200 feet, and under the vegetable earth are thick layers of variegated marl. We continued for twenty minutes to follow the left bank of this geological "fault," which, getting deeper and deeper, separated us from the Djedida Kannoufa. At 4 o'clock 30″ we reached a terrace of ill-cultivated gardens near the village, where the camp had been got ready, but the inhabitants, accustomed to the extortions of marauders and of the servants of the Sultan, afforded us no very gracious reception. While negotiations were being carried on, I endeavoured to recognise the very insignificant ruins which have given the name of Mehdouma to this locality. They are possibly only the last remains of the castle of the Vergoigne mentioned by Leo Africanus, which long ago was built on the road from Fez to Meknas. The inhabitants were very avaricious, as Leo tells us is usual amongst all those who live on the great highways. But in the time of the converted geographer the building was already in ruins, and the land belonging to it cultivated by some poor Arabs.

Marmol calls the place Gemaa El Hanïen,[1] and the distance from Meknas (5 leagues) which he gives, corresponds exactly with the position of the ruins which were about a mile to the west of the place of our encampment at Mehdouma.[2] The whole of this district is topographically of great importance for being situated on the border of the plain or Fhahs Saïs, it thus commands the opening of the valley of Mikkès, which extends northwards along the eastern slope of the Zarhoun.

The inhabitants of this district enjoy the inestimable advantage of being able to sell their goods and agricultural produce both at Fez and at Meknas, from which towns they are equi-distant. There is no doubt that the Romans with their usual geographical acuteness took advantage of this rich plateau to establish some settlement, for Leo and Marmol both speak of the Roman origin of the town of Maghilla, the Maghaila of Edrisi, without mentioning Pietra Rosa, the identification of which has not yet been satisfactorily settled owing to the corruption of the names, and to the fact that the plateau of Zarhoun is absolutely

---

[1] Corruption of Djàma Mosque.
[2] 7° 35′ long. : Paris ; 34° 1′ lat., north.

unexplored. There still exists a tribe of the name of Maghila; this name of Maghila or M'rila, according to the orthography of Renou,[1] is frequently to be met with through the whole of Barbary.[2] Our encampment was not far south from the Dchar Maghila[3] of Tissot's map, although one must go back about six and a half miles south from the position given by the learned archæologist, who however never traversed this middle district from Fez to Meknas, and only prepared the map from information received from others. This would most probably be the great Barbary Dchar of Kannoufa, which would agree with the place occupied by the ancients; unfortunately we were prevented by the presence of such a numerous escort from pursuing any archæological researches, which would no doubt have been most interesting, and we cannot too strongly recommend to any traveller wishing to study the country to take as few people as possible, and especially to do without soldiers.

I returned to the camp for dinner, and we finished the evening with a very animated conversation respecting the political state of the country, and the incursions and robberies of the Beni Methirs. At midnight we were suddenly awakened by a fearful noise, and violent altercations, and remembering our evening's discussion we imagined that we had been surprised, and should have to defend the camp. But it turned out to be only an amusing

---

[1] Description géographique de l'Empire du Maroc. Paris, 1844.

[2] In the town of Salé are still to be found the Meghyly or descendants of Meghyla.

[3] It was at Maghila that Aly ben Youssef (surnamed Abou el Hassan) halted, in 1107, on his way to Fez, then occupied by his nephew, and it was from Maghila that he dated his proclamation to the inhabitants of the capital.

incident. A young musician of the Sultan's army had escaped from the ranks of the militia, and after a rapid flight, had sought refuge in one of the tents of our soldiers; the faithful servants of the Sherif, however, had caught him and wished to make him return to his corps. The young rogue had a piercing and vigorous voice, and by his heart-rending cries had collected together the population of Dehar, who were already inclined to side against the government troops, and as we happened to arrive just at that moment we were made, as it were, responsible for what had occurred.

The old caïd who commanded the escort displayed on this occasion as much diplomacy as warlike energy. A very forcible speech from him, and a plentiful distribution of *mat* quickly put an end to this ridiculous riot. As to the interesting disciple of Mozart he was very summarily invited to take refuge elsewhere with his musical science, and we did him a great kindness in not giving him up again to our men.

Mehdouma is about nineteen and a half miles from Fez, but the road being a very easy one, we were able, after striking our camp at 8·45, to stop about three o'clock at W. Endja,[1] and reached the town at 6·30.

On quitting Mehdouma we saw for a moment across the undulations of the valley of Mikkès, the highest peak of the Tselfatz. It has been often said that the shape of the two summits of Zarhoun at Kannoufa resembles an Arab saddle. I do not know if this simile is too far fetched, but it is quite true that the contour of the mountain is as described. The southern peaks of this chain are entirely bare to the summit, and have a dreary look, the

[1] Or perhaps more correctly Nedja.

numerous ridges standing out with singular clearness, and in summer their sharp outlines and absolute sterility being visible from a great distance.

Here is another proof of the agricultural ruin of the country, for by the most improvident clearing of the trees the irregular course of the waters floods the sloping ground without penetrating the soil, and carries away the vegetable soil, exposing the clayey earth without doing any good. The influence of a wise government would be able to remedy these evils, and if a system of protecting the forests existed, similar to that which France has established in Algeria, these bare regions would be converted into rich districts. In short it would only be to give them back their ancient fertility as it was before the advent of the Arabs. It is admitted that Morocco owes its ruin to two causes, first, from a moral point of view, to a narrow theocracy, the fatal effects of which we have already seen; and secondly, from a practical point of view, to a badly understood pastoral system, and sacrificing everything to the most improvident system of agriculture. The introduction into the Moghreb, by El Mansour, of the nomad Arabs of Ifrikia only increased this deplorable custom of forest clearance, of burning the underwood, and of grazing on the young shoots. The Sultan reproached[1] himself for these things on his death-bed, as well for having built Rabat el Fath, and having set at liberty the prisoners of Alarcos.

Our road now led directly towards some high hills called Dj. Terat, which in the extreme N. E. terminate the plain; these hills are simply the eastern extension of the Zalah,

---

[1] Of course the Sultan never thought of preserving the forests of his country, he only considered these nomad Arabs as another source of sedition.

at the back of which lies the town of Fez. This is the region of the Cherarda, a district of great fertility, but we could only perceive the uniform outlines of a rather low plateau rising again towards the North.[1] We then passed by several heights, one of which is the "Marabout" of Lella Aïcha, or of Madame Aicha, and here we must not omit to notice the homage paid to a holy woman in this country, where women are thought so little of. It must be confessed, however, that this devotion rarely owes its origin to any virtuous action, or to the exemplary and chaste conduct, rather the contrary in fact, and our European modesty would be somewhat shocked if we listened to the exploits and prowess of these "Frenegondish" ladies.

While crossing this plain, whose only vegetation consisted of withered palmettos growing on a rocky soil, we were gradually getting nearer the range of the southern heights. If we can scarcely apply the term fertile to the plateau of Meknas (always excepting the lower valleys), what is to be said of this famous plain of Fez, on which I have never seen the least growth, not from want of labour or from carelessness, for the lands belonging to the tribes of Makhzen are quite near, and the valley of the Mikkès is dotted with their camps and their pastures, but because the soil is a stony conglomerate and truly ungrateful, and we must therefore abate somewhat the enthusiasm of certain travellers. On the heights we passed a number of cromlechs, noticed by Tissot in his learned unpublished notes, and situated not far from a confused heap of ruins,[2] the history of which is unfortunately lost, as so often happens in Morocco.

[1] Fez being in fact 6' further north than the latitude of Meknas.
[2] They may perhaps be the remains of the town of *Banibasil* of Leo, or of *Beni Becil*, according to Marmol, and which these geographers place half-way between Fez and Meknas.

A little while before we had crossed the little W. Soueïr and afterwards the dry bed of a stream where, about two hours after leaving Mehdouma, a solitary palm tree, something like an impertinent black feather broom, shewed us the course of the little W. Endja which is crossed by means of a bridge of 5 arches, in perfect condition.

The river is shallow, but the fresh and limpid current waters some delightful groves of fig trees which afforded us both shade and exquisite fruit. Here we spent three hours killing innumerable tortoises, a sport which I recommend to the tourist, and the most exciting bets could easily be made on the occasion.

Marmol made a great mistake in naming Ain Zore (the Ain Zorac[1] of Tissot) as the source of the W. Endja. The little brook which flows from these blue waters (the translation of Ain Zorac is "the blue fountain") is only an affluent of the Endja, the source of which is much further to the south, and is probably confounded with the W. Hegja which flows near the Qasba of the Qaïd ben Tsami, on the direct route from Sefrou to Meknas. By geographers of the middle ages, the L. W. Endja is called the Hued Neja, and the fact that they place the town of Beni Becil on its banks renders the identification of the actual ruins with those of the town mentioned very probable.

At this season, however, this clear little shallow river presents serious difficulties as regards crossing it, and for this reason the Makhzen has had this bridge built, which at first sight seems much out of place over this tiny stream, particularly as rivers like the Sebou, which are so difficult to ford, are still without any.

At 3 o'clock we resumed our journey, and could discern

[1] Aboul Qassem gives the form *Ain Zoura*.

clearly to the south the Sefrou Mountain or Dj. Kandar, with the neck of the Baalil which form the two remarkable heights on the eastern extremity of the Dj. Mguiled, while the prolongations of the two mountains of Beni Methirs run northwards and rejoin the plateau.

The route crosses the beds of two streams, dry at this season, and in the distance we could see the Douars d'El Atcham encamped on the plain at the time of our journey just before we crossed the plateau on which is built a little "bordj" which protects one of the sources of the W. el Fez; this place is called Ras el Ma (spring of water.)

As to the douar of the Oulad el Hadj, it was at that time quite close to the marshes from which it took its name, Hmian Douïat.

At last, at about an hour's journey from the town, we came to the little outpost of Farradj (Nzala Farradj) which is responsible for the safety of this route. Its success in this direction is, however, doubtful; for, after sunset, when the gates are closed, the robbers seem to have the upper hand, and the watchfulness which our guards bestowed on our last encampment was not, I fancy, a useless precaution.

The Sultan Mula Ismaël had, however, organised a remarkable service of police for the special purpose of protecting the roads in the suburbs of Fez, and thus the fort of El Khemis contained a garrison of Cheraga solely for the protection of travellers.

The commerce carried on between this, the most populous city in Northern Africa, and Cairo, was evidenced by the number of tents which were dotted about on every side; but there was not a single building, nor any sign of cultivation or gardens to indicate from a distance the city of Idris. The plain opened before us until it came to a narrow defile and we imagined that behind the undulations we should at last see the town.

A line of grey walls with the embrasures cut lozenge shaped for staircases, then some minarets, and a solitary gigantic palm tree crowning some "qoubba" shaded by trees, afforded us a confused and unimposing idea of a portion of the town of Fez Djedid; that part of the city which stretches behind on the opposite declivity being entirely hidden. A number of mounted Arabs and Jews on foot were awaiting us and came hastily to meet us, as soon as our arrival was signalled. I must mention here that in the morning we had sent on our staff to prepare a house for us in the town, and to present our letters to the Pacha. Now our new cook, an impudent Algerian, who had taken the place of our Spanish cook, behaved so insolently to the chief functionary of the Morocco Government, that the latter dismissed him, at the same time allotting for our accommodation and that of our suite only a miserable little hut. It was this man who came to meet us with a most piteous mien, but spreading at the same time some report of I don't know what of our official and diplomatic journey, to which story the presence of Mr S——, an attaché to the French legation, gave an air of credibility. On account of this rumour the whole of the influential Algerians and Jewish population came to meet us, and they lavished upon us every mark of attention, but the pale, unhealthy and miserable appearance of some of them roused our pity and made us reflect upon the climate of the town. After a short interview we set off again along the walls of the city in order to go out by the gate of El Mahrouk or "burnt." Morocco is so full of evidences of savageness and religious fanaticism that one is completely surrounded by probatory documents. This gate which leads to the N.E. was built in 1204 and was named El Chezyah, but on the very day it was finished, the body of the unfortunate El Obeïdy, who had raised an insurrection in the district of Rif, was burned under the arch, and to this day are to be seen the iron hooks from which were hung the heads of rebels.

We then reached a square or esplanade, a quiet, grassy spot watered by a tributary of the W. Fez. Here I should have liked to encamp, under the shadow of the high pisé walls, instead of breathing the infected air of the town. But it was ordained that during this journey we were to be nothing more than the slaves of our servants or of our escort, and we were obliged to yield to the arguments of Mr. S., who, athirst for the mysterious East, had been seduced by the numerous temptations offered by our pirate cook.

After crossing a sort of waste land covered with filth of all kinds, we were led through an inextricable labyrinth of lanes, and after being half crushed by the sharp turns of the narrow streets, most truly noxious passages, we came to a lane, darker and more infected still, in which was the most abominable hut I have ever seen. Here we were to lodge, but my protestations were so vigorous that I soon overcame the indolence of the officer who was charged with the task of finding us accommodation, and recommencing our promenade, we were at last installed in a superb dwelling surrounded by a large, dark, shady garden.

CHAPTER XIX.

Our Installation in the City of Mula Idris—A Gaoler and his Houris—Too flattering opinion of an Arab Chronicler—Necessity of following M. Zola's method in describing Fez—The Hydraulic System—Impurity of the Water a certain Factor in Fever and Dysentery—Deplorable State of the Streets—Primitive Method of Cleaning them—Suffocating Temperature—Population—Moral Disorder—The Universities—Destruction of Old Literary Treasures—The Students—Carping Spirit of the Populace—The Feast of Tholba—A Visit to a Pacha—Scandals and Abuses of the Protective System in Morocco—The Principle of Collective Responsibility.

WE were again lucky in our choice of a residence, for at Fez our house had in front of it a beautiful garden, well watered by a running stream, so that even on the very night of our arrival we were able to enjoy the luxury of a bath, rendered still more agreeable after the tropical heat of the day by the fragrant shade of the orange trees. On going out of a large hall we stepped at once on to an esplanade paved with a delightful Mosaic of little many-coloured squares, the tints of which produced a truly Oriental effect—yellow, green, blue, white, and a little black being cleverly blended in interminable complicated arabesques, while in the centre of this "*impluvium*" a beautiful basin of white marble received a jet of water, the crystalline murmur of which was the only sound which disturbed the stillness of the scene. We were charmed at once, though our horizon was somewhat limited, differing in this from Meknas, and, besides, we could not here dream of renewing our escapades on the terraces, the tenant of the house (which was the property of the Sultan) having, with a great noise of keys, bars, and bolts, locked up his flock of houris in the upper rooms, through which we should have been obliged to pass in order to get to the roof. But as we were lost in an ocean of verdure, being only able to perceive the chinks of the wall of the next house across the tops of our orange trees, we were perfectly happy, and had nothing to complain of except the presence of the too scrupulous gaoler.

Our first dinner was somewhat lacking in comfort, for it turned out that our letter from the Sultan did not confer upon us the right to "*Mouna*"[1] in the towns, and the lateness of the hour did not allow of our cook foraging in the remote quarters where provisions were procurable. But our joy at being located in the proud and holy city of Idris made us oblivious of our gastronomic vexations. Were we not at last in one of the few remaining sanctuaries where Islamism—hunted down by what we call civilisation—has taken refuge, and has become even more wild and inaccessible?

After Damascus, Cairo, and Qairowan, does not Fez contain its finest mosques, which no Christian, Jew, or cursed infidel has ever yet desecrated, or even approached?

Were we not in that famous city of which it was said: "O Fez, every beauty is united in thee! With what bless-

---

[1] This distinction between the "amels" of the towns and of the country is sufficiently curious, but in this particular case of "*Mouna*" it is only fair, for if in the country sufficient food cannot be always found for the caravans, in the towns there is enough and to spare.

ings and wealth are not thy inhabitants endowed! Is it thy freshness which I inhale, or is it the health of my soul? Are thy waters of white honey or of silver? Who could paint those streams of thine, which unite under the earth and bear their waters to the market places and on the streets?"

But *pace* the memory of that master of poetry, the learned and distinguished (according to Roudh el Kartas)[1] Romanesque chronicler, Abou-el-Fadhl ben el Nahouy, of whose incantation to his beloved native town the above lines form a part, I must confess that only the realistic genius of a Zola could analyse with sufficient minuteness of detail the multifarious combinations which exist in this famous white honey or this silver—certain factors in the dysentery, fever, and pestilence of this happy Fez. As a matter of fact, the town is most unfortunately situated, its founder, the son of Idris, having shown a singular want of caution in building such a city in a damp and unhealthy spot. The town has increased enormously, and the population increasing also, it is completely ravaged by the germs of frightful diseases.

The geographical position of Fez is tolerably favourable, situated as it is nearly in the centre of the depression which separates the Rifan system from that of the Atlantic; but from a hygienic and strategic point of view its situation is deplorable, under the over-heated rays of a sun which converts the place into a damp furnace as soon as spring appears, a perfect paradise of microbes. Let us, therefore, place the enthusiasm of the Arab chronicler in its true light, and lift the veil which hides the imperfections of the country.

[1] Annals of the Town of Fez, p. 37.

A complicated system of ducts distributes the water through the town, and every house is liberally supplied, but I am far from being reassured as to the water tightness of these ducts. On the contrary, I am convinced that there are many points of communication between the drains and the water we drink, which is tepid, muddy, nauseous, and putrid. Such are the real adjectives to be substituted for the panegyrics of the Moroccan poet.

The former head of the military mission had been in a position to judge of the deleterious effects upon his system of this famous revivifying liquid. He used, therefore, to send his servants every morning for a supply of water from the Sebou, which flows only two and a half miles from the town. They, however, wishing to spare themselves trouble, gossiped away their time in the neighbouring cafés, and dipped their leather bottles into the nearest fountains. The officer was, therefore, obliged to analyse the water every time, and when he found too large a percentage of organic matter, he vented his *chemically* outraged feelings by administering a sound castigation. His operations, however, gained him a great reputation, but he was obliged to continue them during the whole of his stay in order to keep free from fever and dysentery.

The hydraulic system of the two towns is a little complicated, and all the more difficult to study and describe, because part of it is subterranean. It appears that some years ago, by the care of the government of the present Sultan, the reservoir, the aqueduct, and especially the hydraulic wheels[1] which water Fez Djedid, were put into

[1] These wheels are the work of, and invented by, the famous Abd er Rahman, Count de Saulty, the Frenchman whom we have already mentioned, and who lived for such a long time at the Sherifian Court.

repair, but much remained to be done, and now Mulai Hassan is credited with a project for improving the present lamentable state of affairs.

The two towns are situated in a valley watered by the W. el Fez or W. Djonhor ("river of precious stones," although now anything but pearls are found there). This brook takes its rise at Ras el Mâ[1] at the foot of one of the last elevations of the Beni Methirs, only a short distance from the town. On a level with the Imperial Palace, the W. Fez divides into two branches, one of which was canalised some years ago, and, passing under an aqueduct, forms a pretty cascade in the valley at the southern end of the town. The river continues its course and enters the old town by the ancient iron gate called Bab el Hadid, and traverses the quarter known as el Roumelia. At the foot of the last extension of the mountains of Cherarda, about one and a half miles from the ramparts, the W. Fez receives a little streamlet which takes its rise at Aïn el Khemis, in the ravines of the Dj. Zalah, to the north of the town.[2]

[1] There still exists at this place, the Arab name of which signifies "Source," the ruins of a Qasba, mentioned by Marmol. It lies to the south of the road and at a short distance from Fez to Meknas, and according to the author of the Roudh el Kartas, there are about sixty springs there.

[2] Now for the sake of clearness and the better comprehension of the text of the geographers of the middle ages, I may mention—1st. That the course of the W. Fez or W. Djonhor, which runs through Fez el Bali, often takes the name of W. el Kantara—the river of the bridge—on account of the "dyer's bridge" K'antra Sebarin. 2nd. That the lower course of the W. Fez, after it has joined the brook El Khemis, is for some distance called W. Wad el Kebir. The author of the Roudh el Kartas, however, gives it this name as soon as it reaches the town. In the time of this winter, one of the branches of the river—now covered up and unrecognisable on account of numerous substructures, was called W. Masmouda, and ran through the quarter of Andalous—Adowa el Andalous.

The whole system of the water supply of Fez rests upon the fact that the level of the W. Fez is always much the same, and higher than that of the old town, so that the fountains of the houses are easily supplied. At certain hours of the day, and especially in summer, the supply is intermitted, and the surplus is applied to watering the gardens; but favouritism here steps in, and many inhabitants who are not in favour at court see their fountains dry up. The sluices which serve to water the gardens are sometimes opened very suddenly in order to inundate the streets of the town, and wash away all the detritus and filth which the easy-going Arab allows to accumulate. It is the custom to send everything into the sewers, the impurities then flow into the Sebou, and it is easy to imagine what the sanitary condition can be with streets covered with the liquid, putrid, and infectious mud, left behind by the waters after having inundated every corner of the town.

This filthiness which prevails everywhere, proceeds from the want of care and utter heedlessness of the inhabitants, for there are a great number of fountains near the old iron gate (Bab el Hadid), referred to by the author of the Roudh el Kartas, and besides all the baths and reservoirs situated by the great Mosque El Andalous, are fed from the spring which is outside the gate. It is always a subject of astonishment to the new-comer in Morocco to compare the immaculate white robes of the Moorish population with the horrible dirtiness of the streets of the towns. It is difficult to understand how people can take so much care of their persons and yet move about in scenes so repugnantly filthy.

On the other hand the houses are very clean inside, the

pavimentum of "azulejos," which covers the walls, and the squares of glazed tiles which are so frequently washed, rejoice the eye, although hygiene does not gain much benefit when we take into account the long rainy winters which cause a penetrating humidity, still more increased by the frequent washing of courtyards open to the sky, the general arrangement of which is that of the Roman "atrium"; nor is it surprising that rheumatic affections are extraordinarily prevalent even in summer.

During the dog-days the temperature of Fez is stifling,[1] and at the end of July, during our stay there, after five o'clock in the morning the sun produced a perfectly glowing atmosphere. I expect, therefore, that if those chroniclers of the embassies who, on their return, descanted on the mildness and healthiness of the climate, had visited it at any other period than spring or autumn, they would have somewhat moderated their praises. To counterbalance this high temperature the streets are so narrow and the houses so high—sometimes with arcades in addition—that scarcely a bit of blue sky can be seen, and going down one of the smaller streets of Fez is more like descending into a vault than anything else. The inhabitants are in consequence pale, their features drawn, and their bodies emaciated by the confined lives they lead, without air or exercise, and showing distinct traces of the fevers which decimate the population.

But our house, as I have remarked, had luckily a large garden, where the wide borders of verbena, musk, &c., diffused in the cool of the evening a penetrating odour, which, although reminding one of a chemist's shop, was none

---

[1] Frequently 106 Fahrenheit in the shade, often 109 or 110 in the morning.

the less extremely pleasant. Then, too, the rooms were impregnated with the smell of the beautiful odoriferous and precious[1] cedar wood of Atlas, of which the ceilings and most of the woodwork was made.

Unfortunately, in addition to our stay being afterwards cut short by the attacks of fever of my companions, we had some difficulty in enjoying the peacefulness of our abode owing to the frequent visits of the Israelitish and other notabilities of the place, and it was only by stratagem that we were able to put ourselves beyond the reach of their importunities, even to the extent of establishing a bodyguard at the entrance of the garden, with the strictest orders ever received by any Cerberus. The world of shopkeepers and interloping courtiers were always sending us the most cunning of spies, but our Cerberus executed even too conscientiously the orders he had received, which gave rise to a somewhat comical incident. At the end of two days we were informed that the unfortunate tenant of the house having gone out had not been allowed to come in again, and was lamenting at the gate the cries for food which would soon be heard from his beloved harem. This explained the groans of despair which had so much puzzled us from over our heads; they were the complainings of the empty feminine stomachs!

The population of Fez has much increased, and, after Cairo, it is certainly the most populous city of northern Africa,[2] for it contains 100,000 inhabitants. No traveller, geographer, or writer has, however, been able to agree on

[1] In former times this wood came from the Dj. Beni Bazgha, situated about a mile from the gates of the town. The resinous nature of the tree is an unfailing preventive against the attacks of insects.

[2] Fez is the largest and finest city in all Africa, and contains the schools of the sects of Mohammed (Marmol).

this point. M. Feraud, in some learned MSS. notes which he was good enough to entrust to me, speaks of 150,000, while Renou in 1848, basing his computation on the figures given by various travellers, and on the fact that too high a valuation had been made of that of Algiers before the conquest, did not consider that the population[1] of Fez could exceed 30,000 or 40,000, much too low an estimate in my opinion.

The difficulties of estimating, caused by the absence of any census or of municipal administration, and the impossibility of investigating the interior of the houses, are much increased as regards Fez by a circumstance which easily leads to error—that is, the erratic movements of the country folks and of the barbarous tribes, who go there to buy provisions, and cause a sort of perpetual fair. The quantity of shops is, in fact, very large, and the population has to all appearance much increased. However this may be, a few years ago the population of Fez did not exceed 70,000, but the increase is to be explained by the desertion of the country parts owing to the exactions of the Pachas.

It is said that the number of the children of Israel amounts to 15,000: as to Christians, their stay is generally very temporary.[2] There is, besides, a small colony of rene-

[1] The population has undergone various changes, its period of greatest splendour was during the time of the Almohades, the town then possessing 785 Mosques and 82,236 houses. (Roudh el Kartas.)

[2] In our day the number of these at Fez has been much reduced, and with the exception of a queer old Spanish doctor, dressed in black velvet, and with his hands encased in dirty gloves, who lived at Mellah, the Christian element was only represented by ourselves. As, however, the merchants of Tangiers have received permission to establish depots of merchandise in the Arab town, the number will probably increase. In the time of Marmol, however, there was

gades, mostly Spaniards, escaped galley slaves from Ceuta and Melilla. They keep taverns, to which they attract soldiers in order to gamble, smoke *kiff*,[1] drink brandy made from figs, and, in fact, deliver themselves up to every kind of debauchery. They are dens of infamy, and now and then the Sultan has some of them shut up when things go on in them which touch the honour of some family or other.

As regards morals also, Fez enjoys an unenviable reputation, and I can easily imagine that since the period when Leo Africanus stigmatised the shameless vices of the inhabitants as a renewal of the vileness of Sodom and Gomorrah, no amelioration in morals has taken place. We must also take into account the carping spirit of the population, and the bands of undisciplined soldiers of Makhzen. Thus, when a robbery or murder has been committed, and these are not infrequent, it is generally ascribed to the soldiery; but this is only said with bated breath, and no one ventures to search for the culprit for fear of retaliation on the part of those free lances. These latter being able to act with impunity, are also extremely overbearing, and show extraordinary brutality to the citizens, who execrate them accordingly.

In some part or other of the "Garden of Feuillels,"[2] it is said that the inhabitants of Fez are intellectually more acute and subtle than any other of the Moghreb; and that they are very intelligent, very charitable, sly, patient, that they are

a special quarter in New Fez where several free Christians lived with their slaves.

[1] The Sultan, as we shall see further on, has recently forbidden the sale of this intoxicating drug, but its use is still continued clandestinely owing to the connivance of the soldiers.

[2] Roudh el Kartas.

submissive to their chief, and respect their sovereign, and that in times of anarchy they have always maintained an ascendancy over other people by their wisdom, their science, and their religion. But in my opinion these fine qualities are somewhat like the water and climate, for, in the history of the Moghreb, Fez has always justified its reputation for turbulence. Its numerous mosques, its "Zaouias," and the immense number of students who frequent it to learn the science of Islamism, make it the intellectual centre of Morocco, and the principal seat of Moslem fanaticism in Barbary. It is, therefore, easy there to profess ideas of independence, and of resistance to the powers that be, which does not tally very well with the dictum of the author of Roudh el Kartas. Do not the Ulemas reside at Fez? those species of infallible "Bonzes" belonging to the family of the Idrisides, the most holy and distinguished men of Morocco, but whose moral stultification and intellectual decrepitude are absolutely incredible to us Europeans.

There is also a constant opposition to the Sultan on the part of the Idrisides, whose ancestor was the founder of the first Moslem monarchy in Morocco, and who are inconsolable at being now excluded from power. As to the population of Fez, it follows and encourages the ideas of the descendants of their patron. The Shorfas of the Mosque of Idris have, therefore, a strong influence over the already discontented spirits of the town, and as the sanction of this religious areopagus is indispensable to the nomination of a Sultan, it can easily be supposed that they must be conciliated, and, feeling their importance, they set themselves up as supreme judges, and their insolence is unparalleled.

The schools and the Zaouias, or academies, where every sort of theology is taught, are all situated in the same quarter of the town as the famous mosque of Mula Idris, the founder of the town; but you would be strangely deceived if you expected still to find any trace of the libraries or of the intellectual culture for which the town was so celebrated in the middle ages. Here also the degeneracy of the Moorish race, and all the external influences of which I have already spoken, have produced the result of an absolute vacuum.

During our stay at Fez, M. Tissot instituted some very interesting researches as to what might still remain in the famous libraries of the town so much extolled by the geographers of the middle ages. Even in our day it has been mysteriously whispered that they contained precious manuscripts of Livy, the discovery of which would enrich the happy possessor. Why Livy more than anyone else? But M. Tissot has made short work of these theories; he has visited the two great mosques of Mula Idris and El Qairouyin and found the libraries empty. Pillage, assisted by fanaticism, has long since dispersed or burnt everything which had no connection with stultifying commentaries on religion.

This scientific vandalism is of late date, for history tells us that at the peace of Xeres, in 1285, which cost Yacoub two millions of Maravedis (about £48,000), the latter obtained from the King of Seville, Don Sancho, second son of Alfonso X., the restitution of a large number of books—thirteen mule loads—which had formed part of the booty carried off by the Christians in their wars with the Mussulmen, and presented them to the libraries of Fez. And later, in 1326, the Emin Abou Saïd built the great academy of

Fez Djedid, for the accommodation of the large numbers of Tholba, entrusted with the reading of the Koran, and of doctors who wished to study science. At first everyone was fed, and received a monthly allowance, and the Academy was endowed with one-fourth of the revenues received from the harvest, and all this for love of the Most High God and in expectation of receiving great rewards. Besides, was not Fez the most favourable place for strangers, and, as is remarked by the author of the Roudh el Kartas, the centre of union for savants of all kinds, doctors, lawyers, literary men, physicians and poets? and did it not contain more knowledge than the Moghreb?

How times have changed! In our day the most famous Moors savant hardly knew the name of Ibn Khaldoum of Edrisi, or of El Bekri; as orthodox Mussulmen, every new notion seems to be a diabolical inspiration to be guarded against.

The wealth of the middle classes in Fez is very great, as is also their influence in all the interior affairs of the country, and, as I have already said, since they revere their founder Idris as equal to Mohammed, as a result they only listen to the advice of the Shorfas of the great Mosque, and the carping spirit and independent ideas of the citizens give them little sympathy with the warlike spirit of Mulai Hassan—always at the head of an army ready to govern by force. The necessity for managing populaces like these obliges the Sultans to show tolerance even of the most extraordinary customs. One of these, amongst others, is all the more odd because it is only a parody on that Sherifian sovereignty whose power is still so unstable—resting as it does only on a religious prestige which is itself often weak, strongly opposed, and even easily destroyed by rival opposition. The custom referred to—the feast called Tholba—is extremely characteristic of the restless spirit of the people of Fez, and I shall proceed to give a description of it, for I do not believe another like it exists, and as it might become dangerous to the Sultan, containing, as it undoubtedly does, the seeds of revolution, it is an interesting study.

Through all its glorious academical past the University of Fez has maintained a very great prestige in the Moslem world, and students still flock to it in order to drink at the holy sources of the mosques and the "Medarsa," the intellectual felicity and the beatitude of the true believers in the inspirations of the commentators of the Koran. Now the feast of Tholba, although somewhat of a masquerade, rests on a more or less charitable basis, its aim being to increase the pecuniary resources—often very small—of the young students. The Sultan has always preserved this curious custom, which is that in the spring a rival, chosen from amongst the Tholba, acquires the right by paying a certain sum to his fellow disciples, of parodying in every respect the imperial power.

The performance lasts for several days, and the scenery is so well executed that strangers who may happen to visit the town at this particular time cannot distinguish the difference between the original and the copy. I imagine it would be very amusing if an European embassy were to happen to arrive during this feast, and were to present the letters with which it was accredited to the comic student, mistaking him for the real Sultan.

The "tholba" who has for these few days realised the dream of "If I were king," is exempt from taxes for the rest of his life, and as the expense of this privilege never exceeds £10 or £12, he may be said to have really made a good investment. The comedy is carried out to its fullest extent, for the Sultan goes in person to the camp of his rival, and pretends to make his obeisances to the usurper. However, everything has an end, and after this last interview, the two monarchs having prayed together, things resume their ordinary course.

These feasts last about a week, and, ever since the time of Sardanapalus, have been the pretext for great orgies. The Sultan sends splendid "Mouna," and his example being followed by the rich inhabitants of the town, the whole body of Tholba joyously divide amongst themselves masses of the choicest food.

The extraordinary conduct of the cook whom we had engaged to replace the brave Andalusian Antonio, whose ardour had vanished at the idea of going to Tafilalt, enabled us to see at first hand the vices and shortcomings of protection adopted in Morocco. This system is often at the bottom of the diplomatic difficulties at Moghreb, but although, later on, I shall devote a few pages specially to this subject, I wish to quote here some examples which show the abuses to which it gives rise in the interior of the country, where any control on the part of the legations at Tangiers is purely imaginary. However, it gave us an opportunity of paying a visit to that worthy Pacha[1] of the town who died recently at an incredibly advanced age.

The evening of our arrival our cook, an Algerian by birth, or at all events laying claim to the title, and the bearer of a regular diploma, ran about through every quarter of the town, both respectable and otherwise, boasting and assuming the airs of a conqueror. Unluckily for

---

[1] This functionary was the brother of the former grand vizier, the famous Si Mouça, so celebrated for his political abilities.

him he happened to meet with some Moors of a less impressionable nature than those of the coast, from whom he received a forcible correction, in the course of which his face was blackened, and his watch—an article of infinitely small value—broken. The next morning on awakening, we were stunned by his jeremiads and by his lying account of his adventures. His complainings having moved Mr. S., the attaché of the legation, who had accompanied us from Meknas, and he having assumed the entire responsibility of the proceeding, we consented to go with him, simply as spectators, on his visit to the Pacha on the subject.

Our house was situated on the side of the hill which rises to the north-west of Fez el Bali, and we had to go down a succession of little, dark, narrow, crooked lanes in order to reach the seat of government. I trembled now and then for the equilibrium of our horses along the high vaulted alleys, but by degrees as we ascended the hill, we got nearer the centre of activity, and the traffic increased. We were stopped in the middle of the crowd by the impossibility of proceeding, and the people—covered with their white clothing, which made them stand out in the general shadiness[1] of the spot, observed a complete silence, and moved about without any noise of voices as if they had been ghosts. They seemed much surprised at seeing any Christians, not forming part of any embassy, and going about amongst them unconstrainedly. Nevertheless, they were extremely good natured: the shopkeepers smiled at us as we passed, exhibit-

---

[1] This semi-obscurity is in fact a characteristic of the streets of the lower part of Fez el Bali. The houses are generally very high—two or three stories—and in the cross ways or other little places, where the sun might penetrate, they are covered either with trellis work which admits a few stray rays of light, or with dry reeds over which are stretched leaves and rushes.

ing from the other end of their little shops their finest stuffs in order to tempt us, as well as their most ornamental brass work[1] and their richest leather work, so true is it that the commercial spirit softens the most repulsive manners. Then came the turn of the provision quarter, where an abundance of food of all kinds, heaps of delicious fruits and tasty looking appetising fish—the shad and mullet of the Sebou—show by their cheapness that there is no present fear of a famine.

We had gone through part of the district of Mula Idris—the well-frequented shops of which give the town its reputation for richness—when we arrived in front of a porch where some groups of soldiers kept guard over the unfortunate prisoners who were waiting to know their sentence. A fountain of finely serrated stone of the most delicate workmanship occupied one side of the portico. We were admiring this picturesque specimen of Arab art, so delicate, but so overladen with ornaments, when one of the Pacha's slaves came to summon us to the presence of his master. We were naturally followed by our scamp of a protégé, who, intuitively scenting a good windfall for his purse from the goodness of our companion, was servilely civil, a fact which ought to have opened the eyes of our diplomatist. We could scarcely help bursting out into laughter at the sight of the master of the house—a shrivelled up old negro, as small as a dwarf, and as fragile as a doll, which we should have been as much afraid to handle as a Sèvre figure. Imagine to yourself his shaking head, of the colour of dark tobacco, and covered with the

---

[1] These are the "chabel" and "boury," famous even in the days of the author of Roudh el Kartas. Europeans, however, consider them insipid and flabby.

most gigantic turban ever seen, or that could possibly be wound round such a pate. The weight of this stuff rolled round his head must have considerably exceeded that of the skeleton-like form of this old personage. But the unfortunate man was blind, and his dim eyes soon excited our pity and restored us to our normal condition of good behaviour.

The whole of the time of our audience was occupied by the complaints of our domestic; khalif succeeded khalif, and still we were obliged to witness the disagreeable sight of our rogue of a servant affirming and repeating that his broken watch and his stolen purse were worth 200 francs, all in the deepest voice, and accompanied by a whole litany of jeremiads.

The "Moqadem el Homa" of the "adoua" in which the event had taken place was then called, in accordance with the principle of collective responsibility, without which Morocco would be nothing but a den of thieves and cut-throats. This functionary was ordered to find the thieves, and to reimburse the money of the unworthy disciple of Vatel. The affair was at once settled, for the Pacha ordered the sum to be paid out of his coffers, and the greedy hands of the "sauce-spoiler" were soon stretched out to receive a pile of "douros." After all, it was a profitable business; first, for the Pacha, who would most decidedly make his market after we had gone by levying a contribution of three or four times the amount from the inhabitants of the quarter; secondly, for the Moqadem, who would do the same thing to a lesser extent; and thirdly for our protégé.

I have now touched the tender spot of one of the worst evils under which—thanks to the increasing number of those protected—groans the unfortunate inhabitants of the Moghreb. I may add that, for the honour of our caravan, I hastened to dismiss the hero of this affair, for the success of his plan would have encouraged him to try again, and he might some day have seriously compromised us. Some days afterwards I had him reconducted to Tangiers by some soldiers, and the Legation having discovered his deceit, treated him accordingly.

CHAPTER XX.

Strategical View of Fez—Defences of the City—Siege of City by Mulai Hassan—Importance of its geographical position—Historical survey—Etymology of Fez—Invasion of the Merinides—Foundation of Fez Djedid—District of El Qairaouiyn and of Andalous — Commercial Importance — Algerian Influence—Insecurity of the commercial routes—Local Industries—Jewish Brandy—Neighbouring Salt Mines—Illness of my companion—Visit of a great Moroccan personage—The Moroccans at the house of a sick man—The Kiff and native medicine—Preparations for departure—The Consular Agent of France at Fez—Departure from the town—General Aspect—Overwhelming Heat—Route to Safrou—Revolt at South of Empire—The Qasbah of Qçabi ech Shorfa—Aït Isdig and Aït Youssi—Impossibility of continuing journey—Route to Meknas—The Qaria of the Aït Ouelal and of the Beni Methirs—Return to Meknas—A Sultan as photographer—Farewell to Military Mission—Departure for Tangiers—Route of the Ambassadors—Valley of W. Rdem—Plain of Sebou—The Qariya of El Habbassi—The Marabout of Lella Mimouna—Succinct orography and hydrography of the region—Arrival at El Araïsh—History of the town—Spanish Occupation—French Expedition under Du Chaffaut—Estuary of the Kous, and Commerce of the Town—Azila—Portuguese Occupation—Episode in the siege—Passage of the Tahaddart—Return to Tangiers.

NEAR to Fez-el-Bali, on the north and south east, are to be seen two small forts which, although of no importance in the present day, have the peculiarity of possessing no apparent doors; the inhabitants of the town assert, on these grounds, that these defensive works communicate mysteriously with the palace of the Sultan by a long series of subterranean galleries.

The town possesses as fortifications a double enclosure of high walls of concrete blocks, at an elevation of 18 feet by 6 wide and provided with towers, banquettes, and battlements; at certain points, the salients are so arranged, that the nine gates which issue from them, lead into a bent passage. These fortifications are still tolerably well preserved, though they could not resist the assault of even imperfect artillery. These walls have a picturesque air and the walk around them is charming. From the road which rises on the sides of the hills bordering on the town, it is easy to judge of the extent of Fez, of the close grouping of the houses, and of that effect, always so attractive in the East, of the green foliage of the gardens, amidst the white terraces glistening in the sun. But this very facility in overlooking the town on all sides, renders it very open to assault, a fact of which the inhabitants are well aware, happily for the Government of Morocco. Were it otherwise, the turbulent character of the population, which, in a spirit of perversity, obliges each new Sultan to have recourse to force to instal himself, would lead to the gravest consequences.

It is therefore the work of an intelligent policy to leave this town, eminently the most restless in the empire, weakly defended, the small habitations of the Qasbah, which unite on the north the two halves of the city, being directly commanded by the elevated point of the last buttress of Dj. Terat. Mulai Hassan moreover did not escape the usual obligation of laying siege to the town, and although he entered Fez Djedid with little difficulty, he was obliged in due course to undertake the blockade of Fez-el-Bali. The inhabitants, groaning under an increase of taxes, and incited by the opposing religious party of the Ulemas of the Mosque of Idris, had revolted at the instigation of an old blind Sherif, Mulai Abd-el-Malek, who asserted that the new taxes, decreed by the young sovereign, were sacrilegious or "haram." One would think, had the movement been popular, that the siege might have been protracted against the half-hearted army of the government. One day a bomb fell in the camp of the Sherif; the skill of the gunner was remarkable, for it is stated that the projectile fell into a basin in which Mulai Hassan had just finished his ablutions. Finally the town was taken by treason, the "filali" inside having opened a gate to the enemy. It was not long before peace was restored, and the inhabitants laid down their arms.

In the case of a European army entering the Moghreb, whether from Rabat by sea, or from the frontier by Oudjda, it is probable that Fez would be its object. The invader, once in possession of the town, would find in it a valuable base for operations; the country would be divided into two, and by isolating the resistance of either part, the kingdoms of Fez and of Morocco might once more be separated, to the detriment of the power of the Sultan, who would lose the lucrative taxes of the valley of Sebou.

In reality this sovereign is much to be pitied, and deserves the compassion of a too exacting European diplomacy, for being in the painful predicament of either fortifying Fez, and thus affording the means of a terrible resistance to the least pacific of his subjects in the Moghreb, or of leaving the most populous city in the kingdom exposed to the first sudden attack.

Fez was, most probably, the first city founded by the Mussulmen in this country; its site was chosen, as we have already seen, by the son of Idris, whose desire was to rebuild the ancient Roman VOLVBILIS. The Arabs, who in matters etymological or archæological, are much given to romancing, assert with Ibn Batouta, that the name of Fâs (which has become Fez in Europe), or the "pickaxe," was given to it because a fossil hatchet or pickaxe was found there at the time of its foundation in 743. Others assume that the appellation is from "Fedda," money; but Mr. Renou observes that this hypothesis is not at all probable, and that this is the usual Spanish spelling of the name at the present day; thus no one has arrived at a satisfactory derivation, although the author of Roudh-el-Kartas goes into multitudinous commentaries on the analogical etymology of Fez. The reader may refer to them, but we must say with the Arabs, "God alone knows the truth." Let us however add, in order to give some appearance of truth to the legend of the fossil hatchet, that there are numerous caverns in the limestone rock of Dj. Zalah, and that in our days there are still to be found a population of troglodytes. In short, although the whole history of the origin of Fez is very obscure, we cannot ignore the fact that Tangiers, at the time of the arrival of Idris in the Moghreb, was the capital of what we now call Morocco. The chronicler of Roudh-el-Kartas speaks of it as the parent of all the other towns, the handsomest and oldest of the country just then converted by the Mussulman apostle.

In the part played by Fez in the history of the conquest of the Moghreb, we must not forget that on its possession has always depended the entire fate of the Sherifian empire. A convincing proof of this is, that on looking into the annals of the country, we find Fez the primary object of the savage tribes of the Merinides[1] under the command of the virtuous

[1] It is agreed, from an ethnological point of view, that the Beni

and austere Cheikh, Abd-el-Hack. The invasion of the Merinides, wild nomads of the desert, for whom the green pasture lands, watered by the Tingitane, must have seemed a dream of Paradise, must be considered as the slow incursion of tribes who could no longer find food for their flocks. We learn from the historians of that epoch, that about the year 1610 of the Hegira, these invaders arrived, mounted on their camels, as the Lemtouna[1] had come. Finding the Almohadean kings neglecting their business and their duties, addicted to wine, luxury, and self-indulgence, these sons of the desert, after an easy conquest, were not long in occupying the principal Qsour. With great warlike ability they constantly strengthened their position, acquiring territory bit by bit, until they completely destroyed the Almohadean army about 613 of the Hegira (A.D. 1214.) (Vide Poem by Abou Fares, quoted by the author of Roudh-el-Kartas.)

Historians only date the so-called Merinide dynasty from 1248, the year in which Abou Yahya, son of Abd-el-Hack, conquered Fez, considering him for this important act as the real founder of the new reigning family[2]—an evident proof of what I have already advanced, on the great importance of the town of Fez as commanding the south part of the Moghreb.

According to the Arabian chronicler of the annals of the town of Fez, it was in 1275 that the Emir Abou Youssef

---

Meryn are ancient Arabs of the East (confounded with the Berbers from the frontier of Sahara), who lived on a territory situated to the south of African Zab, as far as Sidjilmassa (now Tafilalt).

[1] The Lemtouna, brothers of the Messoufa, were one of the tribes who concurred in the establishment of the Almoravidan dynasty.

[2] Mr. A. Rambaud thinks that a Merinide, by name Abou Youssef Yakoub ben Abd el Hack, used gunpowder for projecting stone bullets against the besieged town of Sidjilmassa.

decreed the building of the new town, since known as Fez Djedid. There is a contradiction on this point between M. Renou, who gives the date as 1220 or 1230, and the Arabian authors. The foundations were laid, tradition tells us, on the banks of the river, in the presence of the Emir on horseback, and a great concourse of people. Nothing was wanting to the ceremony; learned Fekhys cast the horoscope of the town, which was thus placed under the influence of a propitious star, and a blessed and happy moment. How could it be otherwise when the good graces of Allah had been assured to the work, by the massacre of a goodly number of the sons of Israel, who, on the eve of the ceremony, had been slaughtered in a little affray. So says the chronicler of the Roudh-el-Kartas.

The site of the new constructions, judiciously fixed at 1000 feet in the west, was chosen so as to command the ancient city of turbulent reputation. It was first called Medinat el Beïda (the white city), in opposition to Fez il Bali, or Fez the broken down. Since its foundation the latter has undergone remarkable changes. According to Abd-el-Malek el Ourak, it formerly consisted of two towns, each with its encircling walls and gates. The river, which separated them, entered Bab el Hadid by an opening in the wall to which was adapted a gate of "good and fine trellis work of cedar-wood"; the water issued by two similar doors of the name of El Roumelia. Later on, in 492 of the Hegira, Youssef ben Tachefin, having penetrated the town after a vigorous siege, the walls and the gate called Bab-el-Facil, which divided the two Adowa, were pulled down by his orders; thenceforward the quarters of El Andalous and El Qaïraouiyn[1] form one and the same city. This district of

[1] Qairouain, according to Houdas.

Andalusia, which, in these days, is still sharply defined, was founded by 8000 families of Cordoba, who, beaten and driven out of Andalusia by the Imam Hakym ben Hischân, passed over into the Moghreb, came to Fez, and commenced building right and left from Keddân, as far as Roumelïa. Adoua Qairaouwn gave its name to 3000 families of Qairowan who established themselves there at the time of Idris. The most warlike rivalry having existed from the beginning between these two elements of the population, the wise measure of Youssef in razing the dividing walls must be lauded.

The new Qasbah only dates from the reign of Errechid. It was constructed about 1671, in the district of Lemtouna, in the park of Ibn Salah.

Fez is extremely important commercially, owing to its geographical position. It is the last halting place in the plain, before penetrating into the mountains, through which runs the road to Tafilalt, traversing the difficult regions of the Aït Youssi and of the Aït Isdig. It is the emporium for the merchandise of the greater part of the chain of Oases in the valley of W. Ziz. From Fez a whole colony of Jewish brokers, Moorish merchants, and protected agents of European houses carry on a lucrative exchange business with the Aït Youssi, the Beni Waraïn, the Aït Tche-grouchen, and the tribes generally of higher Moulouïa.

The road of Taza, leading to the Algerian frontier, contributes little to the commercial life of the town, owing to its unsafe condition; moreover the Sultan does not care to develop a current of commerce which would give fresh power to the French influence, already so considerable in Fez, in consequence of the great number of

Algerians living there. Nevertheless certain caravans appear at Fez at epochs fixed by the Tlemcen.

The same remarks are applicable to the road of Rif and the port of Melilla, under Castillian influence, which the Makhzen would also like to thwart. Although a certain number of Riffans come to Fez for provisions, the condition of insubordination of most of their mountainous regions paralyses all commercial enterprise. As the rich and populous basin of Sebou has not any real maritime outlet, all the commerce is stationary in the town, though it is the key of intercommunication for all the regions south of Moulouïa; whilst, on the north, the traffic takes the long and costly caravan route towards Tangiers and Larache ("El Araïsh"). It cannot be doubted that a European occupation would develop great prosperity, if canals were made in the course of the Sebou and its mouth dredged. As I have already had occasion to state, this difficulty and the high rate of transport are the cause of the decay of commerce in the most populous town of a region which, with a trade so extensive as that of Fez, ought to yield great profits. The risk of a caravan being pillaged frequently hinders all movement, already impeded by the numerous tolls that must be paid to insure comparative security among the independent hostile tribes bordering on the southern route.

At the present day, the town of Idris shares the stationary or torpid condition of all Morocco. The industry of Fez has, however, always been of high repute, and the different trades are represented by many corporations, each jealous of its privileges and distinguished by great originality of workmanship, especially in ornamentation. At Fez are to be seen embroideries of exquisite delicacy and colouring, also that manufactured leather which comes direct from Tafilalt, whose tannery is highly esteemed. The goat-skin, called by us Morocco, is there called Djild el Filâli; seeds of a shrub belonging to the mimosa family, called Takaout, are used in its manufacture in the Oasis. We must also call attention to the wool and goat-skin of Aït Youssi and of Beni Waraïn. (The Beni Waraïn or Ourain dwell in the mountainous groups, from which arises the Dj. Reggou, and which lies between the territory of the Aït Youssi to the south of Sefrou and the valley of the Moulonïa.)

Fez has the monopoly of those fine and soft haiks, which are unrivalled by any other material, although the shops are full of English and French cloths manufactured especially for the taste of the country; whilst considerable stores of candles from Marseilles and Antwerp, French and German sugar, and slop-goods innumerable slowly but surely penetrate into every house, destroying the picturesque charm and local colouring. The red cap worn by the Mussulmen, which we call the "fez," does not come from here, but from Tunis or Marseilles, where it is largely manufactured. The Jews have created an industry which one is astonished to find in so orthodox a city. They extract brandy from figs, and the business prospers, as all the ne'er-do-weels of the neighbourhood are large consumers of mahïa. The taste of the Morocco ladies [1] for this fiery liquid is also well known, and the government has frequently attempted to effect a reform, but the capitalists of Israel have too many protectors not to get themselves out of any awkward fix.

[1] It is seldom that the dances, for the performance of which tourists pay, come to a conclusion without disgusting drunkenness on the part of the Moroccan Bayaderes.

In the neighbourhood of the city, at a distance of about six miles, are some very remarkable salt-mines, many of which are the property of the Sherif of Wazzan. They occupy an area of 18 miles, and were already celebrated in the ancient days of the author of Roudh-el-Kartas, who speaks of them and informs us that they are situated between the hamlet of Chabry and W. Mesker in the Demmet el Bakoul. They produce a salt coloured by different metallic oxides, but highly appreciated by the Arabs. Not far from here are the famous hot sulphur springs of Ali Yakoub. Unfortunately the geology of this very interesting country is unknown, and, in consequence of its reputation for holiness among the Moroccans, it is very difficult to study it.

My sojourn at Fez, which I had hoped would be long enough to enable me to procure the details of a comparative historical topography, not hitherto done, was unfortunately shortened by the serious indisposition of my companion. The summer heat was suffocating in this valley, where the burning atmosphere was never cooled by any breeze, and I resolved on following the advice of my excellent friend Dr. Linarès (of the French Military Mission who had come from Meknas to give his aid) and go immediately to camp at a little distance to the south, in the first spurs of the Atlas Mountains, at the little town of Safrou, behind the Dj. Kandar, the eastern spur of the Mountains of Beni Methirs.

This illness of my companion was the occasion of a visit from a very important personage in the town, an administrator of the property of the Sultan, who kindly offered us his services. One fine morning he invaded our house, followed by a crowd of servants laden with presents for the patient, and remedies, which in his ignorance of medicine

THE KIFF AND NATIVE MEDICINE.

and his belief in talismans he brought us to combat the fever. The kindness of this proceeding was so manifest that we heartily thanked him for his delicate attention, although we only kept some phials of rose-water which perfumed our things for months, even after our return to Europe. When a Moroccan enters the chamber of a sick man his behaviour is curious. He advances on the tips of his naked toes, incessantly repeating in a low voice "Labass, Labass"—a lugubrious refrain resembling a sort of "de profundis," but which is in reality a conjuring of evil spirits by the assurance that all will go well in this best possible of worlds. We rewarded the zeal of this visitor by presenting him with a revolver, which I had been reserving for this purpose for some time.

On the subject of disease, be it said that, if the health of the country is indifferent in consequence of the dampness of the Tingitanian climate, the sanitary state of a population as dense as that of Fez, is as bad as it can possibly be. To the natural sources of epidemic affections, to the burning heat of summer and the cold nights, must be added the abuses of immorality which exhaust man both physically and intellectually.

Although the Koran, with rare wisdom, has forbidden everything that may trouble the mind and weaken the body, and the Sultan Mulai Hassan, imitating this example, has recently prohibited the sale of kiff, it must be confessed that the greater part of the population of Morocco, especially of the large towns like Fez, give themselves up to the delights of this intoxicating drug. This unfortunate passion, like opium-eating, has the most certain effect in destroying the memory and annihilating all moral and physical energy. It is hardly necessary to mention that kiff is made by the mincing of the tops of the hemp-plant (cannabis indica) which is smoked like tobacco, and which produces a sort of intoxication, much resembling that of opium, and said to be delightful. The meaning of the word kiff is "well-being"—"beatitude."

The orientals call it "hatchich" or divine herb, and certain sweetmeats prepared with it have a disturbing effect; when eaten, this plant only produces a sort of hilarity; it is said to have aperient and anthelmintic properties, especially useful against tænia. According to Arab tradition, the first person who discovered the narcotic qualities of hemp-seed and of hatchich, was an Indo-Persian named Haïdar who made use of his discovery to produce religious ecstasy and hallucinations among the disciples of his Zaouïa and the "Haïdarya" his religious order. The Moqaddem of the Aïssawa also have recourse to intoxicating drugs to produce the necessary condition of enthusiasm.

Shall I mention the medicine of the country? It consists almost entirely of the use of talismans, and its value may be judged by the reasoning of the Arabs, who ascribe every evil to the famous "b'erd"—cold. This is their chief term for designating the disease by which all Moroccans are attacked, and which is caused by the lowering of the natural temperature in consequence of venereal excesses.

In spite of their theological faith and their limited understanding, the people of the Moghreb are fully aware of the superiority of the European Thoubib Roumi or doctor. Few travellers, either in town or country, escape the importunity of poor wretches whose pallor, demeanour, and free confessions, reveal the extent of demoralisation in this strange Moroccan society.

Hygiene is neglected to such a degree that almost all the Arabian children, from their earliest infancy, are attacked with a kind of Tinea, a parasite disease of the hairy parts of the body which leaves great bare patches. This disease is very disfiguring, and becomes chronic; the Sultan himself is not exempt from it, inasmuch as the frequent ablutions commanded by their religion do not include the hygienic customs of an intelligent toilet. If medicine is neglected, the surgery is barbarous; with the exception of a few bone-setters, capable of setting a dislocation, but scarcely a fracture, the Moroccan surgeon treats human beings with red-hot irons, and practises horrible mutilations on them. Veterinary medicine and surgery only progress imperceptibly in the Moghreb.

During the two days preceding our departure from Fez, we were very much occupied by the numerous preparations for our journey. We were obliged to collect quantities of provision and utensils for crossing the Atlas mountains, and to eliminate the many useless impediments with which we were burdened. Having temporarily dismissed the famous cook, we were obliged to seek for a tolerable Vâtel, but all that could be found was a rather stupid sort of Sherif, whose acquaintance with Spanish rendered him valuable. A man who was very useful to us on every occasion was the consular agent of France, a pleasant Algerian, quite up to the ungrateful diplomatic task of protecting, moderating, and pacifying a population of Algerians and protected Jews, who think of nothing but sores, bumps, and indemnities. We had no alternative but to hire the services of El Oudjdi, after having satisfied ourselves of his obliging good-nature. Taking advantage of an improvement in the condition of my friend, I fixed the day of our departure, and sent on the men and animals beforehand, in order not to leave the town until the great heat of the day was over. Starting at 3.30 I hoped to arrive before nightfall at Safrou.

We left Fez by the new gate at Bab Djedid, which is close to the ancient iron gate of Bab el Hadid; near by, from many springs, flows a clear and limpid stream, which is, however, reported to be unwholesome. We then ascended the slopes which on the south command the valley of W. Fez. Passing to the S.E. of Dar Debibagh, we crossed, by the bridge of Errecif, a branch of this stream whose waters feed some of the springs at Fez Djedid. From the plateau we commanded a view of the confused mass of the town. Standing out detached from the groups of houses were three sacred arches, the great mosque of Shorfa, containing the tomb of the Imam Idris ben Idris, the mosque of El Qaïraouiyn, near to the beautiful gate of El Sherky, and lastly, the mosque of the Andalusians. The wood of Merdj Kertha commanded the town near the gate of Beni Massafar.

The heat was overpowering; scarcely had we started than we were overwhelmed by a scorching south wind, accompanied by an impalpable dust which darkened the air, and gave us a foretaste of the desert by making our progress most painful. In short, the wind of Sherky was raging. At rare intervals a slight clearing showed the southern horizon, bounded by the mountains which command the scarcely undulating flat region surrounding the Fhahs es Saïs, known to the Arabs by the generic name of "gour," or plain. At the extremity of a rocky spur we saw the little town of Baalil rising on the denuded slopes of the barren peaks; the name is more correctly "El Bahalil," or the fools. The Moroccans have awarded this amiable nick name to the inhabitants, who claim to be descended from the early Christians. The Khalif, at this time a certain Si Haddou, generally lives at Fez.

At 4.30 we arrived at the Aïn Soumâr (the spring of rushes), beside a small stream of water; hitherto the road had been very flat, beyond the hills which, in the south, command Fez, and the soil hard and stony over the barren steppes. The sun was setting, and as the wind was falling, we unduly prolonged our halt, enjoying with culpable carelessness our refreshing rest. Since our departure from the town we had not met a single human being of whom we could ask news of the column; and as we had not resumed our route until about dusk I felt very uneasy. It was in vain that our kaïd assured us that we were near to Safrou; he hesitated over the direction to pursue; the path was intersected in a thousand directions, and became more and more difficult as the nature of the soil changed. We were approaching the buttresses of Dj. Kandar, the horses could go no further, and, to complete our misfortunes, there was no moon. Before long we had entirely lost our way, and after about two hours of marching and countermarching, we had no other resource but to sleep in the open air, with no other food in prospect than a thin biscuit. The misery of the chief of our escort was extreme, for the road was no longer perfectly certain. He was not long, however, in following our example; having hobbled the horses, he rolled himself in his burnous, and committed himself to the protection of Allah. The darkest visions must have haunted his slumbers.

At day-break on the morrow we perceived the route which we ought to have taken, and which wound among the hillocks until it reached the gardens of Safrou. An hour's journey brought us to the entrance of the town; on reaching the first house on the left, a kind of great caravanserai, we were saluted by one of our soldiers, who, with all the caravan, had installed themselves there to await us patiently. Believing us still at Fez these good folks had prepared a house for us, which we refused, preferring the cool shade and fresh air of the mountains with life in a tent to any palace whatever.

Preceded by a Khalifa, and followed by an escort, increased in number by all the curious of the neighbourhood, we directed our steps towards the enchanting gardens full of great trees which surround Safrou, and make the delights of this oasis, lost in the mountain solitudes at the extremity of the chain of the Beni Methirs. Our only inconvenience was the extraordinary quantity of mosquitos, the bites of which were made more painful by the sun, and with the dust adhering to the perspiration produced painful ulcers of a very persistent nature. The only remedy I found was bathing in a solution of phenic acid and applying an ointment of oxide of zinc, taking care to protect the affected part with linen rag.

This adornment of luxuriant vegetation adds to the commercial prosperity of the little town, which is a considerable emporium of agricultural products. The great number of Jews[1] (1000 Jews to 3000 inhabitants) shows plainly enough that business is not bad. Enormous quantities of fruit, olives, citrons, cherries, grapes, are sent from Fez to Safrou,[2] and even fairly good wine is made there. It is the

[1] "Safrou" and "Demmnat" are apparently the paradise of the Jews of the Moghreb.

[2] The orthography of Safrou varies very much in Europe—Sfrou—Saforo—Sfro—are only euphonic varieties of the correct form Çofroui, according to Edrisi in his journey from Fez to Sidjilmassa. Houdas gives it Safrou.

entrepôt for almost all the oil of the surrounding region, which is as rich in olive-trees as the woods of Zarhoun; there also is stored excellent timber for building purposes, called bellouta, a resinous species of the family of the larch. There are extensive forests in the great mountains of Aït Youssi, and the adjoining territory of the Beni Mguild is also very rich in the same products but less cultivated.

Walking under the shade of superb trees, through a district watered by numerous streams of fresh running water, for a distance of about half a mile from the town, we reached a beautiful orchard surrounded by high hedges; a grove in an expanse of meadows which had been chosen for animals by the intelligent Khalifa. Both man and beast could revel in this ocean of verdure and recover from the effects of long confinement in towns.

The province of Fez terminates on the south in the gardens of Safrou, and this little town being the residence of the governors nominated and imposed by the Sultan on the powerful and semi-independent tribes of Aït Youssi and certain portions of the Beni Mguild, we were able to judge of the complications of this distribution of power. It was not long before we fell victims to the system. In spite of an appearance of perfect politeness and exaggerated amiability every effort was made to prevent us from continuing our journey, and to isolate us by demoralising our servants.

From morning till night we were visited by such personages as the special Qaïd or governor of the town, two Khalifas of the Pacha of the Aït Youssi (Mulai Saleb and Mulai Bou Ali), a Khalifa of the Pacha of the Aït Tsali (Pacha Sidi el Hadj Bougraig), a certain El Hamden, Khalifa of the little village of El Khalowa near to Safrou, and at the same time secretary of the functionary, who, whilst residing at Fez, has the administration of Safrou, all of whom were anxious to know the details of our lives and intentions. One day we were invited to a native *fête*, the lavish display of which astonished the whole population and revealed to them our importance. After the traditional fowls in the couscous, an enormous dish surmounted by a *ghatta*, or ornamental cover, superbly embroidered for the occasion, a whole roast sheep was served up, garnished with lemon-tree leaves, whilst small pieces of meat, on barley cakes, by way of plates, figured as entrées. Then came the *tagins*, or stew made of honey, followed by "msem-men," a kind of butter and honey pan-cakes, and finally a kind of lemon salad. Long after we had finished, our hosts were still at their couscous, all the dishes having been served up at once. They filled the hollow of their hands and ate greedily, breaking up the limbs of the fowls so voraciously that from the very beginning we heartily wished this culinary ceremony at an end.

Our stay at Safrou was prolonged beyond measure; in one month we had perambulated every corner of the adjacent suburbs, unable to get beyond these gardens, and the time seemed the longer because there were no signs of our being able to fix the date of our departure. Insurrections were continuing in the south. The supremacy of the Sultan—which, even in normal times, is so precarious—was still more defied than usual; and it was tolerably certain that we should not be able to pass through the rebel population which lined the road to get at the territories of High Moulouïa, the principal scene of the struggle. Our impedimenta of baggage and European outfit, and our costumes were so many obstacles; and even supposing that the desertion of the road, for the moment, by reason of the rumours of war had removed our anxiety on that account, we might still find ourselves driven on to the mountainous country of Dj. Tsouqt, and the whole mass of the rebels who were cutting off communication with Qçabi. This last strategic point is of the highest importance, as it secures the communication with the chain of oases of W. Ziz. It is the seat of a Qasbah which was established there ten years ago by order of the Sultan. To secure this a Qaïd was sent there from the Abids Boukhari, with a detachment of cavalry with two small pieces of mountain-cannon, hoping thus to maintain communication with Tafilalt notwithstanding that the powerful tribes of the Aït Isdig persist in their evil ways, intercepting the traffic of the road, at their own good pleasure, as at the time of our sojourn at Safrou. We were therefore obliged to renounce our hopes and prosaically pursue the road to Meknas, where a last chance awaited us of profiting by a corps of the Sultan's troops to reach the inhospitable banks of the Moulouïa.

A march of rather more than a day and a half separates Safrou from Meknas, by a straight road which is not safe even at ordinary times, and which runs along the foot of the high mountains of Beni Methirs, and through the Qaria of the Qaïd Mohammed ben Thami of the Aït Wellol,[1] l'aïn Hanseddar, the Qasbah of the Qaïd of the Beni Methirs, and joins the road from Fez to Meknas at a distance of about three quarters of a mile to the east of the ravine of the W. Islem, an hour and a quarter before entering Meknas.

To the west of Safrou the rocky spur projecting from the Beni Methirs Mountains can be crossed by a deep pass.

[1] The Aït Ouellal, Beni Ouellal or Ouellol are mentioned at page 18 of Aboul Qassem, in writing about an expedition made against them in 1667 by Errechid.

This rocky spur is called Dj. Kandar, and on its northern slope lies the little town of Baalil.

Two hours after our departure from Safrou, at a height of about 3000 feet above a rocky ravine, we could overlook the whole of the beautiful valley which separates the two capitals of modern Tingitane. On the east the horizon was bounded by the mountains of the Guerwan, the Dj. Kafès and the range of the Dj. Outita. To the north was the triangular block of the Zarhoun, whose lower slope stretches below the peak of the Kannoufa and the neighbouring spur of the Dj. Kala; the far north-east was encircled by the Tselfatz; whilst to the east, the Guebgueb, the Terat and the Zalah indicated the valley in which lay Fez, which could not be seen at the bottom of the funnel-shaped ravine formed by the mountains. Having then descended the rocky slope we hastened on so as to arrive by one o'clock at the Qasbah of the Qaïd Mohammed ben Thami. This functionary, whose dwelling had certainly never before been honoured by the visit of a European, made us heartily welcome, and told us afterwards how difficult was his position as a civilian in the midst of the incursions of the Aït Youssi. Quite recently, in order to cope with the rebellion of a portion of this tribe, he had been obliged to have the water-supply cut off by diverting the only brook which supplied water to his savage neighbours. And this was only justice according to the usages observed there. In Morocco the water from the rivers, which is directed by means of "Seguïa" or ducts constructed by forced labour, belongs to the Sultan. The Khalifa having observed this small formality had, therefore, the right to exact from the Aït Youssi, who were supplied with this water, the usual tax, that is to say, what remains after the first charge made by the "achour." In case of non-payment the precious liquid is simply withheld. From the Qasbah we had a magnificent view which had hitherto been hidden from us by the Dj. Kandar; we could see the whole group of the Aït Tchegrouchen, of the Beni Waraïn and the greater part of the little known region which lies around the territory of Taza.

The next day we resumed our journey at daybreak. We first skirted a dried-up lake and then rode through a beautiful plain, with scarcely a sign of cultivation. By mid-day we were near another Qasbah called Beni Methirs. About forty minutes before coming to this spot, we had crossed a well-filled brook which springs from the Aïn Hauseddar and flows into the W. Mehdouma. A pretty copse of fig trees looked very attractive and we decided to take our light luncheon in it; after which we at once proceeded on our journey, in the shade to be sure, but in an oppressive damp heat of 100° Fahr.

The Qariya of the Beni Methirs had been constructed to check the incursions of these natives. We had no time to enter it, but I noticed how unsafe the road was, although quite deserted, for our horsemen of the Makhzen had taken off their *chechia* or red government caps in order that, from their resemblance to ordinary horsemen, they might not be thought bent upon tax-collecting and that they might safely pass within range of the guns. Their bravery would not have equalled that of the wild Beni Methirs. At last, having crossed the W. Islem and the W. el Hamria at night-fall we reached that night the residence of the Sherif. We were heartily welcomed, for the Sultan had for some time had a fancy, which his imperial highness wished to satisfy at once, to be initiated into the secrets of photography. He had been told what we had done at our first visit to

Meknas, and remembering that in times gone by he had been presented with a complete photographic apparatus by an Italian Embassy, he had forthwith given orders to dig it out of the dust-heaps in which it lay a prey to oblivion, so that the mechanism might be explained to him and that his Tholba might be taught to excel in the art of Daguerre. Unfortunately the apparatus had been spoiled by damp, time, rats, and in short by all the adverse influences of Morocco. The officers of the mission had spent all their powers of logic and persuasion in explaining to the Sherifian monarch that the disaster was irreparable. At their wits' end they had sent messenger after messenger after us to ask for practical information, but none had fallen in with us. Meanwhile the court remained in the depths of grief at seeing its master—a Sherif—distressed at being unable to penetrate the mysteries of this cursed science of the roumis. Our arrival therefore put matters right.

It must be owned that Mulai Hassan is rather a modern-minded sultan. It appears he has in the storehouses of his palace all the things appertaining to a microscope, to photography, and to other scientific instruments. A chemical laboratory, telephones, everything, has been offered him or thrust upon him. Only lately, for instance, he was presented with a miniature railway, with which he plays as if he were a child. These sacrilegious tastes, however, might bring ill-luck. Some fanatic Idrissite Sherif of Fez, for instance, might get hold one fine day of a flask out of the above-named laboratory and the imperial tea would send the Sultan's soul on its way to the shades of his ancestors. There is no gainsaying that want of sense, and the number of charlatans which crowd round the Makhzen and mix with the colonies of official embassies, are to a great extent

FAREWELL TO THE MILITARY MISSION. 407

accountable for the barbarous state of stagnation in which the government lies.

Having given every possible information and advice for getting the photographic apparatus into working order, we were hoping to obtain as a reward certain facilities for continuing our journey. But on the contrary we had to submit to the wish of the sovereign who immediately requested us by his black grand-vizier not to pursue our plans. It is true the last company which the court would send this season in the direction of Qçabi had just set out, and, unless we could obtain an escort of about 300 men, we should have to accede to the imperial request. And so we did. The doctor of the mission also advised me in the strongest terms to repair as soon as possible to the north, in order to get the benefit of the sea-breezes so as to recover from an attack of dysentery from which I had been suffering severely for the last six weeks.

We left Meknas on the morning of the 25th of September, after having bid good-bye to the French officers whose kind hospitality had been so useful to us. We were to sleep at the Qariya of Qaid Abdallah, at Sidi Kaçem, at the foot of the northern slope of the Dj. Outita, at the entrance of the plain of Sebou. We were to follow the classical road of the embassies, descend into the valley of W. Rdem, cross the Outita chain not far from the small Roman ruins, above the Pass of Bab Tisra Djorf which had been rendered impracticable by recent slips. We had a magnificent view from the top of the peak of the El Khemis whilst the setting sun cast its golden rays over the whole horizon. We could see the valley of Sebou in all its vastness and nakedness stretching from the desert to the ocean. We were to sleep at the house of Qaïd Abdallah ben Chelellh so as to be able to traverse the next day the vast alluvial plain along the road which goes through Sidi Gueddar, Msaada, and Djoumaa el Hawafa. Then we were to cross the Sebou which then was 2 feet deep at the Mechraa bel Ksiri and sleep at the Qariya of Qaïd El Habbassi near which some fine tumuli are to be seen. Then the scene changes, and we come upon the undulating ground of the Beni Melek of El Biban which lies on the north bank of the river-basin. After traversing the valley of the little W. Meda, the one which comes from Dcharchiera, we come to the territory of the Oulad Djelil, which forms a part of the Sefian, on the plateau of the Dj. Dol, whence flow some salt springs.

On the evening of the third day we came to the market of Djoumaa, which is held every Friday, at about a hundred metres from the little mosque and Marabout of Lella Mimoŭna Taguenaout, on a conglomerate elevation in the stony valley of the W. Drader. This district belongs to the Oulad Djeraï, to the Oulad Drader or Bddrader, the Oulad Harid, and the Oulad Bisbahr, these latter being already on the territory called Bdawa. In the middle of the morning of the 4th day we arrived at the plateau of the Oulad Messen, which forms the line of division between the waters of the basin of W. el Kous, and of the little W. Drader, which is furnished with an independent hydrographic system. It runs through a small valley and flows into the Mezdja d'Ez Zerga (or blue lake), celebrated for the Marabout Mula Bou Selham, and its mouth is situated at the cliffs of the ocean, at the spot where M. Tissot thinks he has found the site of the Phœnician MVLELACHA of Polybius.

As to the W. Meda, which is difficult to ford in winter at the place where we crossed—just at the foot and to the north

ARRIVAL AT EL ARAÏSH.

of the hillock of Dj. Bourk, which bears the Marabout of Sidi Aïssa ben Athsen—it was now only a tiny streak running over a pebbly bed of conglomerate. It will be remembered that this brook also forms a distinct hydrographic system in flowing into the Great Merdja de Râs ed Doura. At the moment we crossed the Meda, we followed a route of 14° (magnetic), having the Peak of Sarsar 299°, and the Qoubba of Sidi Aïssa 182° 30′ (magn.)

On the fourth day we arrived at El Araïsh. We halted at 10·30 at Aïn bou Ali, a little stream with a quantity of watercress in it, and close to a *douar* of the Oulad Boucheta. The water issues from the northern side of a slight depression of the plateau of Hawawan, and belongs to the basin of the Kous. A group of fig-trees enabled us to pass away an hour very agreeably; from there we could see a little white house near El Araïsh, and finally, two hours after leaving the spring, we entered the great forest of cork trees, which surrounds El Araïsh. These groups of trees, more than a hundred years old, and which time has partially stripped, are broken up into numerous large glades, which become larger every day owing to the destructiveness of the Arabs. It is to be regretted that the opening up of this precious wood should have been abandoned to the caprice of the careless and improvident Moroccans, the Makhzen having obstinately declined all the offers made to him by enterprising Europeans.

Towards the East the forest ends at the deep ravine of W. Sah'souh, and three hours after leaving Aïn bou Ali, after traversing a long plateau of red sand, we entered the Town. El Araïsh, at the mouth of the Kous, two short days' journey from Tangiers, and with steamboat communication, is too well known to need any description, especially as the town, though picturesque as seen from the sea, is small, Spanish in its characteristics, and inhabited by a most horrible set of Jews. It is probable that El Araïsh, whose name was unknown to the Arab geographers of the middle ages, was built on the site of that other Phœnician town near Lixos—itself a Phœnician Colony—mentioned by Scyllax as a port at the mouth of the river. This hypothesis has also been adopted by Barth, and is all the more probable as the fertility of the surrounding country is very great, while the rocky promontory, on which now stands the Spanish Castle of St. Elme, has always furnished shelter from the west and north-west winds so much to be dreaded on this inhospitable coast. The blacks also talk of a nameless city which used to stand opposite Lixos.

More recently, the chronicler of Roudh-el-Kartas tells us that it formed, with Azila and Basra, a portion of the country, the command of which was entrusted by Mohammed ben Idris to his brother Yahia; and as to El Bekri he has transmitted to us the name of a populous fortified town as being Harat el Ahchîs, and the topographical details which he gives answer in every respect to those of the modern town.

For seventy-nine years—from 1610 to 1689—El Araïsh remained under the domination of Spain, and it still preserves traces of its Christian occupancy. At every turn of the streets one might imagine oneself in the Peninsula, and the copper-work of the doors and many architectural details help to keep up the illusion.

According to the chroniclers, the town was ceded to Philip II. on November 21st, 1610, by Mulai Cheikh, in return for monetary help; but the place was so neglected that the Spaniards never derived any benefit from it during the time of their occupation, and the Moroccan troops easily regained possession by simply digging holes under the walls, on the port side, which they filled with powder. Through the breach made by the explosion of this powder, the Moroccans, probably led by some renegade, expert in the art of mining, penetrated into the city. The Spaniards took refuge in the citadel of El Qebibat where they remained besieged for a whole year, at the end of which the majority were made prisoners, and to the number of 1300 were sent as slaves to Meknas. [1689.]

In 1173 of the Hegira (1764-1765), the French anchored before the town, which they destroyed, but one of their landings was unfortunate. An attacking corps in armed boats penetrated into the harbour, and having burnt the ships which they found there pushed further up the river in order to reach a ship which had remained there. The Moslems, who had posted themselves at the entrance to the port, surrounded the French and stopped their progress; then, having boarded their boats by swimming, they killed or made prisoners every man who was on them; not one escaped. Afterwards the King of Spain[1] made himself acquainted with the whole affair, and obtained the ransom of some of the prisoners in return for a considerable sum of money. This attempt went by the name of the Du Chaffaut expedition from the name of the officer in command.

In 1760 the French seem to have again entertained designs against this port, in fact there is preserved in the archives at Paris a plan of the estuary made at that time by the order of M. de Pointis, commander of the squadron.

---

[1] Translation of Aboul Qassem by Houdas, page 141.

The night of our arrival we walked along the base of the cliffs (on which is erected the Spanish castle which commands the river), amongst enormous boulders of conglomerate, out of which sprang a number of fountains, at the edge of a superb blue sea—altogether a picturesque picture in the twilight. The scene was completed by the groups of Arabs who came to water their horses at troughs cut out in the rocks, and by the elongated mass, so curiously preserved, of the old castle of Notre Dame, which, like some gigantic ship, commands the town.

The town is interesting to the archæologist on account of the proximity of the hillock of Tehemich, on which are situated the ruins of the ancient Lixos of the Phœnicians, which can be seen from El Araïsh. It is not, however, my intention to give any account of the Lixos of Eratosthenes, as we had not time to go to it during the journey the account of which I am just finishing, therefore all we know of the topography of the town is due to the learned researches of Tissot.[1]

The river of El Araïsh is crossed at about 200 metres from its mouth, which is much narrowed by the formation of sand-banks thrown up by the high tides and by the inundations after the torrents of rain in spring and autumn. Some large primitive boats, carrying cattle also, ferried us, at the risk of breaking our legs, over to the right bank.

The displacement of the bed of the Kous has been admirably studied. The windings of the river after the choking up of the peninsula of the Khildj had always rendered it extremely difficult to identify two places famous in antiquity —the altar of Hercules and the garden of the Hesperides.

[1] "Recherches sur la geographie comparée de la Maurétanie tingitane."

Now, thanks to the distinguished geologist, Dr. Bleicher, and to M. de Laroche, a gentleman who, having lived for thirty years at El Araïsh, was thoroughly acquainted with every corner of the estuary, our lamented savant, M. Tissot (assisted by French science), has earned the glory of reconstituting the primitive configuration of these celebrated places. The islet of Rekada is the spot which in ancient times included the altar of Hercules and the forest of golden fruit which surrounded it.

The silting up of the Kous has of late years stopped nearly all the commerce of the town, for the steamers, being obliged to anchor in the open harbour formed by the ocean in the offing of El Araïsh, cannot communicate with the shore. The English and French companies have obviated this difficulty by creating an auxiliary service of small boats, specially constructed in such a manner as to be able to cross the bar at high tide, after having embarked their European goods in the quiet harbour of Gibraltar. The importance of the commerce of El Araïsh fully justifies this complicated arrangement; it is the port for Gharb and Fez, and by that route the marshes of El Gharbïya, on the way to Tangiers, so difficult to traverse in winter, are avoided.

As for ourselves, two routes were open to us in order to regain the shore of the Straits of Gibraltar. The one in the interior through districts which at the eminence of Sidi el Yemeni rejoined the route which we had followed in going from Tangiers to El Qaçar; the other, which we eventually chose, took us almost the whole way along the sea shore, and allowed of our sleeping at Azila,[1] celebrated for its occupation by the Portuguese.

[1] We follow the majority in writing Azila for the sake of the pronunciation, but it cannot be denied that Azīla would be more correct

After crossing the river of El Araïsh, we followed its course for about half-an-hour, until as high up as the Islet of Rehada, we traversed a group of sand hills which appeared to have been there from time immemorial, after which we went along the beach, which is very fine, until we reached the ravine into which the W. Sebt (a name given in its lower course to the W. er Rihan and the W. el Ghenem) empties itself. This river, as we have already seen, runs along the base of the hill of Sidi el Yemeni. The little Marabout of Sidi Bou Mghaits is at the entrance of a tolerably wild valley, which must be traversed in order to regain the interior. We then wound round the heights of Medjlaou above the little W. Touareus es Sahel, to the east of which can be distinctly seen the Dj. Wazzan and the Peak of Sarsar. At about five o'clock we reached some deliciously shady lanes which, meandering through groves of verdure, eventually brought us to the Marabout of Sidi Bourquenaded in front of the eastern gate of the ancient colony of IVLIA CONSTANTIA ZILIS, lying between the sands of the shore and the verdure of its orchards. Zilis—in our days called Azila—was one of the first colonies founded by Augustus; but although certain historical indications lead us to suppose that Zilis was of Punic origin, documentary evidence on this point is singularly wanting.

As far as we can judge from our cursory visits, the circumference of the ancient city was much greater than that of the modern town.

The numerous substructures which are met with in the orchards in the environs show the limits of the Roman town, while now-a-days Azila is only a big village of no

as it approaches more nearly to the Roman form. Houdas spells it Azille, but points out that Aboul Qassem spelt it Asilah.

commercial importance whatever, its port having been filled up with sand ever since the destruction of the dyke which protected it. The population hardly reaches 1200 souls, two-thirds of whom are Jews who live scattered through the town without having any special quarter to themselves. These Jewish families are Andalusian by origin, and speak Spanish. They are very polite, and are more agreeable than the Israelites of the interior, as are all those along the coast as far as Rabate.

The French consular agent, a well-known merchant of the locality, called Ennijar, received us very cordially. The Foreign powers have two representatives at Azila—the one I have just mentioned and another, also a Jew, who represents in his own person England, Spain, Italy, and Belgium! But I must add that these high functions are purely honorary and absolutely gratuitous, but are much sought after notwithstanding, for they place their holders beyond the reach of the governmental molestations of the Pachas. Reduced as it is, the town is still full of the picturesque charm of historical *souvenirs*; its Portuguese castle with its walls still standing, and its windows in the pointed flamboyant Gothic style, recall to our minds its heroic defence by the Portuguese. The town had been in the possession of the Portuguese ever since 1471; but under John III., finding itself obliged to give up all idea of a continental conquest of the Moghreb, the Court of Lisbon confined itself to keeping in Azila a garrison sufficiently strong to repulse the repeated attacks of the Sultans of Morocco. The siege of 1508 was particularly touching, and Marmol has left us an account of the following episode.

The town had been in the possession of the Moors for three days when Don John brought assistance to Azila.

The fleet being obliged to anchor outside the dyke for fear of the Sherifian artillery, and the sea at the time running very high, the commander, before entering the port, wished to ascertain whether the castle still held out; and for this purpose sent a well-armed boat with two tried soldiers to ascertain if by signs or cries they could discover anything. They had a great deal of trouble in getting in, because they were fired upon by the battery which was stationed at one of the gates. (In our day there is only one gate—that which opens on the beach looking towards the north.) At last they got near enough to see, at an open window in the tower, in the apartment of the count, a flag on which was the arms of Portugal, and a woman with dishevelled hair holding a child in her arms. "Portugal! Portugal!" she cried, on seeing her deliverers. Then Don John de Menessez, surnamed the "Thief," son of Count de Cantagnede, gathering together his little army, forced the entrance of the harbour and took the town from the Moors.

But the place was soon abandoned—this time willingly—by the Portuguese Government (about 1516), on account of the enormous cost of keeping up its defences, in return for which there were no compensating advantages to be obtained from this isolated and more or less barren spot.

Previously Azila had been taken by the Arabs, about 712 (94 of the Hegira). Leo Africanus represents it as having been captured by Norman pirates, while El Bekri, who places this expedition of the Northmen in 202 of the Hegira (843-844), considers that this irruption may have been a peaceful one. However this may be, the natives must have then laid the foundations of the fortifications which were afterwards reconstructed by El Kassem Ibn

Idris ibn Idris, and later on were only so far modified as to admit of the use of artillery. The great windows of the keep which fronts the sea—and where the scene passed which I have just described—were remodelled by the Portuguese. Their Gothic arched bays look very curious in the midst of their Arab surroundings, but the walls and the bulk of the building are of the earlier date.

After the departure of the Portuguese, however, the town fell into the hands of a Moroccan administration, and is now in an absolute state of decay. A cannon-ball of clay would knock down the walls, and Azila is perishing within sight of Cape Spartel and the lantern of its light-house, which like a star of civilization lights up this desolate shore.

It is only a day's walk from Azila to Tangiers, but we were obliged to start at two o'clock in the morning in order to cross the estuary of Tahedart at low tide. The local authorities allowed the gate to be opened for us, and we crossed the Portuguese threshold by the light of a superb moon. The route along the sea-shore is now no longer used on account of the difficulty of crossing the Tahedart, but in the time of El Bekri it was the most frequented road in this part of the Tingitane.

A quarter of an hour to the north of Azila we came to the W. el Halou (the W. Acila of El Bekri). It is easily crossed even in winter, by following the sand bank which forms the bar at its mouth. Forty-five minutes further north we arrive at the W. el A Kouès, or *the arches*, which is the name given to the lower course of the W. el Aïacha, after it leaves the ford of Mechráa el Ghrifa on the direct road from Azila to Tangiers in the interior. This deep and rapid river is only fordable at low tide. Some ruins of

Moorish origin cover the banks, while an aqueduct on arches, still in good preservation, and which by extension has given its name to the surrounding country and even to the river, recalls all that is left of that port of Nebroch mentioned by El Bekri.

An hour afterwards we were at the Tahedart, whose deep and rapid channel is impassable in winter except in a boat. An old refuge for the pirates of Barbary, the entrance to the Tahedart (it will be remembered that it was noticed at the commencement of this journey that the Tahedart is formed by the union of the W. Mharhar with the Kharroub which flow into the sea at this estuary) has always been of great importance, and there is no doubt that its vicinity prompted the erection of the Roman city of AD MERCVRI. In winter during the bad weather, it is allowed on a sort of happy-go-lucky system to carry across goods when the communication by the marshes of El Gharbïya with Tangiers is interrupted. After the shipwreck of the large steamer "Abyssinia," belonging to an Italian company, which was lost in a fog on this coast, a knot of intelligent Jews of Azila bought one of its big boats, intending to establish a permanent service at this passage, which in the season would be able to render the greatest services by doing away with the long delays necessitated by the numerous journeys of the little Moroccan skiff. But the authorities, moved by this civilizing invasion, benevolently shut their eyes to the thieves who have taken possession of this new embarkation and who are extending their operations to unknown shores.

We then continued along the coast from the south to the north in the direction of Cape Spartel whose imposing mass could be more and more clearly descried on the horizon. We went along the downs of El Briedj and El Hawara, and at about 9.30 came to the first rocks of the "Ampelusia" of the Greeks. Here we then got into the apology for a road, constructed by order of the committee of the powers, from the lighthouse of Cape Spartel to Tangiers, and at 11.30 we dismounted at the porch of the Legation which we had quitted six months before.

APPENDIX.

Since this work was commenced there has been a remarkable development in means of communication with Tangiers.

The Spanish Government has at length decided on changing the lamentable condition of the Postal Service between Tarifa and Tangiers.

The *Compagnie Transatlantique Espagnole* has established a regular service between Cadiz and Tangiers; a small steamer takes the mail three times a-week; whilst thanks to H.B.M. Legation, a cable has been laid from Gibraltar.

A line of Italian boats has placed Tangiers in monthly communication with Barcelona and Genoa.

Amongst the very apparent changes in the condition of Tangiers it is necessary to call attention to the considerable increase of the Spanish population—but a population of very bad character—people without work and often without any resource—who come to seek their fortune in Morocco. As a matter of course, since this state of things arose, the number of crimes, thefts, and misdemeanours has increased in an alarming degree.

This is conquest by destruction. It is in truth a sad example that Spain gives to Morocco.

April, 1889.

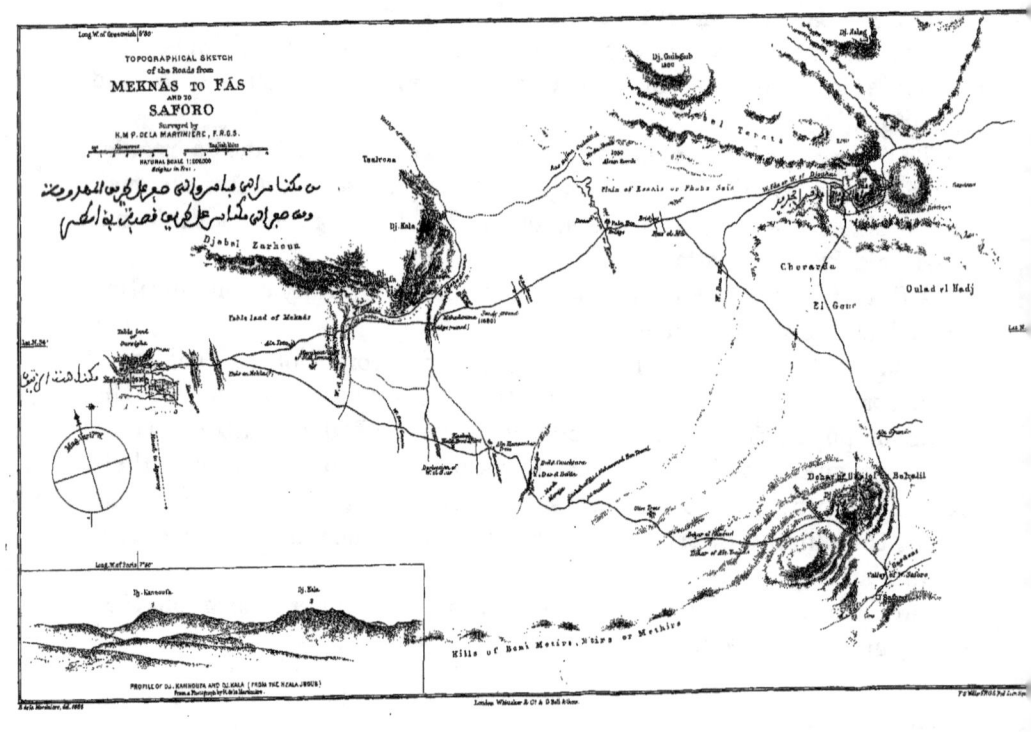

CORRIGENDA.

Page 59, line 21, *for* Tahaddar *read* Tahedart.
,, 69, ,, 15, *read* great tribe of the Sanhadja (omit Betama).
,, 86, ,, 2, *for* Puertoleano *read* Puertollano.
,, 96, ,, 15, *for* Mountain of the Starlings *read* Woody Mountains.
,, 98, ,, 8 from below, *for* Arabia *read* Asia.
,, 171, ,, 5 from below, *for* peak *read* neck.
,, 202, ,, 4 from below, *for* Fay *read* Fez.
,, 231, ,, 5 from below, *for* Allas *read* Atlas.
,, 232, ,, 1, *for* Zedig *read* Isdig.
,, 250, ,, 4, *for* Haranis *read* Harams.
,, 266, ,, 2 of note, *for* Black *read* White.
,, 277, ,, 2 of note, *for* £30 *read* £40.
,, 296, ,, 4 from below, *for* Muley *read* Sidi.
,, 319, ,, 2 of note, *for* Edrisdides *read* Idrissides.
,, 334, ,, 9, *for* Der Raoua *read* Derkawa.
,, 336, ,, 12, *for* Chfa or Filali *read* Shorfa Filali.

Page 36—On the recent death of M. Féraud the French Government nominated M. Patenôtre. The philarabian disposition of the former of these representatives has certainly not given all the diplomatic results that might have been hoped for.

Page 418—AD MERCVRI ought to be written AD MERCVRIVM. The MSS. which have come to hand have either this reading, or that of AD MERCVRIÓS a form which, following the example of Wæsseling and Tissot, we reserve for the Roman post of occupation which lay to the south of the "Sala *Colonia*," the situation of which has not yet been identified.

BIBLIOGRAPHY OF MOROCCO.
[1844-1885.]

Supplement to the "Liste des Ouvrages relatifs à l'Empire de Maroc par ordre Chronologique" and to the "Cartes, Plans et Vues relatifs au même Empire," published at the end of the "*Description Géographique de l'Empire de Maroc, par E. Renou.* Paris: Imprimerie Royale, MDCCCXLVI."

—:o:—

ABDERRAMAN-BEN-MAHOMET—Carta sobre costumbras de Marruecos enviadas desde Larache al diario de Madrid. *El Imparcial.* Año 1875.

ABUL-HASSAN-ALI-BEN ABD-ALLAH—Annales regum Mauritaniæ a condito Idrisidarum imperio ad annum fugæ 726. Illustravit Car. J. Fornsberg. Upsaliæ, 1843-1846, 2 vols. 4to.

ADAMOLI—Viaggio al Marocco. Boll. Soc. Geogr. Italiana. XIII, 1876.

,, —p. 630. Lettere dell'Ing. G. Adamoli, dal Marocco. Publicadas an el *Giornale de Viaggi e Geogr. Commerciale de Milano,* 1878.

AGADIR—Article concerning the town of . . . *Nautical Magazine.* page 600. London, 1881.

AGUIRRE (Ruperto)—Expedición al Riff (Su importancia, necessidad y conveniencia). Madrid, Imp. de Ducazcal, 1858.

ALARCON (Don Pedro Antonio de . .)—Diario de un testigo de la guerra de Africa. Segunda Ed. correg. Madrid, Imp. de V. Saiz. 3 vols. 8vo., 1880.

ALBY, (Ernest)—Les Vêpres marocaines, ou les derniers prisonniers d'Abd-el-Kader. Paris, 2 vols. in 8. 1853.

,, Les Prisonniers Français en Algérie—Aventures du trompette Exoffier. Paris, 1850, 2 vols. in 8vo. (L'histoire des femmes Lanternier—Documents sur la bataille d'Isly).

ALERMON y DORREGUIZ—Descripción del Imperio de Marruecos, (en que se trata principalmente de las instituciones etc. . . .) Madrid, Imp. de Minuesa, 1859, in 8to.

ALVAREZ-y-PEREZ (José)—El país del Misterio. Madrid. Medina edit., 1876, in 8to.

,, ,, ,, —Memoria sobre el comercio que se hace por el puerto de Mogador, 1876, (Publicada in las *Memorias Comerciales, por la Direccion g^{al} de Aduanas*).

ALVEREZ-Y-PEREZ (José)—Vistas y tipos de la Costa del Sus, tomados del natural en la expedicion del "Blasco de Garay." Ano, 1878. La Illustracion Esp. y Americ. : No. xiv., 15 Abr, 1878.

,,   ,,   ,, —Marruecos. Memoria geographico commercial de la demarcacion del Consulado de Mogador. *Bull. Soc. Géogr. de Madrid.* II., page 499, anno., 1877.

AMADEDDIN (Moro)—Historia de los Mahometanos en Africa y España traducida en Castellano por Marco Obelio, con notas originales de Ustarroz. Madrid, M.S., Bibliot. Nac., S. 79.

AMADOR DE LOS RIOS Y RADA Y DELGADO—Victorias de Africa, oda de D. J. A. de Los rios y canto en octavas, con motivo de la Toma de Tetuán por D. J. de Dios de la Rada y Delgado : Composiciones leidas a. S.S.N.N. en presencia de S.S.A.A.R.R. los Sermos, Infantes Duques de Montpensier. Madrid, Ducazcal, 1860, in 4to., 18 paginas.

AMICIS (Edmondo de)—Marocco. Milano. frat. Treves, in 16. 1876, 2'ed., 1885.

,,   ,,   ,, —Le Maroc, trad. de l'italien par H. Belle. Paris. Hachette. in fol. illustré (il existe une édit. in 16.) (A paru dans le Tour du Monde.)

,,   ,,   ,, —Morocco—its people and places (with illustrations). London, 1879, in 4to., Cassell and Co.

,,   ,,   ,, —[Er bestaat ook eene Hollandsche vertaling van dit werk.]

AMOR (Fernando)—Recuerdos de un viaje á Marruecos. Sevilla, 1859, 8vo.

ANDREWS (W. H. C.)—A pamphlet and map of Southern Morocco, or Sūs, and the "Ait Bou Amaran." Edited by W. H. C. A., [giving some account of the present condition of the people and country, etc.,] page 40. London, E.W. Allen, 1884, 8.

ANNALES du COMMERCE EXTÉRIEUR—Aperçu et Sommaire du commerce des Etats Barbaresques en 1866 et 1867. Mouvement Maritime et commercial des ports de Tanger, Rabat Salé, Casablanca, Mazagan et Saffi. Ann. Com. exter. Paris, Août, 1869.

ARTECHE (D. José Gomez de) y COELLO (D. Francisco) Coronels—Descripción y Mapas de Marruecos con algunas consideraciones sobre la importancia de la occupacion militar de una parte de este imperio. Madrid, 1 vol. in 16, 1859.

ATLAS HISTORICO TOPOGRAPHICO—de la guerra de Africa, Sostenida por la nacion española contra el imperio Maroqui en 1859 y 1860. Madrid, 1861. Deposito de la guerra.

ATMELLER (Victoriano)—Juicio critico de la guerra de Africa. Madrid, 1861, in 4to.

AUSLAND—Eine Gesandtschaftreise nach Marokko. N. 37-39, 1876.
„ —Marocco, neue Mittheilungen aus. 1880, N. 11.
„ —Die Scheluh im Atlas. 1885, N. 21.

AZLANDES (Th. Vernes d')—En Algérie. A travers l'Espagne et le Maroc. Paris, 1881, in-12.

AVEZAC. D'—Description et histoire de l'Afrique ancienne, précédée d'une esquisse générale de l'Afrique. (Univers *pittoresque*). Paris, 1845, in-8, cartes et fig.

BACHE (Paul, Eugène)—Souvenirs d'un voyage à Mogador en 1859. *Revue Maritime et Coloniale.* Tom. I, 1861, page 81.

BALANSA (B.)—Voyage de Mogador à Maroc (au point de vue botanique) *Bull. Soc. Géogr. Paris*, No. 27, 1868, p. 312.

BALL (J.)—Mountaineering in the great Atlas. London, *Alpine Journal*, 1873, p. 220.

„ „ —Spicilegium Floræ Morocanæ. London, *Journal of the Linnean Soc.* Vol. xxi., N. 93, page 281.

BALL-MAW-RAMSAY—Geology of the Atlas. *Proceed. of the Geolog. Soc.* London, 1872.

BARBIÉ du BOCAGE (LOUIS)—Le Maroc, [notice géographique.] Paris, 1861, in 8.
„ „ „ —Partie in *Bull. Soc. Géogr.*
„ „ „ —*Nelles Ann. des Voy.*
„ „ „ —*Rev. du M de Colo.*

BARD (Joseph)- L'Algérie in 1854. Itinéraire Général de Tunis à Tanger. Grd. in 8vo. Paris, MDCCCLIV. 251 pages.

BARTH (Dr. H.)—Travels and discoveries in north and central Africa being a journal of an expedition undertaken under the auspices of H. B. M. Government, in the years 1849-1855. New York, 1857, 3 vols. 8vo, map and illust.

„ „ „ —Reisen und Entdeckungen in nord und central Afrika in den Jahren, 1849 bis 1875. Gotha, 1857-58, 5 vols. 8vo.

„ „ „ —Voyages et découvertes dans l'Afrique septentrionale et centrale, pendant les années 1849 à 1855, traduit de l'allem. par P. Itier. Paris, 1860-61, 4 vols. in-8, carte et gravures en noir et en couleur.

BASSET, (René)—Relation de Sidi Brahim de Massat dans le Soûs. *Bull. Soc. Géogr. de l'Est*, 1882, p. 524, et p. 707 (printed separately, 8vo).

BASSET (René)—Documents géographiques sur l'Afrique septentrionale. *Bull. Soc. Géogr. de l'Est*, 1883.

BASSET (René)—Mission scientifique en Algérie et au Maroc. *Bull. Soc. Géogr. de l'Est*, 1883-84.

BAUDOZ et OSIRIS—Histoire de la guerre de l'Espagne avec le Maroc. Publiée sous la direction de M.M. Paris, 1860, in-8 br.

BEAUMIER (Aug)—*(Consul de France à Mogador)*. Le Maroc. *Bull. Soc. Géogr. de Paris* v Série xiv, 1867, page 5.

,, ,, —Excursion de Mogador à Safy. *Bull. Soc. Géogr. de Paris* v Série, xv, 1868, page 305.

,, ,, —Description Sommaire du Maroc. Paris, in 8.

,, ,, —Itinéraire de Mogador à Maroc et de Maroc à Safy. *Bull. Soc. Géogr. de Paris* v Série xvi, 1868, page 231.

,, ,, —Lettre sur le Maroc. *Bull. Soc. Géogr. de Paris.* vi. Série, i. 71, page 131.

,, ,, —Le choléra au Maroc. *Bull. Soc. Géogr. de Paris.* III., page 286, 1872.

,, ,, —Le Maroc, notes de voyage. *L'explorateur Géogr.* II., No. 40, 1875.

,, ,, —Mogador et son climat. Paris, 1875.

,, ,, —Le commerce au Maroc. *Bull Soc. Géogr. de Bordeaux* 1875-1877.

,, ,, —Itinéraire de Tanger à Mogador. *Bull. Soc. Géogr. Paris* vi. Série, xi. 1876.

BEAUMONT (Pedro)—Memoria sobre la plaza de Melilla. M.S. en el Ministerio de la guerra. Madrid, 1869.

BEN-GAZEL (Sidi Mahomet)—Diario de lo mas curioso que o currió en su viaje a la Corte de España y del de D. Jorge Juan a la de Marruecos. Madrid, M.S. Bibliot. nac. S. 259.

BENITEZ (Crist.)—Viaje por Marrueccos, el Desierto del Sáhara y Sudán al Senegal. *Bolet. Soc. Geogr. de Madrid* xx., 1886, page 337, xxi., pag. 7.

BERLINER GESELLSCH. FÜR ERDKUNDE—Artikel über Marokko. Berlin, 1869. IV Band, II Heft, 172.

BEYNET (Léon)—Les drames du désert, scènes de la vie arabe sur les frontières du Maroc. Paris, 1864, in-12.

BIZEMONT (V. Cte)—La France et le Maroc. *L'exploration* xvii., 1884, page 853.

BLACKMORE—A ride to Gebel Mousa in North Western Barbary. Bat. lll. Travels, III, 71, page 15.

BLACKMORE—A Visit to the Sultan of Marocco at Fez in the spring of 1871. *Ibid.* pages 276, 310, 346.

Blackwood's Edinburgh Magazine—Morocco and Moors. May, 1880.

„ „ „ —A Spring trip to Morocco, from Tangier to Wazan. Oct., 1883. [Journey of Major Trotter and Mr. H. de la Martinière to Wazan in March 1883.]

BLANCHÈRE (de La)—Malva, Mulucha, Molochatch, étude d'un nom géographique. Bull. de corresp. Africaine, III, 1884, page 136.

„ „ „ —Voyage d'étude dans une partie de la Maurétanie Cœsarienne. [Rapport à M. le ministre de l' Instruction publique] Paris, 1883.

BLANCO HERRERO (D. M.)—La guerra de Africa, La Atlantida, Poema, por. B. H. Madrid, C. Gonzalez, 1860. 4to.

BLEICHER (Dteur. A.)—Un voyage au Maroc (conférences publique d'Oran) *Revue Scientifique de la France et de l'Etranger*. Paris, 13 févr, 1875.

BLUMENTRITT (F.)—Die Spanischen Presidios an der Nordküste Marokkos. Globus, xlviii, 1885, N. 18.

„ „ —Die neuen Erwerbungen Spaniens an der Atlantischen Küste Nordafrikás. *Ibid.* xlxviii., 1885, N. 20.

BONELLI (Teniente. D. Emilio)—El imperio de Marruecos y su constitucion. Descripcion de su geografia, topografia, administracion, industria, agricultura, comercio, artes, religion, costunbres, razas que lo pueblan y estudio de su importancia politica y militarmente considerada. Madrid, deposito de la guerra, in 8to, 1882.

„ „ „ —Observaciones de un Viaje por Marrueccos (con una mapa). Madrid, Fortanet, 1883.

„ „ „ —Nuevos Territorios Espanoles de la Costa del Sahara (con una mapa). Madrid, Fortanet, 1885.

BONO SERRANO (Gaspar)—Alas Victorias contra Marrueccos, Oda por P. Gaspar Bono Serrano, capellan de honor de S. M. entre los arcades de roma afgero Latmio. Madrid, por aguado, 1860, en 4o, 13 pag.

BOUSQUET (du)—Article sur le Maroc. *Revue française*, p. 277, 280. Avril, 1885. Paris, Chaix.

BROSSELARD (Charles)—Tlemcen et Timbouctou. (Article sur le commerce entre l'Algérie et le Soudan, où il est traité des relations commerciales du Maroc avec cette colonie, paru dans l'Akhbar, et reimprimé dans la revue de Géographie.) Novembre, 79. Paris, Delagrave.

BUGEAUD (le Maréchal)—Relation de la bataille d'Isly (insérée dans la *Revue des 2 mondes*) 1 Mars, 1845.

BUSTILLO (Eduardo)—Romancero de la guerra de Africa. Publicado por la *Gaceta Militar*. Madrid, 1860. En fol., 187 pag. Portadas y orlas en colores y 5 lám. litog.

„ „ —Romancero de la guerra d'Africa. Madrid, 1860. in 4.

BUTLER (Guillermo)—Documentos relativos al cautiverio de españoles en Uad Nun. *Revista medica*. Bomba, 1 Cadiz.

CAMARA (R. da.)—Viagens em Maroccos. Lisboa, 1882.

CAMPOU (Ludovic de.)—Un Empire qui croule (le Maroc contemporain.) Paris, 1886, in 18.

CAMPUZANO Y GONZALEZ (Ramon.)—Sobre la oportunidad de la guerra de Africa. Madrid, 1859, in 4.

CANAL.—La frontière marocaine. *Bullet: Soc. Géogr. de la Province d'Oran*. 1884, pag. 83. [Printed separately.]

„ —Les troubles de la frontière Marocaine. Oran, 1886.

CANOVAS DEL CASTILLO (Antonio.)—Apuntes para la Historia de Marruecos. Madrid, imp. de Maderolas, 1860.

CARAMAN (Adolphe de.)—Lieutenant d'Etat-Major—Itinéraire de Tanger à Fez suivi en 1825—Avec carte de l'itinéraire de Tanger à Fez; 1 vue de Tanger, 1 vue du nouveau Fez; 1 carte itinéraire de Tanger à Maroc et plans des villes de Mogador et Maroc. *Spectateur militaire Août*, 1844, *Paris*.

CARETTE.—Recherche sur l'origine et les migrations des principales tribus de l'Afrique septentrionale. Paris, 1853, en 8.

CARVAJAL (T.)—España y Maruecos. Madrid, typ. Hernan, 1884.

CASTAING (Alph.)—La question marocaine. Brochure, in 8, 1859.

CASTANEIRA (Ramon F.)—Noticias de la expedicion de Mr. D. Mackenzie al cabo, Juby en 1876. *La Academia*, tom. I., pag. 171, 217 y 295.

CASTELLANOS (Fr. Manuel Pablo.)—Descripcion historica de Marruecos y breve reseña de sus dinastias, o apuntes para servir a la historica del Magreb. Santiago, imp. del *Boletin Eclesiastico* à cargo de P. Andrés Fraile, 1878, En 4to., 336 pag.

CASTELLAR (Emilio.)—Cronica de la guerra de Africa. Madrid, imp. de Matute, 1859, in 4to.

CASTILLO (Rafael del.)—España y Marruecos. Historia de la guerra de Africa escrita desde el campamento. Cadiz J. Graciá, Editor, 1859, in 4to., 570 pag.

CASTONNET des FOSSES (H.)—Le chérif de Wazzan. *Revue française*, Janvier 1885. Paris, Chaix.

„ „ „ „ —Les interêts français au Maroc. *Bull. Soc. Géogr. d'Oran* v. 1885, p. 17.

„ „ „ „ —Le Maroc, sa situation actuelle; Bruxelles et Leipzig, 1884.

„ „ „ „ —Les Portugais au Maroc. *Annales de l'extrême Orient.* VIII. 1885, pages 129, 161, 193 [printed separately 8vo. Paris, 1886.]

„ „ „ „ —Le Maroc, ses relations avec l'Europe, 1884. *Revue de droit internat.* Bruxelles.(Marquardt).

„ „ „ „ —Le Maroc. *l'Exploration* XVIII., 1884, pag. 105.

„ „ „ „ —Le Maroc conférence faite à Cambrai. 29 Mars., 1885, brochure in 8, 41 pag.

„ „ „ „ —Le Maroc tel qu'il est. Brochure. Paris, 1887.

CASTRIES (de.)—Notice sur la région de l'Oued Draa [with map.] *Bull. Soc. Géogr.*, Paris, 1880.

CERVERA BAYIERA (D. Julio) Teniente de Ingenieros—Georgrafia militar de Marruecos—Barcelona, 1884, in 16, 184 pag. con. 13 laminas y una mapa.

CHARMES (Gabriel)—Une ambassade au Maroc. *Revue des Deux mondes*, 15 Juin, 1 Juillet, 15 Juillet, 1 Août, 15 Août, Septembre, 1886. (et 1 vol., in 16 Calman Lévy, Paris, 1889).

CHAUCHAR (Achille)—Espagne et Maroc. Campagne de 1859-1860. Paris, 1861. 1 vol. in 8, 500 pages, 3 cartes, [tiré 100 exempl.]

CHAVAGNAC (Cte. M. de.)—Quinze Jours à Wazzan. *Revue française*, p. 360-376. Mai, 1885, Paris, Chaix.

„ „ „ „ —Le chérif de Wazzan, son caractère, son influence, les intérêts français au Maroc. *Bull. Soc. Géogr. Commerciale.* Paris, 1884-1885.

„ „ „ „ —de Fez à Oudjda (1881), avec 1 carte itinéraire au 1/800,000. *Bull: Soc. Géogr. de Paris.* 3 Trimestre, 1887, pag. 269.

CHELI (Nicholas)—Nuestro porvenir en Africa. *Revista Medica.* Cadiz, 1873.

CHERBONNEAU—Les limites réelles de l'Algérie. *Revue de Géogr.* Juillet, 1881. Paris, Delagrave.

CHRISTIAN (P.)—Souvenirs du maréchal Bugeaud, de l'Algérie et du Maroc. Paris, 1845, 2 v. in 8. [L'auteur est M. Pitou, secrétaire du Maréchal Bugeaud.]

,, ,, —Question d'Afrique, le Maroc et la politique anglaise. Paris, in 8, 1845.

,, ,, —L'Afrique française, l'empire du Maroc, et les déserts du Sahara. Histoire nationale des conquêtes, des victoires, et nouvelles découvertes des Français depuis la prise d'Alger jusqu'à nos jours. Paris, in 8, 1846.

COAST.—The African pilot or sailing directions for the Western coast of Africa. 1873. [There is another edition, 1849.]

COELLO (Francisco)—Estudios geográficos en Marruecos. *Bull. Soc. Geogr. des Madrid.* Tomo III., pag. 429. Anno. 1877.

COELLO (Fr.) et COSTA (J.)—Interesses de España en Marruecos. Madrid. Imp. de Fortanet. 1884.

COLAÇO (J.D.)—Colonias portuguezas em paiz estrangeiro, em Marrocos. Bullet. Soc. Géogr. Lisboa, 1881.

COLVILLE (Captain H. E.)—A ride in petticoats and slippers. London, S. Low, in 8vo., 1880.

CONRING (Adolphe de.)—Marocco, Land und Leute; Allgemeine Geographie und Ethnographie; Städter; Land; Bewohner; Handel; Producte; Politik; Die Europäer und ihre Representanten, nach den neuesten eigenen Beobachtungen, mit einer AllgemeinenKarte und einem Plan der Stadt Maroc. Berlin, G. Hempel, in 8, 1880. Neue Ausgabe, 1884. [Dieses Werk ist auch in das Spanische übersetzt.]

CORA (G.)—Due missione afficiali Italiane nel Marocco, 1873, e 1882. Cosmos di Cora VII., 1883, pag. 292.

COSSON (E.), *membre de l'Institut.*—Note sur la géographie botanique du Maroc. *Bull. Soc. Botanique de France.* Paris, 1873.

,, ,, ,, ,, —Compendium floræ atlanticæ seu methodica plantarum omnium in Algeria. Flore des Etats barbaresques: Algerie, Tunisie, Maroc. Tomo 1er, première partie: historique et géographique. Paris, 1881, in 8, avec 2 cartes coloriées.

,, ,, ,, ,, —Illustrationes floræ atlanticæ seu icones plantarum novarum, rariorum vel minus cognitarum il Algeria nec non in regno Tunetano et imperio Marocano nascentium. In compendia floræ atlanticæ criptarum. Fascicule I. Paris, 1883, in fol., avec 25 pl. gravées.

,, ,, ,, ,, —Conspectus floræ atlanticæ seu enumeratio plantarum omnium in Algeria, regno Tunetano et imperio

Marocano hucusque notarum exibens quoque diagnoses specierum novarum et annotationes de plantis minus cognitis. [M. Cosson has published in the 22d volume of the "*Bulletin de la Soc. Botanique de France*" a list including the plants received from his collectors in South Morocco up to the year 1874.]

COSTA (Joaquin)—Articulo sobre el pais de Marruecos, publicado en el "*Tiempo*" diario de Madrid, 15 Setiembre de 1877.

COTTE (Narcisse)—Le Maroc contemporain. Paris, 1860, in 12.

COUTO de ALBURQUEQUE (Luis Mariá do.)—Memorias para a historia da praça de Mazagas. Lisboa, 1864.

COWAN (G. D.) and JOHNSTON (R. L. N.)—Moorish Lotos leaves, London, 1883, in 8., glimpses of Southern Marocco.

COYNE—Une ghazzia dans le grand Sahara.

CRAIG (J.)—Un aperçu sur le Maroc. *Bull. Soc. Géogr.*, Paris v. Série, 1870, xix., page 177.

CREMA (C. F.)—Missione italiana de Tangeri a Marocco e Mogador diretta dal Ministro Comm. S. Scovasso, 1882. *Ebids* vii., 1883, p. 292 ; viii. 1884, p. 11, 44, 108, et *Cosmos di Cora;* viii. 1884, p. 225.

CUBERO (Sebastian)—Vida, crueldades y tiranias de Muley Ismael, Emperador de Marruecos. *Bibliot nac MS.* v. 72.

CUEVAS (Teodoro.)—Estudio general del Bajalato de Larache. *Bollet: Soc. Geogr. Madrid.* Tom. xvi. 1 Semestre, 1884.

  ,,   ,,   —Memoria comercial de la provincia de Abda y puerto de Saffi. *Autografiada*, 1865.

DAMBERGER (F.)—Travels through the interior of Africa from the Cape of Good Hope to Marocco; in Caffraria, the Kingdoms of Mataman, Angola, Massi, Monoemugi, Muschako, Bahakara, Wangara, Haoussa, etc., etc. And thence through the desert of Sahara and the North of Barbary to Marocco between the years 1781 and 1797. London, 1801, in-8. Map and illust. [*A work of fiction.*]

Le Même, trad. en franç. par H. Delamarre. Paris, an IX, 2 v. in-8 carte et fig. gravées par Gaucher.

DASTUGUE (Colonel.)—Quelques mots au sujet de Tafilet et de Sidjilmassa avec une carte générale du Tafilala. *Bull: Soc. Géogr. de Paris,* Avril, 1867, pag. 337.

DAUMAS & FAVAR.—La grande Kabylie, Etudes historiques, avec 1 carte. Paris, 1847, in 8.

DAVIS (N.)—Ruined cities within Numidian and Carthaginian territories. London, 1862, in 8, with maps and illustration.

DAVIES (Lieut. Col.)—The English occupation of Tangier. 1 Vol., fc. London, 1887. Richard Bentley.

DEOUGIS (Docteur.)—Relations d'un voyage dans l'intérieur du Maroc. *Bull: Soc. Géogr. de Paris*, xx.-xxi., 1878.

DELAVAUD.—Notes sur le Maroc. *L'exploration*, xviii., 1884, p. 446.

DELPHIN (G.)—Fas, son université et l'Enseignement Supérieur Musulman. Paris, Leroux, 1889, in 8vo, 121 pages.

DESCAMPS (Alex.)—Le Maroc en face de l'Europe, à propos de la dernière rupture, survenue entre la République Française et le Gouvernement Marocain. Brochure in 8, 1849.

DESGUIN.—Etude sur le Maroc. *Bull: Soc. Géogr. Belge*, 1870, p. 75.

DESJARDINS--La colonie romaine de Banassa et l'exploration géographique de la Maurétanie Tingitane. *Revue archéologique*, xxiv., p. 361, 1872.

DESPORTES et François—Itinéraire de Tanger à Fès et à Meknès (carte dans le texte). *Bull: Soc. Géogr. Paris*, xv., p. 213, 1877.

Deutsches Handelsarchiv, 1881—Marokko, Handel und Schifffahrt des Sultanats und Seiner Haupthäfen in 1880.

    ,,   ,,   1880—Marokko und seine Haupthäfen. Handel und Schifffahrt in 1879.

DIANA (Manuel. Juan.)—Un prisionero en el Riff. Madrid, 1859, in 8.

DIARIO del sitio de Melilla, por el emperador de Marruecos, des de 9 de Deciembre de 1874 al 18 de Marzo de 1875. *MS. en la Bibl de Ingenieros.*

DOZY (R.) et DE GOEJE (J.)—Description de l'Afrique et de l'Espagne d'après la traduction de MSS. de Paris et d'Oxford, avec notes et glossaire. Leyde, 1866, in 8. [Also 2 vols. 8vo, 1848.]

DOULS—Excursion dans le Sahara Marocain. Cpt. rendu. *Soc. Géogr. Paris*, 1887, p. 442-48.

DUMALMONT-MÉGE—Expédition du Maroc [poême en 3 chants] in 8, 1844.

DUPRAT (Pascal)—Essai historique sur les races anciennes et modernes de l'Afrique septentrionale. Paris, 1845, in 8.

DURO (C. F.)—El Hach Mohammed-el Bagdadly (D. José Maria de Murga) y sus andanzas, en Marruecos. *Boll. Soc. Géogr., Madrid* iii., 1877, pp. 117, 193.

    ,,   ,, —Exploracion de una parta de la costa N.O. de Africa en busca de Santa Cruz de Mar Pequeña (Forts). *Boll: Soc. Géogr. Madrid* v., 1878, p. 17.

    ,,   ,, —Nuevas observaciones acerca de la situacion de Santa Cruz de Mar Pequeña. *Boll: Soc. Géogr., Madrid*, vi., 1879, p. 193.

    ,,   ,, —El puerto de Ifni in Berberia (Marocca). *Ebds.* xiv., 1883, p. 119.

Duro (C. F.)—Los derechos de Espana en la costa del Sahara. *Boll. Soc. Géogr.* Madrid, xx., 1886, p. 42.

,, ,, —Noticias de la bahia y ciudad de Mogador, con plano y vistas. *Anuario de la Direccion de Hidrografia,* Ano iii., pp. 259-279, 1860.

,, ,, —Cautivos españoles en Cabo Blanco. *La Illustracion Espanola y Americana,* 8 Sept., 1877.

Durrieu (Xavier)—The present state of Marocco, a chapter of Mussulman Civilisation. London, 1854.

Duval (Jules)—La question du Maroc et les interets européens en Afrique 1. *Revue des 2 Mondes,* 15 Décembre, 1859.

Duveyrier (Henri)—Exploration du Sahara. Les Touaregs du nord. Paris, 1864, gr. in-8, v., portr., carte et fig. [L'auteur a obtenu pour cet ouvr. la grande médaille d'or de la Société de géographie de Paris.]

,, ,, —Sculptures antiques de la province de Soûs—Découvertes du Rabbin Mardochée. *Bullet. Soc. Géogr.* Paris v., Série 12, p. 129, 1876.

,, ,, —La confrérie musulmane de Sidi Mohammed ben'Ali es-Senoûsi et son domaine géographique en l'année 1300 de l'hégire (1883 de notre ère). Paris, 1884, in-8 de 84 p. et une carte, a paru dans le *Bullet. Soc. Géogr.* Paris, 1884.

,, ,, —Historique des Explorations au Sud et au Sud Ouest de Geryville. *Bullet. Soc. Géogr.* Paris, 1872.

,, ,, —Rapport sur le voyage de M. le Vicomte de Foucauld au Maroc. *Bullet. Soc. Géogr.* Paris, 3 Trimestre, 1885.

,, ,, —Note sur les Soulèvements au Maroc [avec esquisse ethnographique]. *Bullet. Soc. Géogr.* Paris, pp. 148-149, 1885.

,, ,, —Note sur l'occupation de la côte du Sahara par l'Espagne. *Bullet. Soc. Géogr.* Paris, p. 519, 1885.

,, ,, —Note sur l'altitude de Fâs. *Bullet. Soc. Géogr.* Paris, p. 590, 1885.

,, ,, —Les chemins des Ambassades de Tanger à Fâs et Meknâs, en 1885. *Bullet. Soc. Géogr.* Paris, 3 Trimestre, 1886.

,, ,, —Positions géographiques dans le nord de l'Afrique. *Bull: Soc. Géogr.* Paris, pp. 8, 25, 29, 118, 135, 137.

DUVEYRIER (H.)—La dernière partie inconnue du littoral de la Méditerranée. Le Rif. *Bullet. de Géogr. Historique et Descriptive.* Ministère de l'Inst. Publ. et des Beaux. Arts., p. 127-149. Paris: Leroux, ed. 1887. No. 3.

DUVEYRIER'S Studies in the geography. *Proceedings of Royal Geogr. Soc.* London, p. 339, 1885.

EBBARCK (Ed.)—Histoire des naufrages qui ont désolé la marine française, position difficile de l'Astrolabe et la prise de Mogador, en 1845. Paris, 1874 in 8vo, 20 pages.

EMBAJADA MARROQUI EN MADRID—Recepcion, visitas, espectaculos, etc. *Gazetta de Madrid,* 23 Nov., 1877.

ERCKMANN (Jules)—Capit. d'artillerie, chef de la mission militaire française au Maroc. Le Maroc moderne. Paris, 1885, in-8, carte du Maroc occidental, 4 plans en couleurs et 6 gravures, 304 pp.

ESTEVANEZ CALDERON (Serafin)—Manuel del oficial em Marruecos o'cuadro geografico-estadistico-historico-politico y militar de aquel Imperio, por D. Serafin E. Calderon, auditor general de Ejercito (Escudo de la Sociedad Economica Matritense). Madrid, imp de D. Ignacio Boin, editor, 1844. Un tomo en 4, 342 pages., y un mapa del Imperio de Marruecos. El mismo del num 63, rectificado con presencia del libro.

EXPÉDITION HYDROGRAPHIQUE sur les côtes du Maroc, en 1854. *Bull: Soc. Géogr.* Paris, 1884, p. 227.

FAIDHERBE (Général)—Sur les tombeaux mégalithiques et sur les blonds de la Libye. *Bull: Soc. Anthrop.* Paris, 15 Juillet, 1869.

FELICE de la PENA (Francisco)—Legenda historica-politica-militar-administrativa-religiosa del Peñon de Velez de la Gomera, con noticia de las expediciones españolas contra la costa de Africa, y memoria sobre la conservación o'abandono de los presidios menores. Valencia Imp. de P. Marianor. Cabrerizo, 1846. En 8, 159 pp.

FERREIRO—Informe al almirantazgo acerca de la bahia de Lobos. (boca del Draa), 1872. *MS. Archiv del ministerio de Marina.*

FILIAS (Ach)—Le Maroc. Vapercau, 1859.
   ,,   ,, —L'Espagne et le Maroc en 1860. Paris, 1860.
   ,,   ,, —Campagne du Maroc—Tanger—Isly—Mogador, 1844. Récits militaires—Alger, 1881. Broch. in 8. avec carte.

FONTPERTUIS (Ad. F. de)—Le Maroc, son gouvernement, ses populations, ses villes, et ses ressources. Paris, "*Economiste Français,*" 27 Août, 81, p. 163.

   ,,   ,, —Le Maroc et son organisation intérieure. "*Nouvelle Revue.*" 1 Mai, 1886, Paris.

FOUCAULD (Vi.Cte Ch. de)—Lettre de M. de F... Sur son voyage, communié par M. Macarthy. *Bull. Soc. Géogr.* Paris, p. 196, 1884.

,, ,, ,, —Tableau d'observations astronomiques observées en Maroc en 83-84. *Bull. Soc. Géogr. Paris*, p. 297, 1885.

,, ,, ,, —Itinéraires au Maroc, 1883-84. *Bull: Soc. Géogr*. Paris, 1887. Septième Série. Tome viii., 1 carte générale.

,, ,, ,, —Reconnaissance au Maroc, 1883-84. 1 vol., in 4o. 1 atlas, 21 cartes [20 itinéraires 1,250,000, 1 carte générale]. Paris, 1887. Challamel.

FOUCAULD'S Journeys in Morocco. *Proceedings of Royal Geogr. Soc.*, London, pp. 547, 548, 1885.

FOUCAULD (Cte de)—Iitinerarios en Marruecos. *Bol. Soc. Geogr.* Madrid. T. xxiii., p. 110-17.

FOURNEL (Henri)—Etude sur la conquête de l'Afrique par les Arabes, et recherches sur les tribus berbères qui ont occupé le Maghreb central. Paris, 1857, in 4.

,, ,, —Les Berbèrs, étude sur la conquête de l'Afrique par les Arabes, d'après les textes imprimés. Paris, S.D., in 4.

FREIHERRN VON AUGUSTIN (Ferd.)—Erinnerungen aus Marokko, gesammelt auf einer Reise in Jahre 1830. Wien, 1838, in-8.

FRITSCH (R.)—Reisebilder aus Marokko, Mitth. der Ver. für Erdkunde zu Halle, 1877, p. 111.

,, ,, —Gleiche Ausgabe, 1878, p. 24.

GALIANO (Pelago Alcala)—Memoria sobre la situacion de Santa Cruz de Mar Pequeña en la costa noro este de Africa. Madrid, 1878.

GALIBERT (Léon)—La Argelia antigua y moderna y el imperio de Marruecos. Madrid, 1859-1860, 3 vols. in 4.

GALINDO y de VERA (Lion)—Intereses legitimos y permanentes que en Africa tiene España. Madrid, 1861, in 4to, 52 pp.

,, ,, ,, —Historia vicissitudes y politica traditional de España respecto de sus posesiones en las costas de Africa. Madrid Tello, 1885.

GATELL (J.)—L'ouad Noun et le Tekna, à la côte occidentale du Maroc. *Bull. Soc. Géogr.* Paris, xviii. p. 257, Oct., 1869.

,, ,, —Viajes por Marruecos, el Sus, Uad-Nun, y Tekna. Madrid.

,, ,, —Description du Soûs. *Bull. Soc. Géogr.* Paris, vi., Série 1., 1871, p. 81.

GAY (Jean)—Bibliographie des ouvrages relatifs à l'Afrique et à l'Arabie. 1875.

GERARD (Jules)—Le Maroc. Paris, in 12, 1860.

GEROME (J. L.)—Santon Marroqui. *La Illustracion Espanola y Americana.* Madrid, 1877, tomo i. p. 377.

GIMINEZ (S.)—España en el Africa Septentrional. Madrid, 1886.

Globus—xxix., 1876. Alte Denkmäler an der Marokkanischen West Küste.

,, ,, —xxxviii., 1880. Colville's Ritt durch das nord westliche Marokko.

,, ,, —xxiv., 1873. Dolmen in Marokko.

GODARD (Léon)—Curé d'El-Aghouat. Le Maroc, notes d'un voyageur, 1858-1859. Alger in 8vo., 1859.

,, ,, —Description historique du Maroc, comprenant la géographie et la statistique de ce pays et le tableau du règne des souverains qui l'ont gouverné depuis les temps les plus anciens jusqu'à la prise de Tetouan, en 1860. Paris, 1860, 2 vol. in 8, 1 carte (Tanera édit.)

GOLTDAMMER (F.)—Note géographique et commerciale sur l'empire du Maroc. Paris, Pougin, 1878.

GOMEZ Y COELLO (Francisco)—Descripcion y mapas de Marruecos. Madrid, 1859, in 8vo., 145 pages.

GORRINGE (Henry H.)—The West Coast of Africa from Cape Spartel to Sierra Leone. New York, 1873.

HALÉVY (Joseph)—Rapport sur l'état des écoles dans les communautés juives du Maroc. *Bull. all. Israel.* Paris, 1877, 1re. semestre.

HANN—Meteor. Beobachtungen in Tanger, Meteorol. Zeitchz, Berlin, iv. Nr. 1, p. 26-8.

HARLACH (H. Th-d'-)—Le Maroc et le Riff, en 1856. Paris, in 8vo., 1856. Ledoyen.

HAY (Sir John Drummond)—Benaboo, *Murray Magazine.* London, May 1887.

HEIN (H.)—Un faux diplomate au xvii. Siècle (ambassade du Juif David Palache à la cour de Louis XIII).—Revue d'Histoire Diplomatique, Deuxième Année N. 1, pag. 27-40.

HODGKIN (Th.)—Narrative of a Journey to Morocco in 1863-64. London, 1866, in 8vo., with a map.

HŒFER (Ferd)—Afrique australe, Afrique orientale, Afrique centrale. Empire du Maroc, in 8, 1848.

Hooker (Joseph Dalton)—Letters on his Ascent of the Atlas. *Proc. of the Royal Geographical Soc.* xv., 1871, page 212.

„ „ and Ball (John)—Journal of a tour in Morocco and the great Atlas, with an appendix including a sketch of the geology of Morocco, by Geoge Maw. London, Macmillan, in 8., 1878.

Horowitz (Victor J.)—Gew. Consulatssekretär zu Tanger-Marokko. Das Wesentlichste und Interessanteste über Land und Leute. Leipzig, W. Friedrich, 1887, page 215.

Houdas (D.)—(Le Maroc de 1631 à 1812, extrait de l'ouvrage arabe d'Aboul Qassem-Ben-Ahmed-Ezziani, publié et traduit par). Paris, Leroux ed., 1866, gr. in-8, texte arabe, caractères maghrébins et traduction française.

Howard Vyse (Mrs.)—A winter in Tangier, and home through Spain. London, 1882.

Hy. L. M.—Union latine dans l'Afrique Septentrionale (France et Espagne au Maroc.) *Revue française* Oct., 1885, pages 369, 373. Paris, Chaix.

Ibn. Batutah—Voyage à travers l'Afrique septentrionale au commencement du xiv. siècle publ. par M. Cherbonneau, Paris, 1852, in 8.

Ibn. Hancal—Description de l'Afrique, traduit de l'Arabe, par le baron de Slane. Paris, 1842, in 8vo.

Idris El Jorichi—Viaje que hizo al Guad nun El Hache Idris El Jorichi El Fasi, Taleb del consulado de España en Mogador en Agosto de 1874, para gestionar el rescate de los cautivos españoles. *Traducido del Arabe por D. Antonio Mariá Orfila é inserto par apendice en la presente conferencia.* Madrid.

Imperio de Marruecos y su Constitucion—*Revista militar Espanola.* Madrid, Aña III.

Interets français au Maroc (Les)—*Bull. Soc. d'Oran,* 1885, pag. 17.

Jackson (James)—Archiviste bibliothécaire de la Soc. Géogr. de Paris. Liste provisoire de bibliographies géographiques. 1 vol. in 8, de viii., 340 p. (1117 articles.)

Jannasch (R.)—Von Schwika über Wad-Draa bis Mogador. *Export.,* 1886. N. 24.

„ „ —Handelspolitisches über Marokko. *Ebds.,* 1886. N. 27.

Jerez Perchet (Augusto)—Viaje á la Costa de África, Melilla, Chafarinas, Cabo del Agua. "*Museo Universal,*" Madrid. 1868, page 150.

Jerez Perchet (Augusto)—Cuatro dias en el Riff. "*Mus. Univ.*," Madrid, 1869, page 291.

Jordana y Morera (J.)—Parte oriental del Bajalato de Tetuan, bajo el punto de vista de la colonizacion. *Bull. Soc. Géogr. Madrid*, page 110, xii., 1882.

Joubert (André)—De Cadiz à Tanger. *Revue d'Angers*, 1869.

Jourdan—L'empire du Maroc. Paris, in 8vo., 1852.

Judas—Sur l'écriture et la langue berbère dans l'antiquité et de nos jours. Paris, 1863, in 8vo.

Juden (Zur Lage der) in Demnat-Marokko. Jeschurun, NF. II., 48.

Juden (Die) in Miknasa. *Jüdisches Literaturblatt*, xii., 1883.

Kerhallet (Ch.)—Manuel de la navigation à la côte occidentale d'Afrique. Paris, 1857.

Kerhallet (Ph. de) et A. Legros—Instructions nautiques sur la côte occidentale d'Afrique, comprenant le Maroc, le Sahara et la Sénégambie. Paris, 1871, in-8 br.

Kersten (L.)—Handel und Verkehr in West Marokko. *Geogr. Nachrichten für Welthandel und Volkswirths*, 1879, page 363.

Kobelt (W.)—Tetuan bei den Saülen des Herkules. *Deutsche Touristen Zeitung* 1883.

Kübb (Ph.)—Voyage des missionnaires en Afrique du commencement du xvi. siècle à la fin du xvii. siècle. Mans., 1863, 2 vols. in 8.

Lambert (P.)—Notice sur la ville du Maroc. *Bull. Soc. Géogr. Paris* v Série xvi., 1868, page 432.

Landa (Nicasio)—La Campaña de Marruecos. Memorias de un Medico militar. Madrid, S.D.

Langles.—Les Maures du Maroc. *Bull de l'athénée Orientale*, 1883. N. 3; 4.

Lanoye (F. de)—Voyages au Maroc résumé des voyages du sieur *Mouette* en 1670. de *Lemprière* en 1789. de *James Richardson* en 1859 avec une carte générale du pays. *Tour du Monde*, 1860. Paris, pages 209 à 234.

Lapie (Pierre)—Recueil des itinéraires anciens, avec un atlas de 10 cartes. Paris, 1844, in 4.

Larmandie (Comte de). Trois semaines au Maroc (conférence faite au Hâvre, 13 Janvier 1887). Hâvre, imp. de la soc. des anc. Courtiers Broch. 20 pag. in 8.

Larousse—*Dictionnaire universel*, article sur le Maroc. Paris.

BIBLIOGRAPHY.

LAVAYSSIÈRE (P.)—Stations dans l'empire du Maroc. Brochure in 12. Limoges, 1865.

,, ,, Stations dans l'empire du Maroc. Limoges, 1870.

,, ,, Stations au Maroc. Limoges, 1876.

,, ,, Stations au Maroc. Limoges, Ardant, 1879.

,, ,, Stations au Maroc. Limoges, Ardant, 1882.

LEARED (Arthur)—Marocco and the Moors, being an account of travels, with a general description of the country and its people, with illustr. London, S. Low. 8vo., 1876. 380 pages.

,, ,, —A visit to the Court of Marocco, with illustrations. London, S. Low. 8vo., 1879.

,, ,, —Marocco and the Moors. London, 1875.

,, ,, —The site of the Roman city of Volubilis. London, *The Academy*, 1878. No. 321.

,, ,, —On a journey to Fez and Mequinez. London, 1878.

LECLERC (J.)—Voyage à Tanger et Mogador. *Revue britannique*, Décembre, 1878 et 1881.

,, ,, —De Mogador à Biskra. Maroc et Algérie. Paris, 1881, in-12 br., carte.

LEE (Sir J. C.)—The north-west coast of Africa with map. (Lies outside and south of Marocco from the Wady Draa in the north, to the Bay of Arguin in the South). *Journal of the Manchester Geogr. Soc.* Vol. II., Nos. 4, 5, 6, 1886.

LENZ (Dr. Oscar)—Die militärverhältnisse Marokkos. *Gegenwart*, 1882. No. 34.

,, ,, ,, —Die Machazniyah in Marokko. *Deutsche Rundschau f. Geogr.* iv., 1882.

,, ,, ,, —Tetuan und die Landchaft Auschira. *Aus allen Welttheilen* xv., 1884, p. 1.

,, ,, ,, —Reise von Tanger nach Fàs. *Ebds.*, xv., 1884, p. 65.

,, ,, ,, —Fàs die Residenz des Sultans Muley Hassan. *Oesterreich. Monatsschr, f. d. Orient*, 1884, No. 4.

,, ,, ,, —Timbuktu, Reise durch Marokko, die Sahara und den Sudan, 2 vol., in 8. Leipzig, 1884.

,, ,, ,, —Timbouctou. Voyage au Maroc, au Sahara et au Soudan, trad. par L. Lehautcour. Paris, 1886, 2 vol., in-8 br., contenant 45 gravures et une carte.

LENZ'SCHE EXPEDITION (die)—*Mitth. d. Afrikan. Ges. in Deutschland.* 1879, p. 246.

LENZ (Oscar)—Conférence sur le voyage de . . . . *Bull. Soc. Géogr. Paris.* Mars, 1881, pp. 199-226, avec une carte.

LERCHUNDI (Fz. José de)—Rudimentos del Arabe vulgar que se habla en el imperio de Marruecos. Madrid, Rivadeneyra, 1872, in 4to.

LIEBERMANN (J.)—Appel à la charité des Juifs en faveur de leurs coréligionaires Marocains, Nancy, Mars, 1860. Imp. de Trenel, in 8vo.

LINARÈS (F.)—Médecin major de la mission militaire française au Maroc. Une epidémie de choléra au Maroc en 1878. Paris, 1879. *Br.* in 8vo, 25 pages, avec carte.

LEVINCK (Mad. A.)—L'osasis de Figuig, avec carte, *Revue de Géogr.*, *Paris,* Dec. '84, Jan. '85.

LEYNADIER ET CLAUSEL—Histoire de l'Algérie avec un précis sur le Maroc. Paris, 2 vols., in 8., 1846.

LLANOS Y ALCAREZ (A.)—Siete anos en Africa. Aventuras del renegado Sonsa en Marruecos, Argelia, el Sahara, Nubia y Abisinia. *Bibl. de instruc. y. recreo.*, 1 tomo 8. Madrid. Sin Ano.

LLANA Y RODRIGANEZ—El imperio de Marruecos. Madrid, 1879.

LONDON (Fr. H.)—Die Berberei. Eine Darstellung der religiösen und bürgerlichen Sitten und Gebrauchen der Bewohner nord Afrikás. Franckfort, 1845, in 8vo.

LOPEZ BOTAS (Antonio)—Los espanoles cautivos en Marruecos. Madrid, 1870, in 4to, 57 pages. Otra edición, 1871. Imp. de M. Martinez.

LOPEZ DOMINGUEZ (José.)—Isly y Tetuan. Estudio militar comparativo. *Revista de Espana* t xxiv. page 523.

LOPES DA COSTA ALMEIDA (Antonio)—Roteiro dos mares, costas, &c., reconhecidos no globo. Lisbon, 1845.

LOZANO MUNOZ (Francisco)—Memoria historico. Comercial de la provincias de Larache, Benahuda. Habbasi, Benishara y Guassans Publicada par la Direccion general de Aduanas en las *Memorias comerciales* 1876, page 125 and 153.

" " " —Apuntes sobre Marruecos, *Diario de Cádiz.* Marzo, Abril, 1872.

" " " —Organizacion Militar de Marruecos. "*Revista de Espana,*" 1872.

" " " —Los tributos y la influencia de las batallas de Isly y de Tetuan. *Revista de Espana.*

" " " —Proclamación del Sultan Muley-Hassan, en 1873. *Revista de Espana.*

Lozano Munoz (Francisco)—Crónica del viaje de la Embajada espanola a la ciudad de Fez el ano de 1877. *MS. en el arch del ministerio de Estado.* Madrid.

Maalem—La question du Maroc. *Nouvelle Revue.* Février, 1888. Paris.

Mackenzie (Donald)—The flooding of the Sahara: an account of the proposed plan for opening Central Africa to commerce and civilization from the North-West Coast, with a description of Soudan. London, Sampson Low, 1877, in 8, 287 pages, with illustrations and maps.

Mac Mahon (Maréchal de)—Souvenir de l'occupation des Zaffarines par les Espagnols. *Bull. Soc. Géogr. Paris,* pp. 375-376.

Mahon—Commerce et navigation de Mogador et Safy en 1879. *Bull. cons. français,* 1881.

Malte-Brun (V. A.)—Voyage de Si Bou Moghdad de St. Louis (Sénégal) à Mogador (Maroc) du 10 Décembre, 1860, au 6 Mars, 1861. *Nouvelles Annales des Voyages,* 1861. Paris.

Maltzan (H. von.)—Die Jahre Reisen im Nordwesten von Afrika.

Marcet (Docteur A.)—Le Maroc. Voyage d'une mission française à la Cour du Sultan. Paris, 1885. In 18 pag. VIII. 298.

Marchessi (V.)—Le relazioni tra la Replubica Veneta ed il Marocco dal 1750-97. Torino, 1886, 56, S.

Mardochee Abi Serour—De Mogador au Djebel Tabayoud. *Bull. Soc. Géogr. Paris,* 1875.

„ „ „ —Les Daggatoun, tribu d'origine juive demeurant dans le Sahara (traduit sur l'hébreu et annoté par Isidore Loeb). *Bull. Alliance Israélite.* Paris 1880, in-12.

Maroc—Agriculture in Marocco. *Unit. States Cons. Rep.,* Oct. '86.

„ —Documents diplomatiques relatifs à la question de la protection diplomatique et consulaire au Maroc. Paris, impr. nation., in-4, de 278 p. 1880.

„ —Etat économique. *Revue française de l'étranger et des colonies,* 1885, p. 158.

„ —Situation militaire, *Bull. Soc. Géogr. de la province d'Oran,* v., 1885, p. 178.

„ —Lettres du. L'affaire d'Agadir, *Gazette Géogr.* N. Serie., xxi., 1886.

„ —Le —— L'Afrique explorée et civilisée, vii., 1886, p. 44.

„ —Mission militaire au. *Bull. Soc. Géogr. d'Oran.,* Tome v., 1885, p. 157.

Marocco, il—Nuova Antologia, Vol. XI., p. 664-71.

Marokko und Schifffahrt der Haupthäfen, 1875.

,, —Producte Handel und Schifffahrt des Kaiserthums, 1869.

Marokkanische Hafenplätze—(Handel und Schifffahrt der)—und insbesondere des Hafens von Tanger. *Deutsches Handels Archiv* 1885. pag. 299-882.

Marokkanische Hafenplätze (Handel und Schifffahrt der) und insbesondere des Hafens von Tanger in J. 1885 II. pag. 825. Casablanca, pag. 830. Mazagan, pag. 832. Mogador, pag. 833. Saffi, pag. 835. Larache, pag. 836. Rabat, pag. 836. *Deutsches Handels Archiv* 1886.

Marokko—Handel und Schifffahrt des Sultanats und seiner Haupthäfen in 1880. *Deutsches Handels Archiv*. 1881.

,, ,, ,, ,, —des Sultanats in 1882 *Deutsches Handels Archiv*. 1883, pag. 558.

,, ,, ,, ,, —Vorgänge und Zustände in— export N. 42.

Marokko—Topographische Werke—Mittheilungen über topographische Aufnahmen in Tetuan, Tanger, El Araish, Arzila, Meknès und Fez durch Spanische Offiziere ausgeführt. Verhandlungen, Dec., 1886.

Marquez de Prado (José)—Recuerdos de Africa o' apuntes para formar la historia general de las posessiones españolas del Africa. Barcelona 1851, in 4.

,, ,, ,, —Recuerdos de Africa. Historia de la plaza de Ceuta Madrid 1859, in 8.

Martin (Ch.)—Commandant des dragons de l'impératrice. Guerres avec le Maroc. Spécialement celle de l'Espagne. *Spectateur militaire*, 1859-1860, Paris.

Martin (Don Luis Garcia)—Espana en Africa. [conferencia dada en la Societad Geografica de Madrid].

Martinière (H. de La.)—Maroc, le Sultan et Son gouvernement. [Aperçu] *Revue française*, Sept. 1885. Paris, Chaix.

,, ,, —Itinéraires d'Alkazar à Ouezzan et de Ouezzan à Meknès. *Revue de géogr.*, Dec. 1885. Fevr. Mars et Avril 1886. Paris. Delagrave.

,, ,, —Le Maroc et les puissances européennes *Revue franç.* Avril 1886.

,, ,, —La France et l'Espagne dans l'union latine à propos du Maroc. *Revue franç.* Dec. 1886.

MARTINIÈRE (H. de La.)—Altitudes hypsométriques déterminées au Maroc. *Bull: Soc. Géogr.* Paris, 1886 pag. 7.

,, ,, —progress of journey of. *Proceedings of Royal Geogr. Soc. London.* 1884, pag. 421.

,, ,, —Aperçu de la question marocaine à propos de la prochaine conférence internationale. *Revue de géogr., Juin,* 1888. Paris, Delagrave.

MARTINIÈRE (de La.)—L'heureux esclave, ou relation des aventures du Sieur . . . comme il fut pris par les corsaires de Barbarie. . . . Paris, 1671, in 12-136 pages.

MARTITEGUI (Yoaguipe de)—Articulo sobre la cintod de Melilla "*La España.*" Madrid, Deciembre, 1857.

MASCARENAS (Jeronimo)—Historia de Ceuta—*Bibl.: nacional M.S.* T. 68.

MAS LATRIE — (Comte de). Relation et commerce de l'Afrique septentrionale ou Magreb avec les nations chrétiennes au moyen-âge. Paris, 1886, in-12 br., 550 pag. Firmin Didot.

,, ,, —Traités de paix et de commerce, et documents divers concernant les relations des chrétiens avec les Arabes de l'Afrique septentrionale au Moyens âge, recueillis et publiés avec une introduction historique ; supplément et tables. Paris, 2 vol. in 4 Klinsieck, 1868.

MATHAN—(Adrien). Voyage au Maroc (1640-1641). Journal de voyage publié pour la première fois, avec notice biographique de l'auteur, introduction et notes par F. de Hellwald. La Haye, 1866, in-8 br. de 87 p. [The journal is in Dutch ; the rest in French.]

MATHIEU (J.)—Le Maroc. *Bull: Soc. Géogr. Marseille,* VIII.-1884, p. 147.

MATTHEWS—Uber die Hülfsquellen der nord west Küste Afrika's *Mitth: der geog Ges: in Lübeck.* Heft 2, 3 1883, p. 42.

MATTHEWS (F.A.)—Northwest Africa and Timbuctoo. *Bull: American geogr. Soc.* 1881, p. 196.

MAUROY—Du commerce des peuples de l'Afrique septentrionale, dans l'antiquité, le Moyen-âge et les temps modernes, comparé au commerce des Arabes de nos jours. 1846, in-8.

,, —Précis de l'histoire et du commerce de l'Afrique septentrionale, depuis les temps anciens jusqu'aux temps modernes ;

précédé de deux lettres du Maréchal Bugeaud sur la question d'Alger. Paris, 1852, in-8.

MAW (G.)—A journey to Marocco and ascent of the great Atlas. 1872.

,, —Geology of Marocco and great Atlas.

MAZADE (Charles de)—La guerre du Maroc avec l'Espagne. *Revue des 2 Mondes.* 1er Janvier, 15 September 1850.

MAZET (du)—Les Ouled Sidi Cheik, et les territoires insurgés de la province d'Oran. *Revue de géogr.* Juin, 1881, Paris, Delagrave.

,, ,, —La frontiére Marocaine. *Revue de Géogr.* Décembre, 1881, Paris, Delagrave.

Du Même—Commerce entre l'Algérie et le Maroc. *L'explorateur* III. 1876, pag. 248-368.

Memoria de Artilleria—Breve noticia del imperio de Marruecos. 1884.

MERCIER (Ern.)—Histoire de l'établissement des Arabes dans l'Afrique septentrionale selon les documents fournis par les auteurs arabes et notamment par l'histoire des Berbères d'Ibn-Khaldoun. Constantine, 1875, in-8, avec deux cartes.

,, ,, —Comment l'Afrique septentrionale a été arabisée. [Extrait résumé de l'histoire de l'Etablissement des Arabes dans l'Afrique septentrionale] Paris, 1874, in-8 18 p.

,, ,, —Quelques notes sur le Tafilalet. *Bullet. Soc. Géogr.*, de la Province d'Oran, v. 1885, p. 79.

MERLE (A.)—L'Angleterre, la France et l'Espagne, à propos de l'ile d'Arguin. *Revue de Géogr. Paris, Mars,* 1885.

,, ,, —La question du Cap Blanc. *Revue de Géogr.* Paris, Mars, 1886.

MERRY (Francisco) y COLOM—Relacion del viaje a la ciutad de Marruecos que par disposicion de l'Excmo. Sr. P. Manuel Pando, Marques de Miraflores primer secretario de Estado, verifico en el mesde Mayo de 1863. Madrid, imp. nacional, in 4 1864.

,, ,, ,, ,, —Un viaje a Fez. Revista de Espana- tom 11. pag. 394.

MEULEMANS (A.)—L'empire du Maroc et ses relations commerciales avec la Belgique, 2me Edition. Bruxelles, 1870.

MEYNERS D'ESTREY—Un Empire qui croule. *Ann. de l'Extrême Orient.* 1887. p. 140-43.

MIRVAL (J. B. J. de)—L'orphelin de Mogador, ou notions sur l'empire du Maroc. Limoges. in-18 avec planche, 1853.

MISSION—militaire envoyeé au Maroc en 1882. *Ebds*, v. 1885, p. 157.
MOGADOR—*Annales hydrographiques* 1867 pag. 137.
,, —*Gesch für Erdkunde* 11. 67 pag. 470.
,, —*Nautical Magazine* 1866, pag. 515-582.
MOLINS (El Marqués de)—El romancero de la guerra de Africa presentado a la reina dona Isabel II. y al Rey. Madrid, Rivadeneyra, 1860 En 16to 394 p.
MONEDERO ORDONEZ (Dionisio)—Apuntes de un testigo de la Batalla de Vad. Ras. Madrid, 1877.
Moniteur Universel—Article sur la ville de Maroc, son histoire et les mœurs de ses habitants, 10 Janvier, 1867.
MONTEFIORE (Sir M.)—Narrative of a mission to Marocco, 1863-64. London 1864.
MOURLON (Michel)—Esquisse géographique sur le Maroc. Brochure in-8 1870.
MURGA (José M. de) Recuerdos Marroquies del moro vizcaino (a) E Hach Mohammed el Bagdady, Bilbao. 1868-in 4.
,, ,, ,, ,, —Duro el Hadj Mohammed el Bagdaly, y su andanzas en Marruecos. *Boll: Soc. Geogr. Madrid* III. p. 117- 1877.
MURRAY (Mrs. E.)—Sixteen years in Marocco, etc. London 1859.
M'RAH OULD BEL HADJI—De Tlemcen au Maroc. *Bull: Soc. Géogr, de Bordeaux*, 1882, pag. 269.

NAVARRO (Manuel de)—Memoria del movimiento maritimo y comercial en este puerto y de las ventajas que à Espana ofiece. *Memoriae comerciales de la Direccion de Aduanas*. Madrid, 1878, pag. 160 [Navarro vice consul de Espana in Casablanca].
NÈVE—Relation d'un voyageur Chrétien sur la ville de Fez, et ses écoles dans la première moitié du xvi. siècle, Gand, 1845.
NOLL—von Lissabon nach der Küste Marokkos und den Canarien. *Westermann's Monatshefte*, 1873.

Oesterreich: Monatsschr, f. d. Orient, 1884. p. 71. El Arisch, die Handelsverhältnisse der Provinz, des Sultanats Marokko.
OLIVEIRA (R.)—A visit to the Spanish Camp in Morocco, during the late war. London, 1865.
OLLIVE (C.)—Géographie médicale, climat de Mogador et de son influence sur la Phthisie. *Bull. Soc. Géogr.* Paris, Oct., 1875—56 pages.

OMBONI (G.)—Le Maroche, antiche morene mascherata da frane Padova, 1878, in 8.

OVILO (P. Felipe) Y CANALES.—La Mujer Marroqui, estudio social. Segunda edicion, illustrada con cromos al lapiz y dibujos a la pluma par Democrito. Madrid-imp. de H. G. Hermandez, in 8. 1881.

P.—Viaje á Fez, desde Tánger, de la embajada de Italia en Majo y Junio de 1875. "La Iborio," Madrid, 1875. Julio.

PADRO (Ramón)—Tipos de la caravanas del Sáhara, según los apuntes traidos por la comision del "Blasco de Garay" en el Año de, 1878. "La Academia" Junio, 1878.

PAILLET (H.)—Histoire de l'empire du Maroc, accompagnée d'une carte du Maroc et de l'Algérie. Paris. Moquet, 1844. In 8.

PALEOLOGUE (Maurice)—Le Maroc, notes et souvenirs. *Revue des 2 Mondes.* 15 Avril, 1885. Paris.

PANET (Léopold)—Relation d'un voyage du Sénégal à Soueira. *Revue coloniale.* Nov. et Dec., 1850, et une carte du voyage. Paris, 1851.

PARADIS (Venture)—Grammaire et Dictionnaire de la langue Berbère composés par feu Venture de Paradis. Paris, 1844, 1 vol. 4in. [Contient à la fin différents itinéraires de l'Afrique Septentrionale.]

PELLIER (J.)—Embarque de peregrinos en Tánger para la Meca. *La Ilustracion Espanola y Americana.* Madrid, 1876, tomo II. pag. 273.

„   „   —Mora en traje de casa. [*Ibid.*] Tomo II. pag. 264. Madrid, 1876.

„   „   —De Tanger à Gibraltar. [*Ibid.*] Anno, 1877.

PERRIER (Amelia)—A winter in Marocco. London. King, 1873.

PERROT (Léon)—Itinéraire de Géryville à Figuig. Paris.

PICATIER (Ad.)—Exploits d'un capitaine français dans le Maroc. 2me édition. Paris, 1871. 108 pages.

PIETCH (Louis)—Marokko, Briefe von der deutschen Gesandtschaftsreise nach Fez in der Frühling von, 1877. Leipzig. F. A. Brockhaus, in 8., 1878.

POLITICA HISPANO, MARROQUI—Y la opinion publica en España. *Boll. Soc. geogr de Madrid.* xvii., 1884, p. 36, 161, 321. xviii., 1885.

POSSESSIONS ESPAGNOLES SUR LA CÔTE DU SAHARA. Les, *Gazette géographique,* 1885.

POSTEL (R.)—En Tunisie et au Maroc. Avec 15 dessins originaux par le Dz L. M. Reuss. Paris, 1883, in-12 de 217 p.

POSTEL (R.)—L'Allemagne et le Maroc. *Gazette géographique*, 1885.

POWER (W.G.)—Recollections, including Peregrinations in Marocco, etc. London, 1850.

PRIMERAUDAIE (LA)—Les villes Maritimes du Maroc, commerce, navigation, géographie. *Revue algérienne*, 1872, 1873.

PREUSS. HANDELSARCH, 1877, No. 20—Marokko, Handel und Schifffahrt in den Haupthäfen, in 1876.

,, ,, 1878, No. 10—Tanger's Handel und Schifffahrt in 1876.

,, ,, 1879, No. 16-29—Marokko, Handel und Schifffahrt des Sultanats, and seiner Haupthäfen in 1877 and 1878.

QUEDENFELDT (M.)—Reise und Reiseverhältnisse im Sultanat Marokko. Verhandl. der Berl. Gesellsch. für Erdkunde, xiii., 1886, p. 440.

QUIJADALJ (J.)—Carta de Marruecos. Descripcion de la Vista que hizo el Emperador a Casablanca en, 1876. *La Illustracion Espanola y Americana* Madrid, 1876. Tomo II., pag. 273.

R.—An article concerning Tetuan. "*Fraser's Magazine.*" London, April, 1875.

R.L.—Espana en Marruecos; Memoria administrativa. "*Revista de Espana.*" Tomo xxxxii., pages. 232 a 250, [fechado en Tetuan en Setiembre de 1873.]

RABAT—Viaje del Emperador de Marruecos a Rabat. Publicado en *El Gibraltar Guardian* de 20 de agosto de 1877 y reproducido por *El Tiempo de Madrid*.

RABUSSON—De la géographie du nord l'Afrique pendant les périodes Romaine et Arabe. Paris, 1856. 2 vols. in 8.

RAE (Edw.)—The country of the Moors. . . . . London, Murray. 1877.

RAWSON (W. R.), K.C.M.G., F.R.G.S.—The territorial Partition of the Coast of Africa, p. 615. [With general map of Africa.] *Proceedings of Royal Geogr. Soc.* London 1884.

REISE DER FRANZOSEN nach Marokko, 1882. N. Militär. Bl. xxv., 1884, pag. 9.

RECLUS (Elisée,) Tome XI—Afrique septentrionale. 2ᵉ partie: Tripolitaine, Tunisie, Algérie, Maroc, Sahara, contenant 4 cartes en couleur tirées à part, 160 cartes intercalées dans le texte, et 83 vues ou types gravés sur bois. Paris, 1886, in-8.

RENOU (E.)—Notes sur le Maroc. *Bull. Soc. Géogr. Paris*, p. 447, 505, 509.

REPORT on the commerce of Tangier during 1866. [*Verzameling van Konsulaire Berichten*] S. 385, 1867.

RESUMÉ de l'histoire ancienne de l'Algérie et de la régence de Tunis et du Maroc avant la conquête musulmane. Paris, 1864.

Revista contemporánea—Estudios politicos y sociales sobre Marruecos. Madrid.

Revue Algérienne—Article sur le voyage au Maroc du Dteur Rohlfs, 1863.

REY (M.)—Souvenirs d'un voyage au Maroc. Paris, in 8., 1845.

RICHARDSON (John)—Travels in Morocco. London, 2 vols in 16., 1859.

RIFF (El.)—Articulo descriptivo de la costa, con propuesta de lo que debiera harcerse para mejorar la situacion y objeto de los Presidios de Africa. *El Pabellón Nacional, Madrid.* Junio, 1878.

RINDAVETS (Pedro)—Descripcion y planos de las islas Chafarinas. *Cronica naval.* t. I. p. 662, 1855.

RIO DE ORO, La colonie espagnole du—Gazette géographique, III., Nz. 16.

RIVIERE (M. A. et Ch.)—Les bambous, végétation, culture, multiplication en Europe, en Algérie, et généralement dans tout le bassin Méditerranéen, nord de l'Afrique, Maroc, Tunisie, Egypte. Paris, in-8 illustré de nombreuses figures.

ROHLFS (G.)—Politische Zustande in Marokko. Ausland, 71 No. 25-40.

,, ,, Fes und Uesan.

,, ,, Mein erster Aufenthalt in Marokko. Bremen, 1872.

,, ,, Die Bevölkerung von Marokko. Berlin, 1872.

,, ,, Höflichkeitsformen und Umgangs gebrauche bei den Marokanern. *Globus*, xxii., 1872.

,, ,, Mein erster Aufenthalt in Marokko und Reise südlich von Atlas durch die Oasen Draa, Tafilet. Bremen, Berlin, 1881, 1873.

,, ,, Adventures in Marocco and journeys through the oases of Draa and Tafilet. London, 1874.

,, ,, Bei den Zeltbewohnern in Marokko "*Globus*" xxvii., 1875.

,, ,, Social politische Zustande in Marokko. *Ausland*, 1881.

,, ,, Reise durch Marokko, übersteigung des grossen Atlas, Exploration der Oasen von Tafilet, Tuat in Tidikelt und Reise durch die grosse Wüste über Rhadamès nach Tripoli, Miteiner Karte von Nord Afrika, 1882.

ROLHFS (G.)—Sigelmasa und Tafilet, Zeitch. der Berl. Ges. für Erdkunde, 1877, p. 335. [Another edition, 4 Aug., Norden (Fischer), 1884.]

,, ,, Gesandschaften von und nach Marokko. *Ausland*, 1877, No. 32.

,, ,, Die Juden in Marokko. Allg. Augsb. Zeit. Beilage, 1880, *Vergl. Jüdisch. Literaturblatt.*

,, ,, Reise in Afrika en 1866 und 67. *Mittheilungen aus Justus Perthes, Num.* 10, 1868.

,, ,, Der heutige Zustand von Marokko. N. von 13 Sept., 1884, *der Köln. Zeitung.*

,, ,, Article dans la *Revue Africaine.* No. 39, Mai, 1883.

,, ,, Résumé historique et géographique de l'exploration de G. Rohlfs au Touat et à In. Calah, d'après les lettres du voyageur insérées aux *Annales des Voyages de* 1866, par V.A. Malte Brun. Paris, 1 vol. in 8vo., 150 pages, avec 1 carte, 1866.

,, ,, Resultate der Rohlfs'schen Höhenmessungen in Marokko und Tuat. Petermann's Mitth., 1866, page 119.

ROLLAND (G.)—L'oued Ziz et la colonisation française au Sahara. Paris, Lacune, 20 p. in 8o.

ROLLESTON (C.) von Schröder (M.)—Tetuan. *Ebds* xi. 1880. p. 292.

ROMANET DU CAILLAUD—Note sur le lieu d'origine de certaines tribus arabes du Maroc. *Bullet. Soc. Géogr.* Paris, p. 123, 1885.

ROSARIO (Fr. Pedro Martin del)—[*Interprete del consulado general de Espana en Tanger, en el primer tercio del presente siglo*]—Segun el P. Castellanos, reunio los materiales necesarios para una gramatica y diccionario del arabe vulgar de Marruecos, materiales que se han extraviado.

ROSELL y FORBES (Isidoro)—Una excursion á Tanger, *La Illustracion Espanola y Americana*, Madrid, 1875, page 78.

ROUDH-EL-KARTAS—Histoire des souverains du Maghreb, et annales de la ville de Fès, traduit de l'arabe par A Beaumier, Paris, in 8., 1860.

ROUSSEAU DES ROCHES—Trois souvenirs, Tanger, Isly, Mogador. Paris, 1846.

ROUTE DU MAROC A TIMBOUCTOU.—*Bull. Soc. Géogr. Paris*, 1886, page 507.

San Javier (Vizconde de).—El Penon de Velez de la Gomera.
La Illustracion Espanola y Americana. Madrid, 1872, page 651.

Sanchez Valenzuela (Joaquin).—Historia de los presidios menores de Africa, 1871. *M.S. en la Bibl., del ministerio de la Guerra, Madrid.*

San Martin (Antonio de).—Costumbres de Marruecos, *El Museo Universal Madrid*, 1867.

 ,, ,, Los riffeños, *La Illustracion Espanola y Americana,* Madrid, 1871, page 574.

Santa Cruz de mar Pequna—*Bull. Soc. Géogr. Paris*, 1886, 590-591.

Schaudt (Jacob).—Wanderungen durch Marokko.
Zeitschr. der. Berl. Ges. für Erdkunde, 1883, page 290-393.

Schickler (F.)—Quelques jours à Tanger. Notes de voyages publiées dans le *Tour du monde*, 1860, page 5 à 10, 28 à 32.

Schlagintweit (E.)—La guerra entra España y Marruecos en 1859 y 60. Leipzig in 8, 1863.

Schousbœ (P.K.A.)—Observations sur le règne végétal au Maroc. Paris, Baillère, 1874.

Schweiger.—Marokko, nach dem Ital., frei bearbeitet. Wien., 1882,

Schweiger und Lerchenfeld.—Ein Bollwerk des Islam. *Oesterreich, Monatsschrift für den Orient*, 1882, No. 6.

Scobel (A.)—Reiseskizzen aus Nord West Afrika. "*Ausland*," 1884, No. 14.

Scott (Colonel).—A journal of a residence in the Esmaïlla of Abd-el-Kader: and of travels in Marocco and Algiers. London, 1842, in-8.

Seux (Docteur A.)—Mogador et son climat, extrait du "*Marseille Médical*," 1871.

Si Bu el Moghdad.—Voyage par terre entre le Sénégal et le Maroc. *Revue maritime et coloniale*. Tome I., 1861, pag. 477. Et une carte.

Snider-Pellegrini (A.)—Du développement du commerce de l'Algérie précedé d'observations sur le Maroc. Paris, 1857.

Solrillet (P.)—L'Afrique occidentale. Algérie, Mzab, Tildikelt. Paris, 1877, in-8. Le même in-12.

Soller (Ch.)—Voyage dans l'intérieur du Maroc. *Société Géogr. Paris*, 1887. p. 442-48.

Solvet (Ch.)—Description des pays du Mogreb. Texte arabe d'Aboul-féda, accompagné d'une traduction française et de notes. Alger, 1839, in-8.

Sotto (Le Colonel Raimondo de)—Apuntes historicos sobre las expediciones de los espanoles al Africa. "*La Asamblea militar.*"

Spanish Campaign in Morocco.—An enormous quantity of publications have been issued in Spain on the campaign in Morocco in 1859-60. But the greatest part having only been written to satisfy public curiosity, they have no geographic, historic, or scientific interest.

Stein—Schilderungen aus Tanger. *Wistermann's Monatshefte* (April, 1865).

Stirling—On the races of Morocco. "*Ausland,*" 1870, cl. XIX.

Stutfield (Hugh E. M.)—El Maghreb: 1200 miles' ride through Morocco. London: Sampson, Low, & Co., 1886, in 8.

Suarez (Diego)—Historia de Berberia, precidida de la vida del autor. *Bibl. Nac. M.S. X.* 216.

T. L.—Le Maroc; notions géographiques [une petite carte du Maroc est jointe]. Paris, *l'Explorateur*, 1876, III. pag. 116.

Tanger—Handels und Schifffahrtsbericht, 1875.

„ (von) nach Fés—*Export*, 1885.

v. Taschek (C. R.)—Aus Tanger. *Wiener Jagd, Zeitung*, 1876, pag. 755.

Territories adquirides para España por la Sociedad Espanola de Africanistas y colonistas en la costa occidental de Africa. *Bull. de la Soc. Géogr. de Madrid*, XVIII., 1885, p. 355.

Tessier (J.)—Voyage de deux bourgeois au Maroc, de Fez à Makinez. Revue de Géogr. 1887. p. 140

Thevenin (Docteur)—Du climat de Mogador sous le rapport des affections pulmonaires. *Bull. Soc. Géogr. Marseille.*

Thomassy (R.)—Demande en mariage par Muley Ismael, Empereur de Maroc, de la princesse de Conti, fille naturelle de Louis XIV., et de Mlle. de la Vallière en 1700. [Article publié dans la *France Maritime*, vol. IV., pag. 173, 1841.]

„ Le Maroc et ses caravanes, ou relations de la France avec cet empire. Paris, in 8, 2me édition, 1845 [contient un aperçu des relations diplomatiques du Maroc avec la France, l'Espagne et l'Angleterre].

„ Des relations commerciales et politiques de la France avec le Maroc, Paris. Bertrand, 1842.

„ La question d'Orient sous Louis XIV. Paris, 1846, in 16.

Tissot (Ch.)—(Ministre plénipotentaire de France au Maroc). Itinéraire de Tanger à Rbat, avec carte du nord du Maroc. *Bull Soc. Géogr. Paris* VI., Série, XII., 1876.

Tissot (Ch.)—Sur les monuments mégalithiques et les populations blondes du Maroc. *Revue d'anthropologie*, X., 1876.

" " Recherches sur la géographie comparée de la Maurétanie Tingitane. *Memoires présentés par divers savants à l'Academie des Inscriptions et belles lettres de l'Institut de France.* Paris, Impr. nat. MDCCCLXXVIII.

Torrijos (Manuel)—Noticia de alguno de los puertos y poblaciones de la costa del Imperio marroqui "*Cronica naval,*" 1860. Tom. X., pag. 332.

Traité conclu entre les plénipotentiaires de l'empereur des français, et les plénipotentiaires de l'empereur du Maroc, Fez etc., 1845. Paris, 1845.

Trotter (Philip Durham)—Our mission to the court of Morocco in 1880 under Sir John Drummond Hay, K.C.B., minister plenipotentiary and envoy extraordinary to his Majesty the Sultan. Illustrated from photographs by the Hon. D. Lawless. Edinburgh. 8vo, 1881.

Urquhart (David)—The pillars of Hercules, narrative of a journey in Spain and Morocco. 1850.

Urrestarazu (Francisco, de, A, de)—Viajes por Marruecos. Madrid, Tip de R..Labajos en 8vo., 230 pags, 1877.

Valbert—Le Maroc et la politique européenne à Tanger. *Revue des 2 mondes*, 1er Decembre, 1884. Paris.

Valbert (G.)—Un voyageur français au Maroc. *Revue des deux Mondes*, pag. 670-681. 1er Avril, 1888.

Valdespino (S.)—La question du Maroc, ce qu'elle a été, est, et sera ; examinée au point de vue espagnol et européen. Traduit avec avant-propos par C. Lamartinière, in 8., 1859.

Vanegas (Pedro)—Relacion de todo al Embajador Pedro Vanegas de Cordoba en el viaje que hace a la ciudad de Marruecos con cierta Embajade que Su Magestad le envia al rey Muley Hamete rey de Marruecos y Fez. MS.—*Sin fecha 5 hojas en fol. Bibliot de la Acad de la Historia: Papeles varios de yesuitas.*

Vasquez Navarro (Y.)—Una proccession en Mogador. "*El Argos*" Diario de Madrid, 1872.

Vereker (C.S.)—Scenes in the sunny South, including the Atlas Mountains and the oases of the Sahara in Algeria. 2 vol. London : Longmans, 1871.

Veth en Kan—Bibliographie van boeken en kaarten die in het Hollandsch over Afrika zyn uitgegoven. Utrecht, 1876.

VIAJE del Emperador de Marruecos à Rabat. "*Gibraltar Guardian*," 20 Agosto, 1877.

VIAJE a la capital del imperio de Marruecos de una comision espanola en el anno 1800. *Boll. Soc. Geogr.*, *Madrid*, 1878, pag. 273.

VIAJE de la embajada española à Fez, 1877, relacion en "*El Imparcial.*" Madrid, 24 Mayo, 77.

VIARDOT (L.)—Histoire des Arabes et des Mores d'Espagne. Paris, 1851, 2 vol. in-8.

VINCENDON-DUMOULIN et Ph de KERHALLET—Description nautique de la côte nord du Maroc. Paris, 1857.

VIVIEN de ST-MARTIN—Le nord de l'Afrique dans l'antiquité grecque et romaine, étude historique et géographique. Paris, impr. impér., 1863, gr. in-8 cartes. [Ouvrage couronné par l'Académie des inscriptions et Belles-Lettres].

„   „   *Dictionnaire de géographie universelle*, article sur le Maroc.

VOYAGE dans les Etats Barbaresques de Maroc, Alger, Tunis et Tripoly, ou lettres d'un des captifs qui viennent d'être rachetés par MM. les chanoines de la Ste-Trinité (publié par le P. Lucien Hérault.) Paris, 1885, in-12.

Voz del Litoral (La.)—Periodico independiente de Madrid. [Various articles in 1878.]

WARREN (T.P.)—Gibraltar and Morocco. A letter, pag. 27. London, 1882.

WARREN (F.)—Morocco. Fortnightly Review, Aug., 1884, pp. 186 to 198. [General description—uneasiness of England about French politics in Morocco.]

WALTHAM (Edward)—Our journey to Fez, pag. 47. Privately printed. London, 1882. 8vo.

WARNIER (Dr.)—Souvenirs d'une mission au Maroc. [Document inédit].

WASHINGTON—Voyageur au Maroc [communic.] *Bull. Soc. Géogr. Paris*, pag. 506.

WATSON (Robert Spence)—A visit to Wazan, the sacred city of Morocco, with illustrations and 1 map. London : Macmillan, 8vo. 1880.

WHITE (H.B.S.M. Consul)—Trade and commerce of Morocco in the year 1871. London, 1872.

WIMPFEN (Gal de)—L'expédition de l'Oued Guir. *Bull. Soc. Géogr., Paris*, 1872. [Also in German in *Petermann's Ausgabe*, 1872, pag. 332.]

WINKLER (A.)—Notes sur les ruines de Bella Regia. *Bull. d'antiquités africaines.* T. III. Année 1885, pag. 112.

WEBER (E. von)—Vier Jahre in Africa, 1871-75. Leipzig, 1878.

WEYLER y LAVINA (Fernando)—Apuntes topographicos sobre la parte del Imperio Marroqui que ha sido teatro de la última guerra con Espana. Palma de Mallorca, 1862.

YRIARTE (Charles)—Sous la tente. Souvenirs du Maroc, récits de guerre et de voyage [L'auteur fut le correspondant du *Monde Illustré* pendant la guerre du Maroc en 1859.] Paris in 12, 1861.

ZAFFARINES [Communication.] *Bull. Soc. Géogr. Paris.* 1886, pag. 379.

ZEHDEN (C.)—Tanger. Deutsche Rundschau für Geogr., vi., 1884, pag. 481.

MAPS AND CHARTS OF MOROCCO.

(The Dimensions (D) are in inches.)

—:o:—

Fessæ et Marocchi, Regna, w. p. o. d., 1600? From Cape St. Vincent to Cape Bojador, and on the east to the Zafarines. The Canary Islands are shown. Antwerp? Br. Mus., 63,905 (2).

On the top and on the left, view of Pénon de Velez D. = 19 × 14. Spanish and German scale, 25 mill. germ. = about 2 inches.

Fessæ et Marocchi, Regna, Africæ celeberr, describebat Abrah, Orteluis, 1595. Antwerp?

Same dimensions as the preceding, embracing the same region. Coloured without scale. On the top, on the left, a map of 9 × 7 in. Congi regni christiani in Africa nova descriptio. Br. Mus., 63,905 (1).

Marocchi Regnum, w. p. o. d.—From Azemor to Cape Nou, on the east to Beniniaraz.

Scale 15 Mill. germ. = $\frac{2}{5}$ inch; D = $6\frac{3}{4}$ × 5. Coloured, and on vellum, The catalogue of the Br. Mus. gives Amsterdam 1620. Br. Mus., 63,905 (3).

Fessæ, Regnum.

10 Mill. germ. = $\frac{2}{4}$ inch D. = 7 × $5\frac{1}{2}$. Outlines in colours. From the Straits of Gibraltar (Estrecho de G.), to the environs of Mazaghan (sic). Molouia figures under the name of Nocorflu. Tangiers is not shown.

Amsterdam, 1620? Br. Mus., 63945 (1).

Estats et royaumes de Fez et Maroc, Darha et Segelmesse, tiré de Sanuto, de Marmol, etc.

By N. Sanson d'Abbeville, geogr. in ordin. to the king. Paris, 1655.

From Gibraltar to the region of the O. Draâ (Darha) on the east to the province of Algiers. Without scale. Coloured outlines.

D. = 20½ × 15. Br. Mus. Barbary Atlas, 117 (58-85).

Fezzæ, et Marocchi, Regna Africæ, celeberrima, describebat, Abr. Orteluis, w. p. o. d.

From Cape St. Vincent to the Atlas (montes claros) on the east to Campos de Anget?

Mil. Germ. Comm. 20 = about 2½ inch. D. = 19 × 14½ Antwerp? Br. Mus., 63,905 (4).

Other copy, coloured outlines, Br. Mus., Barbary Atlas, 117, 58-85.

Other copy, not coloured, is in Br. Mus. in fol. 1000, 1110. S. 69, 13, Antwerp?

Barbaria, w. p. o. d. 1700?

Tunis, Algiers, Marocco, in two parts on the same sheet, few names. Size of sheet 22½ × 19. Wild animals in the desert, South Oran, ships and galleys on the sea. Br. Mus., Barbary Atlas, 117, 58, 85.

Statuum Maroccanorum, Regnorum nempe Fessani, Maroccani, Tafiletani, et Segelomessani, secundum suas Provincias accurate divisorum Typus generalis novus ex variis recentioris Geographiæ adminiculis depromptus et designatus a Jo. Chris Homanno M.D. Noribergæ, Anno 1728.

From Tangiers to the Oued Drâ (Darhariv) and on the east to Oran with the "Touet vel Tuat." General configuration very imperfect. D. = 20 × 14. All the Canary Islands; coloured.

30 miles = about 2¾ inch. At foot views of Morocco (town of Morocco), and Meknés. View of the royal residence. Dimens. of views each 10½ × 4¼. On the top and on the left, title with figures, lions, rock which seems to be Gibraltar. Br. Mus., 63,910, (1).

The west part of Barbary containing Fez, Morocco, Algiers and Tunis by H. Moll. Geogr. 1732.

From Tripoli to the Atlantic. D.=10×4. 4. D=about 1¾ inch.
On Top on the left, plan of Oran. D.=1½×1¼ in 1708.
This map surmounts another one of the same size. The east part of Barbary. Br. Mus. Barbary Atlas, 117, 58-85.

A new map of the Kingdom of Fez, Morocco, etc.
From the Straits of Gibraltar to R. Dras, and on the east to Oran.
Brit. miles, 120. D=8×7. The catalogue of Br. Mus., gives 1750?
Br. Mus., 63905, (5).

A map of the empire of Morocco, comprehending the Kingdom of Fez, Morocco etc., by T. Kitchin. Geogr.
London, 1770? D=6¼ 4½. Br. Mus. 63,905, (6).

Mapa General que comprehende los Reynos de Marruecos, Fez, Argel, y Tunez, compuesto con los mejores mapas, y con lo que escribieron Marmol, Torres, Hædo, Dapper, Abbreville, Davite, La Mote y otros.
By D. Tomas Lopez y Vargas. Geogr. of H. M. etc., Madrid 1775, 2 sheets, of which one specially of Morocco. 10 leguas de Marina=about ⅛ inch. D.=16×13½. From Isla de Hierro, 38° lat. N. to 29 lat. N. ; 6° long.
Coloured outlines. Forms No. 144 of the same atlas. Br. Mus., S., 156, (6).

Cartes des régences d'Alger, de Tunis et de Tripoli avec l'empire du Maroc, comprenant aussi tout le bassin citérieur de la Méditerrannée d'une grande partie des Etats qui forment ses limites européennes, par Hérisson, geogr. 1840.
Scale, myriam. ou lieues nouv. 10=1½ inch. D=30×20. Coloured outlines.
Published at the end of the " Histoire pittoresque de l'Algerie," etc., by Eug. Hatin. Paris, Br. Mus. 793. i. 24.

Karte der Regentschaften Algier, Tunis und Tripoli und des Kaiserthums Fez Marokko, nebst den gegenüberliegenden europaïschen. Küstenstrichen von Herisson, geogr. 1844.

Coloured outlines. Straub, Karlsruhe.

$D = 31\frac{1}{2} \times 20\frac{3}{4}$. Myriametres $10 = 1\frac{1}{2}$ inch Br. Mus., 63,713, (2).

Das Kaiserreich Fez und Marokko nebst eienem Theile der franz. Provinz Algier, 1845.

Sketched by V. C. F. Wenng. Scale 1 to 3,000,000 Berlin? $D = 15\frac{3}{4} \times 10\frac{3}{4}$. Br. Mus., 63,905, (9).

Karte von Marokko, Algier und Tunis, nach der Karte von Algier entworfen im allgemeinen Kriegsdepot unter Leitung des lieut gen. Pelet etc., 1846 ohne Ortsangabe.

Designed, drawn and engraved by Allbrecht Platt. Coloured outlines $1 = 1\frac{1}{4}$ inch. $D. = 26 \times 16\frac{1}{8}$. Br. Mus., 63700 (8).

Carte de l'empire du Maroc, indiquant les communications principales, la division en gouvernements et la répartition de la population des diverses races sur le sol .... par le Capitaine d'état major Beaudouin. Réduite et gravée au dépôt général de la guerre. Dressée avec les renseignements suivants :

1 Renseignements communiqués par M. L. Roches.

2 Document sur l'oasis de Touat réunis par M. de Ligny.

3 Renseignements recueillis auprès des indigènes par M. Beaudouin.

Scale 1, 1,500,000. Paris 1848. $D. = 43 \times 33\frac{1}{2}$. Br. Mus., 63,905, (10).

Marocco, by J. Wyld. Tangier Bay. Mogador. City of Morocco, London, 1859. Br. Mus., 63,905, (11).

Carte du Maroc, dressée d'après les travaux les plus récents, spécialement d'après la carte du capitaine d'état-major Beaudouin. Published in the work of the Abbé Godard on Morocco. 100 kil = $1\frac{1}{2}$ inch. $D = 24 \times 17\frac{3}{8}$. Paris 1860.

Carte de l'empire de Maroc, dressée par A Vuillemin, 1860. In the text of the *Tour du Monde*, 1860. p. 216. $D = 6\frac{1}{4} \times 6\frac{1}{4}$.

Carte de l'Algérie avec plan et environs des principales villes, ainsi, que ceux de Maroc et de Tanger.

Paris, Impr. Bès et Dubreuil, 1868.

Carte pour servir à l'intelligence de la géographie comparée de la Maurétanie Tingitane.

Constructed by Charles Tissot, minister plenipotentiary of France in Morocco 1876, 100 kil = 3 inch D. $24\frac{3}{4} \times 19$.

Carte de la côte septentrionale de la Maurétanie Tingitane de Tamuda à Tingis.
    By the same. 10 kil = $1\frac{1}{2}$ inch. D. = $9\frac{1}{2} \times 6\frac{3}{4}$.

Esquisse topographique de la region comprise entre le Cap Spartel et Azila.
    By the same. 10 kil = $1\frac{1}{2}$ inch D = $7\frac{1}{4} \times 5\frac{1}{2}$.

Les voies romaines de la Maurétanie Tingitane.
    By the same. 30 kil = $1\frac{1}{2}$ inch D = $9 \times 6\frac{1}{4}$.

    These 4 maps are published in the Memoirs, offered by different men of science to the Académie des inscriptions et belles lettres, first series, vol ix. Paris. Imp. nat. 1878.

Esquisse topographique d'une partie du royaume de Fès.
    By the same. Scale of 1, 500,000. D = $18\frac{1}{2} \times 14\frac{1}{2}$. Bull. Soc. Géogr., Paris, Sept. 1876.

A new map of South Morocco, by John Ball., F. R. S. Published in "Journal of a tour in Morocco" by Hooker and Ball. London, 1878. D = $26 \times 14\frac{3}{4}$. Includes the region of the Atlas in the South of Morocco. Scale 10 miles = $\frac{5}{8}$ inch.

General map of Marocco in Arabic letters by Gebbas, Sidy Mahomed ben Mahomed el.
    Scale Geogr. miles to an inch, 20·4. Chatham, 1879.

Karte des mittellandischen Meeres, in 8 Blättern, entworfen von A. Petermann.
    The two first sheets contain Spain, Morocco, the provinces of Oran and Algiers.
    Scale 1-3,500,000. Dimension of the two sheets combined $26\frac{3}{4} \times 17$. Gotha, Justus Perthes, 1880.

Map of the north-west portion of Morocco, showing the route followed by mission, under Sir J. Drummond Hay, K.C.B., 1880, constructed from a sketch map by Capt. P. D. Trotter, and from the map of Tissot.
    Tanger to Fez and Meknès. D = $15\frac{1}{2} \times 12$. Scale 5 miles = $\frac{5}{8}$ inch. This map is published in Trotter's "Our mission to the Court of Morocco." London, 1881.

Map of the Empire of Marocco from the French war department map with corrections according with map given in "Hooker and Ball's Marocco, and the great Atlas," translated into Arabic by Sidi Mohamed ben Mohamed el Gebbas of Fez, and zincographed at the R. E. Institute, Chatham. D=40×27½. Scale of the map of Beaudouin, October, 1880.

Le Sahara central et septentrionale, avec une partie du Maroc, par V. Largeau.
    This map is to be found in the "Algerian Sahara." Paris, 2me édition, 1881. D=15¼×10¼. Scale 1, 2,500,000.

Geologische Karte von West Afrika, nach seinen in den Jahren 1874-77 und 1879-81 unternommenen Reisen, entworfen von Dr. Oscar Lenz.
    D.=19¼×13⅝. Scale 500,000. Petermanns Mitth. Gotha, Justus Perthes. 1882.

Maroc occidental, par Erckmann. Le Maroc moderne, par E. Paris 1885.
    D=14×13½. Scale 1 to 500,000.

Maroc. Carte très générale publiée dans la Géographie Universelle de E. Reclus, vol. xi. pl. III. Hachette et Cie Paris, D=10½×7½. 1886. Scale 1 to 760,000.

    Arteche (D. José Gomez de) y Coello (D Francisio) coronses.
        Descripcion y mapas de Marruecos con algunas consideraciones sobre la importancia de la occupacion militar de una parte de este imperio. (General map of Marocco. Scale 1/5,000,000 and another scale 1/1,000,000, of the kingdom of Fez, to the Algerian frontier. Plans of Ceuta, Melilla, Tetouan, Penon de Alhucemas, Velez de la Gomera. Sale y Rabat, Par el Beïda, Mazagan, Safi, Mogador), 1 vol., 145 pag. Madrid, 1859.

Description of Tanger. Mappe made by the Swedish Captain Martin Bockmer, MS. on vellum, 1600 ?
    Very general plan of the town. Few indications. D=28×24.
        Br. Mus., Barbary Atlas.
    Another MS. on vellum, 1661, seems to be by the same author.

Without title. Gives a general plan of the Bay of Tangiers, with its best anchorage. D=22×16. Br. Mus., Barbary Atlas, 117, (53-85).

A map of the city of Tanger, with the Straits of Gibraltar. Described by Jonas Moore, surveyor to His Royal Hs. the Duke of York.

London 1664, coloured. D=53×26. On the right, at bottom, the English Royal arms; and cartouche containing a dedication to Charles II., partly destroyed. On the left, at the top, the Bay of Tangier. D=14¾×9. On the right at the top, map of the Straits of Gibraltar. D=8¾×8¾.

The map represents a bird's eye view of the town, remarkably executed; it is much damaged.

The citty of Tangier with the lines, etc., when besieged by the Moores, anno 1680. S. L. London? D=18×11, English Royal arms at the right. On the left, on the top, environs of the town. D=6¼×4 with the inscription. "The lines, etc., where ye Earl of Tiveot was killed, anno 1664."

This map seems to be a reduced copy of the preceding one. Br. Mus., 64,040, (4).

The Royal city of Tangier with yᵉ lines and fortifications, when it was ataqued by the Moores in May, 1680, by John Seller, and are sold at his shop in Popes head alley in Cornhill. London.

D=20¼×15¾. Same view as the preceding one. On the top, on the left, same view, without Royal arms; battle in the environs, numerous figures. Br. Mus., 64,040, (3).

A true and exact ground plot of Tanger, with the Lines and Forts exactly laid down with their true distances from yᵉ city. As also the Moors Trenches that was made when the Forts were taken, sold by Will. Berry at the sign of yᵉ Globe, between Charing Cross and White Hall, 1680.

Plan of the walls of Tanger, with the position of the trenches. D.=22×17¾. London. Br. Mus., 64040.

Accurata Regiæ civitatis Tingi, dict. vulgo Tangeræ Molæ, Tabula cum appertinent. a Roberto Thacker, Regiæ Maj. dessignatore.

Anno 1680. Large and remarkable engraving. D. = 74 × 50. Containing 23 views of Tangiers (the 23d. is wanting), during the English occupation. Legend in English explaining the views. Description of the town, at foot the inscription to the Sacred Majesty of Charles, the second king of England, Scotland, France and Ireland, defender of the Faith, etc. Your maj. Loyall and obedient subject and servant. R. T... err most humbly dedicates this mapp. Printed by H. H. especial command. No. 17 gives a plan of the Bay of Tangiers at the scale of 500 perches = $2\frac{5}{8}$ inch. Br. Mus.

The royal city of Tangier, with the lines and fortifications when it was attaqued by y^e Moores in May, 1680, by I. Seller.

London, 1685. D = $6\frac{1}{4} × 4\frac{1}{4}$. Seems to be a reduction from the preceding one. Br. Mus., 64,040, (1).

5 Prospects of Tangiers. I. Oliver fecit, I. Seller, excudit.
During the English occupation. Dimens. $7\frac{1}{2} × 4\frac{1}{2}$.
London? 1585? Br. Mus., 64,040, 5, 6, 7, 8, 9, 10.

Tangiers. Bird's eye view. MS. on paper. No name. 1700?
D = $22\frac{1}{2} × 16$. Br. Mus., Barbary Atlas, cxvii, 80.

View of Arzile. MS., 1700?
With indications in English of depth of anchorage. D = 20 × 16.

View of Salée. MS., 1700?
Seems to be by the same author. D = $19\frac{1}{4} × 10\frac{1}{4}$. Br. Mus., Barbary Atlas, 117, 58-85.

Marocco, Bocanum Hemerum Ptolomaei regni cognominis metropolis, haud procul ab Atlante monte posita.
Same inscription in Dutch. Coloured view of Morocco.

Salla, celebre Africæ Emporium, ad mare atlanticum.
Same inscription in Dutch. Coloured view of Salée.

Tingin, Mauritaniæ Tingitanæ quondam metropolis nunc ruinis suis tumulata.
Same inscription in Dutch. Coloured view of Tangiers. Dim. of each view $10\frac{1}{4} × 8\frac{1}{4}$. These views form part of the Album. Petri Schendii Hecatompolis sive totius orbis Terrarum

oppida nobiliorum exquisite collecta atque eleganter depicta, Inscripta sereniss. ac celeberr. Principi Frederico Wilhelmo, Regni Boruss. et Electorat. Brandeburg Hæredi, &c. 1702. Br. Mus., 960, 1304, S. 119, (7).

Tanger.
> General view taken from sea; seems to be cut at right side. $D = 10\frac{1}{2} \times 4$. On the left legend in German. A town in the kingdom of Fez. Augsburg? 1740? by G. Bodenehr? Br. Mus., 960, 390, S. 122, (3).

Tanger; general view taken from sea. $D = 20\frac{3}{4} \times 13\frac{3}{4}$, w. d. 1750? At foot, following inscription.
> Tangiers, a town situated at the extreme point of the small bay, formerly called Tangiris, and afterwards it obtained the name of Tingitane Mauritanie, and the Straits Tingitaniæ finis terræ; it belonged to the Portuguese, till the King of Portugal gave it as a dowry to his sister Catherine of Portugal, on her marriage with Charles II., King of England. Since then the English have abandoned it, as it was difficult to keep, and the King of the Moors has taken it.

Made by A. Amline Paris at Daumont. Br. Mus., 64,840, 1310.

A view of the island of Mogodore and part of the main on the coast of Barbaria.
> Lat. 31^2 18 N. Long. 2°. 1.0. W. Represents the battle of two English ships against two ships of Salle. MS. 13th May, 1734. $D = 22 \times 13\frac{1}{2}$. Br. Mus., Barbary Atlas, 117, 58-85.

The South Prospect of Tetuan.
> P. Tourdrinier sculp. To his Grace John, Duke of Argyll. $D = 19 \times 6\frac{3}{4}$. On the left, at foot, expl. legend. London, 1749? Br. Mus., 64,045, (1).

Plano de la ciudad, Plaza y fuerzas (de Melilla).
> By D. T. Lopez. Madrid, 1795. The map is in 3 parts; 1, Coast of Africa round Melilla. 2, General plan. 3, Detailed plan. $D = 13\frac{1}{2} \times 14\frac{1}{4}$. Br. Mus., same atlas.

Plan of the town and fortifications of Ceuta, by Lieut. F. Wheatley. London, 1813. $D = 14 \times 9\frac{1}{4}$, MS.

Plan of the town and fortifications of Ceuta.
MS. by Major Napier, 1840. D.=$18 \times 8\frac{1}{4}$. MS. Royal Geogr. Soc. of London.

Plano de la Peninsula de Zeuta y Campo de los Moros.
Spanish MS. on modern paper. 500 Tuesas=$3\frac{1}{2}$ inch. D=$28 \times 19\frac{3}{4}$. Coloured. Br. Mus., Barbary Atlas, 117, 58-85.

Plan de la ville de Maroc. Levé par Paul Lambert, 1867, revu et augmenté par Aug. Beaumier à Maroc, février 1868.
D=$12 \times 4\frac{1}{8}$. Bull. Soc. Géogr. Paris, November and December, 1868.

Ansicht von der Küste Maroccos von Cap Spartel bis Mogador. Hydrogr. office. Berlin, 1876. Br. Mus., G.A.C. (43^b).

Plans. J. Erkmann. Marocco and its environs.
D=$6\frac{1}{2} \times 4$. Scale 4 kil=$\frac{3}{4}$ inch.

Agadir.
By the same D=6×4. Scale 2 kil=$1\frac{1}{2}$ inch.

Tarudant.
Same author. Same dimensions and scale.

Fez and its environs.
Same author. D=4×4. Scale 4 kil=$\frac{3}{4}$ inch. "Le Maroc moderne." Paris, 1885.

Original Karte von Gerhard Rohlf's Reisen in central süd Marokko (Atlas, Tafilet, Draa), 1862-1864, nach Rohlf's Tage buch und persönlichen Ausgaben. Scale 1/200,000. D=$16\frac{1}{2} \times 9\frac{3}{4}$. Petermanns Geogr. Mitth., 1865. Gotha. J. Perthes.

Itinéraire de Mogador à Maroc, de Maroc à Saffy et de Saffy à Mogador, en février 1868, par Auguste Beaumier, consul de France. Scale 1/500,000. D=$15\frac{3}{4} \times 9$. Bull. Soc. Géogr. Paris. Octobre, 1868.

Voyages à la côte du Maroc, de Tanger à Mogador, par Auguste Beaumier, consul de France, 1855, 1875.
Scale 1/800,000. 2 parts on same sheet. D=$16\frac{1}{8} \times 13\frac{3}{4}$. Bull. Soc. Géogr. Paris, 6th Serie, 1876.

Die Französischen militar Expeditionen in Marokko, 1866, und 1870.
    Scale 1/2,000,000. Petermann's Geogr. Mitth. vol. 18, Engr. 18, Gotha, 1872. Br. Mus., P.P. 394-6.

Itinerar von Dr. Oscar Lenz. Reise durch Marokko und die Sahara nach Timbuktu und von da durch den Sudan zum Senegal, 1879-80.
    Scale 1/1,500,000. Richard Kiepert, Zeitschr. der Gesell. fur Erdkunde Vol. xvi., engr. 11, edited by Dietrich Reimer, Berlin, 1831.

Bonelli (D. E.) Viages por Marruecos. De Rabat à Mequinez, Fez. y Tanger en 1882.
    Scale 1/100,000, Madrid.

Itinéraires d'Alkazar à Ouezzann et de Ouezzann à Meknès. H. de La Martinière, 1884.
    D. $=9 \times 8\frac{1}{2}$. 20×8. Scale 1/200,000. Revue de Géogr, 1885, 1886. Paris.

Mapa topografico de los payses, y costas, que forman el estrécho de Gibraltar, con quatro Tablas, para saber por los dios de la Luna, etc., Por D. Tomas Lopez. Pensionista de S. M. 1762.
    Leagues of 1 hour's march 1=about 1 inch. D. $=13\frac{3}{8} \times 13$. Coloured outlines. No. 69 of the *Atlas de Lopez*. Br. Mus., S. 156, 6.

Islas Chafarinas, situadas en el mar Mediterraneo.—por D. Tomas Lopez. Madrid 1788. With coloured outlines.
    200 varas castellanas=about $\frac{1}{8}$ of inch. D.$=9 \times 11$. Br. Mus., same atlas.

Carta esférica de la costa de Africa, en el estrecho de Gibraltar que comprende desde el cabo Espartel hasta Cala Grande.
    Made under the hydrogr. direction, after the works of M. C. A. Vincendon Dumoulin in 1854-1855. Madrid 1860. D$=15 \times 24$.

Carta esférica de los fondeaderos de Ceuta levantada en 1855, por M. C. A. V. D. Published in Madrid, 1860, D$=23\frac{1}{4} \times 16\frac{1}{8}$.

Carta, de la costa de Africa en el estrecho de Gibraltar que comprende desde el rio de Las ostras hasta Ceuta. Signed M. C. A. V. D., Madrid, 1860. D$=34\frac{1}{2} \times 24$.

Araish. Eigentliche Abbildung der starken Festung La' Rache, ein vornehmer Meerhaven in Barbarien, welcher in Nahmen Königlicher Maiest, von Hispanien, durch den Marckgraven von S. Germein ist eingenommen worden, 1610 in Nov.

    Nurnberg (1615). Above, on the right, the Spanish coat of arms. D. = 11 × 7. Zauger is on the Atlantic, and instead of Tangiers, is a town Alcaser, the same as Alkazar serir, facing Larache. Landing fleet attacking. Br. Mus., 64,037, (2).

Africa, north coast, Tangier Bay surveyed by M. Le Saulnier de Vaukello, 1835.

    Admiralty charts, 1849, No. 1912, view of Tangier. D. = $21\frac{1}{4}$ × 17. 3 naut. miles = $1\frac{1}{4}$.

A chart of the coasts of Portugal, Spain and Morocco, from Cape St. Vincent to Mogadore.

    With 1 Jeremias road from cape Spartel to Asillia. D = 8 × $7\frac{1}{2}$.
    2 A view of the entrance to Mogadore.
    3 The Bay and Island of Mogadore. D. = $8\frac{1}{8}$ × $7\frac{1}{2}$. Nautic. miles $\frac{1}{4}$ = 1 inch. London hydrogr. office, 12 Oct. 1812. Capt. Hurd. R. N. D. = 40 × $25\frac{1}{2}$. Br. Mus., Sec. 4 (92).

A Chart of Ceuta and Tetuan Bays, in which are pointed out the most advantageous places of rendezvous for the purposes of victualling and watering a fleet by Capt. Knight of the Royal navy.

    London 1 May, 1800. D. E. Steel, Little Tower Hill. D. = $28\frac{1}{2}$ × $20\frac{1}{8}$. Views of Gibraltar and the Zaffarine islands, with a plan of the Zaffarine islands by Capt. Wolseley. D = $8\frac{1}{4}$ × $6\frac{3}{4}$ $\frac{1}{2}$ mile = $1\frac{3}{4}$ inch. Br. Mus., 64,010, (1).

Chart of the Strait of Gibraltar constructed in 1786, by Breg. D. V. Tof. A. S. Miguel, with additions by J. F. Dessiou, 1806. D. = $25\frac{1}{2}$ × $21\frac{5}{8}$. 5 long $1\frac{1}{2}$ inch.

    View of the mountains of Ceuta, merid. of Cadiz and Greenwich. Br. Mus., 18,440, (13).

West coast of Africa.

    Sheet I. Cape Spartel to Azamor, surveyed by Lieut. Arlett. R.N., 1835. Admiralty chart. London, 1835?
    Sheet II. Azamor to Santa Cruz. Surveyed 1835. Admiralty chart. London, 1844.

Sheet III. Santa Cruz to Bojador. Surveyed 1835. Admiralty chart. London, 1844.

D. of each $=26\frac{3}{8}\times 16\frac{1}{4}$ 15° long. $=1\frac{3}{4}$. Br. Mus., Sec. 11, 1227, Sec. 11, 1228, 1229.

Carte de l' hydrographie française. Dépôt des cartes et plans de la Marine.

- I. 1700. Mer Méditerranée. Côte d'Afrique. Tétouan (Maroc) Levé en 1853. M. M. Duchaxel, Olivier, Tirard. C. C. Vincendon Dumoulin, du cap Negro au Cap et Tour Mazari. D$=23\frac{1}{4}\times 16$. Scale 1,600.

- II. 1701. Détroit de Gibraltar. Côte d'Afrique. Tanger et ses atterrages. Levés en 1854, et 1855, MM. C. A. Vincendon Dumoulin, Philippe de Kerhallet, etc. D$=36\times 23\frac{1}{4}$.

- III. 1711. Mer Méditeranée. Côte du nord du Maroc. Levés en 1855. Les mêmes, 1855, du Mont aux Singes au cap de l'Agua. Same dimensions.

- IV. 1723. Détroit de Gibraltar, côte d'Afrique. Mouillage de Ceuta. Levés en 1855. D$=$about $23\frac{1}{4}\times 16\frac{1}{4}$.

- V. 1748. Détroit de Gibraltar. Mouillages de la côte d'Afrique, de la pointe Malabata à la pointe Blanca, (Cala Grande, Alcazar, R'mel, Almanza et Benzus). Levés en 1855. Les mêmes. Scale, D.$=36\times 23\frac{1}{4}$.

- VI. 1809. Détroit de Gibraltar. Levé en 1854, et 1855. Les mêmes. Same dimensions.

- VII. 1843. Carte de l'entrée de la Méditeranée. Comprenant la côte d'Espagne, de Huelva, au cap Palos à la côte d'Afrique, de Mehediyah au cap Ferrat. Dressée d'après les travaux les plus récents, 1860. Same dimensions.

- VIII. 1165. Côte occidentale d'Afrique, partie comprise entre le détroit de Gibraltar et le cap Ghir. Levée en 1835, par le Lieut. Arlett, de la mar. roy. angl. Dép. gen. de la marine. 1848. D$=37\times 24$, 10 long$=\frac{1}{2}$ inch. Avec vue des côtes, rade de Mogador, levée en 1852, par M. C. A. Vincendon Dumoulin. 1 marine mile$=\frac{1}{2}$ inch.

IX. 1511. Océan Atlantique. Côtes d'Afrique. Mogador. Levé en 1852, par M. V. A. Vincendon Dumoulin. Dép. gen. de la marine. 1856. D=$17\frac{1}{2} \times 11$. Scale 1/13,300.

X. 960. Plan de la rade de Mogador. Levé en 1840, par J. A. Prouhet. Dep. gen. de la marine 1842. D=24×17. Scale 50 m.=$1\frac{3}{4}$ inch.

XI. 1508. Océan Atlantique, côtes d'Afrique, Safi levé en 1852, par M. C. A. Vincendon Dumoulin. Dép. gen. de la marine 1856. D.=$11\frac{1}{2} \times 8\frac{1}{2}$. The direction of the Hydr. of Madrid has published an edition. Madrid, 1860.

XII. 1507. Océan Atlantique, Côtes d'Afrique, Mazaghan. Croquis levé en 1852, par M. C. A. Vincendon Dumoulin. Dép. gen. de la marine. 1856. Same dimensions.

XIII. 1350. Rade de Mazaghan (Maroc) Croquis communiqué en 1837, par M. Simonet de Maisoneuve, L. de vaisseau. D=$9 \times 5\frac{1}{2}$. (Spanish edition 1860). Océan Atlantique, Côtes d'Afrique. Atterrage de Mazaghan d'après la carte levée en 1835, par le Lieut. W. Arlett de la mar. roy. angl. Dép. gén. de la marine, 1851. Same dimensions. 5° long=$\frac{1}{2}$ inch.

XIV. 1348. Océan Atlantique. Côtes d'Afrique. Atterrage de Mehediyah, d'après la carte levée en 1835, par le Lieut. W. Arlett de la mar. roy. angl. Dép. gen. de la marine 1851. D=$9 \times 5\frac{1}{2}$. Same scale. Rade de Mehediyah (imperfect sketch). Same dimensions.

XV. 1710. Océan Atlantique. Côtes d'Afrique. Rade de Larache. Croquis levé en 1855, par M. C. A. Vincendon Dumoulin. D.=$11\frac{3}{4} \times 9$. The direction of hydrogr. in Madrid published an edition in 1860.

XVI. 1347. Océan Atlantique. Côtes d'Afrique. Atterrage de Larche, d'après la carte levée en 1835, par le Lieut. W. Arlett, de la mar. roy. angl. Dép. gén. de la marine, 1851. D=$9 \times 5\frac{1}{2}$, 15° long=$1\frac{1}{2}$ inch. Cap Spartel, baie Jeremias. Levés en 1854, et 1855. Same dimensions.

Afrika, Häfen an der Küste von Marocco. Vermessen von Freih. von Löwenstorn, Lieut. zur See an Bord "Nautilus," 1875.

On the same sheet, El Araish. Scale 1/100,000. D.=11¾×9¾.
,, ,, ,, Rabat and Salé. Scale 1/50,000. D.=10×7½.
,, ,, ,, Mogador (Zuerah). D.=19¼×10.
Published by the Hydrogr. office. Berlin, 1876. Dietrich Reimer. Br. Mus., G. A. C. (43).

Carta esférica de la costa norte de Marruecos c desde el Estrecho de Gibraltar hasta las islas Chafarinas.
    Spanish edition of the map of the French hydrogr., by M. C. V. D. Madrid, 1860.
Planos de Melilla y de la Bahia de Alhucemas y de la Isla de Alboran. Same dimensions.

Carta del Fondeadero de Dar el Beïda.
    Spanish edition of the map of the French hydrogr. by M. C. V. D.

Carta del Fondeadero de Mazaghan.
    Spanish edition of the map by M. C. V. D.
       These two maps are on one sheet. Dimens.=11¼×8.

Carta de la Bahia de Mogador.
    Spanish edition of the map by M. V. C. D., in 1852, Madrid, 1860.

Carta del puerto y rada de Salé.
    Spanish edition of the map by M. V. C. D., 1852. Madrid, 1860.

Carta de la Bahia de Safi.
    Spanish edition of the map, by M. V. C. D., 1852, French hydrogr. Madrid, 1860.

Carta del Fondeadero de Agadir o Santa Cruz.
    Spanish edition of the map by M. V. C. D., 1852. Madrid, 1860.
These two maps each of 39×8, are on the same sheet.

Carta esferica de las islas Chafarinas construida en la direccion de hydrografia segun los trabajos mas recientes.
    Madrid, 1860. D=24×17¾.
    All these maps are to be found in the Atlas 972, 621, S. 207, 3 of the Br. Mus.

Direccion de Hydrografia.
- I. Derrotero de la costa de Marruecos desde cabo Espartel a cabo Bojador, por M. Charles de Kerhallet en 1821. Madrid Imp. Nac. 1860, in 4.
- II. Derrotero de las costas occidentales de Africa, redactado en la direccion de hydr. con presencia de la publ. mas recen. Comprehende desde Tanger hasta la bahia de Algoa. Madrid, impr. Fortanet, 1872, in 4 illust.
- III. Derrotero de las costas occid. de Africa, red. en la dir. de hydr. comp. desde el cabo Espartel hasta Sierra Leone. Madrid, imp. Fortanet 1875 in 4 illust.

Suirah or Mogador harbour, surveyed by Lieut. Arlett 1835.
Admiralty charts, 1844 No. 1594. $D. = 24 \times 18\frac{1}{4}$. 1 naut. mile = 9 yards.

Anchorages on the coast of Morocco, Admiralty charts, No. 1692. Ann. 1878 by Capt. Evans, Zafarin islands.
$D = 13\frac{3}{8} \times 9\frac{1}{4}$, 1 marine mile = $\frac{17}{8}$ inch. View of the Zafarin islands. Mazari Bay. Same Dimensions, 1 naut. mile = $\frac{2}{8}$ inch.
Melilla, general plan. $D = 4 \times 4$, $\frac{1}{2}$ naut. mile = $\frac{3}{8}$ inch.

Part of the West Coast of Africa, from Tangiers to Cape Bojador surveyed in 1835. Published for the Journal of the Royal Geogr. Soc. by J. Murray. London, 1836.
$D = 8\frac{3}{4} \times 7\frac{1}{2}$, $7\frac{1}{2} \times 5\frac{1}{2}$ 2 on 1 sheet. Br. Mus., 64,649 (2).

A map without a title, of the western part of Algiers, together with the adjoining portions of Marocco, 1847. Francke, febr. 1847, at bottom of Map, Br. Mus., 63,775, (2).

Masqueray (E.) Le Sahara occidental. Carte d'après trois pèlerins de l'Adrar. Paris, Challamel, 1880.

MacCarthy (O). Le Sud Oranais et les parties limitrophes du Maroc. Paris, Delagrave, 1882, $\frac{1}{500},000$.

Magno de Castilho (Alexandre). Roteiro da costa occidental de Africa, Lisboa, 1866.

INDEX.

—:o:—

Abou el Aïchibn Ibrahim ibn el Cacem, Poem in honour of, 99.
Abd-el-Djebbar, Sheriff of Wazzan, 112-119.
Abd-el-Hack, the cheik, 389.
Abd el Kader, the Emir, 321.
Abd-el-Malek, 73.
Abd el Moumeïn, reign of, 261.
Abd er Rahman, or Count de Saulty, 320, 369.
Abouam, oasis of, 199.
Abou-el-Fadhlben el Nahouy, the Romanesque chronicler, 368.
Abou Youssef, the Emir, 389.
"Abyssinia," wreck of the, 418.
Acheheb, Dj. el, 157.
Actius, 22.
Administration of the Morrocan army, 300.
Ad Mercvri, 418.
Ad Novas, Roman Station of, 70.
Agadir, Plateau of, 42.
Agbat el Maresfaia, 180.
Ahmet ibn Feth, the poet, 99.
Aïacha, W. el, river of, 64.
Aïcha, Madame, 361.
Ain Daliya, ridge of, 56.
Aïn Soumâr, 399.
Ain Zore, fountain of, 362.
Aïssawa, juggling of the, 119.
  ,, history of the confraternity of, 345.
Aït Isdig, tribe of, 232.
Aït Youssi, tribe of, 41.
Akabat el Hamra, mountain of, 58.
Albinus, the procurator, 22.
Alexander Severus, 22.

Algeciras, gulf of, 2.
  ,, excursion to, 3.
Algeria, conquest of, 28.
  ,, Traders to, 37.
  ,, Mussulman religion in, 116.
Alphonso V. of Portugal, 26.
Alqaçar, point of, 26.
  ,, Battle of, 72.
  ,, Town of, visit to, 76.
  ,, route from, to Wazzan, 80.
  ,, Plain of, 85.
Ampelusia, promontory of, 47, 419.
Andalusian Administration, 3.
Antonio, 72, 73.
  ,, acting as interpreter, 103, 153.
  ,, culinary mission of, 161.
Anna, Mount, 103.
Antæus, Tomb of, 46.
Antoninus, 22.
Ansaldo, Mr. John, 51.
Arabian Nights, Wazir of the, 19.
Arabic tongue, figurative character of the, 10.
Arab Cafés, 15.
  ,, irregulars, 73.
  ,, story tellers, 13.
Arabs and Jews, struggle between, 7.
Arabs, renegade, 3.
Araïsh, El, or Larache, 71.
Arifas, or overseers, 315.
Armament of the Troops, 298.
Armstrong guns, 30.
Artillery, the Sherifian, 283.
  ,, practice, 287.
Asmid, dohar of, 151.

INDEX.

Assada, site of, 157.
Atlas, chain of, 40.
  ,, lions on, 44.
Augustus, founder of Mauritanian Colony, 21.
Azila, or Zilis, 26, 72, 414.
  ,, Siege of, 415, &c.

Bab el Hadid, gate of, 371.
Bab el Mesra, the gate of, 8.
Bagdad, 111.
Bargash, Sidi Mohammed, Foreign Secretary, 16.
Basra, ruins of, 83, 86, 97.
  ,, history of, 92.
Beamier, M., translator of Roudh el Kartas, 202.
Bedouin driver, 9.
B'hareïn, hillock of, 55.
Belisarius, 23.
Beni Aamar, dchar of, 180.
Beni Ahsen, tribe of, 269.
Ben Aïssa, Ambassador to France, 205.
  ,, account of, 347.
Ben Aouda, Qarïya of, 100.
Ben Assouli, family of, 94.
Ben Chimoul, family of, 94.
Beni Hassan, 65.
Beni Mçawars mountain, 56.
Beni Mçara, 103.
Beni Meratz, 180.
Beni Mesgilda, tribe of, 171.
Beni Methirs, rising of the, 217.
  ,, incursions of the, 358.
  ,, Qasbah of, 405.
Beni Meryn, tribe of, 389.
Beni-Tunde, ruins of, 164.
Beni Waraïn, tribe of, 393.
Benouasfer, the, 114.
Ben Reihan, dchar of, 65.
Berber tongue, the, 21.
Berbers, quarrelsomeness of, 90.
Berber costumes, 108.
  ,, Tribes, revolt of, 108.
  ,, Brigands, 131.
  ,, race, the, 160.
Bey of Tunis, administration of, 253.
Beyt, W. El, Valley of, 151.
  ,, river of, 153.

Blois, Mlle. de, afterwards Princess de Condé, 205.
Bokharis, bodyguard, 113.
Bonelli, Capt. D. E., 185.
Boniface, 22.
Bougdour, the hills of Djebel, 152.
Boukhari, influence of the, 264.
Bouquet de la Grye, M., 125.
Bou-Regrag river, 42.
Brooke, Arthur, opinion of cromlechs, 68.
Byzantines, 23.

Cadiz, Boats to, 1.
Canary Islands, Cochineal from, 38.
Cannon, purchase of, 340.
Campou, M. L. de, 169.
Carnero, Cape of, 4.
Cavalry, the Mahzan, 275.
  ,, Tactics of, 281.
Cedar Wood, the, of Atlas, 373.
Centellas, Joachim de, 81.
Cephisias, Lake, 56.
Ceuta, 4.
Chaouch, visit to, 75.
Chechawen, Djebel, 128.
Cheffaut Expedition, the Du, 411.
Cheik, title of, 120.
Cherâd or Justice, 307.
Cherada, tribe of, 272.
Cheraga, tribe of, 271.
Cherf el Akab, plateau of, 42, 44.
Christian Women in the Harem, 36.
Christian Soldiers in Morocco, 305.
Constant, Benjamin, 14.
Constantius Chlorus, 22.
Cotta, Phœnician Town of, 47.

Daaklaou, plateau of, 56.
Dar el Amin, 110.
Darwin, Theory of, 88.
Darzawa, Djebel, 128.
  ,, peak of, 151.
Dcharchiera, olive trees of, 87.
  ,, dchar of, 89.
  ,, Fairs at, 90.
  ,, Tribe of, 104.
Dchar, derivation of, 54.
Dchavénah, 75.
Dellah, or auctioneer, 50.

INDEX. 473

Derkawa, brotherhood of, 334.
Dikr, the, 112.
Djazoulïyn, order of, 127.
Djedida, W., ravine of, 355.
Djemena, Djebel, 163.
Djoumaa, Market of, 408.
Dogs in the East, 12.
Domitian, 188.
Dou-l'-Carnein, the Kingdom of, 25.
Dress of Women, 226.
Dumas, Alexandre, humorous remark of, 85.
Duveyrier, M., 126, 142.

East, life in the, 16.
Edrîsî, description of Africa by, 98.
El Andalous, Mosque of, 371.
El Araïsh, Account of, 409 *et seq.*
El Bekri, 14, 21, 98, 148, 157.
El Fythrâ, compulsory act of charity called, 309.
El Khemis, fort of, 363.
Elyezid, revolt of, 265.
Embarek Ben Chleuh, the Qaïd, 179.
Emir el Moumeïn, the Sultan, 304.
England, intervention of, 29.
Ennijar, French Consular agent, 415.
Erckman, Captain, 302.
Erguille, river of, 107.
Ezaguen, ruins of, 81.

Farradj, outpost of, 363.
Fanaticism at Meknas, 344.
Féraud, M. Charles, 236, 374.
Feudal System in Morocco, 133.
Fez, modern kingdom of, same as Tingitana, 22.
„ Turks at, 111.
„ Treaty of, 215.
„ siege of, 269.
„ plain of, 351.
„ exact position of, 353.
„ commerce between, and Constantinople, 363.
„ residence in, 366.
„ Water supply of, 369.
„ Wealth of the people of, 378.

Fez, fortifications of, 386.
„ etymology of the word, 388.
„ founding of, 390.
„ commercial importance of, 391.
„ manufactories at, 393.
Figs, in North Morocco, 78.
Filali or Haceni family, the, 109.
Foucauld, Viscount Charles de, 311.
France, relations between, and Morocco, 28.
„ policy of, 95.
French Legation at Tangiers, 128.
„ Military Mission, 301.
„ Women in the Harems, 316.

Galba, 22.
Gayland, the, killed, 72.
Genseric, 23.
Gemaa el Hanien, 357.
German protection, 88.
Gharbüja, el, 59.
Ghellaïat, plateau of, 61.
Gibraltar, victualling, 1.
„ Rock of, 5.
„ The "Gaditanum Fretum."
Gibraltar, siege of, 27.
Gilda, site of, 168.
Greek Inscription, 77.
Grévy, M. A., Governor of Algeria, 115.
Guerwan, mountains, the, 177, 221.
"Guichs," the, 258.
„ History of, 266.
Gusman, Alphonse de, 302.

Habiba, mother of the Khalif er Reschid, 316.
Habbisi, tribe of, 156.
Hableur, Spanish, 137.
Habmido, the groom, 67.
Hadjerün, plateau of, 42.
Hadrian, the Emperor, 22.
Haïdar, the discoverer of Hachich, 396.
Hakk, W. el, 29.
Hamaïar, el, 68-73.
Hamdachia, order of, 110.
Hamria, El, plateau of, 200.

INDEX.

"Harams," or forbidden subjects, 250.
Harem of Muley Hassan, 314.
" recruiting for the, 317.
Hassani, Pacha of Algiers, 212.
Hawara, El, plateau of, 42, 55.
Hayâïna, tribe of, 271.
Hay, Mr., British Consul, 28.
" Sir John, 33, 34.
Hedjas, the, 248.
Hel Soual, tableland of, 220.
Hercules, Pillars of, 5.
" Grotto of, 47.
Homa, or chiefs, 345.
Homar, or Homara, town of, 69.
Horses in Morocco, 277.
Houdas, translation by, 352.
Hygiene in Morocco, 397.
"Ibn-el-Khaldum," author of the History of the Berbers, 24.
Idrisides, the, 376.
Idris, Ben Abdallah Ben Haam, 109.
" founder of first Sherifian Monarchy, 185.
El Khemis, peak of, 407.

Iman's pulpit, 10.
Infantry in Morocco, 294.
Ingliz Pacha, 319.
Islem, W., bridge over, 354.
Isly, battle of, 270.

"Jellaba," 10.
Jews in Morocco, 3.
Jews, River of the, or W. Boubana, 46.
Jewesses in Tangiers, 15.
Joan of Arc, a Berber, 231.
John I. of Portugal, 26.
Joinville, Prince de, bombardment by, 26-28.
Julian, 25.
Justice, court of, 306.

K'aaer R'mel, camping place of, 53, 57.
Kacheriyîn, suburb of, 93, 126.
Kannoufa, plateau of, 356.
Karroub, W. el, 58.

Kebaïls of Berber race, 89.
Kermatz, dohar of, 180.
Kiff, intoxication from, 332.
" properties of, 395.
Khouans, atrophy of, 116.
Kous, W. el, 72, 81.
" valley of the, 74.
" account of, 412.
Koran, 117, 248.
Kourt, or Kort, Djebel, 149, 154.

Lalla Rahma el hazwanïa, marabout of, 224.
Lapie, Colonel, 183.
Largeau, M., 141.
Law in Morocco, 307.
Lemtouna Berbers, 24.
Leo Africanus, 98, 99, 416.
Le Vallois, Major, 302.
Libyan tongue, the, 21.
Lixos, 412.
Louis XIV., ambassador to, 205.
Louis Philippe, present of mares from, 279.
Los Molinos, or El R'h'a, river of, 72.
Lucius Quietus, 22.

Maclean, old British officer, 297.
Mahasmouda, Djebel, 147.
" heights of, 155.
Makhzen, the Government administration, 33.
Mahzen, W. el, river of, 72.
Mahzen, the tribes of the, 258.
Malabatta, promontory of, 6.
Mamora, taking of, 210.
Marakesch, residence of the Sultan, 197.
Marcus Aurelius, 22.
Marmol, author of "Africa," 107, 147, 182, 184, 362.
Marmolejo, 85.
Marseilles, wax candles from, 38.
Marshân, plateau of, 45.
Martius Turbo, 22.
Mecca, the Moroccan, 142.
Mechraat-ech-Chedjira, river of, 56.
Mechowari soldiers, the, 260.
Mechráâ Aoucacha, ford of, 157.

INDEX. 475

Mechra'a Erremel, 262.
Meda, W., cascade of, 87, 92.
Mediouna, dchar of, 48.
Mehdouma, dchar of, 353.
Meknas, preparations for journey to, 49.
,, route to, 145.
,, first view of, 194.
,, arrival at, 196.
,, description of, 197, &c.
Mektab school, 249.
Melilla, præsidio of, 112.
"Mellah" or Jewish quarter, 14.
,, the, at Meknas, 214.
Menessez, Don John de, 416.
Mennow, General Hadj, 296.
Mercvri, Ad, ruins of, 61.
Merdja, system of, 88.
Merinides, invasion of the, 389.
Metasseb, an official, 50.
Mharhar, W. el or Wad el Kebir, 56.
Mitkal, story of cows at, 110.
Mikkes, W., water course of, 177.
Military Resources of the Sherifian Government, 259.
Miralaï, or Colonel, 289.
Moghreb el Acsa or Morocco, 23.
Moghreb, bigotry in, 115.
Mohammed, candidate for Sherifian throne, 72.
Mohammed el Bukhari, the author, 261.
Mokhazni, troops of the Makhzen, 274.
"Monkey's Mountain," 4, 44.
Moors, attacks on, 23.
Morisco policy, 32.
Moroccan hospitality, 136.
Morocco, European influence in, 33.
,, saddlery, 38.
,, wintering in, 40.
,, Genesis of native races in, 69.
,, roads in, 82.
,, dew in, 83.
,, modern power in, 113.
Moses, disciples of, 95.
Mosakherin, corps of, 273.
Mouedzenn, explanation of, 48.

Muça, Djebel, 5, 25.
Mulai Abd er Rahman, 270.
Mulai Abdallah es Sherif, 110.
Mulai Abdallah Sherif, 127.
Mulai Abdallah, 217.
Mulai Abd el Malek, 387.
Mulai abd es Selam Ben Machich, 110.
Mulai Ahmed Soueri, 290.
Mulai Boncheta, Djebel, 163.
Mulai er Rechid, 72.
Mulai Hamdan, 109.
Mulai Hassan, 31, 109, 118.
,, going to the Mosque, 324.
,, abilities of, 331.
Mulai Idris, 143.
Mulai Idris, city of, 185.
Mulai Ismael, 27, 100, 202, 204.
,, proposed marriage of, with a French princess, 205.
,, anecdote of, 210.
,, library formed by, 213.
Mulai Mohammed Hadj, 138.
Mulai Taïeb, Order of, 108.
,, Khouan of, 109.
,, account of, 113.
,, initiation into Order of, 121.
"Mulinn dor," or night police, 231.
Mul Muddol, the, 328.
Municipal Guard of Wazzan, 130.
Mzora, 65.
Mzaoug, or Sanctuary, 129.

Ocba-ben-Nafé, or Ok'ba-ben-Nafê, the Emir, 23.
Officials, fraudulency of, 339.
Oppidum Novum, or Alqaçar, 98.
Orghona, tribe of, 102.
Ordega, M., Minister at Tangiers, 115.
Ortega, M., 33.
Oualily or Gualili, or Volubilis, site of, 186.
Oudaïa, account of the, 267.
Oulad Djama, tribe of, 271.
Oulad Djammah Mountains, 179.
Oulad Messen, plateau of, 408.
Oulad Messenana, douar of, 160.

Oulad Migdoul, tribe of, 84, 96.
Oulad Sidi ech Cheiks, tribe of, 140.
Ourd, the, 121.
Outed, El, douar of, 68.
Ouzera in Algeria, 348.

Parisian Modiste, 9.
Pay of the soldiers, 313.
Peregil, Island of, or El Coral, 5, 25.
Photography, mania for, 250.
Photographic apparatus, present of, to the Sherif, 406.
Pointis, M. de, plan made by, 411.
Police, service of, 363.
Pontion, Valley of, 56.
Portuguese, incursions of the, 81.
Pride, the Mussulman's vice, 256.
Prisciana, the, of Mela, 164.
Puertollano, 85.

Qaçar Mahasmouda, 26.
Qaçar Pharaoun, or Faraoun, 187.
Qadrya, order of, 111.
Qaïd of the Sefiyan, 97.
,, of Sidi Kaceno, 179.
,, Embarek Ben Chleuk, 179.
,, El Mechowar, 329.
,, of Meknas, 337.
,, of the northern provinces, 193.
Qariya, of Ben Aouda, 100, 178.
Qasbah, the, at Tangiers, 17.
,, visit to the batteries near the, 30.

Rabat, road from Meknas to, 218.
,, batteries at, 290.
Ras, W., battle of, 29.
Ras el Mâ, ruins at, 370.
Rdat, W., the, 155.
Recruiting in Morocco, 295.
Regnault, Henri, 14.
Rekada, or garden of the Hesperides, 413.
Renan, M., 134, 256.
Renou, M., 106, 388.
Rif, Berbers of, 27.
,, snow on, 39.
,, peak of, 65, 69.
,, Mountains of, 84.

Rif, lands about, 149.
Rifles, various types in use, 130.
Rihan, W. er, or Fah'ser Rih'an, river of, 70.
Rohlfs, the traveller, 97, 141, 185.
Roman Antiquities, 106, 107.
,, baths, 62.
,, Bridge, 23.
,, Way, the old, 184.
"Roudh el Kartas," 202.
Roumis, soliciting alms from, 10.
Roumi, derivation of, 24.
Roumi doctors, 161.
Russell, Mr. John, English Consul General, 215.

Safrou, town of, 394, 400.
" Fête at, 402.
Salt mines, 394.
Sanhadja, the, 164.
Sarsar, Djebel, 71, 96.
Sarsar Mountains, 104.
Schools at Fez, 249, 377.
Science in Morocco, 251.
Sebastian, Don, 72.
Sebou, plain of, 165.
" hydrographic system of, 168.
" basin of, 169.
" mode of crossing, 175.
Sefiyan, Qaïd of, 97.
Septa or Ceuta, 23, 25.
Senousîya, the order of, 120.
Senslo, rocky spur of, 153.
Sherifa, the, 118.
Shorfa, the endless succession of, 115.
Shorfa Hassani, or Saadiens, 111.
Sidi-abd-es-Selam-ben-el-Hadj-el Arbi, the Grand Sherif, 52, 117.
Si Mohammed El Arbi El Djamai the Grand Vizier, 297.
Sidi Aourao, Marabout of, 152.
Sidi Bou Becker el Arbi, Marabout of, 322.
Sidi Boutmin, 178.
Sidi el Arbi, 113.
,, arrival at his house, 94.
,, account of, 133.
Si Mohammed el Arbi, visit to, 244.
Sidi el Yemeni, qoubba of, 69.

INDEX.

Sidi Mohammed, 95.
" visit of, 138.
Sidi Mohammed ben Ahmet, 170.
Sidi Mohammed Ben Ali, marabout of, 64.
Si Ahmet ben Souda, the Qaid, 337.
Sidi Mergo, marabout of, 163.
Sierra Bullones, 4.
Slavery in Morocco, 232.
Sok el Arba, territory of, 154.
Sokhra, a commission, 306.
Soko, market place of Tangiers, 8.
Souani, 54.
Souçac river, 148.
Soudan, communication with, 141.
Sous-el-Adna, 24.
Spain, journey between, and Africa, 2.
" opened for the Arabs, 25.
Spanish Ecclesiastics, Schools under, 11.
" Legation in Tangiers, 10.
" and French post offices compared with the English, 11.
Spartel, Cape, 12, 44, 45.
Spies, female, 317.
Subur river, 168, 170.
Sultan, disloyalty to the, 89.

Tadera, the, or prayers, 337.
Tadla, the, country of, 210.
Tchawan, peak of, 151.
Tafilalt, 141.
"Tagus," the, English Frigate, 28.
Tahedart river, 59.
" estuary of, 417.
Taïbiya, the, 112, 120.
Tangiers, crossing to, 1.
" Bay of, 5.
" Civilisation in, 8.
" Beggars in, 19.
" Inhabitants of, 14.
" Mussulmen in, 16.
" Pacha of, 18.
" Penitentiary in, 19.
" History of, 20.
" transferred to Britain, 27.
" Foreign Minister at, 31.
" Newspapers in, 34.

Tangiers, European colony in, 35.
" Shipping, Trade in, 36.
" Jews in, 37.
" tanneries in, 38.
" climate of, 38.
" game in, 41.
" sport in, 42.
" cooks in, 67.
" Berber population in, 69.
Tarek or Gibraltar, 25.
Tarifa, mails from, 1.
" heights of, 5.
Tartarin de Tarascon, 172.
Tarudant, 24.
Taxes in Morocco, 308.
Taza, 311.
Tea in Morrcco, 37, 96, 136.
Tetuan, taking of, 29.
" mountains of, 103.
Thaleb, or scholar, 105.
Tholba, corp of the, 289.
" the feast of, 379.
Tidikelt, oasis of, 140.
Tingis, 5.
Tingitana Mauritania, 183.
Tingitane, geography of, 147.
" diseases in, 161.
Tissot, M., 20, 47, 56, 61, 70, 76, 88, 98, 106, 157, 164, 167, 168, 188, 335, 408, 412.
Tlata Raïçana, plateau of, 68, 70.
Tobjyah, artillerymen, 287.
Tocolosida, 61, 191.
Torre Blanca, 6.
Torrès, S. M., successor of S. M. Bargash, 16.
Touat, 141.
Trafalgar, Cape, 45.
Travelling in Morocco, 238.
Tremulæ, station of, 98.
Trotter, Major, 52.
Trotter, Capt., P. D., 185.
Tsougt, Dj., country of, 403.
Turpin, Commander, 28.

Ulemas of Fez and the Sultan, 264.
Uniform of officers, 299.

Vallière, Mlle. de la, mother of Mlle. de Blois, 206.

Vandals, 22.
Vandalism, scientific, 377.
"Vatel," adventures of a disciple of, 381.
Vitellius, 22.
Visigoths, 23.
" Iberian Monarchy of, 25.
Volubilis, 182, 188, 191.
Vospisciansæ, Roman post of, 106.

Wargha, W., Valley of, 145, 158.
Warour, W., 73.
Water in Morocco the property of the Sultan, 404.
Wazzan, Sherif of, his wife an English lady, 93.
,, 52.
,, dohar of, 74.
,, history of, 104.
,, religion in, 111.
,, description of, 124.
,, population of, 125.

Wazzan, toleration in, 142.
,, departure from, 144.
,, Djebel, 148.
Windus, S., Sketch of Volubilis by, 188.
Women, condition of, among Musselmen, 219.

Xeres, Victory of, 25.

Yacoub el Mansour, 26, 76.
Yenahoum, W., Valley of the, 169.
Yulan, a Roumi nobleman, 24.

Zarhoun Mountains, 146.
,, first sight of, 156.
,, eastern slope of, 180.
,, geological nature of, 192.
Zaouïa of the Sherif of Wazzan, 83.
Zeggota, Watercourse of, 177.
Zeïtoun, Djebel, 60.
Zemmours, mountains of, 192.
Ziara, or offering, 115.

1750   24/6 89   1875

www.ingramcontent.com/pod-product-compliance
Lightning Source LLC
Chambersburg PA
CBHW050606230426
43670CB00009B/1291